Exploring Futures in Initial Teacher Education
Changing Key for Changing Times

Exploring Futures in Initial Teacher Education

Changing Key for Changing Times

Editors
Andy S Hudson and David Lambert

Book arising from the
Exploring Futures in Initial Teacher Education
International Conference
Institute of Education, University of London

September 1996

Bedford Way Papers

INSTITUTE OF
EDUCATION
UNIVERSITY OF LONDON

First published in 1997 by the Institute of Education University of London,
20 Bedford Way, London WC1H 0AL

Pursuing Excellence in Education

© Institute of Education University of London 1997

British Library Cataloguing in Publication Data;
a catalogue record for this publication is available from the British Library

ISBN 0 85473 531 3

Design and Typography by Joan Rose

Produced by Reprographic Services
Institute of Education
20 Bedford Way
London WC1H 0AL

Printed by Formara Limited
16 The Candlemakers, Temple Farm Industrial Estate
Southend on Sea, Essex SS2 5RX

December 1997

Contents

Contributors

Len Barton, University of Sheffield (Modes of Teacher Education Project)

Graham Butt, University of Birmingham

Sue Butterfield, University of Birmingham

Anne Campbell, Didsbury School of Education, Manchester Metropolitan University

Linda A. Catelli, Queens College, City University of New York

Pat Crockett, Didsbury School of Education, Manchester Metropolitan University

Lisa Dart, University of Sussex Institute of Education

Pat Drake, University of Sussex Institute of Education

Anne Edwards, School of Education, University of Leeds

John Furlong, University of Bristol

Linda Fursland, Bath College of Higher Education

Carol Gray, University of Birmingham

Viv Griffiths, University of Sussex Institute of Education

Peter P. Grimmett, Institute for Studies in Teacher Education, Simon Fraser University

Alma Harris, Centre for Teacher and School Development, University of Nottingham

Jenny Harrison, School of Education, University of Leicester

Ruth Heilbronn, Hampstead School, London, and Institute of Education, University of London

David Hopkins, School of Education, University of Nottingham

Crispin Jones, Institute of Education, University of London

Sue Leach, University of Birmingham

David Lines, Institute of Education, University of London

Norman Lucas, Institute of Education, University of London

Alan Marr, University of Birmingham

Sheila Miles, Institute of Education, University of London

Jan Peckett, Didsbury School of Education, Manchester Metropolitan University

Helen Penn, Institute of Education, University of London

John Piper, Crewe and Alsager Faculty, Manchester Metropolitan University

James Porter, Education consultant to UNESCO, UNDP and World Bank

Roy Prentice, Institute of Education, University of London

John Pryor, Centre for International Education, University Sussex Institute of Education

Jeni Riley, Institute of Education, University of London

Carol Robinson, University of Sussex Institute of Education

John Robinson, Crewe and Alsager Faculty, Manchester Metropolitan University

Ann Shelton Mayes, Director PGCE, Open University

Allan Soares, University of Birmingham

d'Reen Struthers, Middlesex University

Janet Stuart, Centre for International Education, University of Sussex Institute of Education

Ciaran Sugrue, St Patrick's College, Dublin City University

David Taylor, Head of the Teacher Education and Training Team at OFSTED

Michael Totterdell, Institute of Education, University of London

Roger Vallance, University of Cambridge

Marvin F Wideen, Institute for Studies in Teacher Education, Simon Fraser University

Margaret Whiteley, Didsbury School of Education, Manchester Metropolitan University

Caroline Whiting, University of Exeter

Geoff Whitty, Institute of Education, University of London

Anne Williams, University of Birmingham

Mike Willson, University of Sussex Institute of Education

Foreword

Professor Peter Mortimore

Exploring the future in teacher education

Throughout the world, Governments are concerned with raising standards of educational attainment. The idea that the intelligence and the ability to learn effectively of the majority of a country's population will be the key to the future prosperity of a nation has been widely accepted. The implications of this view for the education of teachers, however, clearly have not been fully grasped in all countries. There are few clear patterns of change. In France, for example, recent reforms have sought to place teacher education firmly within the academy (Bonnet, 1996). In England, in contrast, it is the higher education element of teacher education that is most often attacked by critics (Phillips, 1996). The lack of an international consensus is mirrored in the attitudes of different countries to the teaching profession. In Taiwan, teachers are accorded privileged status and, as a result, are excused the payment of income tax (Yung-Sheng, 1994). In the USA, national regard for teachers appears very different: status and pay are relatively low and attacks from the media are common (Lieberman, 1995).

These chapters, which were first written as papers for a conference at the Institute of Education, provide the opportunity for all involved with teacher education to:

- reflect on their practice

- extend their knowledge through contact with colleagues working in different conditions and cultures

- consider future challenges.

It is sometimes forgotten that the history of teacher education in England is relatively short and, in comparison to its continental peers, rather half-hearted (Green, 1990). One hundred and fifty years ago the main opportunity for the study of pedagogy was through the monitorial system, whereby older pupils supposedly 'taught' younger ones what they themselves had been taught by the schoolmaster or schoolmistress. Contemporary HMI Reports, however, described monitors as 'almost as ignorant as the classes whom they instructed' and the first training college for teachers was only opened in 1824 (Lawson and Silver, 1973:286). Since then, the main routes for English teacher education have moved from a two-year sub-degree course to a four-year programme based either on an honours degree with a specialist one-year certificate course or a four-year degree which integrates subject and pedagogical knowledge. In comparison to longer established professions, however, the culture of teaching does not yet sufficiently reflect its intellectually demanding nature. This has not been helped by the refusal by successive British Governments to countenance the establishment of a General Teaching Council (GTC) as the professional body controlling entry and discipline.

Perhaps because of its uncertain professional status and the existence of so many professional bodies representing teachers' interests, the public support for teaching that is so vital is seldom exhibited other than at the individual school. The result is frequent attacks in the media and an emphasis given to any critical comments made by ministers and officials. As if this were not enough, for those involved in teacher education there is an additional problem – experienced in most professions, but frequently singled out in teaching – of practitioner criticism of professional preparation! Added to this list of problems is a genuine underfunding of the system (especially where resources are divided between universities and schools), a tendency for Government overregulation and – not at all surprising in these circumstances – a growing fear that insufficient young people are attracted to the idea of a career in teaching.

For those who are committed to teacher education, however, all is not gloomy. We share a positive sense that through partnership we are developing an approach that can combine the craft knowledge of practice with an understanding of pedagogy so as to promote the development of intelligent, reflective (if I may use that slightly over-worked term) and highly competent practitioners: people who have a philosophy as well as a set of competences and who have been acculturized into a body of knowledge and experiences which define teaching as a vocation as well as an occupation. Our first challenge is to overcome the poor public image of teacher education. We must open ourselves to objective and fair-minded criticism (but we should reject any biased and unethical attempts to attack our work, no matter how cleverly these are clothed in the mantle of public interest). We should be our severest critics. We must learn from other nations and from other professions in our own countries.

Finally, we must improve our efforts to disseminate our achievements. Our critics are often adept at using the media to present their case and we must learn to match their skills so that we can refute false charges whilst we take account of genuine faults. To do all this will take courage, patience and will involve, for some, the learning of new skills. This is why the conference held at the Institute of Education was so important. It heralded a new era for teacher education. As these chapters make clear, if we can be honest with ourselves and intelligent in our strategies, we can be influential in raising the standards for successive generations of teachers and pupils.

References

Bonnet, G. (1996), 'The reform of initial teacher training in France', *Journal of Education for Teaching*, 22(3), 249–69.

Green, A. (1990), *Education and State Formation.* New York: St Martin's Press.

Lawson, J. and Silver, H. (1973) *A Social History of Education in England*. London: Methuen & Co.

Lieberman, M. (1995), *Public Education: An Autopsy*. Cambridge: Harvard University Press.

Phillips, M. (1996), *All Must Have Prizes*. London: Little Brown & Co.

Yung-Sheng (1994), Personal communication from National Taipei Teachers College.

Introduction

Andy S. Hudson and David Lambert

The climate of high anxiety which characterizes 1990s educational politics in Britain, in which rapid and sometimes precipitous legislation has resulted in shifting policy and occasionally bewildering ambiguities for those working in the education service, has had a number of adverse effects. Not least, damage has been done to the self-image of teachers and the image of teaching. Recent years have seen such a flight of experienced teachers from the classroom, that the Government in 1997 is reconsidering its early retirement rules and there is also now a significant recruitment shortfall to secondary initial training courses. Furthermore, the broader community of educationists has suffered a bruising few years during which time they have perceived a sustained external attack on what they do and how they do it, resulting in a crisis of confidence and a form of blame culture, in which the victim always seems to be the education service and its perceived limitations.

There is, nevertheless, common acceptance among teachers and other educationists on the 'inside', as well as politicians, officials and journalists on the 'outside', that the education service is indeed not working as well as it might. Such perceptions are certainly not confined to Britain. Around the world, teacher education and training has been identified – particularly by outsiders – as the vital component in the complex apparatus of the system as a whole, and has come under especially sharp criticism, to which educationists and trainers have had to respond.

This book offers a number of responses, drawn mainly from 'insider' perspectives in an international setting. The collection is future oriented, positive but not, we hope, complacent. Indeed, we start with what Marvin Wideen and Peter Grimmett from Canada describe as a 'wake up call', a warning that unless teacher educators can learn to say what they do with better effect than hitherto, then as a specialist group they will continue to be ignored and may disappear altogether.

What distinguishes many 'insiders' from perhaps most 'outsiders' in such considerations is their tone and trajectory; or as we used to say, where they are 'coming from'. In the case of those outside direct experience of the education business, the tone adopted is often punitive, coming from a position of thinly veiled contempt for what are considered to be the weaknesses of the teaching profession and the supposed inability of its members to operate in the 'real world'. However, the goals of these people, despite the rhetoric of 'world standards' and such like, are unambitious and apparently obsessed with introducing mechanisms for detecting and correcting inadequacy. As we write, the list of statements that specify potential incompetence in teachers trained in England grows ever longer. We suspect that long lists of 'competences' (or at least those that have not been effectively mediated by supportive and creative tutors) exert enormous pressure on both trainers and trainees, resulting in a kind of 'regression to the mean', whereby for every teacher for whom standards have been 'levered up' there is another, possibly outstanding individual, who decides to play safe.

It is important to note what is not being said in the above paragraph. We are not denying the perfect right of those outside the education world to criticise, have a point of view or project their perceptions or diagnosis of what might be at fault. Neither do we (at least consciously) adopt a defensive stance designed simply to ward off others who 'don't understand' what we do, thereby protecting a form of the *status quo*. The inward looking 'fortress' of the expert has in fact now lost its power to repel. For a start, the only thing 'not understood' in such a world was, arguably, the one aspect of the whole business that outsiders did not, in fact, have to understand – namely the arcane language that educationists use to talk to each other. The main *function* of teacher education and training is, surely, understood by all – to create effective teachers. If there is a widespread perception that effective teachers are not being produced, the experts cannot, however tempted, simply turn and exhort that they are (if only the critics would accept 'effective' as defined by the experts). Far from sniping at the critics then, we intend through this book to engage with issues with a new self-discipline and self-imposed toughness. One outcome, we hope, is that those outside the direct experience of the world of education and training (from whom we have accepted the need for hard thinking) will in turn be encouraged to understand and accept a greater level of sophistication in *their* evaluation of effectiveness in the field of teacher preparation.

What this book also argues for is for educational insiders to move beyond a culture of blame. Where outsiders may look for fault and move to eradicate inadequacy, the role that falls to insiders is that of creating, and then striving for, vision. Educationists, in various forms, are the guardians and the advocates of the moral purpose of teaching. As such, they have a profound responsibility. It is possible that this part of the teacher trainer's mission has not been well executed in the past. It may be that teacher trainers have been too content in the past simply to talk to themselves. However, the conception of the teacher as one who is schooled and certified in an approved range of subject knowledge and who is sufficiently competent in its transmission to be licensed by some educational authority does little justice to the nature of knowledge, to the experience of learners or to the efforts worthy of teachers. It needs to be challenged and it by-passes the crucial insights that every event of human understanding is an interplay consciously underway in a three-fold manner amongst student teachers themselves:

- subject studies
- practical teaching experience
- professional learning.

Such lines of thought offer exciting possibilities, the hint of which we hope is present in the title of this book. The 'changing times' alluded to in the above paragraphs require a response from the education world, particularly from those who train teachers, and a response which sounds a significant *change of key*. This book, which is concerned with the initial (or pre-service) education and training of teachers, is not so much concerned with refining the structures and procedures for fulfilling this task as with the reformulation of its goals: what two contributors to this volume have previously referred to as 'reconceptualisation' (Wideen and Grimmett, 1995) and what we intend by the metaphor of a 'change of key'. A number of authors, particularly those in Sections 1 and 2, tackle this theme head on. Later chapters, particularly those in Section 4, are concerned more directly with developing new practice in changing times, but are still driven by a more or less explicit consideration of appropriate goals for the future of teacher education.

Though several contributors throughout the book write with international as well as national expertise, a number of chapters in Section 2 are devoted specifically to providing international perspective out of a conscious editorial desire to place our discussions about the moral purpose of initial teacher education and training on to an international plane. Not only can we learn a lot from each other across boundaries in every continent, but we can also gain strength from each other. It surely cannot be long before threatened teacher education communities across the world wake up to the possibilities of internationally agreed standards and expectations in relation to the preparation of those who teach. Is it too fanciful to imagine an international charter on teacher education? This is a question which we hope this book may help prepare the ground for in some way.

This book has its origins in the First International Conference on Initial Teacher Education and Training, held at the Institute of Education, University of London in September 1996. The symposium itself has emerged from the ITE programme area which recruits around 900 postgraduate trainees annually (primary, secondary and further education specialists working for their Post Graduate Certificate in Education or PGCE) and which works in partnership with 200 schools and colleges in the Greater London region. At the beginning of the 1990s the new partnership ITE programme began to produce Occasional Papers in Teacher Education and Training (OPTET), a series of publications dedicated to maintaining dialogue within the Institute partnership, covering practical – and sometimes not so practical – matters to do with the preparation of confident and competent new teachers. In the early days, this activity was dominated by the perceived needs of the 'higher education' side of the partnership and indeed, in the most part, the secondary PGCE. However, the editorial group began to turn its attention to wider issues:

- the future shape of the PGCE
- the future needs of PGCE students (known as 'beginning teachers')
- the future orientation of schools in relation to teacher education
- the future 'choice and diversity' of routes leading to qualified teacher status (QTS)
- the future role of the higher education institutions (HEIs) in relation to the preparation of teachers.

The editorial group was also keen to examine such questions from a position looking outwards and resist any temptation to regard its own preoccupations as universal or, indeed, London as the universe. Teacher education was certainly going through changing times, but how had this been interpreted elsewhere in the world? Was there a perceptible change of key from educationists who guide and design programmes for beginning teachers? The International Symposium resulted from these deliberations. We hope, following this book, that there will be more international meetings of this kind.

We wish to record our gratitude to all contributors to this volume who responded promptly in the weeks following the Symposium with their chapters. Indeed there were many more submissions than space allowed to publish, a healthy sign that the theme of the Symposium struck a chord to which many people responded with enthusiasm; to those people also go our thanks. A great debt is also owed to Cathy Bird and her colleagues who ensured that the September arrangements were as smooth as they could possibly have been, and to Tara McNicholas whose efficiency constantly kept the editors alive to fight another day. Any errors or oversights, however, remain the sole property of those editors.

The purpose of this introduction has been to set the scene and establish the overarching rationale of this volume. *Exploring Futures in Initial Teacher Education* urges that policy makers, educationists and practitioners should hold up the possibility of reasoned discourse – particularly of assertions which may command provisional assent even though they lack unimpeachable foundation and are, therefore, subject to revision. In order to maintain focus for the reader, we have written a short commentary or orientation at the start of each of the four sections. This is not a book to read cover to cover and readers are invited to find their own way through – the section commentaries are designed to help.

Readers are also alerted to the fact that 1 May 1997 saw a new Labour government in Britain. The papers that form this book were completed in advance of this event and do not therefore take into account changes that may have occurred in the policy landscape in Britain.

Part 1: *Exploring futures in initial teacher education*

The chapters in this section accept the need for change in the way teachers are prepared and are concerned with the challenge of re-conceptualising initial teacher education (ITE).

They explore futures in different ways and do so from the basis of what has been documented about the past and the present. They all propose strategies for moving ITE (pre-service teacher education) forward.

They, therefore, make a positive response to the restructuring of the last 10 years.

Read together, they address Wideen's 'wake up call' and encourage all those involved in teacher education to probe the possibilities of what the future may hold in ITE.

1.1 Exploring futures in initial teacher education – the landscape and the quest

Marvin F Wideen and Peter P Grimmett

Initial teacher education (ITE) typically occurs in higher education supported by some form of school experience.[1] Notwithstanding certain reforms, such as moves in England and Wales to quasi-contractual partnership arrangements with schools, ITE generally involves three semesters of a post-secondary study and leads to a teaching certificate. Generally, ITE has not been viewed as a high point either in the educational experience of beginning teachers or in the perceptions of its adequacy by critics or policy makers. As we shall argue later, most graduates are critical of their ITE experience. As Tyson (1994) points out, the perceived deficiencies in teacher education in the USA have not changed very much. Goodlad's comment that programs of teacher education are 'disturbingly alike and almost uniformly inadequate' (1990:13) sums up the views of many critics.

The adequacy of ITE will ultimately be judged in terms of how well it prepares beginning teachers for their work in schools. Societal pressure on schools to reform along lines that better prepare today's youth to cope with changing social and economic times, places new demands on teacher preparation. However, if ITE is to contribute to meeting that challenge, teacher educators must find new ways to prepare beginning teachers. Otherwise, teacher preparation, as it is currently constituted, will cease to exist.

The landscape – the end of teacher education

A recent book by Horgan (1996) bears the title *The End of Science*. In it Horgan argues that the great era of scientific discovery is over, and that further research is unlikely to yield any more great revelations or revolutions, but only incremental diminishing returns. Science, which he describes as the empirical study of nature, has been very successful. However, we have now exhausted those areas in which science is going to provide additional significant answers. 'Real science' he contends has been replaced with 'ironic science'. Quirky theories and nifty titles catch the media's attention, but those areas cannot be easily tested or proven scientifically.

More recently, Rifkin (1995) has written about the end of work and Postman (1995) has written about the end of education. In these books one finds conflicting arguments. One might argue that these authors are clearly wrong, because science, work and education will go on. Yet that is to miss the point these authors are making, namely that a certain kind of science, a certain kind of work, and a certain kind of education may well be coming to an end. Thus, these authors provide 'wake up calls', alerting us to changes that we might expect from shifting social and economic patterns and their influence on our work and intellectual engagement.

We would like to borrow a page from these authors and subtitle the first part of this chapter, 'The end of ITE'. We do so with the same intent as these two authors have, as a 'wake up call' to bring us to the brink of our understanding of what the future may hold for ITE. Although we might dismiss the claim regarding the end of science or the end of work, the evidence that supports the contention that we have come to the end of ITE cannot easily be dismissed. If science is about to end because it has been too successful, ITE could end because it has not been successful enough. First, we will offer some evidence suggesting that we have indeed come to the end of ITE as it is currently constituted. Then, we will trace why this point has been reached.

The evidence

Evidence that ITE as we currently know it has reached an end comes from a variety of sources. Consider the following.

The diminishing support for initial teacher education

In a recent examination of teacher education policy in the USA, Gideonse (1992) and a group of case workers present a sobering picture of teacher education in that country. Their analysis finds faculties of education holding very weak positions in the policy arena. According to them, the negative feedback about teacher preparation from teachers themselves had opened the door for policy makers to move in and impose simple solutions to very complex problems. Among them were external control over teacher education, testing programs to ensure minimum competency for beginning teachers and limits placed on the number of hours of education courses required for accreditation. These policy makers saw teacher education as overgrown, lacking in quality and not providing an adequate response to the needs of the school and the larger society. In the closing chapter of his work, Clark holds out this problem and challenge:

> No professional can take comfort from the actions by policy makers that challenge the basic utility of their professional activity. To suggest [for example] that less pedagogical instruction will improve teaching is a challenge that cannot be left uncontested.
>
> (Clark, 1992:294)

What appears most troubling in this work was the fact that no-one (neither teachers, university people, nor policy makers) appeared to defend ITE. Other examples can be brought forwards. The shift of initial teacher education from the higher education base to the schools in England and Wales (Pimm and Selinger, 1995) signals the view that teacher education can best be done in a school setting rather than on a university campus. The huge reorganization in Norway that restructured teacher preparation from 129 separate institutions into 29 regional colleges prompted Hauge

(1995) to suggest that teacher education may well become the loser in that system. Academic critics in Australia have undertaken a review of Australian teacher education and concluded that it 'has a weak and questionable knowledge base, a fragmented and shallow curriculum which provides little academic challenge, and does not attract the intellectual high-flyers leaving school at year 12' (Tisher, 1995:34). Tisher also notes that teacher educators have been virtually silent on these very serious criticisms of ITE.

A similar state of affairs appears to have been the case in England and Wales, but with one important difference. Rather than teacher educators *remaining silent*, they appear to *have been silenced*. In a scathing editorial about government misinformation, Stones (1994) claimed that the then British Government and other agencies had set out to discredit teacher education with the naked use of political power. Stones also lamented the supine reaction of English teacher educators whose inglorious reaction to such political depredation by the national Government was to fall into line and scramble for funds to do things with which they may not have agreed. Consequently, the national Government was free to disregard important research findings and to declare that the education system in England and Wales was in crisis and that only market forces could save it. Any attempt by teachers and teacher educators to counter these assertions was treated with contempt. Such contempt (and lack of a viable counterpoint) inevitably leads Governments to restructure. In the corporate world, restructuring is often a euphemism for lay-offs; in teacher education it means closures.

Closures and rumours of closures

As higher education begins to face the financial realities of the 1990s, Faculties of Education appear among the first to bear the brunt of budgetary constraints. In the USA, the department of education at the University of Chicago (that prestigious institution in which Dewey, Jackson, Schwab, Thorndike, Tyler and many other noted scholars conducted their work, and where leading lights in teacher education scholarship such as Eisner and Shulman, etc. were educated) is slated for closure by the year 1999. Such closures are not only the recommendation of policy makers. In 1994, Tyson proposed that many of the smaller institutions preparing teachers should be closed down. Moreover, the Holmes Group (1995) asserted that unless institutions take serious steps to reform teacher education, they should give up their franchise. In Canada, the faculty of education at the University of Alberta became a serious target for closure during an austere period of university restraint (Carson, 1995). In England, Phillips (1996) recently proposed that faculties of education in Great Britain be closed. In a recent interview conducted by one of the authors, a professor of education in a highly respected British university told how he must articulate a 'show-cause' rationale for the continuation of the faculty of education in his next annual meeting with his university vice-chancellor.

Teacher education – a non-player in school reform

Howey, a prominent teacher educator in the USA makes the point quite forcefully that when policy makers turn to school reform in that country, they typically ignore teacher education as a vehicle for such reform (personal communication, December, 1996). He notes that despite the fact that virtually all beginning teachers must go through a period of preparation for teaching, policy makers fail to place much importance on that experience when considering ways to improve schools. Similarly, ITE in Canada is also disconnected from school reform (Sheehan and Fullan, 1995).

In her 1995 presidential address to the American Educational Research Association (AERA), Linda Darling Hammond spoke of the right of students to learn and of the need for the advancement of teaching. She made a impassioned plea for reform in the nation's schools to preserve the USA's capacity to survive as a democratic nation. Teacher education, however, did not feature prominently in her address as a vehicle for that reform or restoration. It received only a brief mention.

This lack of connection between teacher education and school reform in the USA is cause for concern. For Howey (1995), it suggests that the future of teacher education is precariously balanced. He can find no national design for the reform of schools or teacher education. Indeed, the reform of schools occurs independent of teacher education. No incentive exists to bring the two together and the gap appears to be widening. This is unacceptable for Howey. His view is that US teacher education must engage in a fundamental re-examination of the nature of schooling in today's society, of the changing roles and responsibilities of teachers, and of the character of learning desired by today's youth. Without such examination, it becomes highly vulnerable to political attempts to re-engineer higher education.

The re-engineering of higher education

Imig[2] (February, 1995) recently characterized five current trends in US education:

1 the nationalization of US education
2 the transformation of schools
3 increasing diversity in a multicultural context
4 the professionalization of teaching
5 the re-engineering of higher education.

He concluded that the first four of these trends were now moribund and that the only one that mattered under the Republican Contract with the USA was the last one. This realization did not fill him with a great deal of optimism about the future. He saw certain events as foreshadowing tremendous problems in teacher education. For example, the State of Colorado now has legislation in place mandating members of a faculty of education to undertake at least 15 hours per week in school classrooms. A further example lay in the move to place teacher licensure in the hands of local schools so that they can hire whomever they please, regardless of background and qualification. This invidious picture from Washington reinforces the view that the future of university-based teacher education hangs in the balance. It further implies that conventional approaches to certification may soon become an artefact of the past.

The move towards alternative certification

Persistent threats to teacher education based in higher education can be seen in the conservative sponsorship in the USA of anti-credential, alternative certification models for entry into teaching. Such sponsorship has spawned the belief that alternative certification programmes are likely to be more responsive to minority recruitment. Although partially true, this trend can be seen as a right-wing co-opting of the language of diversity and multiculturalism. Threats to teacher education can also be seen in the strong support for school-based professional development programmes and concerted efforts to uncouple teacher salary advancement from the accumulation of university credits.

Pimm and Selinger (1995) describe how Government restructuring has essentially commodified schooling and teacher education in England. Schools, not universities, are seen as the place of learning to teach. Consequently, schools are given a dominant role to play in teacher preparation. The apprenticeship model appears to be back in vogue. Universities become 'service providers' in the marketplace of education. While the British reforms might be represented as a variation of conventional certification, they nevertheless pave the way for alternative forms of certification to flourish. At the very least, the British approach could face some of the problems currently extant in US teacher education, namely a cumbersome organization that spawns a dysfunctional curriculum.

The cumbersome organization of teacher education

Currently in the USA, over 1,200 institutions (not all universities) prepare teachers. There is now a National Commission headed by Art Wise, which is attempting to co-ordinate the policies and practices of this diverse group of institutions. However, a distinct lack of public accountability in the preparation process can be found and this, in turn, leads to an idiosyncratic curriculum. This cumbersome organization in teacher education and its chronic inefficiencies give the impression of a dysfunctional process that has lost its way, inviting external intervention by debt-conscious Federal and State Governments.

The dysfunctional curriculum

Tom (1995) contends that teacher education will only improve when we attend to its deep structures and stop tinkering with the surface patterns of what is essentially a dysfunctional curriculum. He challenges four sets of taken-for-granted structural assumptions around intensity, sequencing, staffing and grouping. He argues strongly for compressed teacher education experiences over the current gradualist approach. He suggests that practice must precede knowledge and that vertical staffing with faculty teams committed to the programme (as distinct from a course) and to team teaching should replace the current emphasis on horizontal staffing, which he sees as exposing students in superficial and disorganized ways to more material than they can possibly absorb, thereby promoting breadth without depth. He is convinced that students need to experience a shared ordeal with a cohort rather than the current emphasis on regrouping.

These changes become necessary because the conventional theory-before-practice approach, grounded philosophically in anticipatory socialisation (i.e. giving prospective teachers answers to problems they have yet to experience) proceeds without any rigorous sense of public accountability.

The lack of public accountability

Tuinman (1995) also argues strongly for public accountability. He contends that formal agreements must be made between the university, its faculty of education and the field to operate jointly teacher education programmes designed to meet local needs. He further insists that faculties of education must make a public acknowledgement of their professional school status and hold the expectation that education faculties be held accountable for having and providing up-to-date knowledge of the practice and profession of teaching. Accordingly, he sees no reason why faculties of education have not and do not become models of good practice. Finally, he contends that universities must direct their scarce internal support for research specific to the mandate of each of their faculties. Such a policy, he claims, would foster the kind of research in teacher education he considers necessary (and currently lacking) in faculties of education. Without these forms of public accountability, the move of teacher education to the university setting becomes intensely problematic.

The unhappy clientele

This problem surfaces when graduates are asked to comment on the value of their pre-service experience in helping them learn to teach. Two quotations taken from a study of a conventional approach to teacher education in a Canadian university (Clifton, Mandzuk and Roberts, 1994) typify the comments made by graduates of such a programme, especially with respect to on-campus components.

Faculty of Education standards are low enough that, after a while, one wonders if this is not the last hope for most people who cannot make it in other faculties.

> I find it very annoying that all the courses and assignments in education are so useless. They are entirely theoretical and in many ways I find them unrealistic. The courses and assignments in this Faculty do not pertain to the teaching profession. What you learn here from your courses is hardly applicable to the teaching field.
> (Student comments cited in Clifton, Mandzuk and Roberts, 1994:86)

Ninety per cent of the graduates surveyed in this study by Clifton and his co-workers provided negative comments about their teacher education experience. Moreover, in summing up the comments made by teachers who appeared before the Select Committee on Public Education created in Texas, Isher said, 'the only thing worse than their pre-service courses was the in-service training they were having to put up with in their current districts' (1992:8).

Comments such as these – which are all too common – typify those made by the graduates of ITE, the clients of the current system of teacher education. Can one imagine a business, or for that matter any organization in which accountability exists, surviving for long when 90 per cent of their clients are unsatisfied?

This evidence supports the argument that ITE *as it currently exists* may well come to an end within the next decade unless significant changes occur. Before proceeding, a caveat is necessary. In using the broad brush treatment to paint teacher education in a certain light, we have swept too quickly past the wedge of progressive practice that is occurring throughout many Western countries. This wedge of progressive practice receives prominence in several chapters of this book and others (Wideen and Grimmett, 1995), which report innovative attempts to improve teacher education. However, as Sheehan and Fullan (1995) point out, such ground level reform has not made any significant breakthrough to this point. Unfortunately, when discussions are made to close faculties of education, the negative broad brush perception wins the day, not the wedge of progressive practice that occurs at the ground level. One of the reasons for this may be the reluctance of teacher educators themselves to enter the policy arena to argue on their own behalf (Tisher, 1995). This has led to the penetration of corporate interests into higher education, heightened competition and reduced funding levels, accompanied by increased regulation and intrusion into the practice and autonomy of professionals (Grimmett, 1995). The Australian context described by Tisher (1995) is equally in a state of disarray. Government restructuring has brought about numerous changes in teacher preparation:

- decreases in the amount of school experience for pre-service teachers
- reduced supervision by university personnel
- a phasing out of concurrent programmes
- a strengthening of subject discipline knowledge in elementary teachers
- the inclusion of business/industry experiences.

How we arrived

How has ITE arrived at this point where one can seriously contemplate that it may come to an end? The story behind it explains why teacher education is now so vulnerable. Teacher preparation, as we know it in

North America, began in the high schools of Massachusetts in 1848 (Larabee, 1992).

These high schools assumed the role of preparing teachers for the elementary schools of the day. Eventually these high schools assumed more responsibility for teacher preparation and came to be known as 'normal schools'. Within these normal schools, which later became 'teachers colleges', the high school concept prevailed. When those teachers colleges were moved to university campuses, the type of initial teacher education which we now propose is ending had its genesis.

This move of teacher education from the normal schools to the university to join either existing faculties of education or to become fully-fledged faculties within the universities themselves, occurred between the years 1860 and 1950 in North America (Cushman, 1977; Myers and Saul, 1974) and later in Europe. Thus, as Larabee (1992) describes, over the period of 100 years, the task of preparing teachers moved from the high school to the university. According to Hargreaves (in press) a similar progression occurred in Great Britain. That move occurred during times of strong economic growth. There was a vision of a better society, which surely rested with education, which in turn rested on obtaining and preparing better teachers for our schools. Schools and better-prepared teachers would be central to a vision of the new society and preparing young people for that new society. It was in the university as opposed to the normal school setting that such improvement would be realised. In the literature in both North America and Europe three types of arguments justify the move and the costs.

The promise

The first argument had to do with the problem of attracting quality students. Teachers colleges did not necessarily attract students from the upper rung of the academic ladder. For many young people (including the senior author), teachers college provided an extension to their high school experience. One could gain entry into a teachers college with a partial high school standing (no more than two failed courses) and a reasonable pulse. By moving teacher education into the university structure, policy makers believed that a better calibre of student would be attracted to teaching.

The second argument held that the problems confronting the schools in particular, and education more generally, could best be resolved through systematic research and inquiry which would normally go on within a university setting. By creating faculties of education, then, such problems could be examined on a systematic basis.

The third expectation held that a different kind of education would result in a university setting. Myers and Saul put it this way: 'the university provides a setting and an atmosphere in which fundamental issues can be examined critically, fresh alternatives can be explored, and promising, imaginative programs can be developed' (1974:38). Thus, the people who would teach the young would be better selected and nurtured within a research-oriented environment by people who were examining issues in education and seeking to develop innovative ways of teaching. Therein lay the promise for teacher education in the university setting. Now we must ask how far teacher education within the university has come towards fulfilling that promise.

The move of teacher education to university campuses led to a period of expansion in faculties of education during the 1960s, 1970s and early-1980s. This expansion in education paralleled the growth in higher education. Both occurred within strong economic growth and a belief in the future.

Those recruited to faculties of education pursued what they saw as interesting and productive work that would gain them respect within the larger university context of which they were now a part. However, gaining that respect meant attending to the norms of the academic and political cultures of the university. Thus, programmes such as administrative leadership, counselling and educational change had more prestige than working with beginning teachers. A case study by Robinson and Ryan (1989) illustrates what happened to teacher education in many North American universities as normal schools became part of the university. Robinson and Ryan (1989) described the programme of teacher education in their faculty in very positive terms in that it involved a combined type of coursework linked to a semester-long practicum. They spoke glowingly about the clinical supervision model that was used in the supervision of beginning teachers in the schools. However, ironically, the point that ended their paper was that the programme occupied the time of only one faculty member. Graduate students and sessional instructors ran the programme; faculty busied themselves with other agendas.

The university that Robinson and Ryan (1989) described was not atypical. At Simon Fraser University the appointment of seconded teachers (called faculty associates) was introduced as a means to bring practitioners and tenure-track faculty together to radically reform the preparation of beginning teachers. In defending this new programme, Ellis (1967) spoke of the powerful synergy that would be created both on campus and in the schools as faculty associates and faculty members worked together to prepare teachers. Curiously, however, 25 years later, the concept of the faculty associate was defended on the basis that it freed faculty members to conduct their research (Dawson, 1995). More often than not, that research had little to do with how beginning teachers learn to teach. Thus, over a period of 100 years teacher education had moved from high school to university status (Larabee, 1992). Yet in making the move, the faculty members had made a type of contract in which the pressure to succeed on campus drew them away from ITE, which became, in the words of Clifford and Guthrie 'ill-regarded work' (1988:4). University status had been gained, but the mission of teacher education which had placed them there in the first place, had been lost.

What was delivered – the good, the bad and the ugly

How well have faculties of education done in terms of fulfilling the mission that created them – the better selection and nurturing of students within a university setting? In terms of attracting better candidates to the teaching profession, the move from the teachers college to the university has been eminently successful. Today in most Canadian universities the quality of people entering the profession is very high indeed. In Ontario and British Columbia entering teaching can be almost as difficult as entering medicine. Students now require close to a first class average, coupled with work experience, to enter a programme of teacher preparation in those two Canadian provinces.

Regarding the second issue – improved research – the score card is equally impressive. The quantity and quality of educational research in most Western countries is outstanding compared to the era before the creation of faculties. Moving teacher education to the university has concentrated people and provided them with resources that they would not have had. Although many would question the type of research that has occurred particularly with regard to its relevance to schools (Clifford and Guthrie, 1988), in terms of sheer quantity a great deal of research activity under the general heading of education presently occurs.

The third issue – creating an atmosphere where fresh alternatives can be explored, and promising, imaginative programmes can be developed – is something at which universities have simply failed. There are exceptions of course, which we will expand on later. For the most part, however, we have adopted the university teaching norms which typically involve the notion of 'stand and deliver'. In fact, in many of the more prestigious US research universities the preparation of teachers has become a very small part of their overall activity (Clifford and Guthrie, 1988). The innovative programmes and fresh delivery have not materialized. Because faculties of education have failed to live up to this expectation, ITE within the university setting is now threatened with extinction.

The provision of knowledge about the various areas of research seen by university people as important has become the dominant model of learning to teach. Indeed, as recently as 1990, Carter defined the process of learning to teach in terms of students acquiring knowledge about teaching. This knowledge utilization approach has dominated university teaching for the last few decades. It is an approach that leads to any number of problems. First, the 'do as I say' syndrome allows professors to talk about teaching without necessarily modelling it. This practice simply reinforces the transmission model of teaching at a time when school reform is being defined in terms of moving away from transmission teaching (McLaughlin and Oberman, 1996). Second, the knowledge utilization approach undervalues the complexities of what it means to learn to teach – beginning teachers do not learn how to teach by listening to professors talk about research findings that frequently have little to do with teaching. Third, the transmission model leaves the control of teaching in the hands of the researchers, the distant rationalists who downplay the craft knowledge of teachers. The curriculum within faculties of education under this transmission model becomes a type of wish-list depending primarily upon the interests of faculty members. In short, the thinking has been, 'I know something about this area, and because it relates to education, then it must be good for beginning teachers.'

This is the model of education that has developed within the university in faculties of education. Although there are exceptions, it remains the predominant model that underpins programmes of teacher education. It is also the model that brings us to the point of seriously considering that the end of teacher education is in sight. We should not suppose at this juncture that ITE will be the only casualty. In a context where the university model of higher education itself has recently become the subject of concern, one could ask, 'If initial teacher education comes to an end, will faculties of education be far behind?'

The move we have just described provides a classic example of restructuring without reconceptualization in teacher education. In fact, Patterson (1984) conducted a case study of a large university where a normal school was moved to a university setting. He found that little had changed. The same coursework instruction from the teachers college simply moved to the university campus. In fact, the instruction may have deteriorated because now teacher educators no longer found themselves the centre of the institution as they were in the teachers college. Rather, they were obliged to compete with other faculties in terms of research and publication, and, over time, adopted the norms of the university where publication was more important than teaching (Larabee, 1992). The anticipation of new and innovative programmes did not materialize because no attempt was made to reconceptualize the concept of learning to teach.

The move away from teacher preparation into fields such as counselling, educational administration, philosophy and sociology was a natural progression because those in faculties of education believed these fields would gain them recognition within the university. In a Canada-wide study (Fullan, Wideen and Estabrook, 1983), the majority of teacher educators surveyed chose the concept of respect within the university community over issues of salary, programmes of teacher preparation and organization. Faculty members also expressed a feeling of alienation in the university setting. As they struggled to gain status with their counterparts in other faculties, they distanced themselves from the schools for whom they prepared teachers. As the two cultures are very different ones, the balancing act often becomes an unmanageable feat. For these reasons, faculties of education have indeed become alienated, both within the university in which they are housed and in the schools for which they prepare teachers.

Thus, while the 100-year-old experiment has created institutions capable of attracting better candidates for teaching and developing a research capability, it has not made much headway in terms of improving the programmes by which beginning teachers learn to teach. In fact, the perceptions of programmes of teacher education are so bad in many Western countries that ITE within the university setting may well end. If it does, much will be lost. The profession itself could be weakened which would ultimately reflect on the quality of schooling. While faculties of education have not been as successful as they might have been, the potential that exists within them is still there. If we lose teacher education within the university, we lose that potential, and teacher education will move back to the schools from whence it came 100 years ago.

Where are we now?

Just as science will not end tomorrow because Horgan wrote a book about it, ITE is not about to end because of what we have presented in this chapter. Even if everything we have proposed were totally correct, simple inertia will carry programmes of ITE for the short term at least, and the public's belief in education at all levels (Clifford and Guthrie, 1988) may continue to support the preparation of teachers within a university setting. Policy makers may not know enough to deal with these issues, or more compelling perhaps, it may not be in their best interests to do anything about them. In any event, it will probably be economics, not reason, that will prevail in the final analysis.

On the positive side of the ledger, a number of developments encouraged by different groups reflect a general concern for ITE. The conference organized by the Institute of Education, University of London, which led to this publication is an example of one university's concern. The efforts of the Holmes Group and the Carnegie Forum in the USA represent deliberate efforts to improve teacher education. While the assessments of these high-profile projects have been less than positive, they do signal a important concern about teacher education on the part of the large research universities. The efforts of the Urban Network to Improve Teacher Education (UNITE) Group (Howey, 1995), with its focus on improving the preparation of urban teachers, signals a recognition that teacher education must adapt to changing societal conditions. However the quest for improving initial teacher education at the ground level, where it counts most, will be enabled by making appropriate use of the knowledge base in teaching and teacher education, and by building on the wedge of progressive practice now evident in many countries.

The quest – beyond power

What then should we now pursue as a new thrust, a new paradigm, a starting point where might we expect a breakthrough? We believe that the quest for improved teacher education must build on the three overlapping stages of research and development in teacher education that we have witnessed over the past four decades. We will mention these briefly as an introduction to what we see as the quest and the parameters needed to guide that quest.

The background on which to build

The research efforts of the last 30-40 years have produced a rich legacy of knowledge on teaching and teacher education on which our quest for improved ITE can build. What remains crucial is how we view that knowledge as a means to assist beginning teachers learn to teach. This knowledge base falls under two general paradigms which we have chosen to call 'utilization' and 'interpreting teacher knowledge'. Although the work in these two paradigms has typically involved practising teachers, what has been learned applies to ITE as well. In addition, something that we have termed a 'wedge of progressive practice' in teacher education has also been occurring. These three paradigms provide different parts of the knowledge base on which to build.

The knowledge utilisation stage

Under this paradigm, research and development focused on what teachers should know and how they should best be trained to know it. Fuller and Bown (1975) summed it up when they indicated that the object of research and development was to find out what teachers need to know at each stage of their development and to seek the most effective ways of training them to use that knowledge. In this tradition, knowledge comes from the findings of research. The research on the teaching movement typified work in this paradigm. Through observation and controlled classroom studies, researchers sought context free generalizations to identify those teaching acts that would produce enhanced student achievement. As Fenstermacher (1994) notes, the results of such positivistic inquiry were then converted to 'imperatives for practising and beginning teachers to follow'. Learning to teach and learning to change teaching then becomes a process of acquiring knowledge related to classroom practice (Carter, 1990).

This stage of research and development carried with it a very prescriptive tone in which power rested with the researchers whose knowledge would inform and improve the practice of teachers. This emphasis on prescription appeared to rest with the belief, as Louis (1981) argued, that the lack of reform in education rested on an inability of teachers – cast as users of information – to put into practice knowledge about teaching developed by researchers. Teachers were seen more or less as 'dumb instruments of social policy' with little power. The students, who often have most to gain or lose in the process, have the least amount of power.

As indicated in an earlier section, this paradigm and the transmissive model of teaching that emerged from it have not worked well in helping beginning teachers to learn to teach. The failure has occurred, not because of the knowledge that has been produced, but because of how teacher educators have thought about and used that knowledge. When presented as a set of prerogatives to follow, this knowledge ignores the complexities of teaching, assuming teaching to be a very simple act of transmission. If this is all teacher educators can do in ITE, they will be replaced with a computer screen.

Interpreting teacher knowledge

This paradigm has seen a shift to an attempt to understand what beginning teachers actually do know and how that knowledge has been acquired (Carter, 1990). Researchers who take an interpretive approach seek to understand the meaning humans attach to the interpersonal and social aspects of their lives within the frame of reference of the participant as opposed to the observer. All human action is seen as being context-bound and, therefore, unable to be separated or understood apart from that context.

For example, Hollingsworth, Dybdahl and Minarek (1993) drew on a six-year conversation between the senior author and two teachers who began the study as beginning teachers. The conversation focused on the dilemmas the beginning teachers faced as they began teaching and how they resolved them. The authors concluded that the knowledge provided during teacher preparation which focused on research-based approaches to literacy instruction was insufficient for preparing these two teachers to teach children in urban classrooms. Rather, it was the teachers' own knowledge that stood out in this conversation. That 'knowing' developed from a sustained conversation that occurred during their teacher preparation and first year of teaching, a belief in themselves, and an ability to look critically at both themselves and the pupils.

This illustration shows teachers' knowledge being actively constructed during the unstable, uncertain, conflicted world of practice (Schön, 1987; Shulman, 1987). Beginning teachers engage in the joint construction of knowledge through discussion, writing and group process. Teacher educators, such as Hollingsworth in this illustration, are obviously part of the process and bring their own normative expectations to bear on the construction of knowledge about teaching.

The type of knowledge to which Hollingsworth, Dybdahl and Minarek refer has been described in various terms by different researchers. Elbaz (1983) was among the first to use the term 'practical knowledge', which then became personal/practical knowledge as Clandinin and Connelly (1987) carried that work forward. Shulman (1987) brought us the notion of pedagogical content knowledge and others, such as Grimmett and MacKinnon (1992) have explored the notion of craft knowledge. Within the context of these forms of knowledge, learning how to teach becomes a much more complex process, confounded by the beliefs and values prospective teachers bring to their education programmes and by the idiosyncratic and seemingly unpredictable effects that programmes have on the views of pre-service teachers.

Still, much of the literature in this paradigm carries strong 'fix-it' overtones. The notion of prescription remains in the voices of many of these researchers. So much attention has been given to teacher knowledge that the sense of purpose, direction and vision for teaching might have been lost. Also, there is unusual acceptance of the value of teacher knowledge that, as Carter (1990) has pointed out, is totally unwarranted. We see this stage as a very conservative one which provides few insights into how we can actually improve the quality of ITE. Nonetheless, it represents an important bridge in our future quest.

The wedge of progressive practice

One of the most promising series of recent developments is at what Sheehan and Fullan (1994) have termed the ground level. These many efforts provide the wedge of progressive practice in ITE that can be found in many parts of the Western world. Typically, such efforts involve individuals and groups undertaking new approaches to teacher education. The work of Coyle at the University of Nottingham (personal interview, 18 September) provides an illustration.

Coyle teaches French as part of the modern languages programme at the University of Nottingham. She believes that the purpose of learning to teach is to empower beginning teachers to significantly alter the quality of learning in classrooms. Autonomy is fundamental to the process of reflection – a person who is not autonomous has no need to reflect. She takes a constructivist perspective, in that she starts with the beliefs of students. As a result of these beliefs, she finds herself teaching the beginning teachers much differently from how she was taught. Very little lecturing occurs in her course. She begins by having the beginning teachers act as learners of a new language for 25 hours. Through discussion groups, awareness raising and other activities that focus on process, she seeks to challenge their preconceived ideas about teaching. Much talk occurs about reflective practice in her course. She sees herself as a reformer.

What is most encouraging about practices such as these is the increasing amount of research now being conducted to understand what students bring to situations such as these and how programmes assist or inhibit the process of learning to teach. Two very positive features of this research stand out. First, it focuses directly on issues of how beginning teachers learn to teach. It examines, amongst others, prior beliefs held by prospective teachers when they enter programmes of teacher education, the pre-service interventions that are occurring and a smaller set of studies that focus on the first year experiences of beginning teachers (see Wideen, Mayer-Smith and Moon, 1997). Moreover, this research is being done by people who work with beginning teachers, who, in short, combine their research with the work they do in teacher preparation. Thus, what is learned can be applied. Unlike the research in teaching paradigm (Doyle, 1989) and the effective schools research (Reynolds, Creemers and Peters, 1988) where the research was done by those removed from the situation and the findings couched in terms that practitioners could not always understand and apply, the people doing this research typically should be able to apply what they learn.

Dittmer and Frischetti's (1995) description of Wigginton's Foxfire approach provides an example of how restructuring a teacher education programme around Dewey's original reconceptualization of teaching as forging connections between curriculum and students' interests/needs proved cataclysmic for some of their colleagues. It caused much resistance and grief because it sanctioned an experimental approach to teacher education that changed the ground rules and challenged the intellectual and cultural assumptions undergirding their colleagues' image of themselves as a repository of expert knowledge. This experience led Dittmer and Frischetti to question whether the university, if it exists for the faculty as they cite Sarason as suggesting, is the appropriate setting for teacher preparation. They go on to articulate how their particular approach embodies the conditions under which preparation involves a school-based, collaborative approach in a professional development school, where university and school personnel team teach courses with a project focus.

The limits to these and other innovative programme developments rest with their rather episodic nature and the fact innovations do not necessarily travel well. As Sheehan and Fullan (1994) pointed out with respect to the Canadian situation, although they could identify plenty of activity at what they termed the ground level, they could not see any major breakthrough. Because of their episodic nature, such innovations tend to tinker with the surface structure of the institution in which they occur. As Tom (1995) recently argued, reconceptualization in teacher education will only occur when attention is directed at the deep structures. Four areas show considerable promise if for no other reason than they appear so prominently in the literature:

• reflective practice
• constructivist theory
• action research
• partnerships.

We will comment very briefly on these four areas because, taken together, they provide potential for a major breakthrough in initial teacher preparation if we go about things correctly.

Reflective practice

The term 'reflection' has found its way into the vernacular of many teacher educators, claimed by them as a goal, and frequently proposed as the means by which programmes of teacher preparation can be improved (Bengtson, 1995; Korthagan and Wubbels, 1991). Various claims are made for the value of reflective practice, from negotiating a satisfying teaching role to transcending the technical aspects of teaching. But the question remains, is reflection a viable construct that can guide research and reform in teacher education?

Valli (1992), Bengtson (1995) and Korthagen and Wubbels (1991) review both programmes and literature related to reflective practice. Valli undertook a comprehensive study of seven programmes consciously designed to develop reflective approaches among participants. Although her study provided a clearer rationale of what constituted reflection and identified ways in which pre-service teachers were becoming more reflective, she also acknowledged the difficulties of influencing other parts of the programmes of teacher education. Bengtson (1995) critically reviewed works that have been produced on reflection. Although she identifies 15 books and special issues of journals on the topic, she describes the literature as being problematic, because with so many divergent views, it is 'fundamentally unclear what reflection is' (1995:25). She argues the need for those doing the reflection to distance themselves from practice. She also questions the presumed relationship between reflection, teacher education and teacher competence. Korthagen and Wubbels (1991) examine their own experience over several years of attempting to develop reflective practice among beginning teachers. They question whether it can be done in programmes of teacher education and whether it matters to teaching. They also report strong differences amongst beginning teachers as to how they engage in reflective practice. In a position paper for this conference, Totterdell and Lambert (1996) also offer an interesting critique of reflective practice.

The continuing interest apparent in the huge amount of work that is currently underway in the area of reflective practice suggests that the approach will continue to underpin both the practice and research of many teacher educators for some time to come. But as these illustrations show, fundamental issues remain. The concept itself represents different things to different people. A number of writers question whether reflective practice can be fostered in a teacher education programme. Nonetheless, if taken as a general direction for teacher education rather than a template to follow, the area represents an important aspect of the quest for improved teacher education.

Constructivism

This theory has provided the new conceptual ideology for many in teacher education, both in terms how research is undertaken and in terms of programme development. Proponents following the conceptual lead, Driver et al. (1994) and von Glasersfeld (1987), reject the positivist view that meaning can be passed from teacher-educator to learner-teacher. Beginning teachers construct their own knowledge about teaching. Yet, as Cobb (1994) warns us, the various forms of constructivism do not constitute foundations from which to deduce pedagogical principles. Thus, although constructivism is not a theory of teaching, both in specific courses and year-long programmes we see 'constructivist experiences' designed for pre-service teachers (Fosnot, 1993). A study by Mayer-Smith and Mitchell (1994) typifies a group of research reports that describe the experiences of teacher-researchers who attempt to promote an understanding of the constructivist perspective of learning. They discuss some of the difficulties associated with promoting an understanding of constructivism within a programme which is structurally fragmented. A positive feature of the work in constructivism, as with reflection, is that it may provide some conceptual consistency to a field that Carter (1990) characterized in terms of diversity and ambiguity. Again, constructivism will not provide the 'silver bullet' to rescue teacher education. At the same time as we cringe at the thought of a centre for teaching (Fosnot, 1993), we applaud the efforts of those who attempt to develop approaches consistent with the theory of constructivism.

Action research

Other researchers point to the need to engage beginning teachers in teacher research. We will only mention it here, because this has been such a long-standing tradition in many countries and because others (see Cochran-Smith and Lytle, 1990; Hopkins, 1987) have explored the concept thoroughly. Our own experience with the use of action research, at both the initial teacher preparation level and at the in-service level as well, has been among the more positive features of our work these past few years. As it is argued in the concluding chapter of this book, when one combines action research with reflective practice and constructivist theory in a context where those notions are shared with our clients (the beginning teachers), we have the potential for taking the next important step in ITE.

Partnerships

Another area where we find a great deal of rhetoric involves partnerships, collaboration or professional development schools. We increasingly see the notion of partnerships being the major reform to rescue ITE on the one hand and reform the schools on the other. This is a tall order to say the least. I have no argument against closer ties and partnerships with schools. Indeed our programme at Simon Fraser has had some of its finer moments as school and university people have worked together in initial teacher preparation. However, the proponents of partnerships and professional development schools speak of the concept in such glowing terms that it causes me to believe that they have never really been involved in them at all. Fullan recently addressed the UNITE group, pointing out that professional development schools were not working very well in the USA. Johnson (1997) testifies to the difficulty in making professional development schools work. All that may be happening is that teacher preparation is being moved into the schools.

We do not see any of these areas providing any particular breakthrough in teacher education. As they are currently being touted, they fall into a type of add and stir routine that is very unlikely to change much. In fact, in many cases proponents in these areas are still tinkering with the surface features as Tom has pointed out (Tom, 1995). We have borrowed and adapted a figure from Kiernan (1995) who applied the iceberg balance sheet to businesses. He argues that most businesses deal with the 10 per cent of the iceberg that appears on the surface. He argues that to really change a business to make it effective, one must probe the part of the iceberg beneath the surface. The same approach applies to initial teacher education. Our problems are not about to be solved by striking up partnerships or by adding some reflection, action research or constructivist theory and stirring the mix. Not that we should not be doing these things. Quite the contrary, we should. However, our problems run much deeper. It is the deep structure to which we would now like to turn.

The processes around which to build

To this point, we have argued that ITE as we have known it within faculties of education is currently being questioned in ways that might see its demise. The main reason is that we have adopted a university model of knowledge utilisation which might have worked at one time, but which no longer has currency with young people or indeed with policy makers. We have argued that teacher educators have missed the chance in the good times to really examine what it means to learn to teach and what it means to learn to change teaching. Rather, they have adopted a simplistic model of learning to teach in what is a very complicated process. As teacher educators, we have pursued our own interests at the expense of initial teacher education.

The quest for a new paradigm must involve development and research working hand in hand. Rather than to describe a new paradigm, we will set out some parameters to apply to our work so that progress can occur. These parameters represent the deep structure of teacher education that must be probed if we are to work towards a new paradigm. Another

Figure 1 The iceberg balance sheet

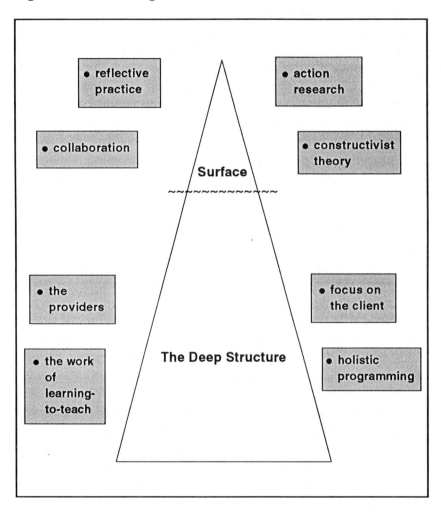

reason for not attempting to describe a new paradigm, rests on our belief that no-one fully understands how it will look as yet. The last thing we need now is premature closure on what is beginning to shape up as an exciting potential breakthrough. As we have just pointed out, we are not starting from ground level. Increasingly, we find examples where ITE works very well. But, we do not know what a reformed notion of teacher education will ultimately look like. We offer you four parameters which, if applied, provide our best bet for arriving at a place where we can look back and see that we have made progress.

Before we begin, we want to argue that making progress requires the best minds we have in our schools and faculties of education in developing new ways of engaging young people in learning to teach. The best minds must also attend to the on-going research necessary to determine what success means and when such success is achieved. Most importantly, we believe, is the need to move beyond the power that we have exercised in the past and to jettison those structures that support that power. We will illustrate that in the following four parameters .

Holistic programming (beyond coursework)

Tom (1995) has referred to this organizational issue as vertical staffing which draws on teams of faculty committed to teacher education. We contend that the future lies not in coursework as it is currently understood, but in combining campus coursework and coupling it with school experience. We make this argument on the basis of our reading of the research, on our own experience at two universities, and also from the belief that it will be for teams of teacher educators to probe the deep structure of teacher preparation. This means that when you have students on campus you simply break down all coursework into one large seminar, or organize the courses so that they are closely connected. We have both observed that process at the University of Regina and have seen its considerable power and potential at Simon Fraser – a programme organized around the concept of a team approach to teacher education.

The value we attach to holistic programming also rests on a reading of the research literature dealing with the assessments of coursework and year-long programmes. Single courses seldom appear to produce any lasting effect. Where they do, those effects were typically washed out by other courses. In Valli's (1992) review of programmes in which reflective practice had been the focus, she acknowledged the difficulty of the reflective skills gained in one part of the programme influencing other parts of the programme. Longer-term experiences, on the other hand, more commonly produced effects (Wideen, Mayer-Smith and Moon, 1997).

The need for a more holistic view extends beyond coursework organization. Capra's notion of creating a new ecological synthesis in science has application to the reconceptualization of teacher education. Central to Capra's new ecological synthesis is systems thinking, which focuses on the interrelations and connectedness among organisms, objects and particles and their contexts. He contends that quantum physics dramatically illustrated that no separate parts exist in any system. What we normally call parts in a system are merely patterns in 'an inseparable web of relationships' (1995:37). This new synthesis stands in sharp contrast to the mechanistic thinking of Cartesian science, the proponents of which believed that the whole could be analysed by studying the parts. Systems thinking rejects this. Capra also argues that as we become aware of different levels of complexity, new properties and insights emerge.

Capra's new ecological synthesis informs the reconceptualization of teacher education. The organization of teacher education around separate parts assumes that learning to teach is an additive process. Beginning teachers acquire knowledge through coursework on a variety of topics believed to be related to teaching. This knowledge is then applied during a school experience. As we have argued throughout this chapter, this approach has met with little success. Applying Capra's notion of systems thinking would see a focus on the connections between areas such as reflection, action research, school experience and perceptions about teaching which beginning teachers bring to the programme. Such connections can best occur where sharp divisions between coursework have been reduced, where teams of teacher educators work with beginning teachers and where improved connections are developed between campuses and schools.

Reconceptualization of teacher education requires change. Holistic programming moves the unit of change from the single course or single teacher educator to a larger set of relationships within the organization. The likelihood of any significant change occurring in teacher education as long as coursework and isolated experiences continue to prevail is about as remote as expecting change to occur through the mandates of policy makers.

A *client focus*

What must become important in initial teacher education if we are to frame a new paradigm is a focus on the beginning teacher, not the teacher educator, not the system, not the rules of the regulatory agencies. In the knowledge utilization paradigm, the beginning teacher is seen as the 'user' of knowledge. The interpretive paradigm, with its focus on understanding how people learn to teach and the contribution of constructivist theory, has shifted our attention to the fact that beginning teachers – as all learners – are actively constructing their own meaning with regards to teaching. Yet we commonly find in the literature references to beginning teachers as 'dumb instruments' who will gladly carry out whatever social policy is set out by policy makers and taught by teacher educators. This became very apparent to me in a recent review in the area of learning to teach (Wideen, Mayer-Smith and Moon, 1996). In that literature, the authors found something that they termed the two agenda syndrome where teacher educators were interested in reform and beginning teachers concerned with survival. Teacher educators expressed the need to prepare beginning teachers so that they would teach very differently than they were taught. Beginning teachers, on the other hand, expressed the desire to simply survive creating a situation where the teacher educator's talk of reforming the schools did not seem particularly appropriate. These conflicting agendas frequently appeared counter-productive in terms of helping beginners learn to teach.

To return to Capra's notion of systems thinking, clearly the beginning teacher cannot be treated as some separate part that can be trained and shaped at the hands of teacher educators. Beginning teachers must become more active players in their own learning so that their individual perceptions of teaching are honoured and built on. Here again, teacher educators must move beyond the power they have traditionally exercized and place themselves on a more equal basis with their clients – the beginning teachers. A useful professional comparison can be made to psychiatry where the emphasis rests on the client and the changes he or she must undergo. That process always involves starting with the client him or herself, understanding those perceptions and building from there. Similarly, beginning teachers enter programmes of teacher preparation with ideas about teaching which they must either learn to put into practice, modify or, in most cases, change. As teacher educators, we learn to work with beginning teachers in ways that honour their entering beliefs and build from there.

What constitutes the work of the beginning teacher?

Drawing on work from the 1980s, Doyle (1989) drew attention to the concept of teaching as work. His analysis signalled a new approach to the study of teaching, one which focused attention on what teachers actually do in a classroom as opposed to identifying what they should be doing. More recently we have seen the emergence of the concept of 'best practice' to describe the best types of working conditions that lead to learning and improved practice (Social Sciences and Humanities Research Council of Canada, 1995). Clearly, ITE has the task of preparing beginning teachers for the work they will be doing as a classroom teacher. We can then ask, 'What work should beginning teachers engage in to best prepare them for that task?' Should it involve classroom teaching? Should it involve listening to lectures or reading great books? Should it involve all of the above? What constitutes 'best practice' in learning to teach? Teacher educators must examine through research and development the type of work or activity that best prepares beginning teachers for the complexities of classroom teaching to reflect the expectations of excellence in teaching and, at the same time, honour the aspirations of the beginning teachers themselves.

Clearly, little attention has been paid to this notion in the past. Many first year teachers (Wideen, Mayer-Smith and Moon, 1997) report that they learned to teach when they received their first teaching position. We can hardly defend the baptism of fire of a new classroom experience as 'best practice' either for the beginning teacher or for the pupils they are teaching. Also, we find it hard to defend having beginning teachers sit in a campus classroom listening to an academic who may not have been in a school for many years extol his or her research interests as 'best practice'. These two approaches reflect the current stock and trade in teacher education. Fortunately, the work of a number of teacher educators and others in related fields have described and reflected on the actual work of beginning teachers in ways that provide instances of 'best practice'. The following illustration reflects the wedge of progressive practice described earlier in this chapter.

Sumara and Luce-Kapler (1996) worked with a team of students and faculty associates to offer a year-long programme to prepare beginning teachers for teaching in the urban environment. They focused on the needs of beginning teachers who were mostly middle-class and Anglo-Saxon whites, many of whom had never experienced the inner city urban environment. Their focus on the students and their work led them to experiment with the notion of a 'curriculum location' – where student views about teaching, what they learn in practice, what they learn in teacher education could come together. Community involvement through volunteer agencies became an important part of that work. The group also learned that the students' own writing provided the most productive source of intellectual engagement for the beginning teachers. This case illustrates several important features of what must occur if we are to frame a new paradigm in teacher education. First, these authors, like others such as Hollingsworth, Dybdahl and Minarek (1993), have developed a new way of working with beginning teachers and also studied their approach through research and made their findings public. Second, they have made the traditional practices in teacher education, such as student teaching and classroom lectures about teaching problematic. Third, they have focused on the clients, the beginning teachers, and the work they can best do to learn how to teach in the urban environment.

Nowhere can the need for a focus on the work of beginning teachers be more important than in the current thrust to build school and university partnerships. The Holmes Group in the USA, for example, in their second report *Tomorrow's Schools* (1995) argued for the construction of professional development schools. If that thrust is to continue, it is incumbent on teacher educators to examine very closely what the work of beginning teachers should be in those schools. If we do not, then students will simple fall into a pattern of apprenticeship in which they are socialized into the existing practices of the school.

We will close this section with a challenge to the reader. Imagine that you have arrived for a visit at an institution that prepares beginning teachers. You are invited into a classroom where 30 beginning teachers are in session. You are asked to do something with them to aid them in the process of learning to teach. What would you do? How would you engage them? That is the essential question. Metaphorically speaking, if, as teacher educators, we cannot move beyond our past patterns to create safe and innovative ways to assist beginning teachers to see teaching in new and interesting ways the invitation to the university teacher educators might not stay open.

Teacher educators – the forgotten players in teacher education reform

Ultimately, the inadequacies of teacher education rest with those who prepare teachers. Despite this obvious point, curiously, little research has been done to understand the beliefs and practices of those who create the experiences that constitute teacher education. Assuming that teacher educators' beliefs influence their practices and that those practices influence student teachers, then the need clearly exists for a concerted examination of the beliefs and actions of those who teach beginning teachers during the pre-service year. For example, Hollingsworth, Dybdahl and Minarek (1993) question the value of traditional forms of knowledge as a basis for teacher preparation. They, like others, argue for approaches more in line with constructivism. However, it seems logical that the success of such proposals inherently rests on whether teacher educators' beliefs can embrace a stance such as constructivism.

If one were to look at any typical institution that provides teacher education, one would see a variety of people who, at one point or another are, or have been, teacher educators. The following three are people I have met. Each is different and each has a different focus when they work with beginning teachers.

Sam is a maths educator. In his work with beginning teachers, he selected a set of readings very carefully for use in his course. He made certain those readings were read by the students and discussed in class. When his students were interviewed the following semester, they could not recall any of the readings or why they had read them in the first place. Harry, has many concerns about schools and teachers. He taught at one time but, in his words, escaped from the school when he received his PhD and moved to the university – a kind of reward. He knows schools, he thinks, but he does not really like them. Sue on the other hand has never taught and has no desire to do so. Still she believes she has a lot to offer to beginning teachers because of the research she does. In her courses, she presents the most recent research findings. That way she argues the teachers will be applying the best and most recent knowledge. The students we interviewed can not see the value in those findings. They do not match what they see happening in schools.[3]

We raise these examples because they reflect who we are in faculties of education. Who we are is part of the problem. Yet we seem to take ourselves as teacher educators and our role as non-problematic. Faculty, it seems, have power and position, and can do no wrong. We believe they need to be part of the deep structure examination in teacher education. The roles played by the teacher educators themselves must become a major focus, if we are to create a new way of thinking about teacher education.

We will end this chapter on a point of irony. Schools have always been the scapegoat for many of the assorted ills of society. Today's criticism seems to have adopted a tone which of late has become stronger and much less forgiving. Politicians, business interests, the press and contributors to talk shows generally decry the state of education. Those in faculties of education have been amongst the strongest critics. Now, however, we see faculties of education having to face the same sort of reform they have been so fondly recommending to those in schools. We find this ironic to say the least.

In short, we can not escape our connection with schools and their perceived successes and failures. How long would a school of medicine last if it had no effect on the health of the nation? How long would a school of agriculture last if it failed to improve the quality of farming? In the final analysis, it is not unreasonable to ask, 'What have we as universities done to make the schools better places for children to learn?' In the end, our survival may well depend on how well we respond to that question. If indeed we can respond to it.

Acknowledgements

We wish to acknowledge Barbara Moon, Jolie-Mayer Smith, Ivy Pye, David Boote and Kathleen Barnard for their thoughtful assistance in producing this chapter. I also wish to acknowledge the suggestions made by the editors. This chapter is based on research conducted under support from the Social Sciences and Humanities Research Council.

Notes

1   ITE occurs in different ways in some countries. What is described in this opening paragraph is the type of initial teacher that is the subject of this chapter.

2   David Imig is the Washington-based Executive Secretary of the American Association of Colleges of Teacher Education (AACTE).

3   This vignette is based on an interview with Dr Coyle conducted by the senior author in September, 1996, at the University of Nottingham.

References

Bengston, J. (1995), 'What is reflection? On reflection in the teaching profession and teacher education', *Teachers and Teaching: Theory and Practice*, 1(1), 23–32.

Capra, F. (1995), *The Web of Life*. New York: Doubleday.

Carson, T. (1995), 'Surviving the Throws of a Budget Crunch'. Paper presented to a seminar of the Institute for Studies in Teacher Education, Simon Fraser University, Vancouver, BC, April.

Carter, C (1990), 'Teachers' knowledge and learning to teach', in Houston, WR *Handbook of Research on Teacher Education*. New York: MacMillan.

Clandinin, D. and Connely, F. (1987), 'Teachers' personal knowledge – what counts as personal in studies of the personal', *Journal of Curriculum Studies*, 19(6), 487–500.

Clark, D.L. (1992), 'Leadership in policy development by policy educators: search for a more effective future', in Gideonse, H.D., *Teacher Education Policy*. Albany, New York: State University of New York Press.

Clifford, GJ and Guthrie, JW (1988), *Ed School*. Chicago, IL: University of Chicago Press.

Clifton, R.A., Mandzuk, D. and Roberts, L.W. (1994), 'The alienation of undergraduate education students: a case study of a Canadian university', *Journal of Education for Teaching*, 20(2), 179–92.

Cobb, P. (1994), 'Constructivism in mathematics and science education', *Educational Researcher*, 23(7), 4.

Cochran-Smith, M. and Lytle, S.L. (1990), 'Research on teaching and teacher research: The issues that divide', *Educational Researcher*, 19(2), 2–11.

Cushman, M.L. (1977), *The Governance of Teacher Education*. Berkeley, CA: McCutchan.

Dawson, A.J. (1995), 'Reframing the clinical professor's role', in Wideen, M.F. and Grimmett, P., *Changing Times in Teacher Education: Restructuring or Reconceptualization*. London: Falmer, 174–88.

Dittmer, A. and Fischetti, J. (1995), 'Foxfire and teacher preparation: practising what we teach', in Wideen, M.F. and Grimmett, P., *Changing Times in Teacher Education: Restructuring or Reconceptualization*. London: Falmer, 163–73.

Doyle, W. (1987), 'The classroom as a workplace: Implications for Staff Development' in Wideen, M. and Andrews, I., *Staff Development for School Improvement*. London: The Falmer Press.

Doyle, W. (1990), 'Themes in teacher education research', in Houston, WR, *Handbook of Research on Teacher Education*. New York: Macmillan, 3–24.

Driver, R., Asoko, H., Leach, J., Mortimer, E.M. and Scott, P. (1994), 'Constructing scientific knowledge in the classroom', *Educational Researcher*, 23, 5–11.

Drucker, P.F. (1994), 'The age of transformation', *Atlantic Monthly*, 53–57, 62–80.

Elbaz, F (1983), *Teacher Thinking: A Study of Practical Knowledge*. London: Croom Helm.

Ellis, J. (1967), 'Who should teach teachers?' *The Chronicle of Higher Education*, 18(4), 423-427.

Fenstermacher, G. (1994), 'The knower and the known: the nature of knowledge in research on teaching', in *Review of Research in Education,* 20, 157–85.

Fosnot, C.T. (1993), 'Learning to teach, teaching to learn: The center for constructivist teaching/teacher preparation project', *Teaching Education*, 5, 69–78.

Fullan, M., Wideen, M. and Estabrook, G. (1983), 'A Study of Teacher Training Institutions in Anglophone Canada, Vol. I: Current Perspectives on Teacher Training in Canada: An overview of faculty and student perceptions', a report to the Social Science and Humanities Council of Canada, 28–9.

Fuller, F.F. and Bown, O.H. (1975), 'Becoming a teacher', in Ryan, K., *Teacher Education* (74th Yearbook of the National Society for the Study of Education, Pt II:25–52). Chicago, IL: University of Chicago Press.

Gideonse, H.D. (1992), *Teacher Education Policy*. Albany, New York: State University of New York Press.

Goodlad, J. (1990), *Teachers for the Nation's Schools*. San Francisco: Jossey-Bass.

Grimmett, P.P. and MacKinnon, A.M. (1992), 'Craft knowledge and the education of teachers', *Review of Research in Education*, 18, 385–456.

Grimmett, P. and Neufeld, J. (1994), *Teacher Development and the Struggle for Authenticity*. New York: Teachers College Press.

Grimmett, P.P. (1995), 'Reconceptualizing teacher education: preparing teachers for revitalized schools', in Wideen, M.F. and Grimmett, P., *Changing Times in Teacher Education: Restructuring or Reconceptualization*. London: Falmer, 202–25.

Hargreaves, A (in press), 'Towards a social geography of teacher education', in Shimahara, NK and Holowinsky, IZ, *Teacher Education in Industrialized Nations*. New York: Garland.

Hauge, T.E. (1995), 'Teacher education in Norway: images of a new situation', in Wideen, M.F. and Grimmett, P., *Changing Times in Teacher Education: Restructuring or Reconceptualization*. London: Falmer, 67–78.

Hollingsworth, S., Dybdhl, M. and Minarek, L.T. (1993), 'By chart and chance and passion: the importance of relational knowing in learning to teach', *Curriculum Inquiry*, 23(1), 5–35.

Holmes Group (1995), *Tomorrow's Schools of Education*. East Lansing, MI: Holmes Group.

Hopkins, D. (1987), *A Guide to Action Research*. London: Open University.

Horgan, J. (1996), *The End of Science: Facing the Limits of Knowledge in the Twilight of the Scientific Age*. New York: Addison-Wesley.

Howey, K. (1995). Narrative report from The Urban Network to Improve Teacher Education, Report submitted to PEW Charitable Trust.

Howey, K. (1995), 'The United States: the context for the restructuring and reconceptualization of teacher preparation, in Wideen, M.F. and Grimmett,P., *Changing Times in Teacher Education: Restructuring or Reconceptualization*. London: Falmer: 67–78.

Isher, R.E. (1992), 'Teacher education policy: the Texas experience', in Gideonse, H.D., *Teacher Education Policy*. Albany, New York: State University of New York Press.

Johnson, M. (1997), 'New shoes for teacher education: trying collaboration and rethinking diversity in urban schools'. Unpublished manuscript: Ohio State University

Kiernan, M.J. (1995), *Get Innovative or Get Dead*. Vancouver: Douglas & McIntyre.

Korthagen, F.J. and Wubbels, T. (1991), 'Characteristics of Reflective Practitioners: Toward an Operationalization of the Concept of Reflection'. Paper presented at the annual meeting of the American Educational Research Association, Chicago, IL.

Larabee, D. (1992), 'Power, knowledge and the rationalization of teaching: A genealogy of the move to professionalize teaching', *Harvard Educational Review*, 62(6), 123–55.

Louis, D. (1981), 'External agents and knowledge utilization: Dimensions for analysis and action', in Lehman, R., and Kane, M. (eds). *Improving Schools*. Beverly Hills,Calif.

McLaughlin , M.W. and Oberman, I. (eds), (1996)*Teacher Learning: New Policies, New Practices.* New York: Teachers College Press.

Myers, D. and Saul, D. (1974), 'How not to reform a teacher education system', in Myers, D. and Reid, F., *Educating Teachers: Critiques and Proposals.* Toronto: OISE Press.

Patterson, R. (1984), 'Teacher education in Alberta's normal schools', in Grimmett, P., *Research in Teacher Education: Current Problems and Future Prospects in Canada.* Vancouver: Center for the Study of Teacher Education, University of British Columbia.

Phillips, M. (1996), *All Must Have Prizes.* London: Little Brown & Co.

Pimm, D. and Selinger, M. (1995), 'The commodification of teaching: teacher education in England', in Wideen, M.F. and Grimmett, P., *Changing Times in Teacher Education: Restructuring or Reconceptualization.* London: Falmer, 47–66.

Postman, N. (1995), *The End of Education.* New York: Alfred A. Knopf.

Reynolds, D., Creemers, B. and Peters, T. (1988). *School Effectiveness and Improvement.* School of Education, University of Wales, Cardiff and the Rion Institute, the Netherlands.

Rifkin, J. (1995), *The End of Work.* New York: G.P. Putman's Sons.

Robinson, S.D. and Ryan, A.J. (1989), 'An Analysis of the Internship Experience, College of Education, University of Saskatchewan'. Paper presented at the annual meeting of the Canadian Society for the Study of Education, Laval University, Quebec.

Sheehan, N. and Fullan, M. (1995), Teacher education in Canada: a case study', in Wideen, M.F. and Grimmett, P., *Changing Times in Teacher Education: Restructuring or Reconceptualization.* London: Falmer, 89–101.

Schön, D.A. (1987). *Educating the reflective practitioner: Toward a new design for learning in the professions.* San Francisco: Jossey-Bass.

Shulman, L.S. (1987), 'Knowledge and teaching: foundations of the new reform', *Harvard Educational Review*, 57(1), 1–22.

Social Sciences and Humanities Research Council of Canada (1995), Strategic Research Network in Education and Training. A request for proposals. Ottawa, Canada.

Stones, E. (1994), 'Editorial: Paranoids of the world unite!', *Journal of Education for Teaching,* 20(3), 259-60.

Sumara, D.J. and Luce-Kapler, R. (1996), '(Un)becoming a teacher: negotiating identities while learning to teach', *Canadian Journal of Education*, 22(1), 65–83.

Tisher, R. (1995), 'Readjustments, reorganization or revolution?' in Wideen, M.F. and Grimmett, P., *Changing Times in Teacher Education: Restructuring or Reconceptualization*. London: Falmer, 34–46.

Tom, A. (1995), 'Stirring the embers: reconsidering the structure of teacher education programs', in Wideen, M.F. and Grimmett, P., *Changing Times in Teacher Education: Restructuring or Reconceptualization*. London: Falmer, 34–46. London: Falmer.

Totterdell, M. and Lambert, D. (1996), 'Designing teachers' futures: an evolving model for developing secondary school partnership in teacher education'. Paper submitted to *The European Journal of Teacher Education*.

Tuinman, J. (1995), 'Rescuing teacher education: a view from the hut with the bananas', in Wideen, M.F. and Grimmett, P., *Changing Times in Teacher Education: Restructuring or Reconceptualization*. London: Falmer, 105–16.

Tyson, H. (1994), *Who Will Teach the Children?* San Francisco: Jossey-Bass.

Valli, L (1992), *Reflective Teacher Education: Cases and Critiques*. Albany, New York: State University of New York Press.

von Glasersfeld, E. (1987), 'Constructivism', in Husen, T. and Postlethwate, T.N., *The International Encyclopaedia of Education* (1st Ed.), Supplement Vol.1, 162–3. Oxford: Pergamon Press.

Wideen, M.F. and Grimmett, P. (eds), (1995), *Changing Times in Teacher Education: Restructuring or Reconceptualization*. London: Falmer.

Wideen, M.F., Mayer-Smith, J. and Moon, B. (1997), 'A critical examination of research on learning-to-teach'. Paper presented to the Annual meeting of American Educational Research Association, Chicago, March 1997.

1.2 Initial teacher education in England and Wales – some findings from the Modes of Teacher Education Project

Geoff Whitty, John Furlong, Caroline Whiting,
Sheila Miles and Len Barton

Introduction

The Modes of Teacher Education (MOTE) project which we commenced in January 1991 was designed to provide a sharper focus to the policy debate about the nature, costs and benefits of initial teacher education (ITE). It involved a national survey of the various routes to qualified teacher status (QTS) in England and Wales at that time and a detailed study of a sample of training courses. These included:

- conventional four-year BEd/BA (QTS) courses
- one-year Post Graduate Certificate in Education (PGCE) courses
- shortened, lengthened and part-time courses
- articled teacher courses
- licensed teacher (LT) schemes.

Among the project's publications was *Initial Teacher Education in England and Wales: A Topography*, which provided a snapshot of the character of ITE at the start of the decade (Barrett et al., 1992). Although the period 1984–92 had seen major reforms in ITE, our study concluded that, while higher education institutions (HEIs) had sought to 'integrate' students' work in the HEI with the world of the school, the formal responsibilities of teachers in the planning and provision of training had not significantly changed across the system as a whole (Furlong et al., 1995).

By the time we began the follow-up project,[1] which ran from 1993 to 1996, further changes were under way, which sought to alter this state of affairs. Circular 9/92 for secondary courses and Circular 14/93 for primary courses (Department for Education, 1992 and 1993) established a new framework for the relationship between schools and higher education providers in the provision of ITE in England and Wales. Through these Circulars, the Government insisted that in the future teacher education courses should be planned and run on the basis of a partnership between higher education and schools. For example, Circular 9/92 stated that the Government expected that partner schools and HEIs would exercise a joint responsibility for the planning and management of courses and the selection, training and assessment of students. Students on PGCE courses were expected to spend two-thirds of their time in school. The Circular also insisted that HEIs, schools and students should 'focus on the competences of teaching through the whole period of initial training' (Department for Education, 1992). The primary Circular insisted on a similar approach, although rather less time had to be spent in school (Department for Education, 1993). The new approach to secondary training had to be implemented by 1994. The changes to primary training were to be phased in by 1996.

Modes of partnership

In the course of our second study, we saw HEIs and schools developing partnership in various ways. Reflecting on the changes we observed in our sample of courses, we identified three 'ideal typical' models of partnership, which we characterized as:

- 'collaborative partnership'
- 'HEI-led partnership'
- 'separatist partnership'.

It is important to emphasize that these models are indeed ideal typical. Any one actual course could embody elements of more than one model. Indeed, mixed models were not uncommon during the period of transition.

Collaborative partnership

Collaboration is probably the model of partnership that is best known within the literature. It is epitomized by Oxford University's secondary PGCE course. As McIntyre (1990) has argued, at the heart of this model is the commitment to develop a training programme where students are exposed to different forms of educational knowledge, some of which come from school, some of which come from higher education or elsewhere. Teachers are seen as having an equally legitimate, but perhaps different, body of professional knowledge from those in higher education. Students are expected and encouraged to use what they learn in school to critique what they learn within the HEI and vice-versa.

HEI-led partnership

The second model of partnership that we identified from our qualitative fieldwork was HEI-led. This model of partnerships was fundamentally different from the collaborative model in that it was indeed led by those in the HEI, although sometimes with the help of a small group of teachers acting as consultants. The aim, as far as course leadership was concerned, was to utilise schools as a resource in setting up learning opportunities for students. Course leaders had a set of aims which they wanted to achieve and this demanded that schools act in similar ways and make available comparable opportunities for all students. Within this model, quality control – making sure students all receive comparable training opportunities – has a high priority.

The motivation for the HEI-led model was either pragmatic or principled. The pragmatic motivation was that local schools were unwilling or unable to take on a greater degree of responsibility for training. Alternatively, course leaders were committed to a model of training that was antithetical to the demands of partnership. They maintained, for example, a strong commitment to introducing students to 'the best' in educational practice within their subject area or to the role of educational theory within ITE. In many such courses, course leaders' aims did not seem to have changed significantly from the past, although the means of achieving them certainly had. If an HEI-led vision of training is to be achieved in the new context, then the challenge is how to achieve it within a highly devolved system – schools and teachers have to be drawn into the process of training in a systematic and structured manner.

Separatist partnership

The final model of partnership that was identified from our qualitative fieldwork was a separatist one, where school and HEI were seen as having separate and complementary responsibilities but where there was no systematic attempt to bring these two dimensions into dialogue. In other words, there was partnership but not necessarily integration in the course – integration was something that students had to achieve for themselves. Interestingly, this is the model of partnership that is put forward within Government Circulars 9/92 and 14/93. The vision of the Circulars is of a division of labour between schools and HEI rather than integration. Within our sample of courses, it seemed that such a model might emerge either from a principled commitment to allowing schools the legitimacy to have their own distinctive area of responsibility or as a pragmatic response to financial constraints. In practice, the separatist model seemed to be emerging more frequently as a pragmatic response to limited resources.

Forming partnerships

From our second national survey of courses,[2] reported more fully in Whiting et al. (1996), it was clear that, in 1995–6, the majority of courses were operating largely on the HEI-led model of partnership.

The model of partnership that it is possible to establish between an HEI and its local schools clearly depends on the availability of schools willing and able to take on the 'partner' role, however it is defined. Respondents to the survey were asked to state the criteria used by their courses for selecting partner schools. Examples of desired criteria included previous relationships and good track records with students, trained mentor availability and, for secondary courses, suitable subject departments. Primary course leaders often mentioned matching philosophy or ethos within the schools and the HEI and availability of National Curriculum expertise.

These selection criteria were often written into partnership agreements. However, difficulty in recruiting schools meant that they could not always be applied. It is not possible to know from this survey how many schools were actually selected according to the stated criteria, but it may be significant that the most common criterion of selection cited by respondents was 'willingness' to be a partner and to sign up.

Over one-third (35.7 per cent) of the respondent courses reported difficulties in recruiting schools. This difficulty was particularly evident in secondary courses and most pronounced in shortened, part-time or conversion courses. This is probably because these courses had a particular subject bias: 44 per cent of them offered maths compared with 16 per cent of conventional postgraduate courses and 39.1 per cent of undergraduate courses. In fact, 20 out of 29 maths courses (69 per cent) reported difficulties in recruiting suitable schools. In addition to problems in maths, difficulties were frequently mentioned in respect of science, technology and modern languages. Art, geography and religious education (RE) were also seen as problematic by some respondents. The point was made, in particular reference to RE, that departments were often small, with no head of department.

In some areas, competition from other HEIs had exacerbated problems with placements – sometimes because schools had signed up to a sole partnership with another HEI, sometimes because they were offering better terms. Where there were schools taking students from more than one HEI, it had sometimes caused complications or even withdrawal of partnership. Many secondary course leaders suggested that some schools were unwilling to take on the added responsibility involved in partnership schemes, especially when funding did not reflect the time and effort required. This was expected to apply even more to primary courses and there was concern about what would happen when the fuller partnership model became mandatory in September 1996. Primary schools were often said to be happy with old arrangements and not to want full partnership and the additional responsibilities it implied.

Teacher involvement

Our survey asked course leaders whether school-based teachers were involved in a number of aspects of their courses. Teachers were certainly becoming more involved in course design and interviewing, but course leadership remained largely the responsibility of HEI-based tutors on all except the pilot school-centred initial teacher training (SCITT) courses run by consortia of schools. The only areas in which teachers were seen as having joint or primary responsibility was, unsurprisingly, in the area of school experience. In other areas of teaching, teachers were often involved, but only in secondary main subject application were they moving towards taking joint responsibility. As for assessment of students, only in practical teaching were teachers taking joint responsibility and, in the case of a few secondary courses, even taking the primary responsibility for it. Teachers still took virtually no role in assessing essays and examination scripts, but did have some involvement in assessing school-based investigations and the development of curriculum materials. They were, however, taking joint responsibility for student profiling, especially when this was based on competences.

The overall pattern was, therefore, one of teacher involvement, rather than responsibility, consistent with the HEI-led model of partnership. It is also consistent with the limited amount of training offered to teachers involved in teacher education. Our survey suggested that very few had received more than three days training for their new roles. Given that much of the training was paid for out of special transitional funding, it seems unlikely that this will change in the immediate future.

Course outcomes

It has recently been claimed by the Major Government[3] that half of the students leaving teacher education courses and a similar proportion of their headteachers are dissatisfied with their training. This is being used to justify further reforms. Yet, even before the 1992–3 reforms had been fully implemented, we found levels of satisfaction considerably higher than claimed by the Government. At the end of the first MOTE Project, we had developed three research instruments to provide data about the outcomes of different modes of training. These were:

- an 'exit' questionnaire administered to students on completion of their training course

- a 'newly qualified teacher' (NQT) questionnaire administered at the end of the trainees' first year of teaching

- a 'headteacher' questionnaire to be completed by a senior member of staff at the NQT's school at the end of their first year of teaching.

Each instrument included a list of 'practical competences' and 'professional understandings'. Respondents were asked to make judgements on a range of professional competences and understandings on a scale of 1 to 3 – well prepared, adequately prepared or poorly prepared. Further items were designed to probe the contribution of the different partners in training to the development of students' practical competences and other professional abilities. The exit questionnaires were distributed to 1,416 students leaving a sample of initial training courses between 1992 and 1994, stratified by mode of provision, geographical region and institutional sector. Of the 567 returned, 248 respondents were primary students and 319 secondary students.

The data yielded by the survey are particularly interesting in view of the Government's proposed National Curriculum for ITE and the then Secretary of State's claims about the inadequacy of the present arrangements for preparing primary students for the teaching of reading and maths. On our exit questionnaire, 82.5 per cent of finishing primary students reported that they were well or adequately prepared to teach reading. A total of 79.5 per cent said they were well or adequately prepared to teach maths, while as many as 89 per cent said they were well or adequately prepared to teach science. This positive picture is consistent with the analysis of recent inspection reports carried out by the Universities Council for the Education of Teachers (UCET) (Furlong and Kane, 1996).

At the end of their first year of teaching the MOTE NQT questionnaires revealed even higher levels of satisfaction in reading and maths:

- 88 per cent of new primary teachers felt they had been well or adequately prepared to teach reading

- 93.5 per cent felt that they had been well or adequately prepared to teach maths

- 88 per cent still felt that they had been well or adequately prepared to teach science.

The responses to the headteacher questionnaire showed that, by and large, headteachers shared this positive evaluation of the competences of new entrants to the profession. A total of 81.5 per cent of primary headteachers felt that their new teachers were well or adequately prepared to teach reading, whereas 93 per cent felt the same about maths. A startling 98 per cent expressed the view that their new teachers were well or adequately prepared to teach science, probably reflecting the lack of confidence in this field among more experienced teachers.

Finishing students themselves also felt particularly confident in a number of other areas – a majority saying they felt well prepared to use a range of strategies and resources, ensure continuity and progression, maintain motivation and interest, and appraise the effectiveness of their teaching. They did, however, feel significantly less well prepared, both on exit and on reflection a year later, in areas such as teaching children for whom English was a second language, special educational needs (although this concern was not endorsed by headteachers), personal and social education, Information Technology and a number of primary non-core curriculum subjects such as music.

In the exit questionnaires students were also asked to rate the differential contribution of schools and HEIs to their training on key professional competences and understandings. In relation to 'professional understandings', students reported almost twice as many positive contributions from HEIs as schools. In relation to practical competences, the same divisions did not emerge – both schools and HEIs were seen as making important contributions across a range of competences.

The data also indicated some significant differences between modes of training. For example, students on school-based articled teacher courses felt they had less understanding of child development than those on conventional courses, but felt better prepared for talking with parents. Data from our 1996 exit surveys should indicate whether there have been further changes in the outcomes of conventional courses as they have responded to the Government's changing requirements. There is clearly a need to collect data in future years to see the full effect of the primary reforms, but unfortunately our own ESRC funding has now come to an end.

Our data clearly have their limitations. They refer only to student, NQT and headteacher perceptions rather than telling us anything directly about the effects of teacher training on pupil outcomes. The response rate, at 40 per cent, was also somewhat disappointing, although similar to that of other recent surveys using a comparable methodology (e.g. Barker et al., 1996). However, there is no reason to suppose that disgruntled students would have been less likely to respond to a national survey than satisfied ones. Indeed, recent negative publicity about the quality of teacher training might even have had the opposite effect.

As far as we know, these are the best data on this subject currently available and they are certainly more up-to-date than those cited by the Government to demonstrate high levels of dissatisfaction. Even if their figures were correct for the early-1990s, our study would seem to suggest that some significant improvements have already taken place. However, even a satisfaction rate of 80 per cent or more is no grounds for complacency. More needs to be done to improve the overall quality of new entrants to teaching, but it is surely best to base this on an accurate assessment of the real scale of the problem.

Our figures are not necessarily an argument against the proposed National Curriculum for primary teacher education, but they do contain a warning that undue emphasis on English, maths and science could put a further squeeze on work in the very areas in which students already feel least well prepared (e.g. the teaching of children for whom English is a second language, special educational needs and non-core subjects in the primary curriculum). Furthermore, the increased time in school required from primary students from 1996 onwards might make the situation in these areas worse. Certainly, the articled teachers in our sample reported less confidence than others in some of these very areas, suggesting that they might not be well covered in school-based training.

Implications for teacher professionalism

One of the issues with which our research was centrally concerned was what the changes we were seeing implied for the future of teacher professionalism. What, we wondered, were the implications of the shift to school-based training and the increased use of competences for definitions of what counts as a professional teacher. In reflecting on these issues, we necessarily move beyond reporting the data, and try to interpret it and extrapolate from it.

It is clear that the British Government has been less than enthusiastic about some features of teachers' professional ideologies, particularly the so-called trendy child-centred teaching of the 1960s. A recurring theme in the pamphlets of New Right pressure groups is the need to challenge the liberal educational establishment, which is seen to have been behind the 'progressive collapse' of the English educational system. This educational establishment, dominated by teacher educators, local education authority (LEA) advisers and teaching unions, is seen as prey to ideology and self-interest and no longer in touch with the public.

Strategies for challenging this supposed self-interest of the profession are particularly evident in the Government's ITE reforms. The preferred strategy of the neo-liberal marketisers is deregulation of the profession to allow schools to go into the market and recruit graduates (or even non-graduates) without professional training and prepare them on an apprenticeship basis in school. The introduction of new routes into teaching and the strategy of locating more and more elements of training in schools has been partly (though not wholly) influenced by such views.

Deregulation also has some appeal to neo-conservative critics who have detected a collectivist (and even crypto-Marxist) ideological bias amongst teacher educators in higher education. However, neo-conservatives are still concerned with enemies within the teaching profession as a whole as well as within teacher education. They believe it is 'time to set aside the professional educators and the majority of organized teacher unions [who] are primarily responsible for the present state of Britain's schools' (Hillgate Group, 1987). Such views, combined with vocationalist concerns about international competitiveness (Hickox, 1995), have meant that the Government has not pursued a policy of total deregulation or a wholesale devolution of teacher training to the schools.

Instead, it has shown some concern to shape the content of teachers' professional knowledge, initially through the introduction of a common list of competences to be required of beginning teachers, regardless of the nature of the route by which they have achieved them, and then by Government proposals for a National Curriculum for primary teacher education. This has given rise to the suspicion that the Government wants to 'deprofessionalize' teaching by ensuring that, wherever they are trained, teachers focus on the development of craft skills rather than professional understanding.

Maclure (1993) has suggested that the downgrading of university involvement in teacher education represents an attempt to dismantle the traditional defences of teaching as a profession. Meanwhile, Jones and Moore (1993) argue that an emphasis on competences will serve to undermine the dominant discourse of liberal humanism within the teaching profession and replace it with one of technical rationality. Adams and Tulasiewicz (1995) complain that teachers are being turned into technicians rather than 'reflective professionals'. Such commentators feel that basing training in particular schools can limit the development of broader perspectives on education, and that specifying a limited range of competences will encourage 'restricted' rather than 'extended' professionality (Hoyle, 1974). More charitable observers, though, might argue that the Government is trying to reform teacher education in order to '*re*professionalize' teaching more in line with what it perceives as the needs of the twenty-first century.

Just as in education reform more generally, there seems to have been a dual strategy involving devolution of *some* responsibilities to schools at the same time as prescribing more things from the centre. Schools and teachers might be 'empowered' to develop their own specialisms or 'local' professionalisms and thus compete with one another, but only within a very narrow frame. To this extent, the last five years might have seen the erosion of an HEI-led definition of professionalism in ITE, not so much to devolve real responsibility to schools as Hargreaves (1994) and Berrill (1994) might suppose, but to impose an alternative and more restricted state mandated one. The role of the Teacher Training Agency (TTA) established in 1994, and part of the 'quango state', is particularly significant here (Mahony and Hextall, 1996). Other potential stakeholders who might foster an alternative collective definition of teacher professionalism, whether HEIs, LEAs, teacher unions or a General Teaching Council (GTC), have been marginalized in the process. This combined use of state control and deregulation to get rid of so-called vested interests is consistent with what Gamble sees as the broader Thatcherite project of creating a 'strong' state and a 'free' economy (Gamble, 1988).

Whatever one may think about the motives behind the reforms, we were interested as researchers, both within our fieldwork and our various surveys, in the extent to which the reforms in ITE were actually bringing about changes in the prevailing view of what it meant to be a professional teacher.

Both our national surveys asked course leaders whether their courses were designed on the basis of a particular view of teaching that could be articulated and potentially held in common by the various contributors to the course. When asked whether their course was based on any particular model of the teacher, 137 out of 211 course leaders in the

1995–6 survey said 'yes' (65 per cent). This percentage was identical to the response of the 'old' universities at the time of the previous survey (Barrett et al., 1992), but significantly lower than that obtained from the (then) polytechnics, where the Council for National Academic Awards (CNAA) had a strong influence on such matters.

We were also interested in the extent to which the existence of an official list of competences, which has often been criticized for embodying technical rationality and neglecting more reflective and critical competences, was actually changing the model of the teacher espoused by teacher educators. We found that 46 per cent adhered to the notion of the reflective practitioner, compared with 57 per cent at the time of the previous survey. Meanwhile, those specifically espousing the 'competency' model had doubled but only to 11 per cent. Even if it was somewhat less dominant than it had been five years previously, 'reflective practice', rather than technical rationality, was still by far the most popular discourse of professionalism within university and college (and indeed school) based courses.[4]

At the same time, however, the use of competences in courses had increased significantly since the previous survey – well beyond the 11 per cent of courses that explicitly espoused a 'competency' model. Indeed, all secondary courses were required to use them at the time of our latest survey and primary courses were gearing up for the requirement. So how can the use of competences be reconciled with the continuing attachment to the reflective practitioner model?

Our survey showed that only about 8 per cent of courses restricted themselves to using the competences specified in the Government Circulars, whereas over 75 per cent had chosen to supplement the official lists with additional competences of their own. This was consistent with our fieldwork, which indicated that there was little continuing objection to the idea of competences among course leaders, but only because they felt that reflective competences could be added to the official list in order to sustain a broader definition of professionality. So course leaders appeared to be able to defend extended notions of professionality, while still conforming to Government policy.

However, it is also clear from our fieldwork that many of the higher education staff who had taken a leading role in developing reflective competences (e.g. those teaching foundations, current issues and teacher as researcher courses) were amongst those most susceptible to early retirement and casualization in an era of retrenchment. This has made it difficult for many courses to maintain this work in practice. 'Core' teacher education staff in both higher education and schools are increasingly becoming those concerned with curriculum subjects and classroom management. This means, incidentally, that the staff left in teacher education in HEIs are often those whose skills are closest to those of school-based teachers, thus potentially undermining any claim for a distinctive role for HEIs in teacher education.

Another question in our recent survey asked respondents to choose three words from a list which would best characterize the sort of teacher their course aimed to produce. Despite some resistance to this question, the responses beyond reflective, professional and competent, were quite varied. However, it is noteworthy that some of the terms that New Right critics often associate with HEI-based teacher education – such as child-centredness and critical – were amongst the least popular choices. Unfortunately, we did not have a similar question on the earlier survey to compare this with, but it might suggest a drift towards the more conservative interpretations of reflective practice.

It is also the case that there is a wide variation of practice in schools in relation to many issues with which teacher education has been concerned. For example, a recent report for the Equal Opportunities Commission found 'wide variation amongst schools and LEAs in the awareness and application of gender issues' (Arnot, David and Weiner, 1996). The shift of more educational and professional studies into schools, with their own 'local' discourses around education, means that treatment of such areas of work in ITE is already becoming highly variable – not only across different universities and colleges, but also across different partner schools of the same university, except where there are strongly collaborative forms of partnership (Furlong et al., 1996).

So what about the future? In the medium term, there is likely to be increased variation and fragmentation in student experience beyond the rather narrow set of mandated competences. There is a danger that school-based training will mean that we move towards a variety of 'local professionalisms' (plural) at the margins, with the common elements of teacher professionalism increasingly confined to the officially prescribed competences and the new National Curriculum for teacher education. It seems to us, though, that a healthy teaching profession will require continuing efforts to maintain a more broadly defined sense of common professional identity if Maclure's (1993) worst fears are not to be realized. That is not to say that current definitions of teacher professionalism do not need to change, but it is to question the appropriateness of the current combination of restricted and localized forms of professionalism and to hang on to a broader collective view of what it means to be a professional teacher.

While some aspects of this may be fostered through HEIs, teaching unions or a GTC, or some combination of those, this can probably not be the whole story as we enter the twenty-first century. We have to recognize that both the state control and market forces strategies are indicative of a 'low trust' relationship between society and its teachers. Media characterizations of teacher unions often tend to encourage popular suspicion of teachers. Furthermore, the defence of the education service has too often been conducted within the assumptions of the 'old' politics of education, which involved consultation between Government, employers and unions but excluded whole constituencies – notably parents and business – to whom the New Right has subsequently successfully appealed (Apple and Oliver, 1996). We need to ask some fundamental questions about who has a legitimate right to be involved in defining teacher professionalism.

It is perhaps indicative of the paucity of thinking on this issue that some of the left teacher educators who, 20 years ago, were criticizing the elitism of the profession should now be amongst those suggesting that teachers should adopt the modes of self-regulation traditionally associated with the conservative professions of medicine and the law. Are state control, market forces or professional self-governance the only models of accountability, or can we develop new models of teacher professionalism, based on more participatory relationships with diverse communities?

In this context, some aspects of the reforms may potentially have their progressive moments. In Australia, Preston and Walker (1993) claim that a non-reductive version of competences can actually help to enhance and legitimate teacher professionalism. Knight, Bartlett and McWilliam (1993) argue that devolution can foster a flexibility, diversity and responsiveness which they quite rightly suggest has been largely lacking in teacher education as it has traditionally been conducted. There has always been a tension between the profession's claim to particular and specialist knowledge and expertise and a degree of relative autonomy and a requirement that it be open to the needs and concerns of other groups in a democratic society. Devolution of decision making could, they suggest, herald the emergence of what they call 'democratic professionalism', which seeks to demystify professional work and facilitate the participation in decision making by students, parents and others within the public sphere.

However, the positive consequences of this envisaged as a possibility by Knight, Bartlett and McWilliam in Australia (at least before the recent Federal elections) seem less likely to be forthcoming on any significant scale in England and Wales, where 'local' definitions of professionalism exist at the periphery alongside a strong core definition of teacher professionalism based on a restricted notion of professionality – supported by technologies of control that include the official specification of competences, inspection by the Office for Standards in Education (OFSTED), TTA funding decisions, etc.

In some ways, the use of such devices may constitute a shift away from conventional techniques of co-ordination and control on the part of large-scale bureaucratic state forms and their replacement by a set of 'discursive, legislative, fiscal, organizational and other resources' (Rose and Miller, 1992:189). Yet, these apparently 'post-modern' forms not only impact on organizational subjectivities and professional identities, they also entail some fairly direct modes of control. The extent to which individual schools can challenge them is likely to be both limited and variable. We can already see in HEIs the ways in which such pressures limit what can be achieved. While our topography shows that most course leaders still aspire to deliver extended notions of professionality, as reflected in their extended lists of competences, the changing structure is making it ever more difficult to do so. It is fanciful to think that individual schools will really have any greater freedom than universities and colleges.

In that situation, any attempt to develop an alternative approach to teacher education reform, even in a context of globalization and 'post-modernity', will require the mobilization of broadly-based national political support and not just professional and local partnerships. The urgent need is for teacher educators to stop being purely defensive or reactive and to begin working with others to develop approaches that relate not only to the legitimate aspirations of the profession but also those of the wider society – and that must include those groups within civil society who have hitherto not been well-served either by the profession or by the state.

Notes

1 The original 'Modes of Teacher Education' (MOTE) project ran from January 1991 to December 1992 with funding from the Economic and Social Research Council (Grant No. R000232810). The follow-up project, which ran from 1993 to 1996, was formally entitled 'Changing Modes of Professionalism? A Case Study of Teacher Education in Transition' (Grant No. R000234185), but the generic title of MOTE continued to be used to encompass the work of both projects.

2 From the 280 HEI-led courses, 211 completed course questionnaires were received, representing a response rate of 75 per cent. Nine out 19 school-centred initial teacher training (SCITT) courses responded to a similar survey, but the results reported here are drawn only from the 211 HEI-led courses.

3 This paper was written prior to the Labour Party's victory in the General Election on 1st May 1997.

4. There are, of course, a number of different interpretations of the concept of reflective practice in teacher education. See Zeichner and Liston (1987) and Hill (1996).

References

Adams, A. and Tulasiewicz, W. (1995), *The Crisis in Teacher Education: A European Concern?* London: Falmer Press.

Apple, M.W. and Oliver, A. (1996), 'Becoming right: education and the formation of conservative movements', in Apple, M.W., *Cultural Politics and Education*. New York: Teachers College Press.

Arnot, M., David, M. and Weiner, G. (1996), *Educational Reforms and Gender Equality in Schools*. Manchester: EOC.

Barker, S., Brooks, V., March, K. and Swatton, P. (1996), *Initial Teacher Education in Secondary Schools*. London: Association of Teachers and Lecturers.

Barrett, E., Barton, L., Furlong, J., Galvin, C., Miles, S. and Whitty, G. (1992), *Initial Teacher Education in England and Wales: A Topography*. London: Modes of Teacher Education Project, Goldsmiths College.

Berrill, M. (1994), 'A view from the crossroads',*Cambridge Journal of Education*, 24(1), 113-116.

Department for Education (DfE), (1992), *Initial Teacher Training (Secondary Phase), (Circular 9/92)*. London: Department for Education.

—   (1993), *Initial Teacher Training (Primary Phase), (Circular 14/93)*. London: Department for Education.

Furlong, J. and Kane, I. (1996), *Recognizing Quality in Primary ITE*. London: Universities Council for the Education of Teachers.

Furlong, J., Whitty, G., Barrett, E., Barton, L. and Miles, S. (1995), 'Integration and partnership in initial teacher education – dilemmas and possibilities', *Research Papers in Education*, 9(3), 281–301.

Furlong, J., Whitty, G., Whiting, C., Miles, S., Barton, L. and Barrett, E. (1996), 'Re-defining partnership: revolution or reform in initial teacher education', *Journal of Education for Teaching*, 22(1), 39–55.

Gamble, A. (1988), *The Free Economy and the Strong State*. London: Macmillan.

Hargreaves, D. (1994), 'Another radical approach to the reform of initial teacher training', *Westminster Studies in Education*, 13.

Hickox, M. (1995), 'Situating vocationalism', *British Journal of Sociology of Education*, 16(2), 153–63.

Hill, D. (1996), 'Reflection in teacher education', in Watson, K. et al (eds) *Educational Dilemmas: Debate and Diversity, Volume 1: Teacher Education and Training*. London: Cassell.

Hillgate Group (1987), *The Reform of British Education*. London: Claridge Press.

Hoyle, E. (1974), 'Professionality, professionalism and control in teaching', *London Education Review*, 3(2) 13-19.

Jones, L. and Moore, R. (1993), 'Education, competence and the control of expertise', *British Journal of Sociology of Education*, 14, 385–97.

Knight, J., Bartlett, L. and McWilliam, E. (eds), (1993), *Unfinished Business: Reshaping the Teacher Education Industry for the 1990s*. Rockhampton: University of Central Queensland.

Maclure, S. (1993), 'Fight this tooth and nail', *The Times Educational Supplement*, 18 June.

McIntyre, D. (1990), 'The Oxford Internship Scheme and the Cambridge analytical framework: models of partnership in initial teacher education', in Booth, M., Furlong, J. and Wilkin, M., *Partnership in Initial Teacher Training*. London: Cassell.

Mahony, P. and Hextall, I. (1996), 'Trailing the TTA'. Paper presented to the British Educational Research Association Annual Conference, University of Lancaster, 13-15 September.

Preston, B. and Walker, J.C. (1993), 'Competency-based standards in the professions and higher education', in Collins, C., *Competencies: The Competencies Debate in Australian Education and Training*. Canberra: Australian College of Education.

Rose, N. and Miller, P. (1992), 'Political power beyond the state: problematics of government', *British Journal of Sociology*, 43(2), 173–205.

Whiting, C., Whitty, G., Furlong, J., Miles, S. and Barton, L. (1996), *Partnership in Initial Teacher Education: A Topography*. London: Modes of Teacher Education Project, Institute of Education.

Zeichner, K. and Liston, D. (1987), 'Teaching student teachers to reflect', *Harvard Educational Review*, 57(1), 23–48.

1.3 Possible futures for initial teacher education in the primary phase

Anne Edwards

The current context of initial teacher education in the UK

Primary school teaching is deceptively difficult and, just as primary school teaching is complex, so is the initial training of teachers to work in the primary phase. Or at least it ought to be. There simply are not any quick fixes. However, there is arguably considerable potential for the development of primary education if primary school specialists turn their collective attention to teacher training.

Quite clearly initial teacher education is important. I am not alone in this belief. The previous Conservative Government agreed and from 1984 did a great deal to harness initial training to its ideologies (Wilkin, 1996). The result is that current emphases in Initial Teacher Training (ITT) on skills, commodified or modularized knowledge and purchaser-provider models of partnership appear to reflect the educational agenda of successive Conservative Governments (Gilroy et al., 1994). However, these formulae have not produced the desired rapid rise in standards and the closing of the skills gap. Apparently the only recourse remaining has been the demonization of ITT and the blaming of it for the ills it has been charged to cure.

If ITT is potentially so powerful a shaper of a nation's future, clearly it is worth taking it seriously. We need to get it right. To do so, I suggest, involves linking ITT to an avowedly communitary agenda aimed at the common wealth or common weal, i.e. the greatest good for the maximum number (Taylor, 1991). Such a move will involve the erosion of a number of the boundaries which currently fragment the education system and which separate the system from the wider community. These boundaries are likely to be eroded in dialogues between stakeholders in education who include policy makers, teachers, parents, student teachers, university staff and local education authority (LEA) advisors. Importantly, these dialogues should allow participants to contribute their own expertise and experience.

One of the contributions higher education can make to educational dialogues on training can be achieved through working with school-based colleagues to provide evidence of what is actually going on in ITT. That evidence can be brought to the conversations as a sound basis for planning the future of training. Hargreaves has pointed out that such is the rapidity of change in English and Welsh education that we have become more tolerant of speculation and have lowered our expectations of substantiation (Hargreaves, 1994). In this chapter, I want to do a little more than simply speculate. First, I will trace the instability of the current contexts of ITT. I will then discuss some of the little data available on initial training in the primary phase. Finally, I will speculate on the lessons to be learnt from the research and the opportunities for development available in current contexts.

Let us start with current contexts and the robust trends or debates to be found within them. The trends are closely linked, but do not necessarily present a consistent pattern. In them we can observe opportunities and difficulties.

There is currently an erosion of the boundaries between the intramural and extramural provision of universities through, for example, workplace learning schemes, the increasing status of applied research, the franchising of provision and the accreditation of prior learning and/or experience. In this context, as Bridges has argued, ITT can perhaps be regarded to be at the forefront of a much wider university development (Bridges, 1996).

The decline in core funding for higher education from 1990 has resulted in a necessarily bottom-line approach to the survival of aspects of university provision. In addition the role of the Teacher Training Agency (TTA) in the funding of ITT in England and Wales has not endeared teacher training to senior managers in universities. Consequently ITT programmes in most universities are under constant review, and those university departments of education which can, are emphasising their research viability within their own institutions.

Current debates over the nature of professionalism within contexts of markets, performance and accountability raise questions about the status of teaching as a profession and inevitably about the lack of a publicly recognized knowledge base underpinning teacher decision making.

Teacher supply is likely to be an increasing problem as the economy improves. The TTA has the burden of ensuring the level of that supply and has continued with a brief of encouraging a variety of routes to qualified teacher status (QTS). It is ironic, therefore, that university departments of education are being scapegoated for the failure of Conservative education policies at the very time that the universities should be being encouraged in their commitment to ITT.

School development planning systems in primary schools have perhaps lagged behind the secondary sector, but are now important features of primary school management. Arguably these systems are now sufficiently robust to allow the full incorporation of ITT commitments into them, but few appear to be doing so.

The themes which appear to be woven through the changing context of ITT for primary schools seem to reflect some of the tensions and contradictions of post-modernity and the uncertainties that it represents. Boundaries slip, goals conflict and identities are not sustained by familiar expectations. Let us pursue just three key themes emerging from the shifts in context just outlined.

The nature of educational knowledge is being called into question as we examine relationships between reasoning about practice in the workplace and theoretical reasoning in universities. The development of educational knowledge will depend on closer research and partnerships between practitioners in schools and universities. However, the role of university departments of education in the development of educational knowledge demands that university researchers move back and forth from the safety of the academic disciplines to the dangers of the margins of engagement with practice at the very time that they are trying to assert their positions as serious research departments within the universities (Edwards, 1996a).

Teachers in schools are asked to adjust their relationships with the students they mentor in school contexts which are not yet geared to recognize the demands or potential of those relationships. Consequently, mentors and students are all too frequently desert-islanded together in the midst of the ocean of school life and connected to universities largely through the rushed ministrations of university-based link tutors (Edwards and Collison, 1996a).

In an attempt to bring the profession of teaching more evidently under central control, the Government and the TTA appear to be by-passing the universities to work directly with individual teachers and schools. At the same time, they criticize what are described as the 'privately arrived at pedagogies' of teachers (Millett, 1996) and require university support in meeting teacher supply targets.

Here we have evidence of a system in flux. Contexts have been disrupted in ways which challenge and shift current identities, break down established relationships and increase links between central Government and individual schools. The centralist thrust of the Government is hard to resist if we are to argue the case for the importance of ITT for the nation's future. However, we do perhaps need to consider alternatives to a form of centralism which depends so much on the fragmentation of the social group, i.e. professional educators, it is attempting to develop. For example, we see a fragmentation or splitting of the ITT community in some school-centred initial teacher training (SCITT) schemes and in the separatist type of training discussed by the Modes of Teacher Education (MOTE) Project (Whiting et al., 1996).

Charles Taylor describes the dangers of fragmentation in a bureaucratic centralism which aims at the control of individuals in the following way.

The danger is not actual despotic control but fragmentation – that is, a people increasingly less capable of forming a common purpose and carrying it out. Fragmentation arises when people come to see themselves as less and less bound to their fellow citizens in common projects and alliances.

(Taylor, 1991, pp 112–3)

These ideas brings us back to the earlier suggestion of a communitary agenda for educational provision of which teacher education is only a part. The TTA is doubtless right to promote a continuum between ITT, newly qualified teaching experiences and preparation for more specialist and senior teaching roles. However, there are perhaps opportunities for wider connections to be made to link ITT and a common agenda for the development of educational opportunities from birth onwards.

Metanoia in initial teacher education

Recognizing these opportunities will require what Peter Senge calls 'metanoia', i.e. a change of mind-set (Senge, 1990). Discussing what besets much industrial planning, Senge argues that what is needed when systems have to take on new challenges is not necessarily an adjustment of existing practices, but rather a fresh look at, or a reperception of, the entire system, followed by adjustments at the level of the system. Interestingly, in the discourse of theology, metanoia means more than simply a reperception, but repentance or a turning from the old life to the new (Edwards and Collison, 1996b).

There is a great deal happening in ITT which is thrusting us forward to a new life or new versions of provision. We can all foresee a number of possibly co-existing futures. They will include school-centred models, partnership arrangements of various kinds. Schemes are likely to be regionally organized through co-operating universities and LEAs, or school consortia, or nationally organized as the Open University (OU) is already. The content of the curriculum could be increasingly provided by distance education from bases outside the UK as well as within. Electronic networks will encourage home-based learning and may discourage widespread debate and dialogue. Large-scale training operations will rely increasingly on technology-driven methods of quality assurance. Student poverty may well create a demand for part-time routes. A number of these developments are likely to lead to further fragmentation of the social world of education and its commitment to particular sets of publicly contestable values.

How can we make the most of these changes in ITT and in primary education more generally? Let us consider some ways forward. First, as Hirst argues, we need to develop the knowledge base of teaching as a form of practical reason which is informed by and informs theoretical reasoning and which is regularly and publicly scrutinized by teachers (Hirst, 1996). Furthermore, we need to ensure that engagement with that knowledge base is a core part of ITT and contributes to how teachers construct their identities as teachers while they learn how to teach. We need to recognize that teaching is a complex activity and provide a training which acknowledges that. Recognition of the complexity of the professional knowledge base should operate alongside a developed pedagogy of teacher training. Accountants, lawyers and doctors are treated as learners for extensive periods of their forms of apprenticeship. Student teachers on the other hand are encouraged to undertake trial and error learning in classrooms. Given Anthea Millett's (Chief Executive of the TTA) attention to pedagogy as 'the last corner of the secret garden' (Millett, 1996), as educational professionals, we should be producing rapidly our own professionally contestable and substantiated knowledge base before one is provided for us. Furthermore, we should be clear, as partners in ITT, about how student teachers master it.

Second, we need to talk more about actual practice, the dilemmas and the commonplace. We need to unpack practice for student teachers and induct them into a professional discourse which recognizes the complexity of the work of primary school teaching. Consequently, we need to accelerate the development of a language of professional practice which allows scrutiny, substantiation and the recognition of significant themes.

Third, we need to recognize the potential contribution that initial training can make to the educational continuum which runs from birth.

We need to exercise metanoia in the way that Birmingham, England, as the learning city[1] has done by pulling together all existing sources of educational improvement in a common endeavour. We need to counter the fragmentation of education which has left ITT as professional preparation so isolated.

What happens in school-based initial teacher education?

Each of these ways forward can be supported in dialogues between those who are currently involved in ITT in schools and in universities. However, having emphasised the importance of substantiation, I need first to provide some substantiation for the three assertions just outlined. To do this, I will draw mainly on two sources of evidence. The first, and main, source is data gathered during a three-year intensive study of the experiences of student teachers preparing for infant school teaching in a pilot training partnership between schools and one higher education institution (HEI) in the north-west of England. Jill Collison was the research officer on the project and data were gathered using interviews, questionnaires, observations and tape recordings of mentoring conversations. Using the MOTE taxonomy of ideal types (Whiting et al., 1996), the partnership we studied employed the rhetoric of collaboration, but operated the reality of a higher education-led scheme. The second source is a current study of the pedagogy of expert primary teachers in Leeds.

A training for a complex role

Like other studies of ITT (John, 1996) we found that the students we tracked over their three year programme entered the primary classrooms where they were intended to learn how to support pupil learning with clear views of what being a teacher meant. Also they usually entered the classrooms with ideas for tasks they wanted to try with children. These tasks were often valued by their teacher mentors as 'useful fresh ideas from the College'.

Student teachers then worked with children on those tasks with the successful implementation of the task as the desired outcome. Successful implementation involved children's apparent enjoyment and their task completion. However when we analysed the curriculum content of the tasks and compared them with the student teachers' curriculum planning and expectations for pupil learning, we found considerable disparity. The most worrying data came from science where only 17 per cent of student-implemented tasks appeared from our observations of children on-task to be dealing directly with the science curriculum. A major problem was an apparent mismatch between the skills and understanding demanded by the task and the children's current capabilities. This meant that the task was either trivialized by pupils who found it easy or was turned by the student teacher into, for example, a cut and paste exercise to simply ensure that the task was seen to be completed. So, for example, in an activity aimed at mastery of the concepts 'transparent' and 'opaque' the pupils spent their time cutting and pasting silhouettes (Edwards and Collison, 1996c).

Two processes seemed to be at work. First, the student teachers were not seeing pedagogy as teaching and learning, but as simply teaching or, more precisely in this case, as task implementation. In this example, engagement with a professional knowledge base, which drew in part on understandings of how children learn drawn from modern cognitive and developmental psychology, would perhaps have encouraged the students to analyse the difficulties with task implementation they were experiencing and have led to their being rewarded for the insights into children's learning they might consequently have achieved.

Second, the student teachers did not seem to be seeing themselves as learners in the public arena of classrooms but, unsurprisingly given the current emphasis on student teacher competence, as performers who had to get it right first time. They were encouraged in this perception by supportive mentors who were generously giving up parts of their classrooms for the students to work in, but were absolutely not interfering once the students had started teaching (Edwards and Collison, 1996a). Teacher mentors told us, for example, that they saw their classrooms as sites for student trial and error learning (Collison and Edwards, 1994).

There were a few mentors who did use different strategies. However, the students resented what they perceived to be interference. The most acceptable and, hence, probably the most effective mentor support strategy was team teaching (Edwards and Collison, 1996a). An alternative strategy of student teachers' observation of the work of their mentors and discussion of that work was so rare as to barely register in the data we collected (Edwards and Collison, 1995; Edwards, 1997).

The analyses of learning in social settings provided by Lave and Wenger (1991) can help us examine the processes at work when student teachers are placed in classrooms in order to learn. Their perspective on induction into areas of skilled and professional understandings offers us some insights for a pedagogy of ITT and the importance of student teachers' intelligent analysis of more expert practice.

Lave and Wenger talk of the areas of skilled understanding as 'communities of practice'. Communities of practice have shared histories, values, practices and principles. Novices are inducted into these areas or communities through a process which they term 'legitimate peripheral participation'. That is, novices are not expected to engage immediately in the practices of the community as skilled practitioners. Their novice status is acknowledged and their rights to stand at the margins of practice to observe, discuss and partially engage is considered a legitimate activity.

In the community of practice of primary teaching in our study, once the student teachers were in schools to practise teaching, the observation of established practices and discussion of those observations was not considered a valid occupation (Edwards and Collison, 1996a). When students did have the opportunity to watch their mentors, elaborate strategies were devised to disguise what might appear to be their lack of busyness in the classroom.

There was, consequently, little attempt made by the students to draw on the expertise that the mentors held about the complex management of pupil learning (Edwards and Collison, 1995; Edwards, 1997). As a result, the overwhelming conclusion from our study was that student teachers were connecting at a very superficial level with the knowledge base from which their mentors were operating as teachers. In part this was due to the need the students felt to be teachers as soon as they entered the classroom.

Interestingly, the teacher mentors saw their role to be primarily one of carer when working with the students. Some also saw themselves as guides but few felt that their function was to challenge the students. That role they believed belonged to higher education, which should take responsibility for what the mentors termed the 'theory' (Collison and Edwards, 1994). Here we return to the theme of fragmentation already discussed. Rather than the development of the practical reason through the illumination of practice by theory advocated by Hirst (1996), we seemed to be observing, in the partnership programme we studied, a further separation of theory and practice – with theory the province of higher education and practice the province of schools.

Talking about practice

The teacher mentors with whom we worked allowed us to tape record some of the conversations they had with the student teachers either before or after the students worked with pupils. We analysed these conversations in a number of ways. First, we looked at what was discussed. Second, we looked at how the interactions operated.

The data about the content of the conversations supported the teachers' descriptions of themselves as carers and sometimes guides. The major part of mentors' talk centred on practical guidance relating to resourcing the students' tasks for pupils. There was little discussion of the pupils as learners and even less of the students as learners (Edwards and Collison, 1995). The topics of the mentor talk were of course mirrored in the talk of the students. There was barely any reference to the teacher mentors' own teaching during the sessions in which mentors and students both taught (Edwards, 1997).

One reason often given for the lack of discussion about pedagogy in the talk of teachers is that so much of the profession's pedagogical understanding is stored as tacit knowledge and is, hence, inaccessible. However, as we are currently discovering in our study of the pedagogies of expert teachers at Leeds, when discussion is centred on a classroom event which has been observed by both teacher and researcher and the tone of the discussion is one of genuine seeking after information by both participants, expert teachers do articulate with considerable clarity well-worked-out principles of practice and pedagogy (Edwards and Hodgson, 1996).

So what was happening in the mentoring conversations? Our second level of analysis, which looked how the interactions operated, gives some insight. Drawing on some of the ideas of Bakhtin in literary criticism, we looked at how the students addressed their mentors. We looked at how they positioned themselves in the conversations about practice that were the mentoring conversations, i.e. which genre of talk they selected to address their mentors (Edwards, 1977). That analysis revealed that the students selected the genre of polite guest addressing an equally polite host when they talked to their mentors. They positioned themselves as guests who had something of value to bring into the classrooms of their mentor hosts. The interactions were so much those of mentor as polite host and of student as guest bearing gifts to ensure their right of entry that it was difficult for the mentors to do anything but care or gently guide. The polite genre of host–guest prevented challenge.

The gifts that the students brought with them were of course the tasks or 'fresh ideas', which were cited most often as the major value to schools of having students in their classrooms. Therefore, the tasks had to work and to fit seamlessly into the rhythm of the classrooms of the host teachers. The tasks had to succeed, with, as already indicated, a consequent emphasis on student teacher performance at the expense of attention to pupil learning. It was also unsurprising that the content of the talk between mentors and students centred on how to set up the tasks.

What was clearly not happening in the conversations was the induction of student teachers into Hirst's professional discourse of practical reason illuminated by access to theoretical reasoning (Hirst, 1996) and, hence, to the public, open-to-scrutiny knowledge base of teaching as a profession. The discourse in operation was one of practical survival in a particular context. Arguably the legitimization of student teachers as peripheral participants in classrooms would have allowed them at times to pay less attention to their own performances and more to the strategies of their mentors or to the children as users of the learning resources available.

Our current work with expert teachers does seem to suggest that conversations about specific classroom events bring to the surface underlying principles of classroom organization, beliefs about children as learners, curricular goals and understandings of how teachers can promote the learning of pupils. Others too have stressed the importance of classroom events as a key to understanding the processes and structures in operation in complex classrooms (Doyle, 1996).

It would seem that alongside reperceiving the student teachers as learners in classrooms, we need to think about their entitlement to mastery of the professional pedagogic discourse of primary school teaching. Their entry into and use of this discourse in direct association with the practice which stimulates it is entirely in accord with Hirst's view that practical reason is developed when practice is illuminated by reference to theoretical reasoning, i.e. when we talk about practice and relate it to substantiated information available in the public domain.

It seems as if the interface between practice and theory, i.e. talk about events in classrooms, would be the site for student induction into a developed discourse of teachers' professional knowledge. The interface is also arguably the site for aspects of the development of the discourse itself and the development of both teachers and researchers. For some people, this is what reflection on practice actually means. However for all the rhetoric of reflective practice in ITT, we found very little evidence of this kind of reflection in discussions between students and their mentors.

At this point let us return to the idea of communities of practice and think this time about university-based researchers in the field of primary education who are also tutors to student teachers. As researchers, they might belong centrally or peripherally to a general community of practice of educational researchers. As tutors, they will belong to a community of teacher educators. However they also have a great deal in common with classroom-based practitioners in terms of shared beliefs, interpretations of meanings and understandings of common histories. Arguably, therefore, higher education tutors who specialize interactively in primary education have the right to be seen as members of the community of practice of primary education. Furthermore, each of the three communities is enriched by the overlap.

Class management dominated a number of conversations between mentors and beginning teachers and featured in all. Subcategories included organization, such as lesson openings and endings, organizing groups and equipment, timing and pace, safety, classroom routines and seating arrangements. A major subcategory was discipline which included discussion about sanctions, late arrival of pupils, sending pupils out, separating trouble makers, off-task behaviour and minor misdemeanours (e.g. chewing, talking or leaving coats or bags around the classroom). The third subcategory, working relationships, covered issues such as use of praise, relationships with individual pupils as well as with whole classes, dividing attention between groups and sensitivity to individuals' needs. A fourth subcategory of miscellaneous comments included assertive discipline, use of sarcasm, the effect of the time of day and seating arrangements in classrooms.

Subject knowledge and assessment issues featured in the dialogue between all the mentors and their trainees, but to varying degrees and with different foci. Further professional development topics were raised by some mentors and students but not by all.

The function of mentoring

A number of writers have drawn attention to the roles fulfilled by mentors, to the multiplicity and complexity of these roles and to the potential conflicts between some of them. Part of the process of developing a conceptual map of the practice of mentoring was, therefore, to explore the ways in which different roles appeared to emerge in mentor–trainee discussions and the extent to which specific roles were identified by mentors and trainees as important.

Mentor roles have been categorized in various ways within teacher education (Campbell and Horbury, 1994; Nolder, Smith and Melrose, 1994; Back and Booth, 1992; Shaw, 1992) and in the broader context of mentoring in the workplace (Hawkins and Sholet, 1989; Burgoyne and Wiggans, 1994; Jowett, 1995). Three common strands seem to emerge from these varied accounts – the first relates to the mentor's evaluative role, the second to the teaching or training role and the third to the formal assessment of students takes place. The extent to which particular competences are the focus of mentors' attention varies and the Office for Standards in Education (OFSTED) has suggested that mentors are more effective in helping students with class management issues than with other areas of competence. They also state that although mentors are effective in bringing beginning teachers to a basic level of competence, many have difficulty in facilitating the further progress of those students with the capacity to be particularly good. Whether these judgements imply a lack of attention to some aspects of competence or ineffectiveness in addressing them is not known.

In order to analyse the focus of our transcripts, lists of the topics of conversation were drawn up and then grouped into clusters which related to Circular 9/92 competences or other categories. The transcripts were then reread in order to establish the extent to which particular clusters predominated and how broadly individual mentors' discussions ranged.

Subject application along with that related to class management dominated discussion. Four broad subcategories could be identified under the subject application umbrella:

- teaching activities
- use of resources
- meeting pupils' needs
- planning.

Teaching activities included discussions about pair work, group work, sequencing, role play, games, questioning and revision – in short about various teaching techniques or strategies. Use of resources involved dialogue about various teaching aids, such as texts, video, Information Technology (IT), worksheets, boardwork, flashcards and tape recordings. Discussion which came under the heading of meeting pupils' needs ranged from levels of challenge, to high expectations of all, differentiation, use of appropriate language and targeting individuals. The planning category included teaching styles, lesson structure, learning outcomes and lesson evaluations.

of the links stem from the often low status of these individuals in their own institutions and their consequent inability to maximize the potential of those relationships.

One UK university has started to develop strong relationships at institutional level between its ITT functions, its continuing professional development (CPD) work, the development planning of local schools and the strategic planning of the LEA (Ashcroft, Davies and Riddell, 1996). Once such a framework is in place at faculty level and at school level in relation to ITT, arguably the pivotal role of mentors as the point of connection to the university decreases and the mentor role becomes more openly part of a school's relationship with its partner university, with attendant opportunities for growth and less fear of rocking the boat.

Of course one can go further and develop the school relationships that professional development schools have with some North American universities. However, what is impressive about some of the more recent attempts at development schools' relationships in the USA is the extensive preparation for collaboration at university faculty level. Universities have obviously learnt from earlier evaluations which suggested that professional development school relationships will demand that the university also changes.

Once the fear of rocking the boat recedes, we might find that mentoring for ITT can be more closely connected to the professional development of teachers and to the development of theories of practice. Most mentors in our study reported that involvement in mentoring made them examine their own practices. If that degree of reflection could be extended so that mentors and student teachers unpack critically classroom events, we might find that not only are students inducted into the professional discourse of teaching but that the discourse itself is developed (Edwards, 1996b).

The discourse is perhaps more likely to be developed if the role of link tutor becomes one that is less focused on student performance and a little more on student analysis of classroom events. With that aim in mind, link tutors too become conversationalists in the discussion of classroom events. Their role there, in Hirst's (1996) terms, is to illuminate reasoning about practice with theoretical reasoning. To do so, they draw on the resources available to members of the communities of practice of ITT and research. Also as Huberman points out, the pay-off for research in this kind of interaction between research and practice is simultaneously high (Huberman, 1993). However, it will cost money!

What are the implications of the small-scale study of one training partnership? As a case study, it can do no more than raise questions to be followed up elsewhere in other studies and evaluations. However, there is also some urgency in finding responses to the more pressing challenges for the education system. Most important of all are serious concerns about the way schooling as currently conceived can cope with the social and economic backwash of late capitalism. Mentoring, as Goodlad warned the USA, cannot stand alone as the way to make student teachers knowledgeable about and expert in teaching and, thereby, solve a nation's ills. He went on to say:

> 'Substantial improvement', means more than tinkering around the edges of what we have now. It means changing our schools in profound ways. The required change will not occur if we continue to prepare teachers for the school conditions that are now prevailing.
> (Goodlad, 1990:27)

Goodlad goes on to argue for the simultaneous development of schools and ITT so that improvements in one may impact on the other and lead to improvements there. Changes in ITT, it would seem from his analysis, need to proceed alongside changes in schools and, of course in most universities.

In conclusion, let us consider what happens if we fail to create strong and overlapping links between the communities of practice of primary education research, ITT and classroom practice. We are perhaps likely to sustain a continuation of what we have now. The MOTE analysis suggests that collaboration in training is not easy to achieve and a highly probable development is a move from higher education-led models of training partnership to more separatist models, where differences between the thinking of schools and higher education will be even more marked (Whiting et al., 1996). Were this to occur, all three communities – primary education, ITT and research – would be impoverished.

The analysis presented in this chapter suggests that forms of training patnerships which do not embody collaboration are essentially forces for the conservation of existing classroom practices. In addition, a system of partnership which separates theory from practice by severely restricting university tutors' contact with the classroom events which are learning points for students also restricts the engagement of student teachers with a professional discourse informed by both theory and practicalities. The separation also does little for the development of relevant theory.

My major concern is that the cohering professional force that might come from a developing knowledge base of teaching and learning will be dissipated if we don't make collaboration our reality. If, for example, we follow the separatist route that Whiting et al. (1996) suggest is advocated by the TTA for the training of teachers to work in secondary schools (TTA, 1996), it is not impossible that ITT could become a form of cottage industry – either school-or home-based – operated through distance learning, where the only quality control is immediate customer satisfaction with the goods (i.e. teachers) produced.

What kind of teachers would a cottage industry produce? Arguably, it is likely to produce practitioners of an unquestioning and unquestioned craft of teaching where attention is on routine performance. Despite the power of central guidelines and expectations, the products, i.e. the newly qualified teachers (NQTs), are likely to represent the cultures of specific schools as the students work hard to 'fit in'.

So let us examine an alternative future. Like Monty Python, let's 'look on the bright side of life'. The alternative involves some metanoia, a reperceiving of the educational continuum and the place of ITT in it. Let us look for real collaboration between universities' ITT staff, schools, LEAs and the agencies who work with them for the general benefit of educational provision for all. ITT provides an important bridgehead in that development. However, having built the bridgehead, we all need to construct something more long-lasting and to move back and forth across it thoughtfully and conversationally in and across the communities of practice to which we belong. What is crucial is that we heal the fragmentation which currently exists.

Let me end, licensed by the talk of futures, with a recipe for the future. Take one LEA which is encouraging area-based school development consortia. Match to those consortia a university education department's mapping of primary school partnership school clusters, each with their own designated link tutor. Let link tutors work with the mentors in partnership schools – with research and development projects (including community development), associated with each consortium, and with school senior management teams as a connection into the university department in response to needs arising in the development planning of partner schools. Add to that a number of regular senior level strategy meetings, which allow connections to be made in long-term planning. Bind those ingredients with a belief that the benefits which accrue to participants are different but evenly spread. Hopefully, this is a recipe which improves the quality not only of ITT, but of primary education as a whole.

What kind of teachers would we expect that kind of environment to produce? I would hope that it would produce teachers who are aware of themselves as learning professionals, confident in the knowledge base of teaching and their ability to challenge it with evidence and sound argument. They would also be profoundly aware of the transformational potential of education in certain local communities, their associated responsibilities and the potential of their own roles for the common good.

Note

1. The City of Birmingham in central England has, since the appointment of Professor Tim Brighouse as Chief Education Officer, designated itself The Learning City.

References

Ashcroft, K., Davies, J.G. and Riddell, R. (1996), 'A New Way of Working: Partnership between a Unitary Authority and a New University'. British Educational Research Association Annual Conference, Lancaster.

Bridges, D. (1996), 'Initial teacher education and the reconstruction of the university', in Furlong, J. and Smith, R., *The Role of Higher Education in Initial Teacher Training*. London: Kogan Page.

Collison, J. and Edwards, A. (1994), 'How teachers support pupil learning', in Reid, I., Constable, H. and Griffiths, R., *Teacher Education Reform: The Research Evidence*. London: Paul Chapman.

Doyle, W. (1996), 'Heard any Really Good Stories Lately?'. American Educational Research Association Conference, New York.

Edwards, A. (1996a), 'Investigating the Complexities of Teaching: Implications for Research and the Teaching Profession'. University of Warwick Seminar Series, The Future of Educational Research, University of Warwick.

— (1996b), 'Can action research give coherence to the school-based learning experiences of students?', in O'Hanlon, C., *Professional Development Through Action Research in Educational Settings*. London: Falmer.

— (1997), 'Guests bearing gifts: the position of student teachers in primary school classrooms', *British Educational Research Journal*, 23(1), 27–37.

Edwards, A. and Collison, J. (1995), 'What do teacher mentors tell student teachers about pupil learning in primary schools?', *Teachers and Teaching: Theory and Practice*, 1(2), 265–79.

— (1996a), *Mentoring and Developing Practice in Primary Schools*. Buckingham: Open University Press.

— (1996b), 'Partnerships in school-based teacher training: a new vision?', in McBride, R, *Teacher Education Policy: Some Issues Arising from Research and Practice*. London: Falmer.

— (1996c), 'Taking Teacher Education to Task: An Examination of Subject Studies in Training Partnerships'. American Educational Research Association Annual Conference, New York.

Edwards, A. and Hodgson, J. (1996), 'Managing Pupil Learning: Teachers' Self-Images, Knowledge and Actions'. European Conference on Educational Research, Seville.

Gilroy, P., Price, C., Stones, E. and Thornton, M. (1994), 'Teacher education in Britain: a JET symposium with politicians', *Journal of Education for Teaching*, 20(3), 261–301.

Goodlad, J. (1990), *Teachers for our Nation's Schools*. San Francisco: Jossey Bass.

Hargreaves, D. (1994), 'The new professionalism: the synthesis of professional and institutional development', *Teaching and Teacher Education*, 10(4), 423–38.

Hirst, P. (1996), 'The demands of professional practice and preparation for teaching', in Furlong, J. and Smith, R., *The Role of Higher Education in Initial Teacher Training*. London: Kogan Page.

Huberman, M. (1993), 'Changing minds: the dissemination of research and its effects on practice and theory', in Day, C., Calderhead, J. and Denicolo, P., *Research on Teacher Thinking: Understanding Professional Development*. London: Falmer.

John, P. (1996), 'Understanding the apprenticeship of observation in initial teacher education: exploring student teachers' implicit theories of teaching and learning', in Claxton, G., Atkinson, T., Osborn, M. and Wallace, M., *Liberating the Learner*. London: Routledge.

Lave, J. and Wenger, E. (1991), *Situated Learning: Legitimate Peripheral Participation*. Cambridge: Cambridge University Press.

Maynard, T. (1996), 'The limits of mentoring: the contribution of the higher education tutor to primary student teachers' school-based learning', in Furlong, J. and Smith, R., *The Role of Higher Education in Initial Teacher Training*. London: Kogan Page.

Millett, A (1996), 'Pedagogy – Last Corner of the Secret Garden'. Lecture at King's College, University of London.

Senge, P. (1990), *The Fifth Discipline: the Art and Practice of the Learning Organisation*. New York: Doubleday.

Taylor, C. (1991), *The Ethics of Authenticity*. Cambridge Mass: Harvard University Press.

Teacher Training Agency (TTA), (1996), *Effective Training Through Partnership: Working Papers on Secondary Partnership*. London: TTA.

Whiting, C., Whitty, G., Furlong., J, Miles, S. and Barton, L. (1996), *Partnership in Initial Teacher Education: A Topography*. Health and Education Research Unit, Institute of Education, University of London.

Wilkin, M. (1996), *Initial Teacher Training: The Dialogue of Ideology and Culture*. London: Falmer.

1.4 The 'applied route' at age 14 and beyond – implications for initial teacher education

Norman Lucas

This chapter is concerned with the development of the 14–19 curriculum in England and Wales and its implications for initial teacher education (ITE). It places the debate about changes in ITE within the context of the changing nature of organisations, work and the new curriculum. I put forward the view that the 'curriculum of the future' requires a broader, more flexible professionalism and discuss the implications for ITE and staff development programmes.

Whilst acknowledging a number of criticisms of General National Vocational Qualifications (GNVQs), I develop the argument that, following the Dearing Report (1996), GNVQs or the 'applied route' are fast becoming an established and expanding part of the post-16 and increasingly the post-14 curriculum. This has important pedagogic implications for teachers and teacher educators because GNVQs emphasize certain aspects of teaching and learning above others and redefine the balance given to the depth and breadth of subject knowledge as well as broader, more transferable skills and knowledge. Dearing recommended that consideration should be given to more specific criteria for courses of ITE covering the 14–19 phase in schools and colleges, including in-service education and training for teachers and teacher educators. The Teacher Training Agency (TTA) is proposing a 14-19 PGCE to start in September 1998.

In this chapter, I will explore some of the difficult issues that have arisen from teaching GNVQs. This revolves around their structure and assessment methods, the teaching of key skills, and the fear that depth and subject knowledge are in danger of being lost in the breadth of vocationalism. I ask whether current ITE courses adequately prepare beginning teachers for the new post-14 curriculum and discuss whether ITE can learn from some aspects of GNVQs (e.g. adopting a common strand of key skills) and what these key skills could be. I conclude with the view that a partnership of schools, colleges and universities is required to assess the challenging pedagogic issues that the new 14–19 curriculum raises.

The context of the changing curriculum

The pressure for change in the 14–19 curriculum can be best understood when put within the context of a society undergoing quite profound economic and structural change. Although there are a number of different views about the nature of social and economic change, many agree that new forms of production using new technology with smaller organizations and management structures require more flexible skills on the part of the workforce. In a recent study of teachers in further education colleges (Young et al., 1995), changes were identified not only in the way teachers worked, but also in their skills and knowledge. This was described as a change from an 'insular' model of professional practice to a new, 'connective' one. The authors characterized these changes as teachers moving:

- from teacher-centred to student-centred pedagogy
- from classroom knowledge to organizational knowledge
- from subject knowledge to curriculum knowledge
- from insular subject knowledge to seeing their subject specialism in a more connective way to other specialisms, including those of non-teaching staff.

Reich (1991) in analysing the skills used by people in new, leading US companies emphasizes four skills that are needed for the future.

- **Abstraction** emphasizes the need to concentrate on discovering new patterns and meanings, rearranging knowledge in new ways to suit new purposes.

- **Systems thinking** is the opposite of compartmentalized expertise and emphasizes the connectiveness and relationship between subjects, theory and practice.

- **Experimentation** is the ability to find new knowledge and new ways of doing things which at present are often discouraged because of the need to 'cover' certain fixed routes of knowledge.

- **Collaboration/communicating and learning from others** is stressed because of the importance of working in teams, sharing ideas and problems.

I would suggest that the pressures for change in production and other professions are similar to those being experienced by teachers learning to manage the new demands of delivering the post-16 curriculum.

The decline in the demand for unskilled and semi-skilled workers has led to structural unemployment, particularly amongst the 16 to 25 year age group. Linked to this has been a massive increase in those staying on in education and training after 16. As recently as the 1970s only one-third of pupils stayed on at 16 and fewer than half of those went on to university. In the 1990s the overall participation rate for 16- to 17-year-olds has increased to approximately 71 per cent in England and Wales. However there is a steep drop at the end of each year of study (Richardson et al., 1995) with only 42 per cent participation at level 3 – equivalent to two A level passes, an Advanced GNVQ or National Vocational Qualification (NVQ). This compares with 58 per cent in France and 70 per cent in Germany.

The challenge for education and training in England and Wales is the transformation of a system designed for the participation of a minority of students beyond the compulsory years, with the focus on academic achievement, to one of mass participation at post-16. This will mean opening up more opportunities to achieve within the vocational as well as the academic tracks.

For the first time, a majority of young people are continuing their education beyond the compulsory years. Sixth forms in schools and further education colleges are having to deal with a far wider diversity of learner needs than was previously the case. Approaching curriculum reform within a 14–19 framework begins to address progression for those young people who at present underachieve. Yet the success of the 14–19 curriculum will presumably depend to some extent on how teachers are prepared to respond to this challenge and address the real problems of large numbers of young people who have been unable to achieve at, or beyond, Key Stage 4.

The Dearing Report

The Dearing Report (1996) on the 14–19 curriculum is not a radical document. It was a report commissioned by the Government to look at reforming the 14–19 curriculum with the clear brief that A levels, or the 'academic gold standard', were to remain largely untouched. Consequently, the report proposes reform and consolidation of the existing three-track system, with its emphasis on separate academic and vocational routes with an applied route starting at 14 years of age.

On the other hand, Dearing does propose a framework which gives a greater emphasis to breadth of knowledge and key skills and suggests overarching national diplomas and certificates at each level to emphasize breadth and parity of esteem between the vocational and academic qualifications. After a generally favourable initial response to the report, criticisms have emerged focusing on the unwillingness to change A levels, the confusion of having 'horizontal' and 'vertical' A/S levels, and the lack of support for modularization. The voluntaristic approach to the overarching certification makes it difficult to understand why students on the academic track should be motivated to broaden their studies to achieve diplomas or certificates unless universities and employers insist on the broader certification; this is extremely unlikely. However despite doubts and criticisms of Dearing, some believe that the proposals do form a basis for a shift towards a more unified qualifications system in the future (Spours and Young, 1996).

For the time being the continued existence of GNVQs or 'applied qualifications' that are quite distinct and different from the academic route are a part of the curriculum for 14- to 19-year-olds and will have an increasing impact on schools and colleges. A recent National Foundation for Educational Research (NFER) Report (1996) showed the take up of GNVQs is exceeding expectations and it has been suggested by University Colleges Admissions Service (UCAS) that if the growth of GNVQs continues, then in five years time one-third of those applying to higher education will have been studying for GNVQs. Indeed, the whole question of higher education admissions is under review (Carvel, 1996) with 35 per cent of students entering universities outside the A level route, although this figure includes mature/adult applicants via Access courses. The framework proposed by Dearing represents a new and complex curriculum departure, particularly for schools because it requires teachers and learners to work in new ways and raises important questions about teacher education and professional development.

Lessons from GNVQs?

Criticisms of GNVQs revolve around their structure, assessment and purpose. The positive side emphasizes how learning outcomes and units of learning have allowed teachers to use tutorials for setting individualized learning targets to encourage independent student learning. Alongside the better guidance for students more diverse approaches to teaching and learning have taken place, requiring teachers to reassess their teaching and amend the models of teacher-centred and or single-subject-centred approaches that have been associated with traditional A level teaching.

The emphasis given to application of knowledge to vocational areas has led to subject expertise crossing and integrating with other subjects. An example (Sharp, 1996) is delivering application of number (applied maths) in GNVQs. This requires non-maths specialists teachers delivering GNVQs to have at least the same skills and knowledge of applied maths as those expected of the students. This would apply to other key skills such as Information Technology (IT) and English. The role of the maths teacher in this context (or subject specialist in another context) would be to support students in overcoming their learning difficulties and to act as consultants and trainer/teacher to non-maths teachers, giving them the knowledge and confidence to implement the key skill of application of number within their subject area.

The implication that all teachers must teach key skills is complex and problematic. The poor completion rates of students on GNVQs has been seen as a result of candidates being unable to reach the required level of key skills (Green, 1997). Furthermore, the combination of key skills being integrated into vocational areas by non-specialists teachers with little or no experience of teaching and assessing these subjects (Office for Standards in Education, 1994) has led to the marginalization and inadequate delivery of key skills. Wolf (1992) points out that successful European systems teach languages and maths as separate subjects, taught by specialists within vocational or applied courses. The integration of key skills into competence-based vocational qualifications could perhaps be replaced as discrete and separately assessed units within GNVQs.

Supporters of the present GNVQ approach would point out that it is precisely because of the separation of subject from application that many students have failed to achieve in these important key areas and that applying knowledge to the 'real world', making it relevant and understandable to students, will help many more students to achieve and progress. To repeat the teaching at Key Stage 4 will not help – resit GCSE results were never very effective. The basic idea behind the development of GNVQs was to create an alternative to the academic way of teaching and assessment that failed so many young people. The applied route throws up many contentious and interesting issues for researchers and teachers of GNVQs and remains a pedagogic challenge. More research needs to done in this area.

Recent research into the implication of GNVQs for teaching and learning found that teachers used different communication styles and teaching methods from those used at A level (Harkin, 1995). Harkin's research found that GNVQ classes had higher levels of student activity and less passive learning. Students on GNVQ programmes perceived that their teachers were 'warmer' and more supportive, explaining things more clearly than teachers on other programmes of study. He found that sometimes the more experienced A level teachers found it difficult to adopt a more interpersonal teaching style. This view is reinforced by research included in the Dearing Report, which looked at student perceptions about quality of teaching (White et al., 1996.) It recorded the student view that teaching styles for A level students and GNVQs were quite different. A levels were perceived to be more lecture dominated and GNVQs less teacher driven with more guidance, independent study and research.

The research showing a greater student activity and interaction on GNVQ courses must be treated cautiously. Observed 'passivity' in a class does not mean that nothing is going on in the student's head. On the other hand, student/pupil 'activity' does not indicate that learning is taking place. Interactive learning, 'giving students more responsibility for their own learning' and 'independent learning' can all be methods which cover poor practice or are a means of cutting course hours to save money with little thought being given to the pedagogic implications of such approaches.

Most would agree that good teaching and effective learning occurs when a variety of learning and teaching methods are used and where students become involved in their own learning. Didactic teaching has, and will continue to have, an important place, but the teaching and learning on GNVQ courses does require a more active, varied and student-centred approach by the teacher. Thus, tutorial, guidance and counselling skills are needed. GNVQs emphasize independent learning, learning in a group or workshop, experiencing activity-based learning through project work and the production of portfolios of work, all of which make new demands on the teacher. These new demands on teachers require teacher educators to ask whether the 'pedagogy of guidance' is adequately emphasized in preparing new teachers for the 14–19 curriculum.

Although there is common good practice between Advanced GNVQs and A levels, there is also a different emphasis (Lucas, 1996) which can be summarized as follows:

- A levels have been single-subject focused (history, maths, etc.), whereas GNVQs focus on case studies and integrated assignments, which cover a range of skills and subject knowledge (including core skills).

- The teaching and learning on GNVQ courses pulls in expertise and knowledge from different subjects and the division between subjects becomes blurred with teachers working in interdisciplinary course teams.

- Good teaching of GNVQs emphasises a variety of teaching and learning methods ranging from a teacher-focused approach, to group learning, more emphasis being given to directed self-learning and a shift towards greater student autonomy.

- Tutorial and learning support is central to the delivery of GNVQs. Each student must have individual learning targets, a portfolio of achievement, and general guidance and counselling. These requirements have produced a shift from the amount of time spent teaching whole groups to more individual tutorial guidance on a regular basis being built into courses.

Of course, there are criticism of GNVQs and a number of issues that ITE should be aware of in preparing for the future. These have focused on the lack of any syllabus, course or guidelines and an overconcentration on the collection of evidence to satisfy the density of competence criteria at the expense of broader knowledge, core skills and learning (Hyland, 1994). This has lead to accusations that GNVQs are highly bureaucratized with narrow and 'overpapered' assessment procedures, leading to an obsession with recording evidence for assessment purposes at the expense of learning and creativity. There are pedagogic difficulties in teaching key skills within integrated assignments and many teachers seem to have resorted to separating off key skills from the rest of the assignments. The Royal Academy of Engineering (Sparks, 1994) argues that GNVQs are not broad enough and do not cater adequately for the development of 'understanding', 'know how' or 'integrative thinking'. There is also criticism that focuses on structural weaknesses (Spours, 1995) emphasizing the lack of clarity about purpose, pointing out that the majority of those candidates at Advanced and Intermediate level want to progress to university and require a general education rather than one that has vocational relevance. Changing the name of Advanced GNVQs to Vocational A Levels, as advised by the Dearing Report will not alter the structural weaknesses. According to this view, GNVQs have failed to achieve parity with academic equivalencies, have failed as an effective vocational qualification and do not appear to be flexible enough to encourage mixing and matching of academic and vocational study.

Pedagogic problems of the applied route

One of the aspects of GNVQs that has inspired many teachers is the way in which specialist skills and knowledge are applied across subject boundaries and related to a student's experience and possible future. Traditional methods of teaching subjects such as maths and science have not been successful for many young people and the applied route opens up some alternatives which are more flexible in their approach.

However, fears have been expressed concerning the danger of losing specialism, whether academic or vocational in the new generic, applied route where key skills are a poor substitute for a good general education (Green, 1996). The problem for many is the ideology behind GNVQs, which assumes that knowledge or theory is only important in relation to the extent to which it 'underpins competent performance'. The assessment of GNVQs is expressed in terms of performance criteria, elements of competence and range statements, content is not defined as in traditional syllabi, with no length of time specified to achieve the qualification. At present GNVQs only treat knowledge in relation to a student's capacity to apply it to performance. Thus, knowledge is not taught separately, but 'embedded' in the process of application.

With academic courses starting from an assumption of the primacy of knowledge; GNVQs start from the primacy of performance. The approach adopted by GNVQs, or more importantly the National Council for Vocational Qualifications (NCVQ), is problematic as it is in direct opposition to the knowledge based focus and assessment of academic qualifications. The separation of 'knowledge' and 'doing' (theory versus practice) reflects the historic academic/vocational divide in the UK and makes it difficult if not impossible to make real equivalences between A levels and Advanced GNVQs.

The issue, discussed above, about whether key skills are best taught and learnt through application or as separate subjects is a very important and contentious debate. A case has been made (Spours, 1995) that GNVQs should be restructured to adopt an explicit subject core with separate units of general education alongside vocational study.

There are arguments on both sides, standards do need to be raised in GNVQs and the level of key skills is worrying. On the other hand, traditional subject teaching has not allowed the majority of pupils/ students to achieve and progress. The pedagogic implications of the applied route and the debate about subject knowledge, particularly in the areas of key skills, strikes at the heart of why young people in this country are not reaching levels achieved by others in Europe.

Implications of the 'applied route' for initial teacher education

Although ITE courses differ in their approach to GNVQs, on balance most ITE programmes, particularly secondary, need to adapt more rapidly to a changing 14–19 framework and ensure that the GNVQ approach to teaching, learning and assessment be considered alongside National Curriculum subject studies. This will mean an examination of the emphasis given at Key Stage 4 to the balance between depth, breadth of subjects and broader pedagogic skills often associated with guidance, counselling and coaching.

Subject knowledge and subject focus are particularly important starting points for beginning teachers and should not be lost in a sea of generalism, however I suggest that the emphasis given in some ITE programmes is unbalanced with subject-focused practical teaching prioritised with insufficient attention given to key professional skills such as working in teams, interpersonal skills and self-review (improving one's own learning and performance). Because of the applied nature of GNVQs, there are some similarities with ITE courses where skills and knowledge are developed through reflection on practice, emphasizing personal and autonomous skills and the negotiated learning targets. These, along with other moves to develop effective profiling in ITE courses, link with the Teacher Training Agency's (TTA) initiative to develop Career Entry Profiles and create a framework which facilitates the negotiation of on-going professional development of teachers in the secondary and primary sectors.

GNVQs emphasize core or key skills for all candidates, yet ITE has not adopted the notion of core or key skills for teachers, which is an important aspect of the debate about the content of a National Curriculum for ITE. Teachers wishing to obtain qualified teacher status (QTS) in secondary PGCE courses are required to pass GCSE maths and English to grade C or above, but this does not mean that they can apply or communicate that knowledge when teaching others (unless it is their subject specialism). Equally, IT competence is not made a key skill – despite its importance in teaching and learning. Is subject skill and knowledge properly balanced alongside other key skills, including broader professional, personal and interpersonal qualities? Anecdotal evidence on secondary and post-compulsory ITE courses would suggest it is not.

I would like to put the view that all ITE courses should, alongside maintaining subject specialization, have a common strand of key skills. This would broaden present programmes and redefine the balance between depth and breadth of knowledge. This strand of key skills would be similar to those of GNVQs and might include:

- communication/language teaching
- maths/numeracy teaching
- IT
- tutoring, guidance and target-setting skills
- personal skills – working with others
- personal skills – improving the management of one's own learning and performance
- problem solving.

Similarly, more emphasis in ITE courses would need to be given to:

- the 14–19 National Qualification Framework
- the assessment methods of the different qualifications
- an understanding of the vocational relevance of a beginning teacher's subject specialism
- a knowledge of school, college and employer partnerships that can enrich the 14–19 curriculum.

Conclusion

Although the focus of this chapter has primarily been on the implications of GNVQs for ITE, it is important to put the debate in the context of the pressure for change affecting other professions. Teachers, like other professionals, work in the context of changing structural patterns of production and employment as well as changing public perceptions and demands.

Many ITE programmes still give primary and overwhelming importance to the delivery of specific and isolated subject specialisms. Whether or not this is appropriate to the National Curriculum, it is increasingly being challenged by the new post-16 curriculum in general and GNVQs in particular.

The challenge for teachers and teacher educators is to reassess and meet the pedagogic challenges of the 'applied route' in a situation where participation becomes the norm for the overwhelming majority of 16- to 19-year-olds. On the one hand, this means recognizing that subject specialism is important and is often the 'intellectual home' of the beginning teacher. On the other hand, it means moving beyond the rather narrow interpretation of teacher as subject specialist towards a more flexible multidisciplinary approach to teaching and learning including the 'pedagogy of guidance'. The question about the key skills needed by teachers for the 14–19 curriculum of the future cannot be avoided. Is it unreasonable to expect all new teachers in schools and colleges to have an acceptable level of knowledge of IT, English and maths and a grounding in their application to teaching? Is it unreasonable that teachers should be expected to have tutoring and personal professional skills alongside important subject-focused skills delivered in the classroom? Training beginning teachers for the 14–19 curriculum is of growing importance for ITE, however it is not without its problems. The applied route is a new departure for many teachers and in-service education and training (INSET) is required. The challenges of the changing 14–19 curriculum and the shifts in the skills and knowledge of teacher described in this chapter cannot be achieved by simply placing beginning teachers in schools and colleges to work alongside experience teachers. Learning from experience alone does not adequately prepare new teachers for the 'curriculum of the future'. The pedagogic implications and challenges raised by the applied route require opportunities to exchange good practice, review practice elsewhere and exchange different perspectives. Further research and a close partnership and dialogue between schools, colleges and universities in ITE and continual professional development (CPD) is required to meet the diversity of learning needs as increasing numbers of students stay on and achieve in education. ITE must change to meet these new and important challenges.

References

Carvel, J. (1996), 'Student profiles could go on line', *The Guardian*, 16 July.

Dearing, R. (1996), *Review of Qualifications for 16-19 Year Olds*. Full Report. London: Schools Curriculum and Assessment Authority (SCAA).

Green, A. (1997), 'Core skills, general education and unification in post-16 education', in Hodgson, A. and Spours, K., *Dearing and Beyond: 14–19 Qualifications, Frameworks and Systems*. London: Kogan Page.

Guile, D. and Lucas, N. (1996), 'Preparing for the future. The training and professional development of staff in the E sector', *Journal of Teacher Development*, 5(3):47-55.

Harkin, J. (1995), 'The Impact of GNVQs on the Communication Styles of Teachers'. Paper for Universities Council for the Education of Teachers (UCET), Conference, School of Education, Oxford Brookes University.

Hyland, T. (1994), 'Upgraded NVQs or vocational A levels? GNVQs and the problems of learning and assessment in the NVQ system', *British Journal of Curriculum and Assessment*, 3, Summer.

Lucas, N. (1996), 'The changing sixth form: the growth of pre-vocational education', in Capel, S., Leask, M. and Turner, T., *Beginning to Teach in a Secondary School*. London: Routledge.

Office for Standards in Education (OFSTED), (1994), *GNVQs in Schools 1993–4*. London: HMSO.

Reich, R. (1991), *The Work of Nations*. Hemel Hempstead: Simon & Schuster.

Richardson, W., Spours, K., Woolhouse, J. and Young, M. (1996), *Learning for the Future: Initial Report*. Institute of Education, University of London and Warwick, Centre for Education and Industry, University of Warwick.

Schaggen, S, Johnson, J, Simkin, C. (1996), *Sixth Form Options: Post-compulsory Education in Maintained Schools*: Slough NFER.

Sharp, G. (1996), 'Post-Fordism, the vocational curriculum and the challenge to teacher preparation', *Journal of Vocational Education and Training*, 48(1): 25-39.

Spours, K. (1995), *The Strengths and Weaknesses of GNVQs: An Analysis of a Curriculum Model and Principles of Design, Learning for the Future Working Paper No.3*. London: Post-16 Centre, Institute of Education, University of London.

Sparks, T. (1994), *14-19 Education*. A Report for the Royal Academic of Engineering. London.

Spours, K. and Young, M. (1996), 'Dearing and Beyond: Steps and Stages to a Unified System?' Paper presented to conference organized by the Learning for the Future Project, Institute of Education, University of London, 11 June.

White, C., Stratford, N., Thomas, A. and Ward, K. (1996), *Young People's Perceptions of 16–19 Qualifications. Social and community planning research, Dearing* Report. SCAA.

Wolf, A. (1992), *Mathematics for Vocational Students in France and England: Contrasting Provision and Consequences, NIESR Discussion Paper 23*. National Institute for Social Research.

Young, M., Lucas, N., Sharp, G. and Cunningham, B. (1995), *Teacher Education for the Further Education Sector: Training the Lecturer of the Future*. London: Institute of Education, Post-16 Education Centre and Association for Colleges.

1.5 'New Rules' for the radical reform of teacher education

David Hopkins[1]

There is a profound paradox in the current debate on the future of initial teacher education (ITE). This irony was well expressed by Michael Fullan[2] when he said that 'teacher education still has the honour of being simultaneously the worst problem and the best solution in education' (1993:105). For too long, however, the focus has been on the first part of the equation – the worst problem. It is now time to take a more positive view on teacher education. One of the key characteristics of a caring and successful society is a dynamic high-quality teaching force; there is no substitute for good teachers. As we look to the future, we need to explore the boundaries of what is possible in teacher education, and its contribution to educational reform. Unfortunately, this is no simple task. If ITE were easy to reform, it would have been done long ago. This observation alone highlights the signal deficiency in many current reform proposals – it is futile to seek simple solutions to complex problems.

I have recently re-read a number of commentaries and research papers on teacher education that other colleagues and myself have written or conducted over the past 20 years and in many different countries. I was struck at how similar the diagnoses and prescriptions were, irrespective of time and context to our own current debate on the future of teacher education. (See Howey, Yarger and Joyce, 1978; Hopkins and Read,

1984.) If we are going to do something about teacher education – if we are going to create the high quality teaching force that we all desire, we need to view teacher education in a slightly different way. In pursuing this more positive theme, I would, therefore, like to propose some 'new rules' for the radical reform of teacher education. I use the world 'rules' advisedly, more in the sense of imperatives or guidelines than absolute laws; as a means of engaging with the complexity of the problem rather than proposing simplistic solutions.

Articulate the moral purpose of teacher education

There is a striking quality about fine teachers – they care deeply about their students. Our recent study of 'quality teachers' in 12 OECD countries found that a key characteristic of these outstanding teachers was their 'love of children' (Hopkins and Stern, 1996). Most teachers came into teaching because they wanted to make a difference. It may well be that for various reasons, many of which may be to do with the context within which teachers currently work, a degree of cynicism and weariness may dull this initial enthusiasm. However, as Fullan recently commented 'scratch a good teacher and you will find a moral purpose' (1993:10).

It is much easier for individual teachers to express their 'moral purpose' when the institutional climate of the universities and schools in which they train and work espouse and articulate a set of coherent educational values. I do not wish to sound pious, but high-quality teachers are committed to the learning of students, so too are outstanding schools. Those exemplary schools with which we work are characterised by a passion for learning and consistently articulate the values on which their curriculum, organisation and teaching methods are based (see Hopkins et al., 1996). In the sense that I mean it here, moral purpose is not a 'wishy washy' idealism, but a ruthless and relentless commitment to the learning of children at both an individual and institutional level. High standards, a low tolerance of failure and a commitment to student learning is the moral purpose that I see in the outstanding teachers and schools I am privileged to meet and visit. I wish the same for our schools of education.

Reform teacher education systemically

It seems to me that the approach to educational reform in the UK is tactical rather than strategic. Despite the radical marketplace approach to educational reform taken by recent Conservative Governments, a closer inspection of the details of the reforms have an independent and 'bitty' feel to them. It also appears that the response of educational institutions to the reform agenda is also tactical rather than strategic. Institutions have tended to change only as much as is needed to suit the specific situation. In my view, piecemeal change is often worse than no change at all. There is also an irony here. For as Joyce and Clift noted more than 10 years ago:

> Paradoxically, the convergence of criticism, the serious proposals for reform, and the recent accumulation of research on teaching and teacher education may have brought us to the point where we can engage in the systematic renovation of the conduct of teacher training, including its governance, procedures for ensuring its continuing renewal, and its structure, substance and process. We believe that developing a process to ensure the continued renewal of teacher education is as important to its health as is instituting any particular substantive or procedural change. We also believe that piecemeal improvements will make little difference and will be ephemeral. Substantial changes must be made to make any real difference or to sustain minor changes.

For their comprehensive proposal for reform of teacher education, see Joyce and Clift, 1984.

The implications of this line of thinking are numerous and in most cases obvious. A systemic approach to educational reform that enhanced teacher education would at a national level co-ordinate and make connections, for example, between proposals for a National Curriculum for teacher education, the criteria for the Office for Standards in Education (OFSTED) inspections of schools and university education departments, and the various Department for Education (DfE) initiatives for 'improving schools'. Similarly, at the school level, very few heads or mentors see involvement in teacher education as a possible strategic response to the challenge of change. At best, it is regarded as a support to the school's maintenance activities, rather than as agent for development. There are many ways in which secondary schools, in particular, could use involvement in ITE as the spearhead of their development strategy. Seeing educational reform as a whole is the *sine qua non* of increasing student achievement.

Establish partnerships between schools and universities

This might appear a strange exhortation in a chapter with the word 'new' in the title. Hargreaves (1990) has been arguing the case for school-based teacher training for some years, and training partnerships in some form are an established feature of teacher education programmes. I, for one, would be the last to criticise the benefits they have produced. This is not to say, however, that the concept could not be deepened and broadened. As I look at current practice, the expression of partnership in secondary ITE seems to be of two types. The first is common in traditional Post Graduate Certificate in Education (PGCE) programmes, where the university establishes partnerships with subject departments. At the other end of the spectrum are the partnerships established between members of the school-centred initial teacher training (SCITT) consortia. Neither, it seems to me, for very different and quite obvious reasons, fully exploit the potential that partnership offers. On the one hand, the whole-school dimension is lacking. On the other hand, there is a very real danger that the frameworks of thought and action into which the best universities can induct neophyte teachers is lost. As Fullan has commented:

> Teacher development and institutional development (of universities and schools) must go hand in hand. You can't have one without the other. If there was ever a symbiotic relationship that makes complete sense it is the collaboration of universities and schools. When all is said and done, reform in teacher education must begin simultaneously in schools and in faculties of education, both independently (because one can't wait for the other) and together

through multiyear alliances (which serve to put pressure and support on both institutions to change their ways and realise their relationship to each other).

(Fullan, 1993, pp 120–1)

What is needed is more of what Rudduck (1992) referred to as 'les liaisons dangereuses'. She concluded that the success of such partnerships will depend on, amongst other things:

- the readiness of the partners to give up their traditional mythologies about each other and to learn to respect each other's strengths and recognize each other's needs and conditions for professional survival
- building a shared commitment to well-judged change, to exploring alternatives and to pushing back the limits of possibility in learning
- building a shared commitment to clarifying principles and purposes, and to understanding the social and political contexts in which those purposes and principles are set to work
- accepting a shared perception of teaching as one of the 'impossible professions' – impossible because it has 'ideas which admit no easy realisation, (and) goals that are often multiple, ambiguous and conflicting
- recognising that the pace of worthwhile change – change that achieves new cultural coherence and significance – is relatively slow and that ways have to be found of keeping up the momentum.

All this suggests that we need to look for innovative responses to the challenge of reform in teacher education. Why, for example, don't teachers and university staff swap roles more regularly? Why don't university schools of education administer SCITT programmes?

Regard teacher education as a lifelong continuum of learning

The dichotomy between initial and in-service teacher education is one of the most self defeating structural aspects of our educational system. The proposals made in the James Report (1972) some quarter of a century ago still have a poignant relevance today. It is as absurd now as it was then to regard teacher education as being complete following a year of professional training. In preparing to give evidence to the House of Commons Select Committee on Education and Training recently, I reviewed surveys of opinion from newly qualified teachers (NQTs) in our local education authorities (LEAs) (Hopkins, 1996). The sense of isolation, anomie and powerlessness that emerged, particularly from the secondary NQTs, was staggering and very worrying. The first few years of teaching are especially critical in laying the basis for continuous learning (or stagnation). This is particularly important for teachers in a post-modern society who must not only learn to cope with forms of change on a continuous basis, but also prepare their students to do so as well.

We at Nottingham in concert with other universities and LEAs have programmes for NQTs; this may be necessary, it is certainly not sufficient. Once again we need to search for structural solutions, such as different routes for certification (e.g. Masters of Teaching degree); the establishing of a General Teaching Council (GTC), and a re-introduction and extension of the probationary experience for NQTs. It may also be time to once again dust off the James Report and generate political and educational will around its, and similar, proposals.

Focus on teaching as the substantive knowledge base

In recent years, I have often commented to public audiences that in secondary education, at least in England and Wales, we are better at transmitting curriculum content than at teaching. By teaching I mean the creation of powerful learning experiences whereby students gain knowledge, understanding, skills and values. We know from experience and research that the most sustained and immediate impact on the learning of students is provided by the quality of teaching they receive. Our OECD study on 'quality teachers' suggested that besides the 'love of children' referred to earlier, outstanding teachers in OECD countries had command of 'subject specific didactics' (i.e. how best to teach maths, English, etc.) as well as a mastery of a repertoire of teaching models and strategies.

It is in this latter domain that we lag behind practice in other industrialised countries. In my experience, 'instruction' or 'pedagogy' are not familiar terms on the syllabi of teacher education courses.

As we have argued at length elsewhere (see Hopkins et al., 1994, Chap. 4) our educational system will not make the dramatic gains in student achievement that we all desire unless educators expand their language teaching. Take, for example, the current debate about the relationship between whole-class teaching and student achievement. A key problem is that the supporters of whole-class teaching infrequently specify what they mean by the term. As a consequence, some think that whole-class teaching implies something similar to 'chalk and talk'. Nothing could be further from reality! The form of whole-class teaching that is best associated with gains in student achievement comprises a far more complex set of teaching skills than the rather reductionist view of whole-class teaching currently being advocated in the popular press and by a wide variety of politicians and their advisers.

Students usually learn more in whole-class situations when a teacher:

• emphasises academic goals, makes them explicit and expects students to be able to master the curriculum

• carefully organizes and sequences curriculum experiences

• clearly explains and illustrates what students are to learn

• frequently asks direct and specific questions to monitor students' progress and check their understanding

• provides students with ample opportunity to practice, gives prompts and feedback to ensure success, correct mistakes and allows students to practice a skill until it is over learned or automatic

• reviews regularly and holds students accountable for work.

From this perspective, a teacher promotes student learning by being active in planning and organising his or her teaching, explaining to students what they are to learn, arranging occasions for guided practice, monitoring progress, providing feedback and otherwise helping students understand and accomplish work.

Despite the impressive gains associated with whole-class teaching of this type, it is not by any stretch of the imagination a panacea. Her Majesty's Chief Inspector for Schools (HMCI), Chris Woodhead, on a recent Panorama programme for example, quite rightly maintained that it should not be used for much more than half the time. So with what teaching approach do teachers fill the rest of the day?

There are many models of teaching designed to bring about particular kinds of learning and to help students become more effective learners, of which whole-class teaching is but one example. Powerful teachers have at their disposal a repertoire of strategies that they can use at different times, with different students, with different curriculum content to achieve a range of learning outcomes. For an extended discussion of models of teaching, see Joyce and Weil (1996). For a more anglicised version, see Joyce, Calhoun and Hopkins (in press). There is no implication that one model is better than another. It is just that one may be more appropriate than another at any point in time, given the learning outcomes desired.

It is also worth noting that models of teaching are really models of learning. As students acquire information, ideas, skills, values, ways of thinking, and means of expressing themselves, they are also learning how to learn. In fact, the most important long-term outcome of teaching may be the students' increased capabilities to learn more easily and effectively in the future. How teaching is conducted has a major impact on students' abilities to educate themselves.

As the TTA grapples with the challenge of creating a curriculum for teacher education, I suggest that they take seriously the point that the acquisition of a range of teaching strategies is not an end itself, but provides a more effective means for students to acquire not only curriculum content, but also a variety of learning strategies. In a similar way, I would encourage OFSTED, in line with the argument made earlier, to expand the definition of 'teaching quality' currently available in the Inspection Framework. Such a move towards a more complete and specific view of teaching would, given the importance of the framework, contribute enormously to the establishing of a 'language of teaching' in this country.

Develop a praxis of teacher education

One of the reasons why teacher education is having difficulty in formulating a future for itself, and sustaining itself against the arguments of its critics, may be because it has insufficiently established the theoretical/conceptual/research basis for its work. Without a clear idea of what its 'principles of procedures' are, it is difficult to either project forward or defend the *status quo*. If there is some truth in this proposition, the irony noted earlier applies here also. The paradox is that the theoretical and practical components of a praxis of teacher education are already in existence, albeit in their singularity. What is needed is a praxis of teacher education, the establishing of a practical theory from research and experience. Some 20 years ago I somewhat grandiosely defended my PhD thesis as being a contribution to the establishing of a 'discipline of teacher education'. My recent review of the literature on teacher education suggests that the emergence of a 'discipline' is a long time in coming.

It is no doubt a crude overgeneralisation, but what I am concerned about is not just the paucity of research on teacher education, but the lack of praxis in the integration of research with practice. The practice of teacher education in our schools of education needs to become enquiry led. This involves not just carrying out research on teaching and teacher education, but self-consciously testing out theory in practice, and using these experiences to refine a theory for teacher education.

As with the universities, so with the schools. For example, a number of schools in the Improving the Quality of Education for All (IQEA) network (see Hopkins et al., 1996) are taking enquiry as the key priority on their whole-school development plan. In practice, this involves time and resources being devoted to a systematic enquiry into the process of learning and the dissemination of the outcomes across the school. In one school at least, trainee teachers are an integral part of this research process.

The idea of the 'reflective practitioner' has widespread currency in many teacher education programmes. Such an emphasis will remain simply a tactic for reform and development, unless such an ethic of reflection, on the part of the beginning teachers, is enhanced by, and intergrated with, teacher training institutions and schools.

Take school improvement as the context for teacher education

It should be obvious by now that these propositions or 'rules' are not independent – indeed, they will only contribute to a radical reform of teacher education if they are worked on simultaneously. When taken together these propositions also contribute to what I would call a 'school improvement orientation' to teacher education. Elsewhere (Hopkins et al., 1994) we have suggested that school improvement is a strategy for educational change that focuses not only on the enhancement of student achievement, but also on the establishing of facilitating conditions at the school and classroom level supportive of high levels of student (and teacher) learning. That teacher education has a major role to play in this enterprise should by now be self-evident.

The achievement of the moral purpose of (teacher) education, enhanced levels of achievement and learning on the part of students, inevitably has a change theme to it. The dialectic between moral purpose and what Michael Fullan has, rather unfortunately, called 'change agentry' pervades these propositions. It underpins the systemic nature of change to which teacher education should be a central contributor; the nature of the structural relationships between schools and universities; the emphasis on teacher education as lifelong learning; the focus on teaching as the essential professional skill of teachers; and the need for teacher education to be enquiry led.

In combination, these propositions provide a set of parameters within which a variety of fascinating policy options for the future of teacher education could flourish. One obvious scenario would be networks of schools within regional settings linked to external support agencies, such as a reconceptualised university school of education with a more explicit research and development function. The purpose of the network would be to support school improvement, teacher education and a variety of other initiatives designed to enhance the achievement of students. The nature of these networks would be characterised by high expectations, low tolerance of failure, collaboration and a thirst for professional/ technical competence. The training of teachers would be provided by school and university/support system mentors whose role would also encompass staff and school development. Much of the curriculum of teacher education, particularly the emphasis on teaching strategies, would be replicated at an appropriately deeper level during staff development sessions for established teachers. Such aspirations would also be reflected in the school's development plans. All this would be conducted within a framework of local/regional/national goals and values, with appropriate accreditation opportunities being provided by the university.

These 'new rules for the radical reform' of teacher eduction provide the context for a series of similar possibilities that respond to a range of individual needs and contextual variables. The super-ordinate idea, however, is found in the links between moral purpose, school improvement and teacher education. As I have already drawn heavily on the writing of Michael Fullan, it is appropriate that, in conclusion, I use a final quote from *Change Forces*:

> The majority of teachers must find their moral niche closer to the individual student. If these teachers can also see the causal relationship between working conditions at school level and their ability to be effective in the classroom, they will be motivated to work with others on school and school system change. I believe that reform in teacher education must focus on developing and bringing together two broad themes:
>
> 1 It must re-establish the moral purpose of teaching (defined as making a difference in the lives of more and more individual students).
>
> 2 It must establish and continue to develop the knowledge and skill-base required to accomplish (1) including knowledge and skills required to change organisations and to contend with the forces of change in complex environments.
>
>   (Fullan, 1993:111)

It is within such a nexus that the future of teacher education lies.

References

Education and Employment Committee (1996), *The Professional Status, Recruitment and Training of Teachers – Minutes of Evidence, Professor David Hopkins, Wednesday 3 July*. London: HMSO.

Fullan, M. (1993), *Change Forces*. London: Falmer.

Hargreaves, D.H. (1990), *The Future of Teacher Education*. London: Hockerill Educational Foundation.

Hopkins, D. and Read, K. (eds) (1984), *Rethinking Education*. London: Croom Helm.

Hopkins, D. and Stern, D. (1996), 'Quality teachers, quality schools', *Teaching and Teacher Education*, 12(5), 501–17.

Hopkins et al. (1994), *School Improvement in an Era of Change*. London: Cassell.

Hopkins, D. et al. (1996), *Improving the Quality of Education for All*. London: David Fulton Publishers.

Howey, K., Yarger, S. and Joyce, B. (1978), *Improving Teacher Education*. Washington DC: Association of Teacher Educators.

James Report (1972), *Teacher Education and Training*. London: HMSO.

Joyce, B. and Clift, R. (1984), 'The phoenix agenda: essential reform in teacher education', *Educational Researcher*, 13(4), 5–18.

Joyce, B. and Weil, M. (1996), (5th Ed.), *Models of Teaching*. New York: Allyn and Bacon.

Joyce, B., Calhoun, E. and Hopkins, D. (in press), *Creating Powerful Learning Experiences*. Buckingham: Open University Press.

Rudduck, J. (1992), 'Universities in partnership with schools and school systems: les liaisons dangereuses?' in Fullan, M. and Hargreaves, A. (eds), *Teacher Development and Educational Change*. Lewes: Falmer Press.

Part 2: Changing key for changing times – national and international perspectives

Whereas the opening section probes into what the future may hold for initial teacher education (ITE), this section concerns the 'here and now'.

Contributions have been grouped, for convenience, under three general themes. Six writers focus on specific age-phases of education and on national issues; three write from international perspectives. All draw our attention to key themes and challenges in these changing times.

The editors have grouped these contributions together, with a significant overview of each particular 'landscape', written by Riley, Lines and Porter respectively, at three key points.

What the chapters have in common is a great deal of hope and determination in their response to the challenge of changing key. They offer critical and often contrasting views of priorities.

2.1 A view of the landscape for teaching children aged 5-11

Jeni Riley

Any consideration of primary initial teacher education is set against a backdrop of intense political and educational interest and concern. In addition, as Edwards (1997) comments:

> Here we have a system in flux. Contexts have been disrupted in ways which challenge and shift current identities, breakdown established relationships and increase links between central Government and individual schools.
>
> (Edwards, 1997)

Concern about the levels of educational attainment achieved by seven- and 11-year-olds in England and Wales in comparison with other countries, has been coupled with serious debate as to the underlying causes for the comparative underachievement and, depending on the individual perspective and the different background, there are myriad proposed solutions. The 1997 General Election provided opportunity and space for the opposing political parties to claim the high ground with affordable policy statements intended to revolutionize primary education and to transform educational standards. The chapters in this publication reflect this diversity of outlook and approach.

Edwards (this volume), writes, 'Primary school teaching is deceptively difficult and just as primary school teaching is complex so is the initial training of teachers to work in the primary phase.' It is worthwhile reflecting on the issues that affect the teaching and learning of primary-aged children in particular ways.

Studies in school effectiveness indicate much wider variation in pupil attainment between classes in primary schools in comparison with those of secondary schools, 'most of the variation among pupils is due to classroom variation' (Stoll and Mortimore, 1995). This central importance of the primary teacher is related to the length of time and exposure of the pupils to one individual teacher's strengths and weaknesses. Primary teachers are responsible for a group of children for at least an academic year, sometimes longer if the age group is mixed. The advantages of this system are clear: the primary teacher has the opportunity to make the curriculum coherent for the class and, through a deep and thorough acquaintance with the pupils, a close match of work to child can be achieved. The disadvantages are also obvious, as the academic progress of an entire class of young children can be slowed down by an ineffective teacher or one with whom certain children do not relate.

In addition to the advantages and constraints of the one class/one teacher organizational structure, there is the challenge that the introduction of the National Curriculum has made on the primary teacher's own grasp of the subject knowledge required. This issue flows from the previous point of the generalist teacher who has the responsibility for the planning, resourcing, teaching and assessing of the entire curriculum of 10 subjects and religious education (RE). Even an effective teacher is unlikely to be equally confident in all aspects of the curriculum. Concern regarding this crucial issue has been indicated repeatedly by Her Majesty's Inspectors (HMIs) for well over a decade (e.g. Department of Education and Science (DES) ,1987 and 1988). These curricular demands are exacerbated by the volume of the content to be covered and despite the recent pruning of the National Curriculum, the overriding reality is that, currently, primary teachers need to be 'Renaissance men and women' (Campbell, 1993:25).

Added to this complex role is the expectation that primary teachers will be responsible for the pastoral and social development of their pupils in addition to meeting the educational needs in often very mixed intellectual ability classes. Children who have special educational needs are frequently in high profile in the classroom, and demanding of the primary teacher's time, energy and expertise. This point on the unrealistically wide brief of primary teachers is emphasized by a report from the International School Effectiveness Research Project (ISERP), a cross-cultural project studying seven-year-olds in schools in Australia, Canada, Hong Kong, Ireland, the Netherlands, Norway, Taiwan, the UK and the USA. An interim-report observed that:

> It is the complexity of the practice that a British (or American) teacher is expected to master that is I think the most outstanding difference between the countries that ISERP has shown. A British primary teacher is likely to start with a range of children, in terms of reading ages for example, with reading ages in some cases 4.5 years below chronological age to, in some cases, three years above a chronological age of eight years. All these children will be in the same classroom, sometimes with a further 1 to 3 adult helpers present who will themselves need co-ordinating. Because much of this work in the class is in groups, and within the groups collaboration is encouraged, a degree of noise from the pupils is tolerated but the teacher is constantly having to monitor the noise level because s/he is aware that it can get distracting. There will be a large number of transactions during the day, when the teacher switches from whole class direct instruction to groups based upon achievement or mixed ability. The teacher will then, for probably 60-70% of the lesson, resource groups which are attempting tasks of different complexity group to group with children of the same levels of prior achievement, or resource groups attempting all the same tasks group to group but with children that are heterogeneous by ability. The teacher will also be allocating children to groups of differing composition all day.

> (Reynolds and Teddlie, 1995:29–30;
> cited in Southworth, 1996:269)

It is the experience as described here of the primary classroom at the end of the twentieth century that prompts Southworth to suggest that 'Primary teachers need to develop not because they are poor, but because their role is challenging and complex' (1996:268) and it is in this context that the requirements of the Department for Education (DfE) Circular 14/93 have had to be operationalized. Edwards in the previous section argues that the resulting partnership models of initial teacher education (ITE) particularly have the potential to provide primary teachers with exactly the opportunity that is needed to develop their own practice by being involved with mentoring beginning teachers. This activity gives primary teachers, traditionally and historically isolated in their own classrooms, a broader professional outlook and access to wider influences. Edwards says:

> The nature of educational knowledge is being called into question as we examine relationships between reasoning about practice in the work place and theoretical reasoning in universities. The development of educational knowledge will depend on the closer research and partnerships between practitioners in schools and universities.
>
> (Edwards, this volume)

Edwards asks that both primary teachers and teacher educators maximize the potential benefit of the changes and challenges in order to undergo a 'metanoia', that is a positive adaptation to the legislative stipulations and not merely a grudging adjustment to them. This metanoia will embrace the complexity of the task of being a primary teacher with a professional knowledge base that is complementary to it in complexity. There is a need to recognize that this knowledge base must encompass rigorous subject knowledge study at the teacher's own level, in addition to a study of pedagogy, in order to equip appropriately the beginning primary teacher in training.

Two chapters in this section focus on the issue of subject knowledge of primary teachers and the opportunity that exists with the advent of collaborative training schemes to enhance the practice in schools. Campbell et al. write:

It would seem that higher education tutors wish to 'regain' their professionalism, to rescue it, from the attacks by Government edicts and Teacher Training Agency (TTA) policies, to discover the core of their professional practices, namely, the promotion in their students of critical review and evaluation, of the development of a pedagogy for teaching, and the development of appropriate subject knowledge. At the same time, teachers are engaged in 'redefining' their professionalism. Redefining arises partly from the barrage of National Curriculum documentation and implementation. It includes their partnership schemes with higher education tutors, which have led many to a radical evaluation of their roles and responsibilities.

(Campbell et al., this volume)

Subject knowledge is explicitly addressed in the chapter describing the development of a Key Stage 2/3 course. Aptly subtitled 'crisis of identity or golden opportunity?', Fursland pursues a line of argument that such a course will enable teachers to address subject issues rather than a preoccupation with age-phase specialism.

Mould breaking involves crises of and even loss of identity ... in relation to Key Stage 2, but it also provides golden opportunities for new developments. When one mould has been broken, another must form or be formed speedily to replace it. It remains to be seen whether the structure of schooling will enable those trained on Key Stage 2/3 courses to fulfil their potential in linking specialist learning across the two age phases, in addition to the subject-specialist contribution at Key Stage 2.

(Fursland, this volume)

Conversely, at the opposite end of the primary age phase, in nursery and reception classes, an overfocus on the demands of the National Curriculum has led to concern regarding the initial preparation for those primary teachers planning to teach in the early years of education. Diminished appreciation of the wholeness of the very young child's learning has lead Penn to feel that Initial Teacher Education (ITE) and National Nursery Educational Board (NNEB) courses neglect at their peril the wider understandings of child development and care. Given the research evidence on the importance of a positive and successful start to education (Aubrey, 1994; Riley, 1995a and 1996), this deficit within the structure of these courses Penn argues vehemently is letting our young children down. The two recent studies seem to indicate that it is as essential for the early years teacher to possess as rigorous and extensive subject knowledge as those working with Key Stage 2 pupils. The class teacher working with reception and Key Stage 1 pupils has to construct and represent knowledge in a way that builds on the understanding that has been acquired prior to formal schooling and thus enables the young child to learn effectively.

Both Aubrey and I have found that it is those teachers who know the most about mathematics and literacy who facilitate the most rapid progress. Aubrey makes the point:

> Rich teacher knowledge appeared to be reflected in the content and structure of lessons, in explicit and well-integrated instruction, varied representations with links to, or connections made with, pupils' existing skills and understanding.
>
> (Aubrey, 1994:68)

In my study, the level of the teachers' subject knowledge indicates a cause for concern when the vast majority of the teacher group studied rank ordered the most valuable literacy entry skills in exactly the *reverse* order of importance from the research findings (Riley, 1996). As Shulman asks:

> What are the sources of teacher knowledge? What does a teacher know and when did he or she come to know it? How is new knowledge acquired, old knowledge retrieved and both combined to form a new knowledge base? How does knowledge for teaching occur?
>
> (Shulman, 1986:8)

But how are practising primary teachers able to improve their own subject knowledge? The level of local advisory support is limited and secondment in order to study for higher degrees is non-existent. Opportunities present themselves to offer support for teaching and learning in schools at the classroom level through 'partnership in training'.

Shulman continues: 'A number of strategic research sites and key events are particularly illuminating for our understanding of how knowledge grows in teaching' (1986:8). 'Since there are no single most powerful forms of representation, the teacher must have at hand a veritable armamentarium of alternative forms of representation, some of which derive from research whereas others originate in the wisdom of practice' (1986:9).

This issue is very pertinent to the discussion of partnership in training.

Research interest is developing in universities which is complementary to the whole-school improvement movement and is focused on more effective teaching and learning at classroom level. These findings can, and must, be shared, directly and as early as possible with the partner schools .

The majority of a university's primary teacher educators will be both subject and age-phase specialists. In-service training offered by such a team as *quid pro quo* for being involved with partnership, is potentially a great resource and energy needs to be given to the most effective ways of harnessing this expertise for the maximum benefit of partner schools. The directed tasks carried out in school, overseen and tutored by the teacher, tutors or mentors can have powerful in-service potential if the school staff are made fully aware of the subject knowledge and teaching issues involved.

Often unexploited in the partnership models is the potential for joint action research projects conducted by university and school staff in the partner schools on topics of interest and use to the teachers themselves.

The new regulations for primary ITE (Teacher Training Agency, 1997) provide universities with the opportunity to redress this imbalance by designing specialist early years courses, which aim to focus on the particular issues connected with the age-phase, in addition to enhanced subject knowledge in the three core subjects.

Partnership modes of ITE cannot, and will not, solve the ills of primary education, but the student–mentor relationship can be used to orchestrate simultaneous development in primary schools and universities.

If primary course leaders in the universities recognize the challenge and focus on the main disabling weaknesses in the system in order to ensure that the primary beginning teachers are rigorously prepared with the required subject knowledge, there can be a genuine exchange of expertise during the school practices. The inter-relationship of initial and in-service training can be a practical reality and mutually reinforcing. In order to achieve this, primary course design needs to be radical. Southworth (1996) believes 'that primary teachers need to be helped to stop doing more and more'. Primary PGCE courses, in particular, can support this view by using the new TTA framework (Teacher Training Agency, 1997) by focusing on the three subjects of the core curriculum plus a specialism in one of the foundation subjects for those beginning teachers training for Key Stage 2. This initiative would be a serious attempt to cover less ground but with more depth. As Goodlad says:

> Substantial improvement ... means more than tinkering around the edges of what we have now. It means changing our schools in profound ways... The required change will not occur if we continue to prepare teachers for the school conditions that are now prevailing.
>
> (Goodlad, 1990: 27)

References

Alexander, R., Rose, J. and Woodhead, C. (1992) *Curriculum Organization and Classroom Practice in Primary Schools – A Discussion* Paper. London: HMSO.

Aubrey, C. (1993), 'An investigation of the mathematical competences which young children bring to school', *British Educational Research Journal*, 19(1), 19–27.

— (ed) (1994), *The Role of Subject Knowledge in the Early Years of Teaching*. London: Falmer Press.

Campbell, J. (1993), 'A dream at conception: a nightmare at delivery', in Campbell, J., *Breadth and Balance in the Primary Curriculum.* London: Falmer.

Campbell, A., Cockett, P., Peckett, J. and Whiteley, M. (1996), 'Across the Great Divide: What Can Be learned from an Investigation of Primary and Secondary Partnerships?' Paper given at the Exploring Futures in Initial Teacher Education Conference, Institute of Education, University of London, September.

Department of Education and Science (1987)*Primary Staffing Survey.* London: HMSO.

—   (1988), *The New Teacher in School: A Survey by HM Inspectors in England and Wales 1987.* London: HMSO.

Department for Education (DfE), *Circular 14/93.*

Edwards, A. (1997), 'Possible Futures for Initial Teacher Education in the Primary Phase'. Paper given at the Exploring Futures in Initial Teacher Education Conference, Institute of Education, University of London, September 1996.

Fursland, L. (1997), 'The Key Stage 2/3 Course: Crisis of Identity or Golden Opportunity'. Paper given at the Exploring Futures in Initial Teacher Education Conference, Institute of Education, University of London, September 1996.

Goodlad, J. (1990), *Teachers for our Nation's Schools.* San Francisco: Jossey Bass.

Grossman, P.L., Wilson, S.M. and Shulman, L.S. (1989), 'Teachers of substance: subject matter knowledge for teaching', in Reynolds, M.C., *The Knowledge Base for the Beginning Teacher.* Oxford: Pergamon Press.

National Curriculum Council (NCC), (1993), *The National Curriculum at Key Stages 1 and 3.* York: NCC.

Office for Standards in Education (OFSTED), (1993), *Curriculum Organization and Classroom Practice in Primary Schools A Follow - up Report.* London: Department for Education Publications.

Penn, H. (1996), 'What Age-groups should Primary Teaching Cover?' Paper given at the Exploring Futures in Initial Teacher Education Conference, Institute of Education, University of London, September.

Reynolds, D. and Teddlie, C. (1995), 'World Class Schools: A Preliminary Analysis of Data from the International School Effectiveness Research Project'. Paper presented at the ECER Conference, Bath.

Riley, J.L. (1995a), 'The transition phase between emergent literacy and conventional beginning reading: new research findings', *Journal for Tutors for Advanced Courses for Teachers of Young Children*, 16(1):155-60.

— (1995b), 'The relationship between adjustment to school and success in reading by the end of the reception year', *Early Child Development and Care*, 114, 25–38.

— (1996), 'The ability to identify and label the letters of the alphabet at school entry', *The Journal for Research into Reading*, 19(2):87-101.

Shulman, L.S. (1986), 'Those who understand: knowledge growth in teaching', *Educational Researcher,* 15(2):4–14.

Southworth, G. (1996), 'Improving primary schools: shifting the emphasis and clarifying the focus', *School Organization*, 16(3), 263–80.

Stoll, L. and Mortimore, P. (1995), 'School effectiveness and school improvement', *Viewpoint*, 2, 1–8, Institute of Education, University of London.

Teacher Training Agency (TTA), (1997)*Training Curriculum and Standards for New Teachers.*

Wilson, S.M., Shulman, L.S. and Richert, A.E (1987), '150 ways of knowing: representation of knowledge in teaching', in Calderhead, J, *Exploring Teaching Thinking*. London: Cassell, 104–24.

2.2 Across the great divide – what can be learned from an investigation of primary and secondary partnerships?

Anne Campbell, Pat Cockett, Jan Peckett and Margaret Whiteley

This chapter describes and discusses lessons from participation in partnership models of initial teacher education (ITE), primary and secondary. It has three objectives:

- to appraise the roles and responsibilities of higher education tutors and teachers

- to focus on the quality of student experience, with particular reference to subject knowledge

- to illuminate instances of professional development for various participants.

The chapter is rooted in:

- research: the Esmée Fairbairn National Project, Mentoring in Schools (1993–5); Manchester Metropolitan University (MMU) Student Subject Knowledge and Teaching in Maths and English Project (1996–8)

- evaluation: Primary and Secondary Evaluation Reports, MMU (1993–6)

- development initiatives: the Associate Schools Projects, (1992–4), and the Teacher–Tutor Project (1995).

All these occurred at the Didsbury School of Education, MMU. Its policy for initial and continuing teacher education states:

> Our understanding of the effective teacher is that of a professional communicator who can, within the context of teaching, think analytically and creatively, who can make decisions and solve problems, can manage and not just survive change, and who can be a significant influence in a democratic and ethical society. Such a view rejects any suggestion that a teacher is a mere educational technocrat without wider responsibilities.

Interpretations of that policy in primary, secondary and continuing professional development (CPD) courses, inform this chapter assisting the authors to examine comparative practice so as to contribute to the growing body of knowledge about partnership models. Central is the notion of collaboration between higher education and schools, to facilitate the professional development of both student teachers and experienced teachers. It would be useful to address the terms 'partnership' and 'collaboration'.

A recent paper, Campbell, Hustler and Stronach (1996), put partnership in:

> the first eleven of politically-weighted, Government-inspired concepts (the rest of the team perhaps – competence, mentoring, empowerment, effectiveness, integration, progression, continuity, coherence, professionalism, dialogue). If we were to name this team of words – perhaps the Weasels?
>
> (Campbell, Hustler and Stronach, 1996:2)

That paper's conclusion, after analysing partnership from ideological, anthropological, philosophical and business management perspectives, was that there was:

> no such thing as meaningful partnership with schools ... There is instead a range of different associations – some of which approach

partnership, and at the other end of the spectrum some which bear more relationship to the 'twinning' of cities: not much more than a notice at the side of the road.

(Campbell, Hustler and Stronach, 1996:10)

Who exactly are the partners, characterized as they are by different locations, involvements and investments? Does partnership include the student teacher? Teachers and tutors, at the level of actually working together at the 'chalk face' to produce the teachers of the future, would seem to be very important. Yet arguably pupils, parents and governors are also partners. Most higher education institutes (HEIs) collaborate with multiple partners. Whiting et al. (1996) in their analysis of modes of teacher education, were sceptical about 'collaborative models of partnership', finding that, in most of these, HEIs were 'in the lead', despite a ministerial and Teacher Training Agency (TTA) press for schools to be so. Evidence from the projects and developments we have researched, and confirmed by the Modes of Teacher Education (MOTE) Project (1996), is that teachers are mostly happy for higher education to take a leadership role, for higher education to be the majority stakeholder, and to confirm moderation and quality assurance roles for higher education. A growing bank of evidence supports the claim that schools do not want to 'go it alone' (Campbell and Kane, 1996; Whiting et al., 1996), but actively desire a strong higher education presence. Considerable diversity in our local partnerships gives a feeling of shifting boundaries and of movement. To some extent, it appears that power taken away from the universities is informally being handed back. Such are the contradictions and paradoxes in the current, turbulent climate, that we find ourselves critical of the collaborations and partnerships at the same time as developing, supporting and defending them.

Within this background of diversity, we propose to develop a number of themes 'across the great divide' to identify and discuss what we have learned about partnership. The themes, arising from papers given by the authors at the Exploring Futures in Initial Teacher Education Conference (see Campbell et al., 1996), can be grouped as:

- Reconceptualizing roles and responsibilities – a new professionalism?

- Messages from partnerships

- Emerging intellectual challenges of school-based training initiatives.

Reconceptualizing roles and responsibilities – a new professionalism?

That professionalism has been lost has become something of a recent truism, especially in the sense that teachers seem to have lost shared belief in the validity of their enterprise.

A major concern about the introduction of school-based ITE or, more accurately, initial teacher training (ITT), was effectively summarized by Elliott (1991), when he voiced the danger that beginning teachers could experience 'very rapid socialization into obsolete practices and cultures' following the Government's proposals, which he described as lacking 'any vision of a coherent and continuous process of professional development'. In short, new teachers would fail to be inducted into the professionalism that Davis (1991) defines as 'how one justifies the way one's work is done'.

Regaining recognition that the intellectual tradition of justifying the way one's work is done by continually discussing and critically evaluating, seems to be an idealistic vision, but a necessary one. We are reminded of a phrase of Barber's (1994): 'Policy should be designed to cherish and restore the sense of idealism which is at the core of all good teaching.' Similarly, Wilkin (1996) writes that critical reflection must remain as the internal dynamic of teacher education. Fish (1995) urges higher education teacher educators to 'reclaim their professionalism' by joining with teachers to fight back against Government impositions which reduce teachers to 'mere technocrats and tutors to administrators of quality control'. To so say is not to confuse idealism with romantic nostalgia for a mythic past where everyone read the English classic texts, spelled everything accurately according to the dictionary, could carry out complicated mental arithmetic and where teachers were at once respected and feared. Those myths belong to the same vision of England as a country of warm beer and small counties, more reminiscent of an Ealing comedy than a vision for a multicultural, participatory democracy.

It would seem that higher education tutors want to 'regain' their professionalism, to rescue it from the attacks by Government edicts and TTA policies. They want to rediscover the core of their professional practices, namely the promotion in their students of critical review and evaluation, of the development of a pedagogy for teaching, and the development of appropriate subject knowledge. At the same time, teachers are engaged in 'redefining' their professionalism. Redefinition arises partly from the barrage of National Curriculum documentation and implementation. It includes their involvement in partnership schemes with higher education tutors, which have led many to a radical evaluation of their roles and responsibilities. It will be useful here to look at how tutors and teachers shape and view their roles by considering the following words from a tutor and a primary school teacher.

> 'Teacher-tutors want the students to produce a better lesson next time – I want them to critically evaluate why things went wrong in order to improve their teaching.'
>
> 'If you've got a good student you should leave them alone – how can you improve someone who is doing really well?'
>
> (Campbell, 1995:13).

Those words neatly summarize one of the major findings of the research at MMU about roles and responsibilities, and pinpoint one of the main differences in the roles of tutors and teachers, namely that of promoting in students, systematic, critical evaluation of practice in order to refine, renew and develop teaching. Students are themselves conscious of their need to discuss and evaluate their practice outside their particular placement school, and can become frustrated if such opportunities are reduced. Doing teaching and critically evaluating teaching are not, of course, mutually exclusive. Both are highly desirable. The current problem is the thrust to accept only one of these, the better lesson approach. That teachers find critical appraisal and evaluation of teaching difficult, and that the culture of the school often does not engender critical analysis, is not new. Those working and studying in continuing professional development (CPD) contexts appreciate the difficulties in supporting teachers to become critically reflective in order to enable students to become so. Failure to challenge students can result in students 'hitting the plateau' as described by Maynard and Furlong (1993). Some problems of accommodating able students in a 'school staffed by average teachers' were raised by headteachers in Campbell and Kane (1996), and there is evaluation evidence (Secondary Monitoring and Evaluation Report, MMU, 1996) which identifies a feature which is beginning to emerge, tentatively referred to as the polarization of mentoring. At one end of the spectrum of variability are the schools which have not absorbed the cultural shift, but which adopt a minimalist attitude, often on the basis that the funding is inadequate. At the opposite end are schools which have seen partnership as beneficial to their own 'team learning' (Senge, 1990). This begs questions. Should all schools be involved in teacher education? Can all teachers be mentors or tutors? Our students would answer 'No' to the above questions, and many mentors would agree.

On the whole, students' views taken from the previously cited research projects, indicated that the experience of being in a school where the teachers had been prepared as mentors or teacher-tutors, was beneficial to their professional development. Our evidence would support the claim that 'mentoring is good for you', with regard to professional development. Our findings show that partnership can lead to mutually beneficial relationships between mentors, students and teachers by providing professional development that enhances the quality of the initial training. An interesting question arising from the MOTE Project (Whiting et al., 1996) was, 'Do these different models of partnership make any difference in terms of the forms of professionalism being engendered in the next generation of teachers?'

Do teachers trained in partnership models of courses have a different notion of professionalism from those who are not? It would be inviting to think that these initiatives would make a difference to the next generation of teachers and that they would shape our notions of professionalism, based on collaboration and partnership, which combined the best practice of schools, universities and practitioner research traditions to form a vision for tomorrow's schools.

Messages from partnerships

Messages from secondary partnerships

Three significant areas of professional development for participants have been identified:

- pedagogical development
- subject development
- managerial skill development.

In pedagogical development, there are both inter- and intra-departmental aspects. The inter-departmental dimension has proved particularly interesting – in terms of first-hand experience – to the central, organizing mentors in the secondary school, often senior managers. Their responsibilities include moderating standards. This requires them to observe students across a range of departments, thereby giving them access to inter-departmental practices (still relatively rare in secondary schools) and the opportunity to identify best practice across the curriculum. Observing students in colleagues' departments can give insight into teaching and classroom observation and improve intra-departmental practices in respect of shared issues and collaborative target setting. Perhaps of the most benefit, is the way in which the agenda of the mentoring role shifts as the student moves towards increasing competence. Discussions based on 'myself as a teacher', shift to discussions about children's learning. One mentor, enthused about mentoring that it has legitimized enthusiasm for practice within the classroom.

In terms of subject development, mentors and students in secondary schools have reported considerable benefit from the subject-grouping days, events involving mentors, students and higher education tutors working on a programme which is subject- and ITT-driven. For some mentors this is the only subject-specific development opportunity available to them. Not only the published agenda for these days is valued. Mentors and students exchange ideas and practices across the region, and readily adopt the different relationship of learning alongside each other. Through assignment work, the student also introduces mentors to recent research in their subject area, which can usefully result in a discussion of subject issues. From our research we know that students retain their subject group identity throughout their Post Graduate Certificate in Education (PGCE) course, despite being in different schools for large periods of time. They appreciate having other students in school, but comment that, 'It's good to have other students in school, we can help each other in general ways, but that's no use when I want to discuss how to teach spelling to 9K.'

More fundamental than the immediate answer to a specific and localized question such as that just posed is the issue of subject beliefs which actually lies beneath the question, namely an ideal opportunity for a subject mentor to engage in an exploration of the complex question of teaching spelling. Such opportunities often are missed according to Dart and Drake (1996), who argue that 'without examination of implicit subject philosophies, many opportunities for intellectual and professional development are lost'.

The management skills involved in mentoring students in initial training have a direct affect on the ability to organize an induction programme for newly qualified teachers (NQTs). Mentors report a better understanding of competences and standards. Links to the appraisal process are also alluded to. Review and target setting are valued by mentors for their own professional support, seeing mentoring skills as being directly transferable to the professional development process. One mentor has described involvement in school-based training as having the Heineken effect: it has reached the parts that other INSET [in-service education and training] cannot reach.

Messages from primary partnerships

Recent partnership developments in the primary phase pose similar concerns about the development of students' critical thinking and evaluation of teaching, as discussed earlier, but they also pose some very different questions with regard to partnership models. Our primary partnerships are very different from our secondary partnerships. One of the most challenging areas of primary ITE, is that of subject knowledge, an area of concern across all ITE courses, and currently an area of contention, nationally. Office for Standards in Education (OFSTED) pronounce weekly on teachers' lack of subject knowledge to teach at Key Stage 2, yet expect schools to contribute to subject teaching on ITT courses in the primary sector. Surely there are some contradictions here? The work of Maynard (1996) raises and discusses the difficulties experienced by primary school mentors of taking on the role of subject mentor to students when they themselves feel they are in need of education and development. Our investigations would support that finding.

Secondary teachers are, on the whole, identified by the subject they teach, whereas primary teachers usually identify themselves as primary or infant/junior teachers (until they take on a management role). Despite considerable pressure from OFSTED, TTA and the Government, there is no great enthusiasm for subject specialism within primary schools, although there are signs of some cautious exploration of the practicalities, in the face of the challenge of the National Curriculum at Key Stage 2. Surveys of our students in their first teaching posts have produced evidence that they are often asked to take responsibility for co-ordinating subjects other than those of their first degree or their main subject in the BEd degree. A situation very rare in secondary schools!

We are at the beginning of a small-scale research project, at Didsbury, exploring some of the issues related to subject knowledge for teaching in the primary school and already a number of questions have been thrown up about roles and responsibilities in partnerships as well as the quality of student experience in university and in schools.

For some people, the definition of subject knowledge in this context is non-problematic. Her Majesty's Chief Inspector (HMCI), Chris Woodhead, when asked what subject knowledge he thought primary teachers needed, reportedly replied, 'The National Curriculum. Do you have any problem with that?' The Draft Framework for the Assessment of Quality and Standards in Initial Teacher Education (1996) refers to 'a secure knowledge at a standard beyond the equivalent of, level 8 of the National Curriculum for teaching at Key Stage 1 and 2. This limited notion of subject knowledge could give the impression that a primary teacher only needs to be a page or two ahead of the pupils to be able to teach effectively. However, in the section in the draft framework on planning, teaching and classroom management, mention is made of selecting learning objectives, content and teaching methods appropriate to the topic taught, and the age, abilities and attainments of the pupils. This implies another dimension to subject knowledge. There are other voices recognizing that subject knowledge, as defined by the content of the National Curriculum, is a necessary, but not sufficient, requirement to produce effective teaching, see Shulman (1987), Bennett and Carre (1993) and Meredith (1995). A key question arising from the above research is whether a degree in a subject promotes better teaching of that subject.

Bennett and Carre (1993) found that graduates in science and maths did not have a subject knowledge base adequate to teach their subject at primary level and attributed this to the essential difference of teachers' needing to know their subject but also to understand it in ways that will help their pupils to learn. We are using Bennett and Carre's (ibid) definition of pedagogic subject knowledge as 'an amalgam of content knowledge; curriculum knowledge; knowledge of learners and their characteristics; and general pedagogic knowledge', and we would tentatively suggest from the pilot study that knowledge of learners and their characteristics, and general pedagogic knowledge, seem to influence students more in their planning, implementation and evaluation of teaching.

Despite acknowledging a lack of teacher subject knowledge, it is recognized that teachers do some things better than higher education tutors. There is ample evidence that vast amounts of support are given to students by teachers. Negotiation, planning, detailed discussion about curriculum, appropriate teaching strategies and resources, together with discussion about individual children, comprise highly context-specific expertise. However, there can be problems. Close relationships between teachers and students, developed through daily contact in the same classroom and with the same children, often can involve the teacher in counselling a student about both personal and professional aspects of their lives. Getting too close to your student was a problem for a significant number of teachers. One result of this was the tension between support and assessment roles, more acute for teachers than university tutors. Daily contact often developed a close bond, causing the teachers to worry about their mentoring as a cause of student failure. Other dangers occur in the close daily support. One student felt like a monkey in a zoo as a result of over zealous supervision.

It would appear from our investigations that what tutors do well is to shift roles from being very supportive, through to developing wider perspectives on teaching and into a more distant and more objective role encompassing assessment. Generally, tutors have a higher level of subject knowledge (based on their work as subject tutors at university) and have knowledge of a wider group of schools, which enables them to bring different perspectives to supervision of students.

The messages from both primary and secondary partnerships make it clear that the potential for professional development for all participants is substantial. To come to fruition, the effective collaboration between schools and higher education must exist, despite the present pressurised educational climate. A look at the emerging intellectual challenges may help to point to the pathways for the future.

Emerging intellectual challenges of school-based teacher education

Edwards (1996), in her keynote speech at the Exploring Futures Conference, commented on the present context:

> Here we have evidence of a system in flux. Contexts have been disrupted in ways which challenge and shift current identities, breakdown established relationships and increase links between central government and individual schools.

Much of this chapter has been concerned with investigating and appraising the establishment and development of effective relationships with schools, when the 'system is in flux' and when fragmentation is occurring in types of training (Whiting et al., 1996). At the same time, we are experiencing a bureaucratic centralism, which aims at the control of individuals and to which Edwards (1996) and Taylor (1991) alert us.

> To attempt to identify an agenda for the intellectual challenges for the future is difficult, to try to sustain our own innovative practices in the face of the prospect of yet another major change in policy – the National Curriculum for ITE – seems impossible, but some major issues for consideration can be isolated (Edwards, 1996).

Deciding what beginning teachers ought to know is a good place to start. Any list produced cannot account for how subject knowledge brought from degree work (or other subject-specialist work) must be reconceptualized and informed by explicit theoretical understandings to make it appropriate to pupils in the classroom. It is in the process of regular, systematic reviews with both mentor and tutor that students are guided in their emergent recognition of the complexities of teaching, towards critical evaluation and revision at increasing levels of sophistication. Constructing the opportunities for intellectual discussion does not mean that they will be fully realized, but a gradual move towards fuller professional dialogue needs to occur. The difficulties of this dialogue are discussed in the full by Edwards and Collison (1995) of what primary teachers tell (or rather don't tell) students about pupil learning. Opening up a discussion and investigation of the quality of discourse between students, teachers and tutors in order to make more explicit talk about teaching and learning must be a major feature of the partnerships of the future, and one which will, hopefully, aid the professional development of all participants and have an impact on the quality of pupil learning experiences in the future.

Another major challenge for the future is how to cultivate quality professional development for students, teachers and tutors in school-based partnerships without disadvantaging anyone – particularly pupils. How can we take existing partnerships in ITE programmes into and beyond the development of a new partnership or collaboration in CPD and practitioner research? This question is currently exercising the minds of higher education personnel as they reel from the impact of funding for CPD being moved to the TTA, seemingly intent on imposing a yearly bidding process within a tight list of nationally imposed priorities and creating a two-tier profession. How do we sustain the critical appraisal and evaluation perspectives in ITE within such a framework? A tentative suggestion would be to provide opportunities for CPD through mentored action research in the classrooms, a proposal from a local headteacher, aimed at providing an opportunity for schools to participate in a long-term school-based professional development programme, one focusing on action research in the classroom and pupils' experiences. It is the development of these types of initiatives which will also help to tackle the theory–practice divide. By creating an interrelationship between theory and practice without a simplistic locational divide, e.g. higher education equals theory and school equals practice, it could be hoped that better opportunities for professional development would arise and conditions for what Senge (1990) calls 'metanoia' (i.e. a change of mind-set) would be ripe, so that education and educators might be transformed. Edwards (1996) makes a strong case for the development of 'a knowledge base for teaching', which would be made public. We would support this call and stress the need to make explicit the complexity, the problematic features and the dilemmas involved in the profession. Senge reminds us of the need to regain the professional agenda of intellectual debate by encouraging continued enquiry into complex issues:

> School trains us never to admit that we do not know the answer, and most (institutions) reinforce that lesson by rewarding the people who excel in advocating their views, not inquiring into complex issues.
>
> (Senge, 1990:76)

Practical ways of realising what initially looked Utopian are already being explored and may go some way to achieving Kress's (1995:22) first principle of curriculum innovation:

the curriculum should envisage, project and aim to produce an individual who is at ease with difference and change, whose fundamental being values innovation and is, therefore, able to question, to challenge, and above all to propose alternatives, constructively.

Replace 'individual' with 'beginning teacher' and we have an agenda for ITE which will take us into the next century.

References

Barber, M. (1994), *Times Educational Supplement,* 18 March.

Bennett, N. and Carre, C. (eds), (1993), *Learning to Teach.* London: Routledge.

Campbell, A. (1995), *Evaluation of The Teacher–Tutor Scheme.* Didsbury School of Education, Manchester Metropolitan University.

Campbell, A. (1996), 'What Have We Learned so far from Partnerships with Primary Schools?' Paper at Exploring Futures in Initial Teacher Education Conference, Institute of Education, University of London, September.

Campbell, A. and Kane, I. (1996), 'Mentoring and primary school culture', in McIntyre, D. and Hagger, H., *Mentors in Schools: Developing the Profession of Teaching.* London: David Fulton.

Campbell, A., Hustler, D. and Stronach, I. (1996), 'The Theory and Practice of Partners in Education: How Many Partners can One Word Have without Getting a Bad Reputation?' Paper given at BERA Annual Conference, Lancaster, September.

Dart, L. and Drake, P. (1996), 'Subject perspectives in mentoring', in McIntyre, D. and Hagger, H., *Mentors in Schools: Developing the Profession of Teaching.* London: David Fulton.

Davis, J. (1991), 'Professions, trades and the obligation to inform', *Journal of Applied Philosophy,* 8(2).

DfEE (1996), *Draft Framework for the Assessment of Quality and Standards in Initial Teacher Education*, London: HMSO.

Edwards, A. (1996), 'Possible Futures for Initial Teacher Education in the Primary Phase'. Paper at Exploring Futures in Initial Teacher Education Conference, Institute of Education, University of London, September.

Edwards, A. and Collison, J. (1995), 'What do teacher mentors tell student teachers about pupil learning in primary schools?', *Teachers and Teaching: Theory and Practice*, 1(2).

Elliott, J. (1991), 'A model of teachers' professionalism and its implications for teacher education', *British Educational Research Journal*, 17(4).

Fish, D. (1995), *Quality Learning for Student Teachers*: London: David Fulton.

Furlong, J., Whitty, G., Whiting, C., Miles, S., Barton, L. and Barrett, E. (1996), 'Redefining partnership: revolution or reform in initial teacher education?' *Journal of Education for Teaching*, 22(1).

Kress, G. (1995), *Writing the Future: English and the Making of a Culture of Innovation*. NATE.

Maynard, T. (1996), 'Mentoring subject knowledge in the primary school', in McIntyre, D. and Hagger, H., *Mentoring in Schools: Developing the Profession of Teaching*. London: David Fulton.

Maynard, T. and Furlong, J. (1993), 'Learning to teach and models of mentoring', in McIntyre, D., Hagger, H. and Wilkin, M., *Mentoring: Perspectives on School-based Teacher Education*. London: Kogan Page.

Meredith, A. (1995), 'Terry's learning: some limitations of Shulman's pedagogical content knowledge', *Cambridge Journal of Education*, 25(2).

Senge, P. (1990), *The Fifth Discipline*. New York: Doubleday.

Shulman, L. (1987), 'Knowledge and teaching: foundations of the new reform', *Harvard Educational Review*, 57(1).

Taylor, C. (1991), *The Ethics of Authenticity*. Cambridge, Mass: Harvard University Press.

Whiting, C., Whitty, G., Furlong, J., Miles, S. and Barton, L. (1996), *Partnership in Initial Teacher Education: A Topography*. London: MOTE Project, Institute of Education, University of London.

Wilkin, M. (1996), 'Reasserting professionalism: a polemic', in Furlong, J. and Smith, R., *The Role of Higher Education in Initial Teacher Education*. London: Kogan Page.

2.3 The Key Stage 2/3 course – crisis of identity or golden opportunity?

Linda Fursland

The first section of this chapter examines the political and educational contexts which have given rise to the opportunity to develop Key Stage 2/3 courses. An attempt is made to unravel the various political imperatives underlying this development, including the need for action regarding projected teacher shortages, debates about standards of teaching and learning at Key Stage 2 and, consequently, the education of teachers for this age group.

The second section discusses the issues and dilemmas faced by those in planning and implementing Key Stage 2/3 courses and reaches some conclusions about their potential future contribution.

The planning context

The phase-based nature of initial teacher education (ITE) was fostered by the Council for the Accreditation of Teacher Education (CATE), from its inception in 1984. This agency, set up by Sir Keith Joseph to oversee ITE, emphasized the provision of ITE courses for pupils aged either 3/5 -11 in the primary phase or 11-16/18 in the secondary phase. The CATE criteria implied that only very limited time spans outside the identified age phase would be acceptable in course structures, as is clear from the statement in DES Circular 24/89 that 'courses should prepare students to teach either wholly or mainly in primary schools or wholly or mainly in secondary schools'. This contrasted with practice in the previous decade, prevalent in the early-1980s, when it was not uncommon to find ITE provision for the middle years and/or for junior/secondary.

A significant difference between courses of initial teacher training for the two phases, as they developed according to the mandatory CATE criteria, was that whereas secondary courses were required to prepare students to teach one or two subjects, primary courses were expected to cover all the subjects of the primary curriculum. In addition, primary courses, were required to include subject studies focusing on one or two curriculum areas in order to prepare students to be 'curriculum leaders' (DES Circular 24/89). Some ambivalence, then, about the role of the primary teacher was evident in those early CATE criteria, which otherwise required distinctive provision of courses of ITE for primary and for secondary teachers.

The onset of the National Curriculum from 1988 onwards served to reinforce the age-phase division between primary and secondary education. The separation between Key Stages 2 and 3 at age 11 strengthened the case for transfer at the end of Key Stage 2. As a result, middle schools began to disappear quietly as local education authorities began to reorganize along primary and secondary lines.

The reform of teacher education in the 1990s and the requirement to base courses for mandatory periods of time in partner schools, widened still further the gap between primary and secondary courses of ITE. Two different Circulars, Department for Education (DfE) Circular 9/92 for secondary, and Circular 14/93 for primary, set out differentiated requirements in terms of school-based time and focused on different competences to be achieved by the student teachers, which were, nevertheless, set within a common framework.

DfE Circular 14/93 did attempt to break down the prevailing notion of primary provision as training for general coverage of the whole curriculum, by opening up the possibility of specialist primary ITE courses. These courses were required to include preparation to teach the core subjects of English, maths and science, but were not mandated to cover the full range of subjects within the primary curriculum. It was left to the discretion of institutions to pursue the option of subject-specialist primary courses or otherwise, although there was strong encouragement from the Secretary of State to pursue this line.

It is expected that for the time being most courses will continue to prepare students to teach the full primary curriculum. However, more courses may be developed to cover parts of the primary curriculum in greater depth. The Secretary of State welcomes such fresh approaches to teacher preparation. The new criteria do not, therefore, require all courses to cover all subjects of the primary curriculum.

(DfE Circular 14/93)

The effect of the DfE Circulars on middle schools was to restrict them in the main to partnerships with either primary or secondary courses. Given the numbers of middle schools still in existence in many areas of the country, 859 in 1995 (*The Primary Education Directory*, 1995), a strong case could have been made in the 1980s for the provision of courses of ITE for the middle years. However, it has taken the impending severe shortage of secondary teachers in the subject areas of maths, science, design and technology, Information Technology (IT), modern foreign languages and religious education (RE), projected for the end of the millennium, to galvanize the Teacher Training Agency (TTA) into action in this respect.

With the secondary shortages in mind, the TTA in December 1995, after the original bids for secondary courses had been submitted, probably recognising it was not able to meet its targets for expansion for 1996, came back to institutions with an invitation to bid for Key Stage 2/3 courses in shortage subject areas. These courses would be funded as for secondary courses, an important incentive in encouraging institutions to pioneer this development. The TTA recognized that the existing DfE Circulars for primary and secondary courses would be inappropriate for this course and later the primary DfE Circular 14/93 was amended to fit the requirements of courses preparing students to teach the middle years (seven–14). Originally requiring only 18 weeks in schools for Key Stage

2/3 courses, as for primary Post Graduate Certificate in Education (PGCE) courses, this document in its final form was modified to bring the time in schools up to 24 weeks, as mandatory for secondary PGCE courses.

Another factor in the political and educational contexts within which this planning took place was the debate about the quality of primary teaching at Key Stage 2. Concerns with standards of literacy and numeracy at upper primary level, resurfaced as media attention focused on Office for Standards in Education (OFSTED) reports, such as that on the teaching of reading in primary schools in the London Boroughs of Islington, Southwark and Tower Hamlets. The debate about teaching strategies at primary level, crystallized by the report of the 'Three Wise Men' – Alexander, Rose and Woodhead (1992) – has also continued to preoccupy the media.

A further concern, given less media attention but one of which the education world has been aware for some time, is the issue of continuity and progression between Key Stages 2 and 3. Attention has been drawn to the difficulty of promoting these across the primary and secondary sectors, as emerged in the TTA/OFSTED/SCAA (1996) research paper 'Teachers make a difference' for Key Stages 2 and 3. A SCAA document reflecting these concerns, entitled 'Promoting continuity between KS 2 and 3', was also published in 1996.

At the same time as the above debates were surfacing, a rift was developing between the views of primary ITE courses as depicted by Her Majesty's Inspectors (HMIs) as judged to be generally good and very good, arising from the results of the 'primary sweep' inspection of all primary courses in 1995–6, and the DfE's refusal to accept these results. This led to the decision to re-inspect primary PGCE courses, and to the DfE pronouncement concerning the introduction of a National Curriculum for ITE, to be implemented from 1998.

Whether by attrition or by full-frontal assault, the ethos and culture of the primary school has been placed under threat from the cumulative effect of these criticisms. The topicality of the concerns about teaching and learning at upper primary level may not originally have had such a significant influence on the TTA's decision to allow institutions to develop Key Stage 2/3 courses, as the concern with teaching shortages. What has become clear recently, however, is that the issue about the greater use of subject-specialist teaching in the upper primary sector is now part of the official DfE rhetoric which justifies the introduction of those courses:

> The TTA has advised the Secretary of State that new courses should be developed to cover Key Stage 2/3. These will enable greater use of specialist teaching at Key Stage 2 and provide additional opportunities for primary schools to introduce timetabled subject teaching from teachers with specific subject strengths.
>
> (Undated letter received in July 1996 from Sheila Scales, Head of Teachers Supply, Training and Qualifications Division, DfE. This letter accompanied the criteria for ITE for Key Stage 2/3.)

It has become evident in recent months that by inviting institutions to bid for additional student numbers ring-fenced to PGCE Key Stage 2 specialist courses, as the TTA has done in the 1997–2000 round, it has given a political steer to the bidding process by ensuring that from 1998 onwards any increase in the numbers of students in primary ITE is devoted exclusively to PGCE primary subject specialists.

Issues and dilemmas in planning for Key Stage 2/3 courses

Key Stage 2 issues

The debate about the age at which children should be entitled to specialist teaching in core areas of the curriculum is of recurring significance in Britain, fuelled by international comparisons (Office for Standards in Education, 1996). The argument that certain subjects – maths, science and technology – should be taught to children in Key Stage 2 by 'expert' teachers and should incorporate specialist methodologies, has increased in credibility recently in the debates about standards referred to above.

Pupil attainment in these subjects, particularly compared with other countries in the European Union (EU) and the wider world, is frequently the object of media attention because of the perception of these subjects as crucial to economic development. This argument is reinforced by the status accruing to these curriculum areas as being difficult to master and, thus, needing to be taught by 'experts' before children move to the secondary phase of education.

The philosophy of specialist teachers in the primary school is not one, however, espoused by all or even, I suspect, many institutions involved in primary ITE or their partnership schools. Recent discussions with partner primary schools in course planning meetings at Bath College of Higher Education in relation to DfE Circular 14/93 and to the draft Key Stage 2/3 criteria, have always established the priority to be given to the development of the primary generalist teacher, able to cover the whole curriculum, with the capacity to take responsibility for the co-ordination of one or two particular curriculum areas, as 'curriculum leader' (24/89) or 'subject co-ordinator'. The possibility of moving beyond the 'subject co-ordinator' to the 'specialist' primary teacher has appeared a disturbing prospect to many primary tutors involved with ITE, as much as to their partner schools, in representing a threat to the established ethos of primary education. This notion of the primary teacher as a generalist, covering the whole curriculum, rather than a specialist, would seem to be central to the identity of the primary teacher and many in primary education have forecast the loss of an essentially primary ethos arising from a move in this direction, in spite of the encouragement to do so in Government pronouncements.

However, the notion of the primary teacher as a generalist, albeit a generalist able to carry out a subject co-ordinator's role, involves educating student teachers to cover the whole primary curriculum. The conception of the primary Key Stage 2 teacher as a specialist is likely to preclude being able to teach the whole curriculum, particularly if the post also requires liaison/teaching with/at Key Stage 3. This was the decision reached by the planning team for the Key Stage 2/3 course at Bath College of Higher Education. It was decided that the course should prepare students to teach their specialism, science, and the other two areas of the core curriculum, as required by the Circular for Key Stage 2/3 courses, with the addition of the closely related foundation disciplines of design and technology, geography, physical education and IT.

It was the omission of certain subjects and selection of others from the primary curriculum which provoked most debate, amongst primary members of the planning team and in the consultation with primary tutors and teachers. Concerns centred on the extent to which schools could accommodate this model, both in school experience placements and in the availability of future teaching posts, thus affecting the career prospects of those completing this course. It was also considered that the 'hidden curriculum' of such a course would undermine the status and worth of the subjects not covered and damage whole curriculum developments such as work on equal opportunities.

Handling such concerns during consultation with primary headteachers involved with the various steering and course committees was a delicate matter. It was important to reiterate that such a course should not attempt to serve the same purpose as a primary PGCE course or jeopardize the career openings of that cohort. Cynically, the view was expressed on a number of occasions that the course was 'towing the party line', possibly from financial motivation. It is worth noting, however, that at the end of each comparable discussion at least one participant argued how much a Key Stage 2/3 core subject specialist would have to offer to a primary school, particularly a larger school. Apart from the advantages accruing from subject specialism, this initiative was also welcomed as probably bringing more men into primary schools.

The full involvement of primary schools in the training of subject specialists for Key Stage 2 is fundamental to planning and implementing a Key Stage 2/3 course, as is the obvious benefit to be derived by student teachers from experiencing the liaison across the primary/secondary divide.

Key Stage 3 issues

Consultation over the draft criteria for Key Stage 2/3 courses included partner secondary schools and the 68 middle schools in the surrounding counties. The response was somewhat lukewarm from secondary schools, which may regard such developments as marginal to their more pressing concerns, particularly in the light of the dearth of school experience placements even for ITE secondary students which exists in many areas of the country (Fursland and Green, 1996). However, some far-sighted comments did recognize that such courses will have something to offer, if the implementation of the Dearing Review of post-16 qualifications produces greater coherence for the 14–19 curriculum, thus enhancing the significance of continuity and progression for the 7–14 age group. One inner city secondary school, which had been asked to consider reorganization as an 'all age' school, found the idea of Key Stage 2/3 courses interesting, but more secondary schools approached were concerned about the difficulty of absorbing student teachers unable to teach at Key Stage 4.

The middle schools, however, in responding to the consultation exercise, acclaimed Key Stage 2/3 courses as what they had been waiting for, disenfranchised as they had been from partnerships in ITE across the full age phase represented by the middle school.

Middle schools are certainly the natural school base for this course, but although we are clear about primary and secondary schools, their ethos, culture and organization, it is less obvious what a middle school is. Such schools tend to vary in the exact ages they include, usually from 8–12 or 9–13, but never including the whole of Key Stages 2 and 3 (i.e. from 7–14 years). They differ too in the extent of specialization adopted, some aligning themselves more to teaching by primary generalist teachers and others introducing specialist teachers to year six children, with specialist rooms and equipment. Some middle schools, indeed, try to do justice to the ethos and organization of both primary and secondary within the one school. The other difficulty with middle schools is that they have tended to be, in the age of the National Curriculum, a dying breed, and there are areas of the country where there are none at all. This tends to reduce confidence in the employment prospects of the students and to render more difficult the ensuring of comparable and consistent school experience placements.

It would seem then that although middle schools represent the most natural home for student teachers on Key Stage 2/3 courses, exclusive use of middle schools would be both problematic and inadequate. It is clearly essential to draw in and involve secondary schools in partnerships for the training of such students, however cautious about the final outcome, or preoccupied with secondary ITE, these might be. Not to enable these students to experience secondary schools would certainly deprive them of the opportunity to experience the full range of the upper age group and possibly that of being able to teach their subject under full subject-specialist conditions. It would more than likely also undermine the employment prospects of these student teachers. Moreover, many secondary schools have very well developed and successful primary transfer arrangements, providing models of good practice which student teachers can study in order to gain insight into continuity and progression across the age phases.

Conclusion

One of the greatest challenges for the Key Stage 2/3 course, especially that of one year's duration, must be to prepare teachers, as the DfE criteria require, 'to work as subject specialists with 7–11 year olds in primary schools, with 11–14 year olds in secondary schools, or in middle schools with pupils within the 7–14 age range'. Teachers trained to teach the 7–14 age group will need to cast off age-phase blinkers and transcend the primary/secondary divide, in order to exploit the golden opportunity for promoting continuity and progression between the Key Stages which this course provides.

The development of Key Stage 2/3 courses has broken the mould of the phase-based approaches to ITE which have prevailed in the last decade or more. Mould breaking involves crises of and even loss of identity, as this chapter has attempted to show in relation to Key Stage 2, but it also provides golden opportunities for new developments. When one mould has been broken, another must form or be formed speedily to replace it; it remains to be seen whether the structure of schooling will enable teachers trained on Key Stage 2/3 courses to fulfil their evident potential in linking specialist learning across the two phases, in addition to the valuable subject-specialist contribution at Key Stage 2, or whether this initiative is destined to remain antipathetic to the primary school sector, marginal to the secondary sector, but a cause for rejoicing in the middle schools.

References

Alexander R., Rose, J. and Woodhead C. (1992), *Curriculum Organization and Classroom Practice in Primary schools – a Discussion Paper.* London: HMSO.

Department of Education and Science Circular 24/89 *Initial Teacher Training: Approval of Courses.* London: HMSO.

— Circular 3/84 *Initial Teacher Training: Approval of Courses.* London: HMSO.

Department for Education, *Initial Teacher Training (Secondary Phase), Circular 9/92.* London: HMSO.

— *The Initial Teacher Training of Primary School Teachers: New Criteria for Courses Circular 14/93.* London: HMSO.

— *Criteria for Initial Teacher Training (Key Stage 2/3).*

Fursland, L. and Green, P. (1996), 'A study of the factors influencing partnership between schools and HEIs in relation to school-based secondary PGCE courses', *Forum*, Spring, 26–8.

Office for Standards in Education (OFSTED) (1996), *Worlds Apart? A Review of International Surveys of Educational Achievement Involving England.* London: HMSO.

The Primary Education Directory (1995), Redhill, Surrey: The School Government Publishing Company Ltd.

Teacher Training Agency (TTA), Office for Standards in Education (OFSTED) and Schools Curriculum Assessment Authority (SCAA) (1996), *Teachers Make a Difference: A Research Perspective on Teaching and Learning in Key Stages 2 and 3.* Research papers for Conference, March.

2.4 What age groups should primary teacher training cover?

Helen Penn

I wish to open this chapter with a lengthy quotation:

> In the eyes of both central and local authorities a school is a place where children learn to sit still, to obey orders, and where they receive instruction in reading, writing and arithmetic. The old fashioned manager or inspector looks on such things as (child-centred education) as fads; the beginning and end of elementary education is 'teach 'em to read'. (In the infant classroom) a blackboard has been produced and hieroglyphics are drawn upon it by the teacher. At a given signal every child in the class begins calling out mysterious sounds: Letter A, Letter A, in a sing song voice; or Letter A says Ah, as the case may be. To the uninitiated I may here explain that the former is the beginning of spelling, and the latter is the groundwork of word building. Hoary headed men will spend hours discussing whether c-a-t or ke-ar-te are the best means of conveying knowledge of how to read cat. I must own to indifference on this point myself and I sympathize with teachers who are not allowed to settle it for themselves ... without attempting to follow further the effect on the poor child's brain I would most earnestly discuss the uselessness, nay, worse, the harmfulness of the whole system.

What possible good is there in forcing a little child to master the names of letters and numbers at this age? The strain on the teachers is terrific. Even when modern methods are in vogue and each child is presented with coloured counters or shells, beads, or a ball frame, the intellectual effort of combining three plus one to make four ... has no value at such an age. The nervous strain must reduce the child's physical capacity, and this again reacts unfavourably on the condition of the teeth, eyes and digestion ... The child is in a close (poorly ventilated) room – he is bent forward, his back is all crooked, and his body is all sideways ... the talking is done by the teacher, not by the child, the subject and meaning are fixed by her explanation, and only one child at a time may respond to a question. The others must sit motionless, and with arms tightly crossed, waiting for a notice, that in many cases, never comes.

Are we not slaves to tradition – slaves to custom – slaves to our own regulations. Of what possible use is all this routine? In my opinion ... little children require nurses rather than teachers, and lady doctors rather than inspectors ... In the infant schools ... the whole atmosphere has been made into a forcing house for the schools for older scholars. Even where kindergarten methods are better understood, the teachers are hampered and hindered by a masculine love of uniformity and order. The discipline expected is military rather than maternal, and can only be maintained at the expense of much healthy, valuable, and as far as the children are concerned, necessary freedom.

(Bathurst, 1905b:818–24)

I have quoted this piece at length because, despite being written nearly 100 years ago, it echoes down into our own time. It makes some very pertinent points. It is part of an argument for separate nursery schools rather than infant classes which admit three- and four-year-old children. It regards nursery education as being essentially concerned with physical fitness and well-being as much as with cognitive and social development. It considers that children of four are too young to entertain – or be entertained by – National Curriculum requirements. Finally it argues for women who have been trained differently from primary school teachers to work with young children.

When this diatribe was first published, it met with a great deal of sympathy and, for a time, nursery schooling did indeed follow the pattern that Katherine Bathurst suggested, that is with separate full-day nursery schooling, a real concern with the physical well-being of children, a very open-ended and relaxed regime, and nursery teachers who received a separate and distinct training from primary schooling. The hoary headed men with military leanings were for a while at least kept at bay.

The watershed which changed this view of nursery education was the Advisory Council headed by Plowden (1967) and the subsequent 1972 White Paper. Plowden's Committee was heavily influenced by two major theorists, Piaget and Bowlby. Piaget stressed the cognitive above all – he was not concerned with whether children ate properly, exercised, had fresh air, had any kind of physical freedom or received care whilst their mothers were working, so long as they were exercising their minds. Plowden adopted this new theory whole-heartedly. Children should be stimulated to think and learn by nursery education. On the other hand, Bowlby emphasized the attachment of young children to their mothers and Plowden also interpreted this to mean that nursery education should not be used in such a way to separate young children from their mothers; they should only have this intense thinking and learning experience at nursery school for two hours in the morning or two hours in the afternoon. So part-time nursery education was given its raison d'être in Plowden, and the White Paper following it tartly pointed out that it was much cheaper to attach part-time nursery classes to primary schools than to have them free standing. So, inadvertently, the case for nursery schools was lost again; if children were at school anyway in nursery classes, it was still cheaper for local authorities to put children aged four in reception classes. Primary teachers could easily teach four-year-olds or even three-year-olds – and, by the end of the 1980s, the kinds of initial and refresher training for nursery education which had been developed were mostly abandoned. The introduction of a subject-based teacher training further eroded the attention paid to early years. Then a change of tone by the Government, with a new emphasis on the rigidities of classroom teaching, as has happened recently, and the hoary headed men have got their revenge. We are back where we started, with Kathleen Bathurst protesting about the unsuitability of the classroom regime for young children, albeit conditions slightly better than they were in 1905.

I use this potted history to illustrate that the arrangements we make for young children are not necessary but accidental. I could equally well have used material from the European Union to show how much countries differ in their interpretation of what young children need and how it might be provided.

So the starting point I have arrived at rather laboriously is that there is no *a priori* reason why things are as they are, and if we were to reconsider, 25 years on from Plowden, and in the light of today's circumstances, what would best suit children's and families' needs, what would we come up with? This question is addressed in Moss and Penn (1996), which is based on work already going on in the UK and in Europe and which offers a very practical blueprint for a more rational, humane and communitarian system for the care and education of young children before they reach school age. School starting age it is argued should be five going on six, as in Scotland, not four years old as in England. Like Katherine Bathurst, the argument is that early childhood services would make more sense and be better able to articulate their own rationale if they were detached from primary education not merely viewed as an appendage to it and subject to its rules and regulations. Early childhood is considered to be a distinctive period warranting its own pedagogy.

As part of this blueprint for a comprehensive, coherent system of care and education for children aged 0-6, Moss and Penn looked at the patterns of training currently available to those who work with young children. (See *Table 1*, pages 152-153).

The picture is one of great muddle. Different staff receive different training and experience different conditions of work – yet all deal with children of the same age. Moreover, children's access to these various facilities is grossly unequal. Just over one-quarter of children of eligible age attend nursery education, although rather more than three-quarters of them start primary school at four years old.

The following summarizes the arguments against the present system.

1 Current teacher training requirements focus on children of school age and the needs of children under five are marginalized in the present system

Teacher training is subject based, but there is no evidence that very young children benefit from subject-based teaching. The School Curriculum and Assessment Authority (SCAA, 1995) suggests that there should be a certain number of desirable outcomes from attendance at an early years service. These outcomes prefigure the National Curriculum, but even so there is little time on conventional teacher training courses to include material on these outcomes, and how they might be developed and measured. In fact, evidence from a recent survey carried out by Hurst (1996) suggests that the majority of teachers working in nursery education or reception classes have *no specific training* to deal with this age group.

2 The poor training received by non-teachers

A recent study I carried out for the Department for Education and Employment (DfEE) as part of a wider Organization of Economic Co-operation and Development (OECD) study on childcare as a gendered occupation suggested that much childcare or nursery nurse training was aimed at low achievers and had a remedial function, and that generally the level of attainment of those who received this qualification was poor (Penn, 1997). Yet this group constitutes the majority of those who work with young children. A DfE Paper (1996) talks of the need to set up a national training body for those working with young children. However, the exclusion of teachers from this proposal will tend to perpetuate the existing system.

Table 1 Staff working in early childhood services

	Teacher	Nursery nurse education	Nursery nurse social services
approx no. employed	7,000 (excluding reception)	7,000	7,500
generally acceptable qualification	BEd or degree/ PGCE minimum 4 yrs post-18	certificate/diploma in nursery nursing (NNEB/BTec) 2 yrs post-16	certificate/diploma in nursery nursing (NNEB/BTec) 2 yrs post-16
age-range	3-8, 3-11	3-5	0-5
adult:child ratio	1:13	1:13	1:3 (0-2), 1:5 (2-3);
contracted weekly hrs	1,265 hr/ 195 days per yr	35 inc breaks	37-9 without breaks
contact hrs with children	average 25-30 hrs per week	average 25–30 hrs per week	37-9 hrs per week
shifts/working hrs	9–3.30/4, no shifts	9-3.30/4, no shifts	8-6pm, 2/3 shifts
overtime pay if extra hrs	no	yes	yes
holidays	12 wks	12 wks	3-6 wks
sick pay/pension	LA conditions	LA conditions	LA conditions
career prospects	promoted posts	no promoted posts	9 grades promoted posts
parity with other groups	with teachers	none	none
basic pay scale (1993)	£11,880/ £13,500-£18,000	£9,300- £10,797	£8,226- £21,357
recognized unions	NUT/NASWT	Unison/T&G/GMB	Unison/T&G/GMB
line manager	only teacher	only teacher	NNEB/social worker
staff facilities, staffroom, etc.	yes	yes	yes
supply cover arrangements	yes	yes	yes

From: Moss and Penn (1996).

Playgroup worker	Childminder	Private day nursery
40,000	*100,000*	*25,000*
no legal requirement: local playgroup foundation course/playgroup practice diploma/NVQ	no legal requirement: local childminding course 6-10 weeks, 1 session per week. NVQ	no legal requirement: usually senior staff NNEB/NVQ
2-5	0-8	0-5, 0-8
1:8	1:3	1:3 (0-2), 1:5 (2-3); 1:8 (3–5)
average 5-15 hrs per week	average 50 hrs, no breaks	37-40 without breaks
5-15 hrs per week	50-60 hrs per week	37-40 hrs per week
average 9-11.30 no shifts	8-6pm continuous	8-6pm 2/3 shifts
no	maybe	usually
12 wks (unpaid)	3 wks (half pay)	3-4 wks
none	none	unusual
none	none	no national scale
none	none	none
hourly rates, approx £2/3	hourly rates, approx £2/3	£6- £18,000
none	none	none
none/mgmt committee	none	private employer
no	no	maybe
none	none	maybe

3   *The overwhelming majority of provision for children under the*
     age of five is in the private and voluntary sector where relatively
     few teachers are employed

Currently, most expansion is taking place in this sector. Over 104,000
new early years places have been created in the private and voluntary
sector in the last 10 years (DoH 1996) funded through various inner
city regeneration bids as well as through private capital, although
this expansion is ignored by most local education authorities (LEAs)
as somehow being less than *bona fide*. Nevertheless, it is where an
increasing number of children are receiving their pre-school
education and it makes sense, therefore, to argue that those who
work with them are sufficiently well trained. Trained teachers are
equipped to work in private schools at primary and secondary level,
and they could similarly work in the private and voluntary early
years sector. Indeed, if this were recognized as a reasonable outlet
for teachers, it might also upgrade the pay and conditions in this
sector. However, teacher training, by virtue of its current regulations,
cannot recognize work in such settings as a respectable source of
practice, despite it being a more common form of practice than
nursery education.

4   *The need to address the situation of children of under three years*
     of age, an increasing number of whom are in daycare

The division between over threes and under threes is a bureaucratic
division rather than one based on children's needs. Children do not
become magically more able to start learning or to cope with school
on attaining the age of three. There is tremendous variation amongst
young children as regards the extent to which they can tolerate or
benefit from group settings. In fact, the greatest pressure to provide
places is for children under the age of three. Labour Market Trends
(1996) suggests that the number of women with children under five
is now over 52 per cent, the biggest increase being from women

returning to work after maternity leave. If a majority of mothers now work, then it is peculiarly short sighted to have education services oblivious of that fact. As a result, young children who most need continuity, are shunted from one type of provision to another, under threes to over threes, to a childminder, to a playgroup, to a nursery class plus a childminder and onto school (and even then the shunting continues with out-of-school services). Children are active learners from birth, gradually increasing their self-awareness and control, but they are only presumed to exist by the education system at three years and, a year later, they are exposed to the rigours of full-time school – hardly an accurate or logical mirroring of the progress children themselves make.

5   The variety of training models

Oberhuemer (1997) draws attention to the different models of training for early years throughout Europe. She argues that policies and types of delivery of services influence training – that its level and length, the degree of age specialism, its fit or lack of fit with primary and secondary education relate directly to the kind of service which is provided. Just as our system of part-time nursery education is a British idiosyncrasy, so are the systems of training for early years. Britain is unique in regarding primary school training as sufficient to cover nursery education. In those countries where education and care are seen as an integrated service rather than as a supplementary service outside the home, the training is broader and reflects the nature of the partnerships between professionals and between parents and professionals. These differences are highlighted in Table 2. (See pages 156-157)

So my argument is that present training is on its own terms inadequate. It is a fragmented and bipartite – I might almost say apartheid – system which does not address the needs of young children at present. But if we were to develop a more comprehensive and coherent system of early

Table 2 The parameters of early years services

Policy: aims and objectives	Legal and fiscal framework	Level of decision making/ local autonomy	Process of decision making	Support and monitoring arrangements
NZ 'Educare' service for children 0-5 stressing community involvement	Education system of per capita funding according to age of child and hrs of attendance	national framework institutional discretion	national bicultural discourse: chartering, multiple stakehold at level of institution	national education inspectors
Spain: To provide continuous education 0-16 for all children	LOGSE: infant education 0-6 as first stage of education system. Funding as and when available	national framework but discretion at every level – regional, commune, nursery	professional discourse at every level	national education inspectorate
Denmark: Childcare service for all children who require it	social welfare legislation funded; but all children who require a place obtain one	loose national framework, left up to nursery	stakehold negotiation within nursery	minimal
UK no coherent policies	part Children Act, as part of reception into care procedure: education outcomes linked to vouchers	prescriptive national frameworks little local autonomy no institutional autonomy	national experts/ civil servants	education inspectorate social services inspectorate

Basic training	Types of provision	Who delivers service	Vulnerable children	Curricular objectives
3 yrs post-18 educare degree	various: hours also vary	trained educare workers	integrated	5 aims: • well-being, • belonging, • contribution, • communication, • exploration
3 yr post 18 teacher training	centre based nurseries 0-3/0-6 plus nursery classes: all provision full-time	100% trained 3-6: some trained 0-3	integrated	
3 yrs 6 mths post-18 social pedagog	mixed,0-6, age integrated centres 0-12, all provision full-time	60% trained	integrated	left up to local centre, general aim of happiness and well-being
4 yrs post-18 for teachers in education 2 yrs post-16 for SS day nurseries, otherwise no clear requirements	fragmented many types of provision with different aims and objectives: little full-time provision	varies, majority minimally trained or untrained	little full-integration	prescriptive

years provision, free-standing nursery schools which provided care and education for children aged nought–five, then the need to devise a new model of training for early years becomes still more urgent. We have few precedents and the training would have to reflect the new priorities of a coherent inclusive system – more of a focus on health and well-being, more of a focus on co-operation and solidarity, more fun and rather less insistence on cognitive development, learning and curriculum. There are many models of training one might look at for inspiration – the Danish social pedagogue model (Davies Jones, 1994); the Spanish Educational Act (1989) or New Zealand bipartite education model (Carr and May 1993), or the insistence of the Italian educator Malaguzzi (1993) on the importance of relationships and dialogue between all the participants in the service – children, parents and staff alike. The European Commission, in a recent discussion document, *Quality Targets for Early Years Services* suggests it would be reasonable to aim at an early years workforce of 60 per cent staff qualified at a three-year post-18 level, which modular training available on an in-service basis for the rest.

Whatever we do, I suggest we should go back to the drawing board because what we have at present lets most young children down.

References

Bathurst, K. (1905a), 'The need for national nurseries', in Van der Eyken, W (1973), *Education, the Child and Society*. London: Penguin, 119–25.

—   (1905b), *The Nineteenth Century and After*.

Carr, M. and May, H. (1993), 'Choosing a model. Reflecting on the developmental process of Te Whariki: national early childhood curriculum guidelines in New Zealand', *International Journal of Early Years Education*, 1(3), 7–21.

Davies Jones, H. (1994), 'The social pedagogues in Western Europe – some implications for European inter-professional care', *Journal of Interprofessional Care*, 8(1), 19–28.

Department for Education and Employment (DfEE), (1996), *Work and Family: Ideas and Options for Childcare.* London, HMSO.

Department of Health (1996), *Children's Day Care Facilities at 31st March 1995.* London: Government Statistical Service.

European Commission Childcare Network (1996), *Quality Targets in Services for Young Children.* Brussels: European Commission.

Hurst, V. (1996), 'Preliminary findings of the Early Education Research Project'. Personal communication.

Labour Market Trends (1996), *Women in the Labour Market.* London: Market Trends.

Malaguzzi, L. (1993), 'For an education based on relationships', *NAEYC Journal,* Washington, November 1993.

Ministry of Education and Science (1989), *Project for the Reform of the Educational System.* Madrid: Ministry of Education and Science.

Moss, P. and Penn, H. (1996)*Transforming Nursery Education.* London: Paul Chapman.

Oberhuemer, P. (1997), 'Who Works with Young Children? Concepts and Issues of Staffing and Professionalization in European Countries'. London. Paul Chapman.

Penn, H. (1996), *Childcare as a Gendered Occupation.* London: DfEE Research Report No.RR23.

Plowden, B. (1967), *Children and Their Primary Schools.* London, Central Advisory Council for Education: HMSO.

School Curriculum and Assessment Authority (SCAA), (1995), *Desirable Outcomes for Children's Learning and Guidance for Providers.* London: SCAA.

2.5 A view of the landscape for teaching students aged 11-19

David Lines

In trying to describe a view of the landscape for teaching students aged 11-19, one is struck by the consistency with which the authors of the chapters which follow describe upheaval and challenge, threat and insecurity. Fortunately, they also offer hope and a determination to rise to the task, building on a belief that what teacher education offers is more than worthwhile – that it is in fact essential.

Totterdell and Lambert suggest that the pace of change in the British education system is difficult to follow. A convenient starting point is the Educational Reform Act (ERA) of 1988, because of its fundamental, if unequal, impact upon the education community (Wragg, 1994).

The National Curriculum's introduction changed the professional life of teachers to a far greater extent than it did teacher trainers'. In addition, the fact that schools were reformed before training institutions can be seen, in some senses, as the ultimate rebuff. After all, it would be a reasonable assumption that a radical Government would have introduced a National Curriculum for teacher training before, or at least simultaneously with the one for schools, had it felt that teacher training exerted a crucial or significant impact on what was taught to and learnt by school students, but it did not.

Such marginalization may support Wideen's contention that when it comes to school reform, teacher educators are seen by policy makers as non players (this volume), but an alternative view is that the central Government, by exerting such self evident power and control through the forced introduction of the National Curriculum, made it clear that it would brook no criticism. With as colourful a phrase as one might wish to encounter, especially from one of Her Majesty's Inspectors (HMIs), Taylor wonders 'if the National Curriculum has eviscerated us of the guts of educational thought' (this volume). However, the existence of this book and the conference which preceded it, suggest that even if the body is at risk from the surgeon's knife, at least the soul remains intact!

This 'view' of the 11–19 landscape is, then, an attempt to bring together the contributions of a number of authors, variously concerned with inspection, curriculum control and teachers' futures. Rather than describe each in turn, it is instructive to identify themes, so that our view is indeed a 'landscape'. The fine detail can be found in the readings themselves.

Globalization

Piper and Robinson's chapter introduces Ritzer's term 'McDonald-ization', which refers to the attempt by central authorities to achieve efficiency, calculability, predictability and control in education. They argue that this is a world-wide phenomenon, but that such an attempt will fail, not least because some of its objectives are contradictory or at least antipathetic.

Take 'the market' in education, for instance, which is advocated by its proponents as a guarantee of efficiency – a means of increasing choice and allocating resources in a manner which is both objective and apolitical, and, therefore, above criticism. Although the market may well increase efficiency, its results are unpredictable. It cannot be controlled. It is, after all, 'free'. Thus, a 'free market' in examination setting and marking has resulted in a perception of lowered standards and a pro-market Government arguing for what amounts to a 'nationalization' of examination boards (Tooley, 1996).

Nevertheless, the hegemony of market economics following the fall of communism requires Governments to look at economic performance in a deeper and more searching way than ever before. As Porter argues (this volume) educational and economic performance are increasingly linked. Thus, international comparisons of levels of literacy and numeracy are intensely studied, though often with scant regard for different cultural backgrounds and testing regimes (Eckstein and Noah, 1993). As Taylor points out, 'the ideal of highly-educated citizens is also the pragmatic and economic necessity of a highly skilled workforce'.

Totterdell and Lambert, whilst recognizing the force of globalization, argue that it is something to be harnessed, rather than attempting to return to former structures, hence their term 'globalization from below'. Certainly if one accepts the premise that it is technology which has caused globalization there can be no stopping it; what must be targeted are, in their words, 'wider "ecological" dimensions of professional endeavour' (this volume).

Technological change

Of course, the very technology which has created world-wide markets also offers opportunities to satisfy people rather than groups. In the 1980s, multinational car manufacturers designed 'world cars' which were produced in countries with lowest costs and shipped to the mass markets of Europe, North America and the growing ones of the Pacific Rim. As the 1990s have progressed, the idea of a world car has faded – technology allows low-cost production runs to suit the differing demands of different countries, but it has not stopped there. Cars are now built to the unique specifications of individuals. The industry is now as far away from Henry Ford's dictum, 'any colour as long as it is black' as it can go.

This phenomenon is not unique to cars. Marketing is aimed at you and me, not us. Our names are word processed on the top of the mail-shot which lands on our doormats because of that innocent questionnaire which we answered when we bought our last washing machine or computer, or when we joined a book club or enjoyed a weekend away. Technology allows this to happen and it is important, not only because we are more likely to receive the goods we want but also because it opens the way for small-scale, niche producers to survive and even flourish.

Flexibility and fleet footedness are the keys to entrepreneurial success, but it is also necessary to have a workforce which is both aware and unafraid of technology. This, of course, is where education should play a key role. Unfortunately, our view of the landscape contains at least one blot – in this case, the debate over education versus training which has bedevilled curriculum development in England and Wales, and which Sir Ron Dearing attempted to address in his 16–19 Report (Dearing, 1996).

Lucas explores this debate in some depth in Part 1 of this book. He quotes the work of Reich in industrial contexts and Young in educational ones to show how demands have changed and how colleges have adjusted to take them into account. He is critical of General National Vocational Qualifications (GNVQs), which 'start from the primacy of performance', as opposed to academic courses, which start from an assumption of the 'primacy of knowledge', but he makes the point that GNVQs may be of relevance to initial teacher education (ITE) courses, 'where skills and knowledge are developed through reflection on practice, emphasizing personal and autonomous skills and negotiated learning targets' (this volume). In so far as GNVQs represent 'applied qualifications', so a similar teaching and learning style in ITE represents an applied route to qualified teacher status (QTS).

Initial teacher education or initial teacher training?

This then takes us into deeper waters – is it to be initial teacher *education* or initial teacher *training*? Piper and Robinson are clear – on the one hand there is the 'professional model of teacher education, subscribed to by most teacher educators in HEIs [higher education institutions]' and on the other 'the technician model emanating from right-wing sources such as the Centre for Policy Studies (which has underwritten much central Government policy since 1979)' (this volume).

The technician model emphasises competences and subject knowledge (DES 9/92;14/93) and, as Piper and Robinson show, there is some evidence that students also regard these as the most important aspects of learning to teach. But then these same students are 'adults, knowledgeable about classrooms and teachers, but less knowledgeable about classroom teaching and learning' (this volume). Such a criticism could equally apply to the rest of the adult population, including politicians, and this perception is important because 'the ideological driven determination of much of the content of ITE courses has been undermined by an equally ideological determination to pass major elements of the courses over to "real" teachers in "real" schools' (this volume).

HEIs, therefore, face a dual challenge from both customers and funders who have to be persuaded of the virtues of what they are doing – of adding value above both the financial and opportunity costs of the courses themselves. Falling back on a reflective model as a counter to what might be seen as hard-nosed reality is asking a lot, perhaps too much. As Totterdell and Lambert put it:

> Can reflective practice really function as a 'root paradigm' or 'habitas' for initial training? Does not the 'traffic' it exhorts between action on the one hand and analysis on the other, betoken a rather one-sided emphasis on cognition over action and being? Is this not to perpetuate a disparaging view of practical activity as an intrinsically inferior sort of thing?
>
> (Totterdell and Lambert, this volume)

Paradigm clash or dialectic?

If the positions of Government and HEIs are seen as competing paradigms, then it is reasonable to suppose that there will be winners and losers, but perhaps the process should be seen more as a dialectic. Taylor believes that:

there are common aims shared by those with a stake in education, whether teachers, industrialists, politicians or parents. This has underlined, on the one hand, a widespread resentment of all teaching which is driven by ideological fads and fashions, and, on the other, a support for teaching which gets results.

(Taylor, this volume).

Furthermore, Taylor believes that a national curriculum for initial teacher training (ITT) (sic) will, given sound inspection, allow for a system which 'while marked by diversity and flexibility, still does enough to ensure consistent standards and common experience and content with the training providers' (this volume).

Of course, tensions remain. Lucas (in Part 1) suggests that a review of the entire 14–19 curriculum is required, rather than the piecemeal tinkering of A levels, GNVQs and so on which have occurred up to now (Dearing, 1996; Lines, 1996). This being so, he argues:

Further research and a close partnership and dialogue between schools, colleges and universities in initial training and continual professional development are required if we are to meet the needs of increasing numbers of students who stay on and achieve in education.

(Lucas, this volume)

Piper and Robinson are more pragmatic. They suggest that schools simply are not willing or indeed able to shoulder the burden of initial training alone, and as the process of transfer gains pace, all the players will come to recognize this and step back.

Thus, in the true spirit of dialectic, synthesis will be achieved, although as Totterdell and Lambert argue, only if teacher educators 'exhibit a largesse of spirit' (this volume). Many would go further and suggest that such largesse should apply equally to both 'sides' in this particular debate. It is simply too important to have victor and vanquished, because in the end everyone will lose – teachers, teacher trainers and especially the young people sitting in the nation's classrooms on whom, ultimately, we all depend.

References

Dearing, R. (1996), *Review of Qualifications for 16-19 Year Olds.* London: SCAA.

Department for Education (DfE) (1992), *The Initial Training of Teachers (Secondary Phase) Circular 9/92.* London: DfE.

— (1992), *The Initial Training of Primary School Teachers Circular 14/93.* London: Department for Education.

Eckstein, M.A. and Noah, H.J. (1993), *Secondary School Examinations. International Perspectives on Policies and Practice.* New York: Yale University.

Lines, D.R. (1996), 'A-train is going too fast', *Times Educational Supplement: Secondary Curriculum,* 22 November, 21.

Tooley, J. (1996), 'Beware this State control', *The Times,* 13 December.

Wragg, E.C. (1994), 'Foreword', in Radnor, H.A., *Across the Curriculum.* London: Cassell, vii.

2.6 The role of inspection in initial teacher training

David Taylor

The history of Her Majesty's Inspectors (HMIs) of Schools goes back over 150 years. After a long period of comparative stability, during which time the HMIs' responsibilities spanned schools and further and higher education, there was the creation, through an Act of Parliament in 1992, of the Office for Standards in Education (OFSTED), in which HMIs were to operate as the specialist arm. Simultaneous changes led to the establishment of new funding councils for further and for higher education. These hived off a significant portion of HMIs' work, which consequently centred on the managing and regulating of a new system designed to ensure the regular inspection of schools.

In addition, the legislation gave the Secretary of State for Education the power to assign additional inspection functions to Her Majesty's Chief Inspector (HMCI), the head of OFSTED. One of these was in the field of initial teacher training (ITT) and these functions were endorsed through subsequent legislation (1994). This also added a significant new feature to the teacher education landscape through the establishment of the Teacher Training Agency (TTA), a body set up to manage the funding and allocation of places for ITT, with other responsibilities including continuing professional development (CPD), otherwise known as in-service education and training (INSET). The TTA is required to take account of, amongst other things, the evaluations provided by OFSTED through its programme of HMI-led inspections. An important distinction between OFSTED's inspections of schools and those of ITT is that, whereas school inspections are conducted by inspectors who are not OFSTED employees but who work under contract to OFSTED, inspection of ITT is carried out largely by HMIs working full-time for OFSTED, mostly in the Teacher Education and Training (TET) Team, although additional inspectors (including some from higher education and schools) are also employed on these inspections.

There is, then, a close link between the work of the quality assessments from inspection and the responsibilities of the TTA for accrediting ITT providers and funding training places. This has been formalized by the joint production by OFSTED and the TTA of the 'Framework for the Assessment of Quality in Initial Teacher Training' (November 1996 and September 1997, revised edition). The purpose of this Framework is to ensure that the criteria used for assessment are fully understood by inspectors, the TTA and those who provide the training. It is also designed to support the 'audit' by the TTA, or others, of significant features of provision, while at the same time offering a series of prompts which can be used by the providers of training to carry out self-assessment.

Questions of consistency, reliability, intelligibility and openness to scrutiny have no less weight in ITT than in school inspection and, hence, there is a need to share inspection methods and criteria with the providers who are being inspected. Not surprisingly, such processes are not entirely free from misgivings or suspicions – not least in view of the significance of inspection findings for trainers' funding and allocations, and even their accreditation as providers: an unsatisfactory inspection now triggers the TTA's withdrawal of accreditation procedures, a fact which irresistibly recalls Samuel Johnston's excessively quoted dictum on the effects of the prospects of hanging. Inspection of ITT is a serious business and one which cannot be tempted to veer towards cosiness or complaisance.

Hence the importance of ensuring the quality of inspectors' work, which embraces a variety of forms of inspection in both ITT and INSET, and the defensibility of their judgements. Concerns may remain that such judgements may be seen by some to hold a quasi-sacrosanct status, not susceptible to challenge or amendment. In a sense, of course, judgements are neither more nor less than the best professional assessments of which the inspectors are capable. No-one pretends to perfection – all we can do is use training, moderation, standardization procedures and all other available techniques to minimize any risk of subjective eccentricities, and submit all inspection processes to internal and external scrutiny. What in the end may prove difficult is where a significant difference occurs between a self-assessment and that made by an external agent, such as an inspector. Each side may have access to the same evidence-base and the same criteria and yet there may remain disagreement about the appropriate judgement expressed in the admittedly imperfect form of a single grade. One crucial point about OFSTED practice is that it uses the evidence and experience inspectors have acquired across the whole country in order to place one course, or aspect of a course, in relation to others. That national perspective does not guarantee infallibility, but it does mean that the determination of quality is carried out in the context of the inspectors' collective knowledge of the whole system. Moreover, with the comparatively small number of inspectors involved, vital issues of 'inter-rater reliability' are more easily addressed, though never able to be taken for granted. Systematic processes, including joint working, training in the application of criteria and moderation of different inspectors' judgements have been put in place in order to seek to establish the greatest possible confidence in this respect.

OFSTED has a frequently-stated commitment to 'improvement through inspection', a slogan which has been much discussed and has attracted some sceptics' attention, particularly in the case of school inspection. While the inspection of ITT by OFSTED is manifestly not the same as the inspection of schools, it is certainly not wholly distinct, since the inspection of ITT is itself geared fundamentally to improving standards in schools. Apart from the need for OFSTED to be internally and transparently consistent in its criteria and judgements across schools and ITT, there is a clear sense in which a very good lesson in a school is essentially the same as one taught by a teacher undergoing training on final assessed practice. If it is good, it is good for the same reasons – and we need to be very clear, and share that clarity very publicly, about what it is that we judge makes it so. Putting this at its simplest, a very good lesson is one in which most or *all* pupils manifestly learn what they are meant to learn, where that learning is of something worth learning, and where they learn in a manner characterised by coherence, durability and purposeful engagement with the subject-matter. There are also implications for training partnerships, which mean that in inspecting ITT the need to focus on schools' training roles and how these relate to the roles of higher education is paramount. When we inspect ITT, we do not, of course, subject each schools to a 'mini-OFSTED'. However, not least because there continues to be considerable professional debate about how and what schools should best contribute to ITT, OFSTED needs the best possible evidence on the quality of their involvement.

An additional point is that we have a very keen interest in the articulation of the strands of teacher education – the 'three Is' of initial training, induction and INSET – and to discuss how progression *to* qualified teacher status (QTS) and, then, progress *from* it are to be maintained. Here the work of the TTA in establishing the standards for newly qualified teachers (NQTs), set out in Circular 10/97, and in looking at key points in a teacher's professional career is of particular importance and will merit close scrutiny. Inspection of INSET will continue to focus both on the effectiveness and value for money of provision, from whatever source, and on the way in which teachers' further professional development needs are addressed.

Our contention is that we shall best be able to ensure that inspection, and specifically that of teacher education, is likely to be seen as leading to improvement both in schools and higher education institutes (HEIs), if we do the following:

- set out very clearly the high standards and expectations which are the basis of our judgements. If we judge an aspect of provision very good – Grade 1 – it must be really clear what it is that makes us think it so. Developing and sharing criteria for excellence present important and continuing challenges;

- focus sharply on how well students are developing into fully effective teachers from whom pupils are learning consistently and well. At the same time, we should consider carefully the 'value added', in terms of what students are adding to pupils and classes as well as at what providers are adding to students, and in terms of how involvement in ITT can itself have an impact on the quality of schools;

- contribute fully to debate about the content and methods of teacher training, including questions on the structures of educational discourse and on how to make these permeate effectively the practical work of teachers. We surely need to understand how practice is underpinned by a clear sense of *why* we teach and learn what we do (it is tempting at times to wonder if the National Curriculum has eviscerated us of the guts of educational thought), and of *how* we counter pupils' social or individual learning blocks, so that teachers show both a personal commitment to ensuring progress for their pupils and the practical and technical expertise to do so;

- finally, acknowledge that our inspection of teacher education will make its fullest possible contribution to improvement only if there is a real sense of dialogue and co-operation with our colleagues and fellow-professionals in higher education institutes (HEIs) and in schools. This should be designed to ensure that the providers feel the greatest possible confidence in and respect for the processes of inspection. That co-operation is not easy and it certainly does not depend on cosy collusion or pulled punches. Inspectors need to gain respect through the clarity of their vision, the firmness of their judgement, the conviction of their censure and the cogency of their commendation, as well as by the professionalism of the relationships established.

These, then, are some principles for seeking to make sure that inspection is as effective as possible. There remain for consideration the key issues which are arising from that inspection. These are disseminated in a variety of ways, through papers, talks, discussions and reports, both those on individual providers and those which survey the national scene more broadly. These key issues include:

- the development of training partnerships

- the introduction of new routes to QTS, especially school-based training routes

- the tendency for too many students on their training to stop short of achieving very high standards of teaching skills

- beginning teachers' subject knowledge

- the role of assessment in ITT.

These are considered in turn. A central issue, touched on above and which is the subject of other chapters in this volume, is that of training partnerships. It is clear from inspection and other evidence that schools and HEIs are seeking to respond positively to the initiatives which have led to the setting up of such partnerships. These are now becoming increasingly well-established, although securing the involvement, in sufficient numbers, of schools and subject departments willing and able to share in the task of training teachers continues to present challenges, especially – and ominously – in the secondary shortage subjects of maths, science, technology, religious education (RE) and modern foreign languages. While there are signs of good progress being made in developing primary partnerships, it is too soon to make definitive judgements on their effectiveness (the relevant Circular became mandatory only in September 1996). A key element in their success will be the extent to which schools see themselves as having an 'action research' function, to which training can contribute, and see teaching as a 'research-based' profession.

Another key issue is that of the development of school-centred ITT schemes (SCITT), which has been strongly encouraged in recent government policy, as part of the exploration of new routes into the teaching profession. The most recent Annual Report of Her Majesty's Chief Inspector (4 February 1997) commented that SCITT had continued to expand, albeit slowly, and that there were now some 20 consortia offering primary or secondary training. It added that many courses were still becoming established, so that inspection judgements often referred to an early stage of the development. There are problems to be faced, many of them common to all ITT providers, but also some encouraging signs that these new routes can both attract new teachers and offer worthwhile training experiences.

A principal focus of inspection is the quality of the teaching of students who are coming to the end of their ITT courses. Inspectors have sometimes expressed concern that students are not always reaching the highest standards of which they are capable. The most recent inspection evidence confirms that a comparatively low proportion are able to demonstrate very high professional competence by the end of their course. Some students, indeed, appear to peak, in terms of classroom performance, well before their training is completed, thereafter marking time rather than improving the quality of their performance. It is apparent, therefore, that although there are undoubted successes within the system (individual students, courses and institutions), the system as a whole is not producing sufficient numbers of NQTs of the highest quality. It is important to investigate causes for such 'underachievement', whether within the structures of courses, which inevitably – especially in the one-year Postgraduate Certificate in Education (PGCE) – have limitations on what can be covered in depth, or whether related to the quality of the intake of students or to the effectiveness of training processes. There are complex issues here, some related to the quality and scope of students' first degree courses, and they are worthy of close professional scrutiny.

Issues connected with teachers' subject knowledge are, of course, closely connected with those of standards, whether of teaching or learning. In the field of primary ITT, inspection has recently shone a spotlight on the preparation to teach maths and English and, more specifically, to teach number and reading. In the case of reading, the evidence from the recent primary inspections points to some specific – and absolutely fundamental – weaknesses in some students' competence. Either they lack sufficient confidence and skill to plan, implement and evaluate a programme to teach beginning reading, or they are insufficiently attuned to the ways to develop the advanced reading skills of those who are fluent decoders and who, therefore, need a challenging range of reading materials and approaches to them.

There is currently some dispute as to exactly how many NQTs have reservations about their confidence and competence in teaching reading, but no dispute that it is an issue for some. However, self-perceptions are not enough. We all know of students who think they are teaching perfectly well when no actual learning is taking place and, conversely, it is quite possible that some highly competent students undersell themselves. We are asking how to make as sure as ever we can that the training in teaching pupils to read, both initial and in-service, is as rigorous and precise as it can be. The work of the National Literacy and Numeracy Centres will be of particular significance in this area. We need, therefore, to look closely at the particular methods employed, at students' own knowledge, at the books from which pupils are taught, and the attitudes and practices of students and teachers in schools. This close look must of course be seen clearly as one which is not ideologically committed to the universal applicability of a single theory or method. There are, however, some basic analytical tools of the trade, some key research findings on the tools learners need to handle an alphabetic system with the particular phonic characteristics of English, and some 'tried and tested' approaches to the overcoming of reading blocks. Moreover, a rich reading environment, the close involvement of a skilled parent, other adult or older child and the integration of talking, listening, reading and writing are surely needed in order to underpin the specific methodology of acquiring phonetically-related skills.

Other concerns over subject knowledge occur in both the primary and secondary field, and are highlighted with particular prominence in subjects where there are shortages in the number of students presenting themselves for training and where many students who *do* present themselves have studied for degree courses in subjects which have at best tenuous links with the National Curriculum requirements which they will be expected to satisfy. There are also the long-familiar difficulties associated with the training of primary teachers competent to teach across nine National Curriculum subjects and RE, to the end of Key Stage 2 (pupils aged 10–11).

Issues of *assessment* (providers' assessment of beginning teachers and their assessment of pupils) lurk never far below the surface. Practices in assessing, recording and reporting on pupils have been under the scrutiny of inspectors and, rightly, form an integral part of the Framework for assessing the standards reached by student teachers. There is much to commend. Indeed, it is by no means unknown to encounter trainee teachers who use assessment in a systematic and rigorous way to plan their teaching, which may shame some more established teachers and from which many may themselves be able to improve their practice. However, we are also interested in the assessments which providers make on the students: how consistent and clear-cut are the judgements made by the providers and, within them, the very large number of tutors, mentors and examiners? Do only those who deserve to do so receive QTS? Are the marking and assessment of students' work constantly characterized by rigour, concern for high standards and the clarity and helpfulness of the comments? How reliable are the judgements of external examiners and do these always have the skills, knowledge and experience required? Teasing out these matters is essentially the business of the 'quality assurance' processes which, increasingly, providers have firmly in place. Yet they may lack the capacity to calibrate their own practice against a clearly-defined national 'currency' and even the – much to be welcomed – introduction of national standards will not in itself guarantee comparability or consistency at the level of individual assessments.

Such issues deserve continual probing if the end-product is to be a high-quality ITT system which, although marked by diversity and flexibility, still does enough to ensure consistent standards and common experience and content within the training providers. The development of a National Curriculum for ITT is one measure designed to help give this assurance, and inspection can play an important part in this probing of practice.

To a very large extent, it now appears that there are common aims shared by those with a stake in education, whether teachers, industrialists, politicians or parents. This has underlined, on the one hand, a widespread resentment of all teaching which is driven by ideological fads and fashions and, on the other, a support for teaching which gets results – teaching that motivates, inspires and challenges pupils, certainly, but also teaching that unlocks whatever impedes their progress and equips them with a secure grounding in the essentials of language, maths and other foundations of successful education.

Until we have achieved a training system which prepares our teachers to impart the necessary knowledge and skills with rigour and success, and to do so to all our pupils, the spotlight on teacher education will remain, irrespective of the colour of the political party in power, not least because the ideal of highly-educated citizens is also the pragmatic and economic necessity of a highly-skilled workforce.

2.7 Designing teachers' futures – the quest for a new professional climate

Michael Totterdell and David Lambert

Introduction

The pace of change in education has been so fast and furious that it is little wonder that some in the profession have found it difficult to keep up. Moreover, many have found the changes threatening and consider their overall thrust to be regressive in terms of the aspirations of a democratic society. Some go further and link the educational change to 'a broader political strategy aimed at reversing the democratic advances achieved through the intellectual and political struggles of the nineteenth and twentieth centuries' (Carr and Hartnett, 1996:16). Nevertheless, it is important to set this educational change and the dilemmas it has created in a context of international developments and the current globalization of the economic order. We cannot escape the demands of a modern economy and other broad structural constraints. However, we might consider whether a better response would be to seek a 'globalization from below' as the way forward. This would set its sights on a more realistic and, thus, comprehensively liberating and empowering agenda than a yearning to return to the *status quo ante*.

Nowhere has the impact of educational change been more keenly felt than in the field of initial teacher education (ITE) and training. Ironically, as Hargreaves (1994) observes, the general reaction by teacher educators has not been consistent – an adversarial rhetoric from them at one level has been accompanied by effective reorientation of courses at another, leading to some highly innovative and auspicious practice developing on the ground. This is evidenced by a flurry of publications (Reid, Constable and Griffiths, 1994; Blake et al., 1995; Griffiths and Owen, 1995; Hustler and McIntyre, 1996) and confirmed by the findings of the Office for Standards in Education (OFSTED) and the Modes of Teacher Education (MOTE) Project (OFSTED, 1995; Whiting et al., 1996). Accompanying such developments, has been the emergence of a breed of tutors and co-operating teachers, who are 'in two minds'. On the one hand, they resent intervention from the centre and what they perceive as the 'imposed' structures of the market. On the other hand, they celebrate having risen to the challenge of restructuring pre-service courses around the axes of school-basedness and competences in such a way as to reinvigorate ITE. The upshot is that the educational community feels both buoyant and deflated at the same time, There is also a pervading sense that in 'surviving', its members may have sold their birthright for a mess of 'managerial' pottage (Phillips, 1994:54).

The purpose of this chapter is to make a modest contribution toward recovering a sense of 'single-mindedness' amongst teacher educators. We suggest there is a need to reconcile the general and the particular by achieving a much more fundamental reconceptualization of ITE and training by tutors, teachers and beginning teachers than anything previously envisaged. We offer our analysis, believing that the circumstances that have engendered doubt in the *psyche* of teacher educators can be the precursor to 'the restless probing of curious minds' for a better way of responding openly and effectively to change. Our motive is nicely captured in some famous lines of Tennyson's *In Memoriam:*

> He fought his doubts and gather'd strength,
> He would not make his judgement blind,
> He faced the spectres of the mind
> And laid them: thus he came at length
> To find a stronger faith his own.

Tracking the maze or charting a course?
The need for high calibre entrants to teaching is paramount. Possessing the right mix of qualifications, experience and personal qualities is

considered the *sine qua non* for gaining admission to the corpus of tomorrow's teachers (Millett, 1996b). However if one presses the question, 'Who should teach?', it quickly becomes apparent that there is no unanimity and little consensus on precisely what sort of task teaching is. Is it a science or an art? Is it a craft or a profession? Does it require education or only training? Is it competence based or fundamentally a moral gesture requiring appropriate values and dispositions? Does it essentially involve only transmission or more significantly interaction and transformation? Is it theory dependent or independent? And so the litany of questions could go on.

On turning to the related matter of 'How we make or create tomorrow's teachers', we find a similar range of dissonant voices and differing views. For some, the making of a good teacher is quintessentially a matter of emulating the 'pied pipers' of teaching. It involves coaching novices in tried and tested methods of teaching and understudying a master teacher – assuming their persona, adopting their charismatic style and, eventually, taking on their mantle. For others, guaranteeing that the system does not propagate any 'bad teachers' seems to be the overriding priority. The quest is for a guaranteed formula of technically proficient practical training that will assure a basic threshold of 'quality' and 'standards' in those charged with preparing pupils for 'the world of work'. For yet others, becoming a teacher involves a broader conceptualization of professional practice which emphasizes principled understanding and deliberation. Professionals must be able to utilize a variety of frames of reference and adhere to the principle of political independence of mind and action in pursuit of the wise conduct of education for a more just and equitable society (Carr, 1995; Bottery, 1996).

Much of the recent literature surveying the field (Bolton, 1994; Reid, 1994; Pimm and Selinger, 1995; Blake, 1995) rehearses these questions by doggedly tracking through a maze of conflicting perspectives, agendas and Government initiatives in order to plot the contours and patterns of this labyrinth from some all-embracing point of view. In effect, we are offered what is claimed to be an 'overview', which is, of course, the ubiquitous 'view from nowhere'. Although this approach rightly raises issues, often by way of critique, it invariably fails to address these issues or engage with them in a serious or fundamental way. Moreover, it has the misleading effect of implying that teacher educators can somehow transcend the grubby Hobbesian world of education so portrayed, either by subtly forming a culture of resistance or by recasting themselves in the role of an *avant garde* – transformatively enlightened outside agents of change.

By way of an alternative approach, we will chart a course for improving the professional preparation and formation of teachers from within rather than outside of the ambit of things. The realities of intervention from the centre, educational reform, pressures for greater accountability, school-based practical teaching experience, models of partnership and competence-based assessment will be taken as operative givens with which to interact because they represent a global set of transformations (Wideen and Grimmitt, 1995; Townshend, 1996). Our standpoint is grounded in the supposition that any comprehensive reflective practice must embrace wider 'ecological' dimensions of professional endeavour – institutional, socio-political, economic, environmental and ethical – and must move beyond a single conceptual paradigm to the consideration of others. Our argument is that any adequate reconceptualization of ITE and training will need to be advanced on several fronts and carried on at different levels – policy, theory and practice (Humes, 1996). We believe it should have as its overriding consideration the need to improve practice itself and to give central prominence to the quality of learning experienced by students – both student teachers and pupils in school. We identify and address three broad domains of activity in which teacher educators could better manoeuvre in order to make more coherent and convincing their distinctive contributions to achieving a high-quality teaching force.

The positioning of initial teacher education – policy perspectives beyond 'playing politics'

We have already alluded to our belief that teacher education is, perhaps belatedly in the 1990s, beginning to benefit from rigorous challenge and re-examination. Yet in one respect, teacher educators remain in a quandary. How should they position ITE in relation to the political currents of our times? At a time when policy and politics are becoming increasingly conflated, the challenge is to avoid polarising national agencies and educationists into communities of educational correction and resistance respectively. The imperative is to forge greater consensus around pressing questions such as 'Who should teach?' and 'What are the best ways of preparing them?' Even more challenging questions centre on the kind of professional preparation which can enable beginning teachers to continue learning and adapt to change with a sense of vocation and with broader sensibilities.

Teacher educators have been said to be prone to producing critiques 'which combine *parti pris* with philosophical naivety to an extent which any non-ideologue would find astonishing' (Taylor, 1996:1). Thus, to sharpen the focus, how can educationists avoid appearing to be defensive and reactionary, reluctant to acknowledge any merit in externally driven reforms? Indeed, there may be an opportunity to carve out a central channel to guide policy, working 'with the culture' and its existing tariff of values and judgements even whilst promoting change for the better. However, can educationists exhibit greater positivity (see Ormell, 1995)?

It is obviously incumbent on educationists to engage with complex questions about the role of education in a modern democratic society and to consider what forms it should take. But is it legitimate to do so while refusing to rethink sets of beliefs about equity and equal opportunities or about the inherent worth and fitness for purpose of curriculum models? (Noddings, 1996). Perhaps there is still one more lesson to be learned from Dewey (1927): because public debate is risky and unpredictable, it is therefore educational. It is only by subjecting our preferences and projects to the test of debate that we come to understand what we know and what we still need to learn. In this sense, argument is the essence of education and democracy is the most educational form of government. We must challenge the media's status as arbiters of public discussion and engineer a better informed public debate about teacher education. For, as Taylor rightly reminds us, 'that there is a connection between the standard of public debate and the efficacy of policy is a central concept to democracy' (1996:3).

Some help is available from recent historical and sociological analysis by Wilkins (1996), centring on the role of ideology in teacher education. Unfortunately, Wilkins too narrowly defines ideology as the principles which govern the policies and practices of political parties *per se*. She misses the sense that is common to most definitions, namely that of a belief system that mobilizes people to action in the body politic, and the rehabilitation of a more positive view of ideology along the lines suggested by Geertz (1973), reopens the possibility of subjecting moral and political issues to more serious discussion. It provides a way of refuting those (positivists *or* post-modernists) who deny the possibility of intelligently defending any moral or political position on education. To the extent that ideologies express universal aspirations and have the capacity to speak to enduring human needs and desires, their critics have to argue on the same grounds and not just dismiss them as self-serving rationalizations.

Wilkins rightly recognizes that ideologies are necessary and even useful, as putatively providing a better 'map' of reality, a more reliable guide to action. However, her identification of government with 'ideology', the teacher training community with 'culture' and the training curriculum as interactively mediating the 'dialogue' between the two over theory and practice is contrived. Her argument that the curriculum is a fulcrum for change which is 'cyclical, reciprocal and mutually beneficial' is too selective in its historical purview and ultimately fails to be convincing. A more apt depiction is provided by the social critic Yankelovich (1981), when he says that social (educational) trends do not move in straight lines of decline or ascent, nor do they occur in cycles. He suggests instead a 'lurch-and-learn' model. Ideologies, cultures and communities change by gross, ungainly reactions to new circumstances ('lurching'). When some prophetic voice or community of conviction points out their overcorrecting ('learning'), a fresh lurching begins in a new direction.

The role of teacher educators in the public sphere should not, therefore, be construed primarily as dialogical (*pace* Wilkins), but as prophetic and pedagogical – as befits the moral character of teaching as a profession. It involves both a critical perspective on the conduct of educational affairs, and a prospective shaping of perceptions about what kind of educational life there should be. Critique and design belong together: criticism should be a precursor to developing understandings that may help us shape or fashion the kinds of futures we think we want to have (Kress, 1997).

Given the foregoing terms of engagement, the key components of an effective response at the political level to the present situation have recently been outlined by Humes:

- challenging the prevailing character of teacher education reform by exposing inconsistencies and incoherence in official policies at the conceptual level;

- providing a reasoned justification for having a high-quality corpus of professional teachers – thoughtful, humane and discerning as well as technically proficient, who have a durable sense of identity and community;

- articulating the importance of the higher education link in that it helps teachers keep open channels between their day-to-day activities and the realm of ideas and innovation; this performs a vital function in shaping future practice and the capacity to be adaptable to change;

- developing a stronger sense of audience so as to convey arguments effectively and communicate persuasively with those other than fellow-professionals – educationists need to cultivate a sense of themselves as 'public intellectuals', capable of communicating outside of their academic enclaves.

Underlying any such responses, there will need to be a radical questioning of the extent to which it is legitimate for those who 'teach the teachers' to assume 'that any educational standpoint must take its purposes and orientation from some substantive conception, or ideology' (Hogan, 1995:11) – be it social democratic liberalism, radical 'counter-culture' politics, classical humanism, market philosophy, or whatever (see Carr and Hartnett, 1996). Only by refusing the custodial heritage can educators legitimately elaborate and defend an educational orientation, accompanied by the rediscovery of an 'effective integrity of purpose' (Hogan, 1995:11) based on a conception of the sovereignty of learning. Such a reorientation of teacher educators could provide the generative foundation for 'change capacity' and 'personal vision building, inquiry, mastery and collaboration' (Fullan, 1993:3)

Re-modelling initial teacher education – broader theoretical perspectives

Several models of ITE have held currency in the last 50 years and each has spawned its own definition of what is involved in the task of preparing teachers for work in schools and to what end (Humes, 1996:4). A brief review of some key features and weaknesses will provide a useful backdrop against which to make a proposal for a rubric that gives due emphasis to the professional preparation of teachers.

As long ago as 1972, the James Committee warned that teacher education was in danger of becoming too academic and of losing its link with professionalism and the improvement of practice in schools (Porter, 1996). Ever since, debate has continued to centre on a fundamental disagreement about the priority respectively of operational and academic competence (Barnett, 1994), of instrumental action as against cognitive interaction. As Humes avers, one of the lessons of our own recent history is that 'there are grounds for thinking that teacher educators have been insufficiently self-critical with regard to their own role in changing conceptualizations of the work they do' (Humes, 1996:5, citing Russel and Korthagen, 1995).

The disciplines model, associated with the 'forms of knowledge' philosophy of education pioneered by Hirst and Peters (1970), insisted that teaching must transcend the apprenticeship mode and sought to place 'education studies' on the solid foundation of academic theory. Its complementary components were 'subject methods' and 'school practice'. The synthesis of these elements was to be achieved by trainee teachers who were given opportunities to integrate theory and practice through coursework. The model dominated teacher education from the late-1960s to the early-1980s, although it became increasingly vulnerable to critique from the sociology of knowledge (Young, 1971), which pointed to the arbitrary claims of any concept of 'foundationalism'. Its overreliance on analytical philosophy provided little by way of assistance to beginning teachers coming to terms with the practical problems of the classroom. Its proteges emerged sensitized to the new shibboleth of 'race-gender-class' and articulate in relation to the difficulties inherent in 'schooling', but with limited experience and competence in the practicalities of teaching. In retrospect, it is clear that the model was unduly idealist and rationalistic. It was captivated by an analytic attitude and critical sensibility which served the interests of academics rather than the needs of trainee teachers and had the effect of separating learning from everyday experience.

It was partly in reaction to this model that the 'reflective practitioner' model arose. As instigated by writers such as Schon (1983) and von Manen (1977), the model envisaged a process of pedagogical problem solving, whereby teachers apply different approaches to see whether a particular one 'fits' the problem at hand. They should use past experience to 're-frame' an unusual situation and then decide whether methods used previously are effective in application to the new context. There are a number of refinements to the approach which themselves incorporate implicit criticisms. Thus, Griffiths and Tann (1992) not only suggest that there are different levels of reflection, but also stress that it does not happen in a vacuum: it needs some form of technical base in which to ground itself. Others, such as Zeichner and Liston (1987) suggest that there are levels of reflection which must move beyond techniques of practice to incorporate an institutional or societal dimension of practice.

Nevertheless, there remains a difficulty in specifying 'reflection' in relation to practice. Can reflective practice really function as a sort of 'root paradigm' or 'habitas' for initial training? Does not the 'traffic' it exhorts between action on the one hand and analysis and interpretation, betoken a rather one-sided emphasis of cognition over action and being? Is this not to perpetuate a disparaging view of practical activity as an intrinsically inferior sort of thing? Humes thinks that the notion of reflective practice can once again 'be used to justify an approach which serves the interests of teacher educators rather than the professional needs of trainee teachers' (1996:7). As he sees it, reflective practice leads to 'over-conceptualization and over-subtle deconstruction of unremarkable events'(1996:7). It runs the risk of 'false interpretation based upon inappropriate conceptual categories' (see Sockett, 1987). Moreover, it is potentially self-indulgent because 'it focuses on the teacher's experience rather than the learner's. Actions and events are interpreted in terms of the meaning they have for the teacher rather than in terms of the value they have for the learner' (Humes, 1996:8). It is increasingly clear that reflective practice cannot provide an epistemology of 'everyday professional practice' nor act as a theoretical underpinning for ITE (Eraut, 1995).

Both the 'disciplines model' and the 'reflective practitioner model' have their genesis in the academy. Both manifested a proclivity to become 'essentially inward-looking and self-regarding' (Humes, 1996:8). They have made the teacher educator community vulnerable to outsiders who think instrumentally in terms of accountability, outcomes and measurable results. Reacting against the overacademic and overreflective approaches to the professional preparation of teachers, Government sponsored agencies have sought to introduce a school-based model, with competences providing the framework for the curriculum of training, and profiling of competences the vehicle for demonstrating these have been achieved. The model is policed by OFSTED for compliance and inspected for 'standards'. The results form the basis of published 'performance tables', which will purportedly provide a 'quality indicator' of providers.

There can be no gainsaying the fact that this new model 'has had a galvanising effect on the quality of training' (Millett, 1996b:7). There are good academic and professional grounds for strengthening the role of schools in teacher education – formally acknowledging classrooms as the dominant context for trainee teachers' learning and recognizing the important contribution practising teachers make to the fostering of professional skill, 'craft' knowledge and understanding. Nevertheless, the model is iconoclastic and unbalanced, and therefore of limited professional relevance. In emphasizing 'vocational competence' as reducible to a set of practical manoeuvres, it de-professionalizes teachers. It renders teaching an atheoretical occupation conducive to being 'managed' and 'calibrated' systematically, with a premium on producing effective classroom operatives and efficient functionaries. It underestimates the requirement for knowledge and understanding of complex and subtle kinds, if learning (of pupils, but also of teachers) is to be effective. It also overlooks the fact that teaching is pre-eminently a moral gesture. Teaching implies a commitment to certain values – justice, truth and respect for civic life – and the outworking of certain dispositions to rationality, to the interests of those taught and to 'humility in the face of the venturesome infinity of knowledge' (Hogan, 1995:254). Under the auspices of the current model, measuring teaching's outward show eclipses the deeper and weightier overtures of qualitative experience. Yet, ironically, it is precisely in getting the 'epiphanies of learning underway and sustaining them in practice' (Hogan, 1995) that then we equip teachers 'to communicate to their pupils with passion, conviction, understanding, discrimination and scholarship' (Taylor, 1996:5). Therefore, we have to find an approach to ITE that moves participants beyond an interpretation of competence that resembles little more than learning to cope effectively – a characteristic which may go some way in explaining Taylor's observation (in this volume) that beginning teachers often 'peak' early in their preparation.

If there is to be any prospect of a 'new model' pre-service training being developed which is more adequate to the task, then it will have to be something more than a recovery of the university college-based ethos or a reconstituted version of what now obtains. It is not just that 'what is needed is an honest acknowledgement by teacher educators of the limitations of previous conceptualizations of their work' (Humes, 1996:14). It is also the fact that the 'public face of teaching' requires of us a moral purpose and 'change agentry' (as Fullan calls it) which can discern larger causes, consequences and relationships: we need to undertake a thorough reappraisal of the roles of education, training and experience in the making of teachers (Millett, 1996b).

At the heart of challenge facing us is the acquisition of a more perspicacious understanding of the business we are in. Academic and vocational notions of competence, both of which involve reductions of human endeavour, should be subsumed under a broader professional conception of competence. This would include a sense of 'calling' as opposed to 'career', implying a belief in the intrinsic value of a given line of work and its link to the public good combined with the skills and virtues required to undertake it effectively. As such, 'competence' would have rich moral overtones.

Equally consequential would be a move away from what Kemmis (1995:13) describes as the 'one-sided, rather rationalistic view of theorising, emphasising the power of ideas to guide even direct action'. There is a growing recognition that theory should be conceived not primarily as underpinning, informing or fashioning practice, but rather more as 'supporting, enriching, and stimulating people' (Furlong and Smith, 1996:7) The precedence of practice over theory would emerge less ambiguously and generate a form of 'rationality-in-action' which always owed something to the background perspectives and orientations of its participants who are in some senses indebted to, or encumbered by, substantive pre-judgements of a moral-practical character. Thus, practical judgements can become 'candidates in practice' for universal worthiness and will certainly have the potential to challenge the contemporary creed of 'performativity' (Hogan, 1995).

Towards a re-working of practice in initial teacher education

Recent years have witnessed the emergence of a number of examples of pre-service programmes which seek to transcend the dichotomies of theory and practice, reflection and competence, rationaiist and technicist impulses (Rotheiser 1966; Lambert and Totterdell, 1995; Hundey, 1996). These programmes have responded to external pressures by developing an ethos from within, embodying 'a sense of mission based on identifiable values and principles' (Sultana, 1995). They share a common core of attributes:

- commitment to the 'principled understanding and deliberation required for the wise conduct of education' (Carr, 1995)

- an understanding of 'who should teach' which involves a set of core personal and professional qualities which should be manifest 'in the practice of teaching' in the classroom and the school

- a notion of professional development as progressive and continuing with an implicitly ethical and moral attitudinal stance as well as a cumulative portfolio of experience; a collaborative spirit of inquiry and a reciprocal notion of partnership with co-operating teachers

- a learning-focused concern which drives pedagogical and curriculum design.

All that apart, though, there remains much work to be done if what Wideen and Grimmett (1995) call the 'wedge of progressive practice' is to be extruded, grounded in the culture of teacher education and made congruous with the aspirations of a wider range of parties who have a stakehold in teachers' futures. Four spheres of practice require re-engineering, starting again from first principles:

1   the communicative act or discourse of teaching
2   the pedagogy
3   the curriculum
4   the institutional context.

1   *Discourse*

The anatomy of teacher education has traditionally reflected the 'culture of critical discourse' which typifies higher education and the 'new knowledge class' (Gouldner, 1979). Increasingly, under the impulse towards greater accountability, this has been supplanted by the more operational, functional and utilitarian discourse of the market culture. It is, of course, easy for users of either to parody the other within their own terms of reference. Crucially however, it is the concrete linguistic style within which education is now being commodified that is the more intelligible to the non-specialist, the media and politicians. For educationists merely to critique this situation by reviewing the discourse, so as to highlight inherent limitations, is to proffer an inadequate response. It simply invites a rejoinder of *tu qoque*! Rather the limited semantic reach of both critical and technicist discourse should be acknowledged, leading to the privileging instead of ordinary language as being 'the only secure semantic base we possess' (Ormell, 1995b:31). As the Philosophical and Educational Renewal (PER) Group has opined, by allowing ordinary language to be the final touchstone for any kind of genuine analysis, 'we may hope to find an interpretation which is maximally motivating for us as teachers and for our pupils and students, whilst being minimally vulnerable to partisan attack' (PER, 1995:8). This is the best way, we might add, to generate mutual respect within a partnership of learners.

2 *Pedagogy*

This has been identified variously as 'the neglected strand of education' (Simon, 1994) and 'the last corner of the secret garden' (Millett, 1996a). Yet it is in relation to pedagogy that teacher educators may yet have the most worthwhile contribution to make to professional knowledge and practice. For it is here that the profession most needs to openly assert and exhibit its expertise. Taking stock of what we know – about the principles of human learning, about the tried and tested methods of effective teaching, about the role of assessment in relation to improving learning and raising achievement, about the place of technology in enhancing the learning environment of schools and classrooms, about the structure and dynamics of subject distinctive aspects of the disciplines, and about the power of the institutional context and organization to affect teaching and learning – is surely long overdue. We need to fashion a pedagogical framework and translate this into a pedagogical vision that helps teachers understand anew their professional world and hence produce a considerable body of professional knowledge for the public good. What better place to begin to effect this than with the pedagogical problems of lessons construed by beginning teachers, working together with experienced teachers and tutors to solve them. (See Stones, 1994.)

Moreover, it is here that education needs to resist becoming parasitic on other disciplines, or on the conceptual foundations and underlying values of the mainstream impulses of culture. Pedagogy should neither be a slave to the social sciences and critical methodologies of the university, nor by-pass higher education and, thereby, forfeit a forum that will demand a cogency and profundity it sorely lacks at present. Educational reflection on pedagogy needs to take place in an open forum, yet within an established framework of rationality: the public arena provides an important set of social and intellectual checks and balances, and centres of higher learning provide a set of distinctive normative guidelines or 'approved norms' for sustained critical inquiry. Neither the 'epochal horizon' of socio-economic context nor the 'canonical horizon' of a tradition of learning should take precedence over the other. Each can, nonetheless, be regulative of the other. Educationists, in the 'conversation' with the rest of the profession, should participate not with the intention of gaining approval from the academic community, but for the sake of gaining clarity and precision in order to produce depth (not ease) of understanding. Failure to do so, will inevitably mean that here, as elsewhere, the slogan takes the place of the substance. It serves not as a distillation of a complex discussion but as a substitute for it.

3   Curriculum

Re-shaping the curriculum of teacher education is clearly a priority in the minds of many, although not by any means for the same reasons. There is a growing consensus that the key questions revolve around:

- identifying aptitude to teach, defined primarily as characteristics of the person/situation interaction, not as characteristics of the person alone (see Snow 1992);

- identifying what trainees need to know in order to become good teachers;

- identifying the pedagogical procedures and skills trainees need to possess so as to become competent teachers;

- identifying the core educational values and attitudinal dispositions beginning teachers need to demonstrate (implicitly or explicitly) in their dealings with pupils, colleagues and the wider community;

- identifying the processes (learning opportunities and experiences) that will best promote, cultivate or develop the required knowledge, skills and dispositions in sustainable ways;

- forging a consensus on the ends to which the knowledge, skills and dispositions should be directed and the kind of ethos (monist or pluralist) the mediating structures of the educational system should exhibit.

However, in recent years, the attempt to find cogent and convincing answers for these questions has been pre-empted by preoccupation with demands of assessment and accountability. Curriculum design moves from *pre-hoc* planning activities to *post-hoc* evaluation, with the emphasis on justifying and explaining teaching and other activities in relation to quality assurance mechanisms or anticipated performance indicators. The issues are framed and prescriptively pre-specified by external agents, and curriculum philosophy responds to perceived 'tweaks' from the centre. This has led some to believe that curricular reconstruction without prior contextual change is not really viable (Humes, 1996:19). But, difficulties aside, we suggest that curriculum and context be viewed as two arms of the same strategic action, to be pursued concurrently. Specifically, we should consistently establish the priority of practice and adopt an approach to curriculum design which reflects the internal perspective of practitioners – for example, the phenomena encountered in classrooms, the enacting of teaching and learning activities per-hoc, and the moral character of teaching as an activity – thereby maintaining the independent tradition of the profession (Sockett, 1987). In doing so, we could pay attention to a number of neglected factors, including:

- the rhythm of the school year and the manner in which pupils make their way through secondary school (Hughes, 1995);

- the connections between subject studies, general professional studies and practical teaching experience;

- the problem of individual differences and distinctive cultural symbol systems amongst student teachers and pupils in developing proficiency in communication (Reich, 1992);

- the challenge of adaptive classroom teaching/learning and the related need for an 'aptitude development programme' that promotes the personal learning abilities and effective personal styles that underpin learning to teach (Wood and Thomas, 1996);

- the multidimensional nature of the task falling to the student teacher, viewed as both the ability to use knowledge synthetically (construct meanings) and to engage in subject specific modes of thinking (Mansilla and Gardner, 1997).

4 *Institutions*

The institutional dimension of teacher education is often inhibitive when it should be generative and supportive. In few HEIs or schools does ITE figure prominently in mission statements or development plans. The dominant mood is one of 'studied ambivalence'. The main ray of hope for turning this situation around is the impetus which is now gathering behind the realization that, as there is 'no turning back from "partnership"', it may be something worth exploiting to our mutual benefit. This is likely to encourage institutional dialogue in HEIs (see Harland and Lambert, 1997) and schools, as well as to renew efforts to strengthen co-operation between the two. As Alexander (1990) stresses, such co-operation must aim to move beyond 'enabling' functions to 'action' factors, but the road to multiple-level and multifaceted partnership on a reciprocal basis is daunting (Kirk, 1996), unless the parties involved are committed to exploring new patterns of interface and will risk allocating resources in order to create greater resources in the longer term.

Of course, re-invigorated institutional involvement with teacher education could bring with it a research and development rationale leading to significant benefits for a 'learning profession'. In HEIs, status might be given to individuals who can think what teacher education is, what kinds of courses are provided, how best they can be delivered and what form of teacher education is needed for the future. A new 'scholarship of teaching' might emerge which, in recognising that 'the spirit of inquiry is as essential an element of good practice in teaching as it is in research' (Rowland and Barton, 1994), would be interactive in nature and enhance the research by which it was informed. The scholarship of teaching would articulate teaching in the light of the social context in which it takes place and seek to transcend the split between intellectual substance and teaching process (Rice, 1992). In secondary schools the notion of the 'expert teacher' as pedagogic leader and mentor of fellow-professionals might be revived. Schools could gain access to research findings and to alternative perspectives on educational endeavour. HEIs could gain access to contextualized knowledge and an evidence base against which to test research claims. Both partners would gain a more circumspect honesty and a fresh understanding of the 'pursuit of excellence'.

Conclusion

Teaching has a critically important social function (Kirk, 1988). The task of the teacher is to foster and nurture the human capacity to learn. The process of teaching is such that our schools should be places where we build a culture embodying the biological and anthropological sense of the term. They should be a medium for growing minds and also encompass a shared way of life that recognizes both differences and what we have in common. Thus, teaching is necessarily an intellectually demanding activity which includes an understanding of features of the major traditions of human inquiry, for example:

- an understanding of children – their motivation, development, learning and the factors which influence it;

- an understanding of the planning, organization and management of learning – its implementation, sequencing, facilitation and evaluation.

It requires a 'professional climate', with specialized skills, expertise and a substantive knowledge base with which to offer a specialized service.

What is needed, therefore, to help improve the quality of a professional pre-service programme and the continuing professional development of teachers is partnership between policy makers, educationists and teachers, through professional dialogue for shared understanding of the overall purpose, professional relevance and progression of teacher education courses. To take one relevant example: educational research is essential to the initial training of teachers if academic rigour is to be retained in the culture of education, and a foundation provided for further professional development. Uncoupling professional education from higher education would be a short-sighted and doctrinaire strategy of desperation. However, educationists should not succumb to paranoia. They must instead reiterate the necessity of understanding the nature of the specialised skills and expert knowledge they putatively possess. At the same time, they must provide credible evidence of sustained attention to the quality of student learning, for teachers-to-be and for their pupils. Only then can teacher educators hope to check and overcome the suspicion of self-interest to which all professionals are subject.

Finally, teacher educators should try to exhibit a largesse of spirit. Educationists do not have all the right answers, nor do they always ask the right questions. When they do give the right answers to the right questions, they often corrupt their claims by bad manners. Open discourse

Learning to teach

The increased regulation imposed on the institution will undoubtedly be felt by those who work with beginning teachers. The regulatory bodies may have come to believe that in these times it becomes necessary to identify outcomes and ensure that faculties of education develop those. These practices are justified by those who perceive that ITE has not been effective. Learning to teach then becomes a process of working towards specified outcomes set out for certification purposes. As regulatory agencies set out such competences, alternative routes to certification may become more tempting to policy makers. In fact, according to Imig (1995), alternative routes to certification are being proposed in the USA as a means to attract minority students. Although this might sound like a step in the right direction, Grimmett (1995) assesses this move as an attempt to achieve ends-means education by co-opting the language of diversity and multiculturalism.

The need for an extended practicum and closer links with schools might be the result of this scenario, as has been the case in England. ITE might then become more closely aligned with schools. The English experience has seen increased funding provided for schools where teacher education occurs. Conceivably, under this scenario pure and simple apprenticeship may emerge as the *modus operandi* for teacher education in the next millennium. However, that scenario does not necessary follow. As Tisher (1995) reports, in Australia policy makers reduced the actual time for which beginning teachers could receive credit for working in the schools.

Amongst the more difficult challenges facing teacher educators within such a scenario will be to retain the freedom to explore alternative approaches to ITE. Barnett's (1994) comment with respect to the UK experience in higher education illustrates the concern. He points out that the State has involved itself deeper in the life of academic institutions – in terms of what experiences students have and how they interact with professors. The problems with such imposition will be seriously felt on the work of teacher educators, for example, who attempt to reflect constructivist views of learning in their teaching.

despite warning cries from educators that these practices will result in a downgrading rather than an upgrading of teacher quality.

Imig's (1995) concern with the Republican Party's *Contract with America*, that Wideen and Grimmett described in the first chapter provides another example of government control of HEIs. The proposals emanating from the *Contract with America* made Imig very uneasy about the future of teacher education within higher education in the USA. In Great Britain, school-centred initial teacher education has been given more generous financial provision at the expense of university based teacher education. These developments are cause for considerable concern within the teacher education community – Grimmett (1995) considers that they seriously threaten university-based teacher education.

The type of attention to higher education to which Imig refers was illustrated recently in the Province of Manitoba, Canada. There, according to the most recent issue of the *CAUT Bulletin*, the Conservative Government abolished the Grants Commission and created a new Council on Post-secondary Education. While the former Grants Commission had a mandate to ensure that adequate post-secondary education was available, the newly created organisation has been set up to possibly reduce accessibility. The previous act recognised that the University Grants Commission could not interfere with the basic right of the university to formulate academic policies. However, the new Council 'shall determine priorities and allocate funding not just to universities and colleges but to programs within them' (Canadian Association of University Teachers:1). The new Council will also now determine the criteria for judging the work of professors.

These illustrations from four different countries show how institutions for ITE might become increasingly regulated by Governments. Unfortunately, such regulations often reduce the effectiveness of institutions to improve their work because they take away the freedom and the agency of those within the organisation necessary for such improvement. Thus, no improvement occurs. In fact, problems may even become worse through increased regulation. It becomes increasingly difficult for teacher educators to improve programmes within an atmosphere of increasing constraints.

Hughes, M. (1995), *Teaching and Learning in Changing Times*. Oxford: Blackwell.

Humes, W.M. (1996), 'Towards a New Agenda for Teacher Education'. Paper at the Association for Teacher Education in Europe (ATEE) Conference, Glasgow, 1–6 September, 1–22.

Hundey, I. (1996), 'Symposium on the OISE/UT Two Year Initial Teacher Education (Secondary), Program'. Paper at the Exploring Futures in Initial Teacher Education Conference, Institute of Education, University of London, September, 1–17.

Hustler, D. and McIntyre, D. (eds) (1996), *Developing Competent Teachers*. London: David Fulton.

Kemmis, S. (1995), 'Prologue to Wilfred Carr', *For Education: Towards Critical Educational Inquiry*. Milton Keynes: Open University Press, 1–17.

Kirk, G. (1988), *Teacher Education and Professional Development*. Edinburgh: Scottish Academic Press.

Kirk, G. (1996), 'Partnership: The Sharing of Cultures?' Paper at the Association for Teacher Education in Europe (ATEE) Conference, Glasgow, 1–6 September, 1–17.

Kress, G. (1997), 'The university and its social responsibility', in Harland, J. and Lambert, D., 'Exploring the role of educational studies: perspectives from the Institute'. *Academic Board Occasional Papers*, No.1, London: Institute of Education, University of London.

Lambert, D. and Totterdell, M. (1995), 'Training tomorrow's teachers today', in Blake, D. et al., *Researching School-Based Teacher Education*. Aldershot, Avebury Press.

Mansilla, V.B. and Gardner, H. (1997), 'Of kinds of disciplines and kinds of understanding', *Phi Delta Kappan*, 78(5), 381–6.

Millett, A. (1996a), 'Pedagogy – Last Corner of the Secret Garden', Kings College Lecture, 15 July, 1–14.

Millett, A. (1996b), 'Untitled Paper', Teacher Training Agency Chief Executive's Annual Lecture, London, October, 1–15.

Noddings, N. (1996), 'Rethinking the Benefits of The College-Bound Curriculum', *Phi Delta Kappan* , 78(5), 285–9.

Office for Standards in Education (OFSTED), (1995), *Partnership: Schools and Higher Education in Partnership in Secondary Initial Teacher Training.* London: HMSO.

Ormell, C. (1995a), 'Editorial: the need for positivity in education, the possibility of positivity in education', *PROSPERO,* 1(1/2), 2–3.

—   (1995b), 'Cannonical Modelling, the natural form of modern knowledge.' PROSPERO 1(V2).30-33.

Philosophical and Educational Review (PER), Group (1995), 'Initiating as acting-with-conviction: a method approach to teaching', *PROSPERO,* 1(3), 6–9 and 22.

Phillips, D. (1994), 'Research mission and research manpower', in *The Universities in the Twenty-First Century.* London: The National Commission on Education.

Pimm, D. and Selinger, M. (1995), 'The commodification of teacher education in England', in Wideen, M.F. and Grimmett, P.P., *Changing Times in Teacher Education: Restructuring or Reconceptualization?* London: Falmer Press.

Polanyi, M. (1973), *Science, Faith and Society.* Chicago: University of Chicago Press.

Porter, J. (1996), 'The James Report and what might have been in English Teacher Education and Training'. Seminar paper at the Centre for Studies in Comparative Education, Department of Educational Studies, University of Oxford, 1–12.

Reich, R.B. (1992), *The Work of Nations.* New York: Vintage Press.

Reid, I. (1994), 'The reform: change or transformation of initial teacher training?', in Reid, I., Constable, H. and Griffiths, R., *Teacher Education Reform: Current Research.* London: Paul Chapman.

Reid, I., Constable, H. and Griffiths, R. (eds) (1994), *Teacher Education Reform: Current Research.* London: Paul Chapman.

Rice, R.E. (1992), 'Towards a broader conception of scholarship: the American context', in Whinston, T. and Geiger, R., *Research and Higher Education: The United Kingdom and The United States.* Buckingham: SRHE/Open University.

Rotheiser, C. (1996), Partnership and Programme Renewal: Moving Forward.' In: D.W. Booth and S.M. Steingelbauer (eds) *Teaching Teachers: The Faculty of Education*, University of Toronto 1906-1996. Toronto: Caliburn.

Rowland, S. and Barton, L. (1994), 'Making things difficult: developing a research approach to teaching in higher education', *Studies in Higher Education*, 19(3), 367–74.

Russell, T. and Korthagen, F (1995), *Teachers Who Teach Teachers: Reflections on Teacher Education.* London: Falmer Press.

Schon, D. (1983), *The Reflective Practitioner.* New York: Basic Books.

Simon, B. (1994), 'Why no pedagogy in England?', in Moon, B. and Shelton Mayes, A., *Teaching and Learning in the Secondary School.* Milton Keynes: Open University Press.

Snow, R.E. (1992), 'Aptitude theory: yesterday, today and tomorrow', *Educational Psychologist*, 27, 5–32.

Sockett, H. (1987), 'Has Schulman got the strategy right?', *Harvard Educational Review* , 57(2), 208–19.

Stones, E. (1994), 'Assessment of a complex skill: improving teacher education', *Assessment in Education*, 1(2), 235–51.

Sultana, R.G. (1995), 'Developing a Vision for Teacher Education Programmes: A Values-based Approach,' *European Journal of Teacher Education*, 18 (2/3), 215-229.

Taylor, D. (1996), Transcript of talk given at SCETT Conference on the 'Improving Schools Programme', London, 23 November.

Townshend, J. (1996), 'An Overview of OECD Work on Teachers, their Pay and Conditions, Teaching Quality and the Continuing Professional Development of Teachers'. Paper presented at the International Conference on Education: Forty-fifth Session, Geneva, 30 September– 5 October.

von Manen, M. (1977), 'Linking ways of knowing with ways of being practical', *Curriculum Enquiry*, 6(3), 205–28.

Whiting, C., Whitty, G., Furlong, J., Miles, S. and Barton, L. (1996), *Partnership in Initial Teacher Education: A Topography*. MOTE Project, Health and Education Research Unit, London: Institute of Education, University of London.

Wideen, M.F. and Grimmett, P.P. (eds) (1995), *Changing Times in Teacher Education: Restructuring or Reconceptualization?* London: Falmer Press.

Wilkins, M. (1996), *Initial Teacher Training: The Dialogue of Ideology and Culture*. London: Falmer Press.

Wood, K. and Thomas, L. (1996), 'Assessing Meaningful Learning'. Paper at the UCET Autumn Conference, Market Boswell, November, 1–8.

Yankelovich, D. (1981), *New Rules: Searching for Self-fulfilment in a World Turned Upside Down*. New York: Random House.

Young, M.F.D. (1971), *Knowledge and Control: New Directions in the Sociology of Education*. London: Collier-Macmillan.

Zeichner, K. and Liston, D. (1987), 'Teaching students to reflect', *Harvard Educational Review*, 57(1), 23–48.

2.8 Curriculum control, quality assurance and the McDonaldisation of initial teacher education

John Piper and John Robinson

Introduction

Dramatic changes in the policy and practice of education have been taking place on a global scale. Ginsburg notes that these reforms are the consequence of ideological and social struggles taking place in the context of contradictory economic, political and cultural dynamics (1991:xv). McWilliam (quoted in Steiner, 1996:27) suggests that modern teachers (and modernist education systems) are trying to cope with post-modern children. Various commentators have tracked these reforms and the dynamics within which they operate. Peddie (1995), for example, comments on processes operating within the context of school curriculum reform in New Zealand. Angus (1995) refers to the reforms of governance of schools in Australia. Wylie (1995) refers to a change towards school-based management of schools in New Zealand. Steffy and English (1995) and Neubert (1995) comment on the politics and practice of school reform in the USA. Ben-Peretz (1995) gives an analysis of educational reform in Israel. In the more specific context of teacher education, Zeichner (1994) refers to changes taking place in the USA, Canada, Australia, Austria, the Netherlands, Norway, Thailand and the UK. Gilroy et al.

(1994) have explored these ideological struggles with regard to initial teacher education (ITE) in England and Wales.

Collectively, Ritzer (1993) argues, these changes in educational policy and practice amount to attempts by various agencies of reform operating at State level to achieve efficiency, calculability, predictability and control over both formal and informal systems. Ritzer refers to this as the 'McDonalisation of society', which may ultimately lead to the 'dehumanization of education, the elimination of a human teacher and of human interaction between teacher and student' (1993:142). Hartley (1995) uses Ritzer's conceptual framework as an heuristic device to analyse the marketization of British higher education. For Hartley, one of the strongest indicators in British higher education of incomplete McDonalisation is the fact that 'higher education in Britain has not had to forgo its curricular autonomy' (1995:420) as it moves towards a market system (Ball, 1991). However, within ITE, in England at least, this autonomy has become largely illusory in relation to the more professionally focused elements of student experience, as higher education providers (in partnership with schools) implement the decisions of central Government contained in Circulars of the Department for Education (DfE) – Circulars 9/92 (Department for Education, 1992) and 14/93 (Department for Education, 1993). Together, these have established the parameters of the ITE curriculum, with limited scope for flexible interpretation.

It might be argued that the DfEE, has a more substantial hold on the curriculum of ITE in England (in the sense to which Ritzer refers to control) than over the rest of higher education in the UK, as Hartley (1995) suggests. However, in this chapter we argue that the relative DfEE control over ITE has produced a paradox, by creating a diversity of provision which is actually beyond control. By examining mechanisms for quality assurance in 'school-based' ITE programmes, we suggest that ITE has escaped the McDonaldisation of higher education.

This point and the analysis which follows might appear somewhat parochial in that they focus on what is happening in England. However, changing mechanisms of control over ITE in England are, as Aspin suggests 'part of a set of much wider international trends, tugging training out of the institutions and back – or forwards – towards the idea of education in the workplace' (1993:326; see also Carmichael, 1992; Hager, 1995). There are two broad and contradictory international trends developing in ITE – greater control as a consequence of neo-conservative educational policies and a sharper focus on a practice orientation which necessitates increased individualization of the curriculum.

These trends are illustrated in developments taking place in many countries. For example in Australia the National Office of Overseas Skills Recognition is evaluating and accrediting the assessment of skills and competences developed and articulated by the National Training Board (Aspin, 1993). In Papua New Guinea, central Government is seeking to develop much higher degrees of control over teacher education (McLaughlin, 1991). In Spain, a new and centrally driven curriculum for teacher education is currently being implemented (Ruiz and Marcos, 1994). In British Columbia the State Government is acting in a similar fashion (Grimmet, 1994). At the same time, research in South Africa demonstrates a need for practice-oriented ITE to focus on the individual, to recognize the importance of local context and to appreciate the centrality of the student teachers own personal biography at the heart of the programme (Penny and Harley, 1995). Thus, the local concerns from which the current argument developed should be understood in a broader international context. Initially, a brief account is offered of the context within which these contradictory dynamics are working in the English context, through a discussion of the process of learning to teach in 'school-based' ITE courses.

Learning to teach in school-based initial teacher education

With over 20 years of experience of validation and quality assurance in non-university higher education institutions (HEIs) behind it, as one of its last acts before closure, the Council for National Academic Awards (CNAA) forwarded to the new Higher Education Quality Council (HEQC) a valedictory paper 'Quality Assurance: An Agenda for the Future' (Council for National Academic Awards, 1992). This commended a number of potentially problematic issues to the attention of the HEQC and the newly expanded university sector. Of seven issues identified, three are directly related to the subject of this chapter:

• 'teaching and learning outwith the campus'

• 'assessment and competences'

• 'the External Examiner system'.

The CNAA suggested that (without appropriate action) problems might occur when the imperatives of growth and diversification outstrip the capacity of institutional quality assurance systems. The implication was that such imperatives would come from within institutions. The current concern, however, is with particular implications of the regulations for ITE referred to above. These raise serious issues about teaching, learning how to teach and quality assurance in ITE. Quality assurance appears to be a relatively neglected aspect of current writing on ITE, although the Modes of Teacher Education (MOTE) Project, Whiting et al. (1996) and McClelland (1996) do discuss such issues.

The idea that student teachers learn to teach in HEIs, only coming into contact with schools during 'teaching practice' has not been true for some considerable time. However, the new regulations bring into sharp focus the nature of the partnership between HEIs and schools in ITE and the quality assurance of this process. Whilst ITE was essentially HEI-based, it was relatively easy for HEIs with effective quality assurance mechanisms to check quality, but the growth of school-based ITE raises questions about quality and the procedures by which it can be assured. To illuminate them, we must clarify what is being assured in quality assurance within ITE and identify what is meant by learning to teach.

Hodkinson and Harvard (1994) distinguish the professional model of teacher education, subscribed to by most teacher educators in HEIs, from the technician model emanating from right-wing sources such as the Centre for Policy Studies (which has underwritten much central Government policy since 1979). The latter model emphasizes teacher skills and subject knowledge, placing a lower value on teacher awareness of and critical reflection on their practice and broader social issues. These two aspects of teaching and learning to teach are given more equal status in the professional model, in which the notion of reflective practice is central (Schon, 1983 and 1987; Fish, 1989; Graves, 1990; Griffiths and Tann, 1992; Zeichner, 1994). But there is no consensus about the nature or recognition of practice based on reflective process. Also problematic – for conceptualization and implementation – is the view that reflective practice entails both private theory and practice (Eraut, 1994; Griffiths and Tann, 1992; McIntyre, 1993).

Learning to teach involves acquiring the ability to deal professionally with a series of new and distinct situations, utilizing specific skills/ knowledge and broader awareness/reflection. The focus should be on enabling student teachers to act like learners in relation to both skills and awareness. For Fish (1989) the duality of focus, as teacher and learner simultaneously, can be a powerful aid to professional development. However, it can also bring tensions if the two aspects of the process are not equally valued. There is some evidence (Robinson, 1993; Aspinwall, Garrett and Owen-Jackson, 1993; Dunne, 1993a and 1993b) that student teachers consider subject knowledge/skills as the most important aspect, particularly in the eyes of the pupils and there is evidence (Bennett 1993) that ITE has little impact on the orientation of some student teachers to teaching.

There has always been pressure on the student teacher to be a skilful performer, but this tendency is accentuated in school-based ITE. Student teachers are adults, knowledgeable about classrooms and teachers, but less knowledgeable about classroom teaching and learning. Their preference is for being where the action is, for being accepted. They see teaching practice as an initiation rite where 'doing teaching' is more important than learning to teach (Robinson, 1993). The paradox is that student teachers need to behave like adults, but act as learners. School-based ITE (for all its advantages) does not encourage this duality. Haggar (1995) refers to the twin paradoxes of learning to teach in that student teachers want to get hold of what is real in schools (which means behaving in ways that are unnatural to teachers) and at the same time they have an ambivalent attitude to the rules and procedures for accessing mentors' professional craft knowledge because it makes them stick out like 'sore thumbs'. There is a danger that survival during school experience becomes the determinant of professional socialization and opportunities to experiment are considerably reduced, yet experimentation is a key component of learning through experience (Kolb, 1984; Jamieson, 1994).

In the context of school-based ITE, this raises an important issue. Are classrooms and staffrooms the best environment for 'learning to teach'? Research suggests that the context and culture in which learning takes place is of prime importance (Brown, Collins and Duguld, 1989; Proctor, 1993). Yet there is little research on the influence of school on learning to teach or on how that will change as schools become paid partners in ITE. However, experienced classroom teachers will become an increasingly important resource for student teachers, although their craft knowledge is often difficult to access (Edwards and Brunton, 1990; Terrell, 1993). Student teachers lack the means to discover that craft knowledge and to relate it to broader issues encountered elsewhere in their courses. In school-based ITE the student teacher will be more dependent on the nature of (and effective immersion in) the particular culture and practice of staff in specific schools. As a corollary, the relatively universal aspects of ITE may be diminished, as may the link between the student and a commonly experienced 'course' in HE.

There must be a division of labour between the HEIs and the schools (Grace, 1994). Distinctive skills and processes in the education and training of teachers in HEIs have developed over a long period of time. These are worthy of respect and for reasons of social justice should not be cast aside uncritically. The professional model of the teacher may be at risk in the context of school-based ITE, unless course management and quality assurance reflect the new technician-oriented reality. In any context, ITE should produce students who are rational, questioning and capable of testing preconceptions against evidence. Experienced teachers are an important resource for student teachers, owning knowledge and experience which was often neglected in HEI-based ITE. What is required is partnership between HEIs, student teachers and experienced teachers, to achieve the objectification and articulation of this 'craft' knowledge in the context of broader professional awareness.

A 'real partnership' (Hake, 1993) between HEIs, schools and colleges, and student teachers based on well-understood, complementary, but distinct, role performance is of critical significance for ITE in the new context. In its absence, school-based ITE will emphasize locally determined professional socialization of student teachers into a skills/performance-based *modus operandi*. This concern is supported by the research evidence and it can be expected that an (unintended?) consequence of school-based ITE will be to undermine 'issues'-based components when 'learning to teach subjects' takes precedence. (see the Council for Accreditation of Teacher Education (CATE) 1994; and the Teacher Training Agency (TTA) 1994; Robinson 1995; Robinson and Heyes 1995). In this context, quality assurance must monitor the balance of universalistic and particularistic aspects of teacher education courses (e.g. student teachers' awareness of issues such as social justice and equality and their ability to think critically, as well as their performance). Thus, school-based ITE shifts the balance both in learning to teach and in prioritizing the quality assurance of the process.

Quality assurance in school-based ITE

It has been argued that school-based ITE changes the balance between subject knowledge/skills and awareness/critical reflection in the experience and priorities of student teachers. This changes the task of quality assurance, but the change is more fundamental since the new context introduces a multiplicity of distinct environments into the course. The student teacher must be oriented and relate to particular local factors, rather than focusing on HEI-based aspects of the course. For course management and quality assurance (both the prime responsibility of the HEI) this poses difficulties since *de facto* control of much of the student experience rests with partner schools and their staff. For quality assurance, this suggests that the normal focus on inputs to the course (and the course process itself) is redundant, and that a focus on individual and locally defined outputs is more useful. This calls into question the priority given to universalistic standards in contrast to particular, locally defined requirements.

Arguably, since student teachers have individual strengths and weaknesses, treating them all the same cannot be fair when it overrides individual needs. If setting explicit standards risks the creation of clones of 'good practice', how can we achieve flexibility and responsiveness and the professional autonomy of the reflective practitioner? Matching schools/colleges to students is unacceptable, as the reflective practitioner should be capable in a range of learning environments. Further, the test of being 'fit for purpose' cannot be applied uniformly when individual needs and strengths, and the context in which they are manifested, are so variable. Since effective ITE recognizes individual differences (in students and schools) and provides for flexibility/responsiveness and diverse opinions, it will not be characterized by a uniform student experience. Rather, it should assure an individual student experience which is *reasonable*, *just*, *fair* and *equitable* (given many 'local' variables), while ensuring effective inputs of a more universal nature.

Evidence of quality resides in outputs defined by the student experience and their developing academic, professional and personal capability, but as Whitty has suggested 'in learning to be capable the quality of the experience and the quality of the outcome are extremely difficult to disentangle in practice' (1992:43). Furthermore, the idea of identifying which outputs are to be 'measured' remains problematic because ITE courses vary so widely in their philosophical underpinnings (see Whiting et al., 1996). This issue is more acute in courses where, for extensive periods, student teachers are dispersed into varied environments so that their key interactions are either with particular school-based colleagues or with visiting staff from the HEI. In this situation, the student teacher represents the only viable focus for quality assurance activity, since the range of alternatives on which attention could focus (i.e. the extended staff team across many schools and colleges and subject departments, in addition to the team in the HEI) is daunting. Although all stakeholders should be given a voice in conversations about quality, if it is accepted that students in ITE courses are the primary stakeholders and arbiters of the quality of the partnership between the HEI and schools and colleges, then quality assurance practice should reflect this. Stakeholders in quality assurance in secondary education have been discussed by Freeman (1994).

A report by the Quality Support Centre on the development of students' subject area knowledge and skills in the workplace, stressed that 'the quality of delivery can only be evaluated through analysis and reflection upon a flow of feed back from the actual process of teaching and learning, including responses of the various stakeholders' (Quality Support Centre, 1994). This echoes advice given to the former National Advisory Body for Higher Education by its Continuing Education Working Party, recently referred to by Robertson (Higher Education Quality Council, 1994b:173). In considering the quality of complex course provision, 'institutions and validating bodies should approach the question from the perspective of the individual student rather than as an observer analysing a particular course from the outside' (National Advisory Board 1984:37), a recommendation which challenges the idea of a universalized 'student experience'.

However, structural characteristics of the new context in ITE make such an intention highly challenging. In partnership-based ITE, all partners share responsibility to determine what is reasonable, just, fair and equitable. Although the HEI is the ultimate arbiter through 'ownership' of the award, partner institutions must be represented in decision making so that they feel empowered to contribute at all levels. Ensuring commitment to quality assurance mechanisms must involve sharing of power across a wider range of interest groups and achieving agreements on key issues, including the relative weight to be ascribed to universal, academic, vocational and local conceptions of quality. This may be feasible in smaller courses, but it is difficult for dozens or hundreds of schools to exercise their partner obligations in substantial school-based ITE courses. The implications for the conduct of external examiners and boards are significant.

There are other important characteristics of partnership-based ITE to be considered. Although formal responsibility for quality lies with the institution that bestows the award, the ability to exercise this authority is considerably reduced in the context of partnership, no matter how good the communication and teamwork. This will not be mitigated by the passage of time, as suggested with more optimism than is shared amongst many ITE colleagues by Blake (1994). National news items reinforce this view (THES, 8 July, 1994:1). The level of input to the quality of student experience in schools from HEI- or school-based colleagues will inevitably vary in nature, level and intensity at various times. It will also vary between different schools and between departments and individual teachers within the same school. The implications of this increased local, particularistic focus remain to be fully assimilated into quality assurance systems in school-based ITE courses. This omission will continue while HEIs seek inappropriately to apply their 'normal' processes to the new context.

A taken for granted premise of 'normal' quality assurance systems operated in HEIs is that there is a clear structure of line management, authority and responsibility within which course delivery and management takes place. Responsibility for any issue is defined and this responsibility is backed by power and authority in various forms. Bluntly put, all those who contribute to most courses are employed by the same institution and are subject to the constraints and influences contingent on that fact. In school-based ITE courses the 'course team' works for a variety of institutions, with distinct priorities, politics and procedures. Although formal agreements specify the division of responsibilities, resourcing and control, these agreements are typified by good intention and expediency, and are essentially untested. Indeed, there are factors which make it unlikely that they will be enforced in such a way that course management and quality assurance can be comparable with a 'normal' course. HEIs will wish to assure themselves that all partner schools offer a truly appropriate context for school-based ITE. However, given the importance of funding related targets, they may be forgiven some inconsistency in the way that such criteria are applied, since current DfEE regulations place them at a disadvantage in establishing partnerships. There is no requirement for schools to participate, but HEIs are required to work with those schools which declare themselves willing partners. In this situation 'it is incumbent on

HEIs to seek partners and to develop partnerships which are intrinsically attractive to schools' (Wright, 1994:1).

Substantial variation in the ability of schools to provide an appropriate context for the course, even though covered by a common agreement/ contract, is only one aspect of the problem. Within the same school, the ability of different departments to provide an appropriate school experience will vary, as will the commitment of staff to the partnership agreement. For HEIs, with most of the responsibility but less of the power, the imperatives of balancing quality with target numbers and funding make heavy demands on professional and academic integrity. This will be exacerbated as HEIs realise that the proportion of funding for ITE students passed on to partner schools makes school-based ITE a relatively unattractive business to be in. There is growing concern that the funding mechanism for school-based ITE permits HEIs to cover their staffing inputs, but not to make a normal return to capital overheads and central services, including libraries, etc.

These factors have contributed to well-publicized problems for some HEIs. The response from an officer of the Universities Council for the Education of Teachers (UCET) when one withdrew from a school-based course is informative.

> Many Universities are having to go into partnership with schools which they would not have thought twice about in the past, yet those schools have control over much of the quality of the course.
>
> (THES, 1994:8 July, p1)

This scenario makes the criteria by which the Office for Standards in Education (OFSTED) seeks to assess school-based ITE appear optimistic and detached from reality (Office for Standards in Education, 1993). Stated characteristics of quality provision simply cannot be guaranteed, even though many HEIs in partnership with carefully chosen schools will demonstrate compliance (and beyond) with these criteria and provide a high-quality experience. However, aspirational statements of the ideal by OFSTED do little to inform the complex situation within which school-based ITE is being developed. Rather, the application of allegedly universalistic criteria to courses which are inevitably local and particularistic serves as an ideological mask, maintaining an illusion of controlled and standardised course content and student experience, supported by system-wide quality judgements and meaningful national overview. It suggests the continued existence of a coherent system when what has been created is more akin to a marketplace. It also gives an unhelpful lead to quality assurance processes in HEIs. A more output-focused inspection regime would be a major shift of policy (and not without its problems), but would more effectively match the needs of the situation.

Similar points relate to the role of external examiners, traditionally responsible for both formative and summative judgements on the nature of student experience and achievement. The effective coverage of a course by external examiners, when a large proportion of student activity takes place in varied and dispersed contexts and where the application of subject expertise across a large number of schools is essential, will not be delivered through 'normal' processes. Enlarged external examiner teams could not achieve a valid assessment of course quality or outcomes, and could make matters worse. This confirms the suggestion that the process and structural characteristics of school-based ITE pose significant problems for 'normal' quality assurance in HEIs.

Conclusion

In principle, the assertion of the 'Robertson Report' that 'we do not believe that the quality assurance "off-campus" learning should be regarded any differently in terms of rigour and consistency from the arrangements for institutional academic quality control' (Higher Education Quality Council, 1994:194) is clearly correct. However, school-based ITE courses offer a fundamental challenge to quality assurance in higher education and suggest a need to revisit debates referred to previously. The search for consistency of provision, process and experience (as typified by OFSTED inspection criteria and practice) appears misguided and in reality obscures the extent of actual variation. Rather, the emphasis must be on outputs demonstrated by the successful student teacher, through assessment and subsequent professional progress. Such an approach recognizes the inevitability of a local/ particularistic emphasis and a focus on skills and performance, but maintains a proper interest in more universalistic professional concerns.

Although only student teachers can be the arbiters of quality in school-based ITE courses, to expect them to shoulder such responsibility without having made explicit the purposes and goals (academic, professional, personal, etc.) sought through the course is unrealistic. Given this precondition, to focus on the student experience, perception and achievement (i.e. on outcomes rather than process and inputs) may be the most effective approach to quality assurance. These strategies mirror those suggested for work-based courses by the Quality Support Centre (1994), which supports the position being advanced regarding quality assurance.

In order that school-based ITE can be efficient, calculable and predictable, quality assurance must be focused on the students, their perceptions and achievement, throughout and at the end of their courses. This is a reaffirmation of the true purpose of ITE. To play their part, student teachers need to engage critically with their mentors on a one-to-one basis, thus establishing a humanization of the process, reaffirming the interaction between student and teacher – in contradiction to Ritzer's (1993) more pessimistic predictions. However, student teachers, as learners, may not be in a position to exercise this power. Work by Hodkinson and Hodkinson (1995) based on their analysis of trainees on a Training Credit Pilot Scheme gives grounds for some doubt. Yet the development and encouragement of knowledgeable, responsible, reflective and self-critical practitioners, able to work effectively in a variety of contexts appears to be both the goal of ITE and also the precondition for gaining assurance that the goal is met through school-based courses.

Success in the area of students' critical, self-reflective development in a school-based context leads to the paradox referred to in the introduction to this chapter. For Ritzer (1993) the McDonaldisation of society, or ITE, requires four elements of the process to be established. The proposition that ITE programmes should be efficient, calculable and also (in the sense of student entitlement and opportunities for equality and social justice) predictable is difficult to argue with. However, in seeking to reform ITE by putting it in the hands of schools, the DfEE has lost the ability to control. The paradox is that in insisting on the structure and organization of the delivery of the curriculum, the DfEE has forfeited the ability to control actual curriculum content and quality. It appears that the ideologically driven determination of much of the content of ITE courses has been undermined by an equally ideological determination to pass major elements of the courses over to 'real' teachers in 'real' schools. Thus, mutually contradictory policies have been implemented. The HEIs have to field the problems thrown up by the contradictions.

We have suggested that the paradox which lies between curriculum control and the partnership arrangements for school-based ITE, wherein 'associate tutors' take greater control over curriculum content, delivery and quality assurance, challenges the ability of any central body to control ITE. This raises an interesting issue in relation to any move towards a National Curriculum for ITE. The implementation of the National Curriculum for schools in England and Wales depends on stating the content of the curriculum and also on enforcement through high-profile inspections and publication of results. Whereas schools need to teach pupils to stay in business, universities do not need teacher education in the same way. If a similar enforcement regime became a possibility then, as Hartley (1995) suggests, vice-chancellors appear unlikely to co-operate. Yet there is no viable alternative to HEI-led ITE and further devolution to schools would render successful enforcement of a National Curriculum for ITE still more unlikely.

Whatever the outcome of these tensions, the proper approach to quality assurance in school-based ITE requires early resolution. Initial success may be difficult to sustain as school-based ITE courses threaten to outstrip schools' capacity to collaborate. Although well-managed course teams have fostered a high-quality relationship with partner schools, based on collaborative engagement with a new concept, there are signals that the managerial requirements of school-based courses are placing strains on HEIs, their staff and their quality processes which are too heavy to bear over an extended period. School-based ITE course teams will recognize the constraints placed on the 'normal' exercize of quality assurance processes in their particular context and develop appropriate responses. This reorientation of quality assurance processes may be a necessary precondition for the long-term success of school-based ITE, but in itself may not be sufficient. However, it seems likely that such a reorientation will preserve a degree of autonomy within the HEIs beyond the control of the DfE and further deflect the prognosis offered by Ritzer.

To return to the international context, recent analyses of social change have noted a globalization of culture. Archer (1990) and Wallerstein (1990) point to a globalization of world economies, involving the establishment of global financial systems and networks of technological innovation and change facilitated by telematics. Lyotard (1986) has drawn attention to the 'mercantalization of knowledge' as part of this globalization process. An aspect of this process is the expansion of curricular ideas and pedogogies from Europe to the rest of the 'Westernising' world (Heidegger, 1971). It is within this context of globalization that the McDonalisation of teacher education systems is best considered. However, therein lies the paradox of control and individualization to which we have drawn attention. As national systems become increasingly similar and cross-referenced, so at the level of individual action can local-community-focused development be expected to take precedence (Appadurai, 1995).

References

Angus, M. (1995), 'Devolution of school governance in an Australian state school system: third time lucky', in Carter, D.S.G. and O'Neill, M.H., *Case Studies in Educational Change: An International Perspective.* London: Falmer Press.

Appadurai, A. (1995), 'The production of locality', in Fardon, R., *Counterworks: Managing the Diversity of Knowledge.* London: Routledge.

Archer, M. (1990), 'Foreword', in Albrow, M and King, E, *Globalization, Knowledge and Modernity.* London: Sage.

Aspin, D. (1993), 'Quality, teacher education and internationalization: a challenge in cooperation in teacher education', in Gilroy, P. and Smith, M., *International Analyses of Teacher Education*. JET Papers One, Oxfordshire, England: JET/Carfax.

Aspinwall, K., Garrett, V. and Owen-Jackson, G. (1993), *In at the Beginning: A Report on the Student Mentoring Programme*. Sheffield: Sheffield Hallam University.

Ball, S. (1991), *Politics and Policy Making in Education*. London: Routledge.

Bennett, N. (1993), 'Knowledge bases for learning to teach' in N. Bennett, and C. Carré, *Learning to Teach*. London: Routledge.

Ben-Peretz, M. (1995), 'Educational reform in Israel: an example of synergy in education', in Carter, D.S.G. and O'Neill, M.H., *Case Studies in Educational Change: An International Perspective*. London: Falmer Press.

Blake, D. (1994), 'Quality assurance in teacher education: a case study', *Quality Assurance in Education*, 2(1), 26–31.

Brown, J.S., Collins, A. and Duguid, P. (1989), 'Situated cognition and the culture of learning', *Educational Researcher*, 18(1), 32–42.

Carmichael, L. (1992), 'The Australian Vocational Certificate Training System'. Report of the Skills Formation Council, Canberra, Australia: NBEET.

Council for Accreditation of Teacher Education (CATE), (1994), *Profiles of Competence: Draft Note of Guidance*. London: CATE.

Council for National Academic Awards (CNAA), (1992), 'Quality assurance – an agenda for the future'. Paper submitted to Higher Education Quality Council. London: CNAA.

Department for Education (DfE), (1992), *The Initial Training of Teachers (Secondary Phase), Circular 9/92*. London: DfE.

— (1993), *The Initial Training of Primary School Teachers Circular 14/93*. London: DfE.

Dunne, E. (1993a), 'Learning to teach – the impact of curriculum courses', in Bennett, N. and Carre, C., *Learning to Teach*. London: Routledge.

Dunne, E. (1993b), 'Theory into practice', in Bennett, N and Carre, C, *Learning to Teach*. London: Routledge.

Edwards, A. and Brunton, D. (1993), 'Supporting reflection in teachers' learning', in Calderhead, J. and Gates, P., *Conceptualizing Reflection in Teacher Development*. Lewes: Falmer Press.

Eraut, M. (1994), 'The acquisition and use of educational theory by beginning teachers', in Harvard, G. and Hodkinson, P., *Action and Reflection in Teacher Education*. New Jersey: Ablex.

Fish, D. (1989), *Learning Through Practice in Initial Teacher Training*. London: Kogan Page.

Freeman, R. (1994), 'Quality assurance in secondary education', *Quality Assurance in Education*, 2(1), 21–5.

Gilroy, P., Price, C., Stones, E. and Thornton, M. (1994), 'Teacher education in Britain: a JET symposium with politicians', *Journal of Education for Teaching*, 20(3), 261–301.

Ginsburg, M.B. (1991), 'Preface', in Ginsburg, MB, *Understanding Educational Reform in a Global Context: Economy, Ideology and the State*. New York and London: Garland Publishing Inc.

Grace, G. (1994), 'Education as Scholarship: On the Need to Resist Policy Science'. Paper at the Standing Conference on Studies in Education: Role of Theory in Educational Studies, London, November.

Graves, N. (1990), 'Thinking and research on teacher education', in Graves, N., *Initial Teacher Education: Policies and Progress*. London: Kogan Page.

Griffiths, M. and Tann, S. (1992), 'Using reflective practice to link personal and public theories', *Journal of Education for Teaching*, 18(1), 69–84.

Grimmet, P.P. (1994), 'The control of teacher education in British Columbia and Scotland: two cases and a comment', *Journal of Education for Teaching*, 20(1), 5–7.

Hager, P. (1995), 'Lifelong Learning: An Idea Come of Age?' Paper at the Australian Association for Research in Education (AARE) Annual Conference, Hobart, Australia, November.

Haggar, H. (1995), 'Limitations for Mentoring: Or Doing What Comes Naturally'. Paper at the annual British Educational Research Association/European Conference on Educational Research (BERA/ ECER) Conference, Bath, England, September.

Hake, C. (1993), *Partnership in Initial Teacher Training: Talk and Chalk.* London: The Tufnell Press.

Hartley, D. (1995), 'The "McDonalisation" of higher education: food for thought?', *Oxford Review of Education*, 21(4), 409–23.

Heidegger, M. (1971), *On the Way to Language.* London: Harper and Row.

Higher Education Quality Council (HEQC) (1994), *Choosing to Change.* London: HEQC.

Hodkinson, P. and Harvard, G. (1994), 'Perspectives on teacher education', in Harvard, G. and Hodkinson, P., *Action and Reflection in Teacher Education.* New Jersey: Ablex.

Hodkinson, P. and Hodkinson, H. (1995), 'Markets, outcomes and the quality of vocational education and training: some lessons from a youth credits pilot scheme', *The Vocational Aspects of Education*, 47(3), 209–25.

Jamieson, I. (1994), 'Experiential learning in teacher education', in Harvard, G. and Hodkinson, P., *Action and Reflection in Teacher Education.* New Jersey: Ablex.

Kolb, D. (1984), *Experiential Learning.* New Jersey: Prentice Hall.

Lyotard, J.F. (1986), *The Postmodern Condition: A Report on Knowledge.* Manchester: Manchester University Press.

McClelland, V.A. (1996), 'Quality and initial teacher education', in McClelland, V.A. and Varma, V., *The Needs of Teachers.* London: Cassell.

McIntyre, D. (1993), 'Theory, Theorizing and Reflection in Initial Teacher Education,' in J. Calderhead, and P. Gates, (1993), *Conceptualizing Reflection in Teacher Development.* Lewes: Falmer Press.

McLaughlin, J. (1991), 'Teacher education in Papua New Guinea', *Journal of Education for Teaching*, 17(1), 33–9.

McNiff, J. (1993), *Teaching as Learning: An Action Research Approach.* London: Routledge.

McWilliam, E. (1995), *Times Educational Supplement*, 24 November. p.8.

National Advisory Board (NAB) (1984), *Report of the Continuing Education Group.* London: NAB.

Neubert, S. (1995), 'Texas educational reform: Why? Why Not? Who? What? and So What?', in Carter, D.S.G. and O'Neill, M.H., *Case Studies in Educational Change: An International Perspective*. London: Falmer Press.

Office for Standards in Education (OFSTED) (1993), *Working Papers for the Inspection of Secondary Initial Teacher Training*. London: The Office of Her Majesty's Chief Inspector of Schools.

Peddie, R. (1995), 'Culture and economic change: the New Zealand school curriculum', in Carter, D.S.G. and O'Neill, M.H., *Case Studies in Educational Change: An International Perspective*. London: Falmer Press.

Penny, A.J. and Harley, K. (1995), 'Broadening the experiences of teachers in training: a South African study', *Journal of Education for Teaching*, 21(2), 163–76.

Proctor, K.A. (1993), 'Tutor's professional knowledge', in Calderhead, J. and Gates, P., *Conceptualizing Reflection in Teacher Development*. Lewes: Falmer Press.

Quality Support Centre (1994), 'Developing students' subject area knowledge and skills in the workplace', *Newsletter 2*, Phase 2, September 1994. London: Quality Support Centre/Open University.

Ritzer, G. (1993), *The McDonalisation of Society*. London: Pine Forge Press.

Robinson, J. (1993), 'Students' Perceptions of School Experience'. Paper at the Educational Research Seminar Group, Manchester Metropolitan University.

Robinson, J. (1995), 'The Impact of School-based ITE on Beginning Teachers Attitudes to Issues to do with Ethnicity'. Paper at the Standing Committee on the Education and Training of Teachers (SCETT) Conference Teacher Education 2000+, Dunchurch, England, October.

Robinson, J. and Heyes, I. (1995), 'Conflicting models of teacher training in multi-ethnic classrooms: journal of a mentor', *Language, Culture and the Curriculum*, 9(1), 19–26.

Ruiz, I.G. and Marcos, A.R. (1994), 'Initial teacher education in Spain: a critical analysis', *Journal of Education for Teaching*, 20(3), 313–24.

Schon, D. (1983), *The Reflective Practitioner*. London: Temple Smith.

Schon, D. (1987), *Educating the Reflective Practitioner: Toward a New Design for Teaching and Learning in the Professions*. San Francisco: Jossey-Bass.

Steffy, B.E. and English, F.W. (1995), 'Radical legislated school reform in the United States: an examination of Chicago and Kentucky', in Carter, D.S.G. and O'Neill, M.H., *Case Studies in Educational Change: An International Perspective*, London: Falmer Press.

Steiner, M. (1996), '"I prefer to see myself as a Global Citizen": how student teachers can learn to teach for justice', in Steiner, M., *Developing the Global Teacher*. Stoke-on-Trent: Trentham Books.

Terrell, C. (1990), 'Practical school experiences: who teaches the student teacher?', in Booth, M. et al., *Partnership in Initial Teacher Training*. London: Cassell.

Times Higher Educational Supplement (1994), *Teacher Scheme Failing*, 8 July, p.1.

Teacher Training Agency (TTA) (1994), *Profiles of Teacher Competences: Consultation on Draft Guidance*. London: TTA.

Wallerstein, I. (1990), 'Culture as the ideological battleground of the modern world-system', *Theory, Culture and Society*, 7(2/3), 31-55.

Whiting, C., Whitty, G., Furlong, J., Miles, S. and Barton, L. (1996), *Partnership in Initial Teacher Education: A Topography*. London: Institute of Education, University of London.

Whitty, G. (1992), 'Quality control in teacher education', *British Journal of Educational Studies*, XXXX(1), 38–50.

Wright, N. (1994), 'Quality Assurance in Partnership'. Communication to the Society for Research into Higher Education, Teacher Education Study Group Conference, London, October.

Wylie, C. (1995), 'The shift to school-based management in New Zealand – the school view', in Carter, D.S.G. and O'Neill, M.H., *Case Studies in Educational Change: An International Perspective*. London: Falmer Press.

Zeichner, K.M. (1994), 'Conceptions of reflective practice in teaching and teacher education', in Harvard, G. and Hodkinson, P., *Action and Reflection in Teacher Education*. New Jersey: Ablex.

2.9 A view of the landscape from international perspectives

James Porter

The three contributors that follow write from the perspectives of the USA, Ireland and three countries on the continent of Africa.

Catelli describes a holistic perspective for partnerships between higher education and schools. Her account notes the increase in the number of partnerships from 1,200 in 1989 to over 2,300 in 1995. The quantitative expansion has been accompanied by a qualitative change and the emergence of closer and more comprehensive relationships between schools and universities. Catelli describes the positive effects of such partnerships on the quality and reconceptualization of teaching at all levels. However, she also makes clear that the recent drive for partnerships is often forced by the 'massive budget cuts of state run university systems'. The prevailing political climate favouring a free market and tax cutting is popularised by the cry of 'do more for less'. Forced 'partnerships' can form part of the response of the authorities to such pressures.

However, Catelli remains on the high ground of professional development through her description of a programme that genuinely subscribes to organic relationships between partners with the aim of development and reform in the whole educational system. The 16-year-old School-University Partnership, entitled Project SCOPE and SCOPE program based in New York, illustrates the powerful influence of a long standing and integrated partnership in establishing new professional roles from within the school/university framework.

By contrast, Sugrue writes of an Irish situation that is still becalmed by the failure to address basic questions relating to the location of teacher education, teaching practice and mentoring and the content of initial and in-service education and training (INSET). Her contribution illustrates the distance between the practice of many traditional systems that are beset by continuing elitism, inertia and inadequate resources and the theoretical perspectives of those who call for reform, renewal and reconceptualization in teacher education. The frank description of the problems posed by the situation in Ireland also underlines the urgency for an informed international dialogue to assist those who seek change and development in their own national systems.

Pryor and Stuart discuss the continuing influence of educational ideas from the North on the practices of education in Africa. They consider the effects of such ideas as school-based training, competence-based assessment and the association of teacher training and higher education. Illustrations are provided from Malawi, South Africa and, particularly, Ghana. The authors point to the difficulties which arise from the rigid control of education by central Governments. Although they consider that the slow development of action research is a positive sign, they accept that present training programmes do not encourage the teacher to acquire the necessary independence and professionalism that such research requires. Neither does the political and economic context within which both school and universities operate.

Context

The political and economic pressures under which education and, more specifically, teacher education operate, are illustrated by many of the contributions to this book. However, the global nature of such pressures are most obvious when viewed from an international perspective.

Although it is a fact that 20 per cent of the world's population consumes 85 per cent of the world's income, it is not only the gross and increasing disparity between rich and poor countries that limits the possibilities for education systems. Increasingly, a set of economically crude but powerful judgements supply the framework within which education is expected to operate. The fundamental 'principles' that dictate education policy towards countries in the South, are vividly laid out by the World Bank (1988). This report, quoted at length in the UNESCO World Education Report in 1993, states that the two elements of an adjustment programme for education and training are diversifying the sources of funding and containing unit costs. The first imperative is to 'acquire from the beneficiaries of education and training a much larger share of the real costs of providing these services'. Countries are encouraged to increase the operation of privately owned and funded institutions of secondary and higher education, make students or their families responsible for the costs of food, lodging and living expenses, require students themselves to perform a variety of instruction-related support tasks and introduce tuition fees in public institutions to cover at least part of the costs of instruction.

The containment of unit costs is regarded as the most important component and 'should be aggressively pursued at all levels of education in both capital and recurrent costs'. The World Bank and UNESCO go on to recommend policy options such as:

• reductions in teachers' pay where there is a sufficient supply

• a reduction in the minimum entry qualifications for teachers

• more intensive use of teaching staff

• a reduction in construction costs of educational buildings and an increase in their utilization.

Such are the recommendations for the poorest countries in the world. Many of the countries have to accept such 'restructuring' in return for financial support from the World Bank and other agencies. There is also a message for education policy makers in all other countries.

The influence of thinking derived from the concept of the global marketplace is also clear when the purposes of education are delineated by the international agencies. The World Bank (1993) declares that education should improve people's ability to acquire and use information. At the same time as acknowledging the importance of personal enrichment and greater understanding, the writers focus sharply on the fact that education improves the choices that people make as consumers and producers – increasing their productivity and their potential to achieve a higher standard of living. They assert that more highly educated workers have a big advantage in the dynamic and uncertain environment of technological change.

Most revealingly, the report places the promotion of entrepreneurship at the centre of the ways in which education can improve economic productivity. They comment that, in 'market economies entrepreneurs are the link between innovation and production'. Entrepreneurial ability is characterised as a combination of moderate risk taking, individual responsibility, long range planning and organizational ability. Education, the report states, promotes all four.

This is not the place to consider larger questions, such as the impact of globalization on the capacity of individual countries to dictate the purposes of education systems, or to predict the likely effects of Information Technology (IT) on the ways in which individuals will acquire knowledge in the twenty-first century. However, the contributions to this book do illustrate the pervasive influence of a competitive, individualizing and financially based ideology on the provision of education and on the policies that are being pursued by Governments around the world. It is salutary to observe that the leading exponents of the attack on those publicly funded institutions set up for the common good, are those publicly funded international agencies that are charged with the responsibility for asserting that the:

> ultimate goal of education should be to develop the human personality – for its own sake, to serve the unique purposes of a particular culture and to contribute at the same time to a global culture of peace and mutual understanding.

> (UNESCO, 1993:6)

Although the rhetoric may remain in place, the ability of developing countries to change key for changing times will require a fundamental shift in the policies and practices of international agencies and the Governments they so powerfully influence.

References

UNESCO (1993), *World Education Report.* Introduction by Federico Mayor, Director General of UNESCO. France: UNESCO Publishing.

World Bank (1988), *Education in Sub-Saharan Africa: Policies for Adjustment, Revitalization and Expansion.* Washington DC, USA.

World Bank (1991), *The Challenge of Development: World Development Report.* Washington DC, USA.

2.10 An holistic perspective on school-university partnerships in the twenty-first century: theory into practice

Linda A Catelli

There is no doubt that US society today, its Government and its institutions, are undergoing a major restructuring initiated by economic problems, enlightened self-interest and a collective awareness of cultural and political factors. All sectors of US society are engaging in a mass reconceptualization and a redefinition of values, structure and purpose. A global perspective permeates every facet of US business along with a new and more intense focus by a first-term presidential administration on such domestic issues and problems as health, crime, education, human rights, child welfare, poverty and the economy. Hierarchical organizational structures and corporate managerial patterns once found to be productive to an 'industrial society' have now advanced to more integrative patterns and co-operative, networking structures representative of an 'information and service society'.

In education, obstacles and barriers between and within academic institutions are slowly collapsing and substantial changes in the infrastructure of many educational programmes and departments are occurring – often conducted, ironically, by groups of educators that were once polarised or isolated from one another and often caused by institutional 'downsizing'. In the past few years, whether motivated by shrinking budgets, enlightened self-interest or a serious concern for education reform for the twenty-first century, the academic community has witnessed the emergence of more alliances, co-operative ventures and school-university partnerships than in any other period in US education.

My intent in this chapter is two-fold. First, it is to describe briefly the partnership movement in the USA and the events that have led to a new phase of the movement. Second, it is to propose a 'holistic perspective' on school-university partnerships in the twenty-first century. The perspective advanced focuses on educational integration, change and improvement. The holistic perspective was developed in 1980 for a school-university partnership programme entitled 'Project SCOPE'. Still operating today, the project targets the separate domains of the school's curriculum and staff development programme, and the university's pre-service and in-service teacher education programmes, and then integrates them to effect change and improvement in education. The holistic perspective and model approach to education proposed has evolved from my 17 years of experience as founder and director of the partnership program. Some of the underlying notions and themes come from ideas that date back to my work at Teachers College, Columbia University with Joyce (1969 and 1972). Others have come from later work and discussions with Jane Anne Hannigan of Columbia University and Vandergrift (1990 and 1994), who now resides at Rutgers University. The holistic perspective presented and its accompanying conceptual framework for the partnership project, as I see it, is appropriate to the educational needs of the twenty-first century and critical to reforming education.

Presented first is an overview of the school-university partnership movement in the USA and the events that have significantly contributed to the emergence of a 'fourth phase' of the movement. The first section serves to provide the historical context and rationale for an holistic perspective on partnerships. Second, an holistic perspective and the conceptual framework for the school-university partnership Project SCOPE are explained. Finally, the outcomes and accomplishments of the project are identified along with a final comment on school-university partnerships for the future.

The partnership movement in the USA

Since the appearance of the US report *A Nation At Risk* (NCEE, 1983), academics have initiated and conducted a surprisingly large number of partnership ventures to change and improve education. In 1989, a second national survey of partnerships in education sponsored by the American Association for Higher Education (AAHE) revealed that there were over 1,200 US colleges and universities that had entered into partnerships or collaborative arrangements with schools and faculties (Wilbur and Lambert, 1991). By 1995, when a third survey was completed, a total of 2,322 collaboratives were operating (Wilbur and Lambert, 1995). The large number and diverse nature of the partnership activities identified by the survey reporters range from such national efforts as the Holmes Group (1986, 1990 and 1995), created to reform the US education system, to more 'local' efforts made by educators to initiate change and improvement in teacher education, school curriculum or improvements in student achievement.

According to Haycock, in her closing address at the AAHE's 1990 conference on school-college collaboration, partnership participants were into the 'third wave' or phase of collaborative activities (Haycock, Hart and Irvine, 1992:4). Whereas in the first phase, partnerships focused to a large extent on minority and poor students in high schools programmes, basically as a recruitment strategy for colleges, the second phase targeted teachers at varying levels of education in specific subject areas emphasising excellence in instruction through more equitable and collaborative arrangements between college and school personnel. As we moved further into the second phase of the partnership movement in the late-1980s, a larger number of collaborative programmes emphasised the infusion of changed instructional practices and the development of dissemination strategies, plans and mechanisms to improve a system. Entering into a third phase in 1990, the newer partnerships were characterised by more comprehensive approaches that sought to transform institutions, change policy, revolutionize education systems and, most importantly, emphasise student outcomes and achievement (Haycock, Hart and Irvine, 1992; Stoel, Togneri and Brown, 1992). Many participants of these types of partnerships envisioned a K-16 education system and strived to collapse barriers between colleges and schools. Two such partnership endeavours that exemplify the ideals of the third phase of the movement are:

• the Pueblo Community Compact For Student Success supported by the Pew Charitable Trusts and the AAHE's Education Trust

• the Bronx Education Alliance, funded by the Ford Foundation.[1]

Promoters of third-phase partnership programmes, although relatively few in number, were interested in 'mainstreaming' partnership activities into the infrastructures of both universities and schools. They often included parents and community business leaders in their operation. Since their inception, they have had a respectable measure of success, given their complexity and the scope of the problems they face.

In 1994, as we raced toward the new millennium, what I saw emerging was a 'new phase' of the partnership movement. Initiated in this fourth phase of the movement were many school-university partnerships that were even more comprehensive than those previously. Their systems included representatives from a variety of social and health agencies as well as families, business and community leaders, and politicians. The inter- and, intra-professional collaborative models that were infused in the fourth-phase partnerships were more often than not designed for low socio-economic areas of the USA. The Options School in MacAllen, Texas, and the Washington-Heights, Intermediate School 218, conducted by a partnership between The Children's Aid Society and the New York City Board of Education are examples of the newer partnerships. These on-going partnerships serve to reform systems while concurrently attempting to solve the USA's more serious societal problems (see Stallings, 1995). Their goals and expectations are enormous, as are their problems. Research on their effectiveness is extremely difficult because of their multifaceted nature and their interrelated component-parts (Knapp, 1995; Stallings, 1995).

Also, in this fourth phase of the partnership movement there is currently a dramatic surge of interest on the part of schools of education in the USA to transform the education of teachers and, in so doing, to include more personnel from surrounding school districts. Initiated in part by accountability problems and sometimes motivated by budgetary concerns and downsizing agendas, schools of teacher education and their chief administrators are now busily restructuring their programmes, departments and remaining personnel. New paradigms and forms of teacher education involving K-12 schools are being proposed, some in the context of existing school-university partnerships, some in newly fused or downsized departments. Others are housed in autonomous agencies, centres, institutes and professional associations. Constructivist (von Glaserfeld, 1995; Fosnot, 1996) and cognitive theories (Bruer, 1993; Gardner, 1991 and 1993) as well as social and developmental views of education and teacher education (Zeichner and Gore, 1990; Rosenholtz, 1991) are all emerging alongside long lists of state-sponsored K-12 learning standards and assessments of pupil achievement (New York State Education Department, 1995).

In comparison with the third phase of the partnership movement, what we are currently seeing in this 'fourth phase' is:

- more 'mainstreaming' of partnership activities into the infra-structures of both schools and universities – not outreach programs (Nicklin, 1996)

- more books on collaboration and what it means to collaborate (Trubowitz and Longo, 1997)

- massive budget cuts of State-run university systems (McKenna, 1996)

- the downsizing of public and private institutions of higher education

- increased pressure from communities to reduce school taxes

- attempts to either eliminate tenure for teachers (LaMonica, 1996) or eliminate tenured faculty (Professional Staff Congress, 1995)

- political activism by educators to secure monies for programs that represent deeply-held values of education.

The current economic climate was caused to a large extent by the 1994 elections in the USA, which put more Republican representatives in State Governments and in the Federal Congress (McKenna, 1995). The Republican agenda, which emphasised cutting taxes, created an unfavourable situation for public universities and schools, and it helped to popularise the saying in education 'do more with less'.

What differentiates the third from the fourth phase of the movement is the fact that monies have now actually been taken away from public programmes and institutions, thereby causing educational change – not necessarily progress – to occur in a tight and desperate economic climate. Whereas in the third phase the notion that 'smaller government is better' and the idea that 'leaner institutions can be more productive' were only proposed plans, in this fourth phase they are operating principles and mindsets acted upon by chief administrators. As a result, what we have in this fourth phase is the presence of 'forced' collaborations of people and institutions for survival purposes alongside of third-phase partnerships originally formed voluntarily and from a different ideological vantage point. These forced collaborations or 'shot-gun partnership marriages' are competing for the same monies as the other partnerships. Unfortunately, they may push out of existence many partnerships that probably should remain. The highly competitive, economical-political climate today is not only shaping the partnership movement, it is also causing the creation of alliances in the academic sector that are based on questionable motives. It is clear that higher education is now in the public spotlight, whereas in the third phase, K-12 education was the target of criticism and change. The adjusted public focus on higher education is causing fierce battles between boards, administrators and faculties. The battles are over accountability issues and issues of institutional governance, tenure and curriculum (Kennedy, 1995; Healy, 1996; Magner, 1996; Scott, 1996).

Taken separately and together, the recent events – the results of the 1994 elections and the subsequent impact of a Republican agenda, the presence of competing Democratic-Republican agendas in Government, and competing agendas in higher education, a public focus on higher education, the intense competition for partnership funding, and the removal of monies causing continual downsizing of public institutions – are in essence the 'areas of reality' that are currently shaping a fourth phase of the partnership movement in the USA. For schools and universities a major theme is relevance to society's needs, accompanied by accountability to a State's citizenry, and a reconceptualization of academic disciplines, faculty productivity, rewards, union contracts, governance policies, laws and practices. Thus, as new school-university partnerships are formed, and as existing ones change and adapt, they will need to confront the above realities together, in an integrative, educational and common-sense way. They will need to keep an 'academic' focus in the midst of political and economic forces that threaten to do otherwise. And they will need to remind politicians and institutional managers in schools and universities that 'progress' in lieu of change comes with a strong democratic and educational foundation. In this fourth phase of the movement, it is no longer two institutions (a school and university) coming together to form a partnership, each with their own set of laws, policies, rewards, contracts, etc. Instead, it is two 'changing' institutions working out these realities together in an uncertain economic future. If we are genuinely honest with one another, and if we intend change to mean progress, then what we need to do is to build partnerships on a more educationally sound basis than we are presently doing. We need to do it in a more integrative, interpersonal, and interinstitutional-systemic manner.

I probably have taken more time and space to describe the partnership movement and its new phase than I first intended. However, I want to set the stage and provide the historical context and rationale for an holistic perspective on partnerships. At the very least, I want to explain why I believe an holistic perspective on school-university partnerships is particularly appropriate now and in the twenty-first century. There is no doubt that an analysis of the recent events clearly indicates that the academic sector of society has entered into a new and critical phase of a partnership movement that is aimed, most definitely, at transforming and reconceptualising the US education system as well as redefining the profession of teaching. Participants of the new partnerships in the twenty-first century will require new roles, new professional relationships, new conceptual models for education and new and different teacher preparation. Educational change is now happening on a large scale. What Bellah has termed 'a new level of social integration' is called for – one which fosters 'interdependence' and functional 'connectedness' amongst the levels of education and one which eliminates the unnecessary fragmentation and 'cultural isolation' that has existed for far too long in US education (Bellah et al., 1985, pp 275–96; Gaudiani and Burnett, 1985/6:5). It is from this vantage point that an holistic partnership is offered as a viable model for meeting these challenges.

An holistic partnership

Since its inception 17 years ago, Project SCOPE was and is an holistic, conceptually-based, evolving partnership, which seeks to change, integrate and improve the quality of professional education and K-12 schooling. As an holistic enterprise, it fosters the notion that an organic or integrated whole has a reality independent and greater than the sum of its parts. The partnership's parts – its programmes, people and institutional levels – constantly strive to function in an interdependent manner toward a common goal and for the benefit of the whole.

By way of explanation, in an holistic partnership the relationship between and amongst people and programmes is organic and not symbiotic. In a symbiotic relationship there are two equal parties, a school and university, who work together to satisfy their mutual self-interests (Goodlad, 1988; Schlechty and Whitford, 1988; Catelli, 1990). Each party remains in the relationship or arrangement until the desired goal is achieved. Once the goal is achieved, the relationship ends and the partnership ceases. Such school-university arrangements are temporary and lack the stability necessary to bring about lasting educational change and reform. In an organic relationship, the two parties and their programmes operate in a more integral and intimate fashion. Their relationship is on-going, and their work is directed at the improvement of an entire education system. As aptly described and promoted by Schlechty and Whitford in their work on collaboration:

In organic relationships the parts fulfill unique functions, sometimes in a semi-autonomous fashion, but the purpose of these functions is to serve the body of the whole. Indeed, each part has a major investment in the survival of the whole because ill health of the body has potentially devastating effects on each of the separate parts. Thus, unlike symbiotic relationships, which emphasize mutual self-interests, organic relationships stress the common good above all else.

(Schlechty and Whitford, 1988, pp 191–2)

Hence, an 'organic' relationship between a school and university is the key element of a holistic partnership. All members of the partnership work interdependently for the common good and health of the partnership's educational system. This is the perspective on which activities, practices and policies are designed. This is the vantage point from which a professional culture is developed. In an holistic partnership the parties involved also act as equal partners in the relationship. They assume joint ownership of programmes, and responsibility for commonly agreed agenda goals and their associated problems. At the outset, a school and university agree to work together, sharing physical resources, personnel and administrative decisions. Functional connectedness among the levels of education is essential and planned integration of programs, personnel and content is paramount.

To put these ideas in operation on a small scale, Project SCOPE was started in 1980. The project is a partnership between university professors and school practitioners representing schools in the New York City area. The partnership targets the separate educational domains of the school's curriculum and staff development programmes, and the university's pre-service and in-service teacher education programmes, and then integrates them to effect change and improvement in education. The overall goal is to improve and reform K-12 schooling and professional education subject field by subject field. As an holistic partnership, SCOPE's underlying belief is that each educational domain needs to be intertwined with the others in a meaningful way in order for fundamental change to occur in education.

The conceptual framework for the project, illustrated in **Figure 1**, identifies the three educational domains (A, B, C) which form a 'dynamic triad' inclusive of programmes, content, students and teachers. The conceptual framework was founded on three assumptions from which all project activities were designed:

1 that closer links between, and eventual fusion of, the major domains will result in improving education at all levels

2 that the quality and effectiveness of a university's teacher education programme is dependent on its meaningful connection to schools and educational practice

3 that the development of teaching as a profession and its knowledge base is best served by a more participatory and organic relationship amongst school and university personnel (Goodlad and Sirotnik, 1988; Schlechty and Whitford, 1988).

These three assumptions are the agenda goals for the holistic partnership project. They operate as the guiding principles for all collaborative activities and action-research studies impacting one or more of the domains.

As a triad and as a coherent and integrated whole, SCOPE promotes the idea that each domain relies on the others to accomplish the agenda goals. For example:

1 if instituting major changes in a school's curriculum necessitates the implementation of new pedagogical skills, then the training of such skills for the practitioners responsible for the curriculum relies on the school's staff development programme for its accomplishment

2 if student teachers who will be assigned to the school are expected to demonstrate the new pedagogical skills, then this requires that the university's teacher education programme include in its course content and experiences adequate preparation of such new skills

3   if co-operating teachers at the school are expected to facilitate the student teacher's performance of the skills, then the acquisition of supervisory knowledge for the development and assessment of such skills requires the university to provide adequate in-service training for the co-operating teachers.

The point is that for substantial change and improvement to occur each domain is dependent on the others. Whether new education practices are initiated by research findings or a revised school curriculum based on pupil needs, or by the practical wisdom of school practitioners and teacher educators, all parties must be involved in a co-ordinated fashion for its success and implementation. Similarly, all parties must be involved in the production of new knowledge for the profession of teaching.

Central to SCOPE's holistic foundation and ideals is area 'D' of the conceptual framework. Area 'D' represents the point at which the programmes, personnel, content and resources are 'fused' or come together on common ground for the improvement and reform of professional education and K-12 schooling. It is the area in which co-ordinated project activities, courses and action-research studies that involve pre-service and in-service education students, school practitioners and professors are conducted. As an evolving process, SCOPE has slowly moved toward increasing the size of area 'D', while improving and revitalising professional education and the school curriculum. This is the area that has placed educators from schools and the university in a new configuration where their roles and relationships are defined differently. Such new professional roles for teachers as *action-researcher, student teacher supervisor, university course instructor, change agent, curriculum developer, proposal writer, conference speaker* and *author of professional articles* are intertwined and often jointly participated in by members of the partnership (Catelli and Nix, 1992; Catelli, 1995; Catelli et al., 1995). For professors, *partnership director, staff developer* and *research co-ordinator* are the roles engaged in an holistic partnership. The new professional roles and their associated activities are critical to achieving the ultimate goals of the partnership.

Figure 1: Conceptual Framework for Project Scope

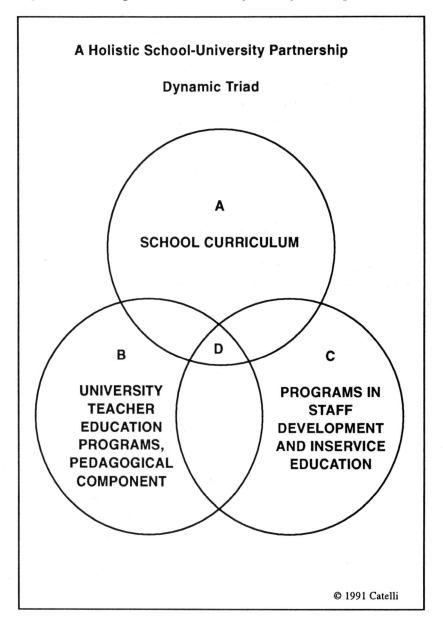

A Holistic School-University Partnership

Dynamic Triad

A

SCHOOL CURRICULUM

D

B

**UNIVERSITY
TEACHER
EDUCATION
PROGRAMS,
PEDAGOGICAL
COMPONENT**

C

**PROGRAMS IN
STAFF
DEVELOPMENT
AND INSERVICE
EDUCATION**

© 1991 Catelli

Since its inception, the school practitioners of the partnership have participated in the restructuring of education courses, assessment tools, and competences of the teacher education programme (Catelli, 1992; Catelli et al., 1987; Catelli et al., 1996). They have joint ownership and shared decision making of the pedagogical component of the teacher education programme. During the 17 years of the project, practitioners have been formally educated in the dimensions of the programme, and then hired by the university as adjunct instructors to:

- teach education courses

- supervise student teachers

- conduct after-school seminars for student teachers

- assist in the early clinical field experiences for pre-service students.

All of the partnership's school practitioners have agreed to a written contract. The education courses included in SCOPE's partnership programme are offered either at the university or collaboratively taught by the director and teachers at a SCOPE-affiliated school.

The holistic partnership programme has received national recognition. In 1990, the project and the director were amongst 56 from around the nation selected and honoured by the AAHE[2] for pioneering efforts in school-university collaboration. In 1991, the director received the City University of New York Faculty Achievement Award for creative achievement and pioneering work in school-university collaboration. In 1995 an article about the partnership and the action research studies conducted by the partnership members was published in *Action in Teacher Education* – the US journal of the Association of Teacher Educators.

Over the 17 years of the partnership, the students, professors, and school teachers of Project SCOPE have produced more than 25 collaborative works and engaged in a number of collaborative research studies. Some of their accomplishments have included:

- five action-research studies for the improvement of teacher education and school curriculum

- 11 collaborative paper presentations at national and international professional conferences by professors, school practitioners and teacher education students of Project SCOPE

- 11 published articles in professional journals

- one research symposium on school-university action research at a regional conference

- the development of the *Pedagogical Component of the Pre-service Teacher Education Program* – inclusive of education courses, teaching competences, materials, assessment and evaluation tools

- the development of a curriculum programme for a SCOPE-affiliated middle school and two articles about the curriculum, published by two major New York City newspapers

- the preparation of over 300 pre-service teacher education students using SCOPE's holistic approach (75 per cent have graduated and subsequently received tenure in teaching positions in the New York City area)

- the preparation and participation of SCOPE's school teachers in new professional roles for the twenty-first century (e.g. action researcher, change agent, student teacher supervisor, university course instructor and curriculum developer)

- the development of a *Process Model for Linking Learning Standards, Assessment, Instruction and Curriculum Change* (Catelli et al., 1996),

- provision of services to 15 schools and 5,000 pupils.

As a combined school–university team, members of SCOPE have successfully achieved a healthy, personal and professional working relationship, which has led to tangible outcomes and the establishment of reciprocal mechanisms for improving and integrating professional education and school curriculum. The benefits as voiced by SCOPE teachers have included such comments as:

- 'SCOPE has provided me with a sense of ownership in the teacher education programme that has engendered a true sense of empowerment'

- 'SCOPE has become a source of professional renewal and rejuvenation'

- 'it has increased my self-esteem and professional pride'

- 'the partnership has provided opportunities to keep up-to-date with new content and teaching methods'

- 'SCOPE gives me an opportunity to give back to my chosen profession and prepare the next generation of teachers'

- 'SCOPE has improved my own teaching which has led to improved learning experiences for our pupils'.

What is important to note here is that, with very little financial[3] and administrative support, the members of SCOPE have effectively demonstrated that an 'holistic', school-university partnership approach can work and it can be long-lasting.

The work of SCOPE affirms that an holistic approach is a viable model for a twenty-first century school-university partnership that seeks to bring about change and reform in education. If we are serious about reforming an education system, I believe we need to look more holistically at partnerships and design them from the perspective of a working framework that targets the separate educational domains and levels, and then links them to form a functional whole. With this holistic model approach, teacher education operates as a component part of a larger schema, which promotes change and improvement. With this type of partnership, the education domains do not operate in isolation from one another, but instead are interdependent in function and purpose. Finally, with an holistic partnership, the school's K-12 curriculum and the university's pre-service and in-service programmes are not viewed as separate points or 'isolates' along an education continuum. Instead, they are critical components made of the integration and fusion of people and content in meaningful and productive ways to form a new education system.

Notes

1   For information about The Pueblo Community Compact For Student Success, interested readers should contact the co-ordinator of the Compact, LeeAnn Withnell, at the University of Southern Colorado, 2200 Bonforte Blvd, Pueblo, Colorado 81001–4901, USA. For information about The Bronx Education Alliance, contact Anne Rothstein, Associate Provost, Lehman College/CUNY, 250 Bedford Park Boulevard West, Bronx, New York 10468, USA.

2   It should be noted that the AAHE has pioneered the school-university partnership movement in the USA. The AAHE operates a school-college office which conducts annually a national conference on school-college collaboration.

3   All financial support for project activities is achieved internally and through the efforts of the Queens College, City University of New York's Center for the Improvement of Education, directed by Paul Longo.

References

Bellah, R., Madsen, R., Sullivan, W., Swidler, A. and Tipon, S. (1985), *Habits of the Heart: Individualism and Commitment in American life.* Los Angeles, CA: University of California Press.

Bruer, J. (1993), *Schools for Thought: A Science of Learning in the Classroom.* Cambridge, MA: The MIT Press.

Catelli, L. (1989), 'School–college partnership: an insider's view'. Unpublished manuscript. Flushing, NY: Queens College.

— (1990), 'School-university partnerships: the transference of a model', in Vandergrift, K. and Intner, S., *Library Education and Leadership: Essays in Honor of Jane Anne Hannigan.* Metuchen, NJ: Scarecrow Press, 127–140.

— (1992), 'Against all odds: a holistic urban school/college partnership – Project SCOPE', *Action in Teacher Education*, 14(14), 42–51.

— (1995), 'Action research and collaborative inquiry in a school-university partnership', *Action in Teacher Education*, 16(4), 25–38.

Catelli, L. and Nix, W. (1992), 'Project SCOPE: an urban partnership venture - descriptions and predictions', in Graham, G. and Jones, M., *Collaboration between Researchers and Practitioners: An International Dialogue – Proceedings from the 1991 AIESEP-NAPEHE World Congress.* Atlanta, GA: International Association of Physical Education Schools in Higher Education (AIESEP) / National Association for Education in Higher Education (NAPEHE), 105–10.

Catelli, L., Anslow-Chakrian, N., DeCurtis, P., Johnston, D., Jordan, J., McLaughlin, P., Mongiello, B., Moskowitz, K., Nix, W., Shurgin, S. and Stack-Lennon, M. (1987), 'Competency-based teacher education: the pedagogical component'. Unpublished document. Flushing, NY: Queens College of the City University of New York.

Catelli, L., DeCurtis, P., Nix, W., Johnston, D., McLaughlin, P., Mongiello, B. and Moskowitz, K. (1995), 'Collaborate: become a new professional', *Strategies*, Nov/Dec, 8–12.

Catelli, L., Franco, M. and Mongiello, B. (1996), 'Linking assessment, instruction, and curriculum change: a collaborative school–college process model', in Fay, T., *Designing Assessment.* Latham, New York: New York Sate Association of Health, Physical Education, Recreation and Dance (NYS-AHPERD), 12.

Fosnot, C. (1996), *Constructivism: Theory, Perspectives and Practice.* New York: Teachers College Press.

Gardner, H. (1991), *The Unschooled Mind.* New York: Basic Books.

_____ (1993), *Frames of mind: The Theory of Multiple Intelligences* (10th anniversary Ed), New York: Basic Books.

Gaudiani, C. and Burnett, D. (1985/6), 'Academic alliances: a new approach to school/college collaboration', Monograph, *Current Issues in Higher Education*, No.1. Washington, DC: American Association for Higher Education.

Goodlad, J. (1988), 'School–university partnerships for educational renewal: rationale and concepts', in Sirotnik, K. and Goodlad, J., *School-university Partnerships in Action: Concepts, Cases, and Concerns.* New York: Teachers College Press, 3–31.

Goodlad, J. and Sirotnik, K. (1988), 'The future of school–university partnerships', in Sirotnik, K. and Catelli, L., *School–university Partnerships in Action: Concepts, Cases, and Concerns.* New York: Teachers College Press, 205–25.

Haycock, K., Hart, P. and Irvine, J. (1992), *Improving Student Achievement through Partnerships*. Washington, DC: American Association for Higher Education.

Healy, P. (1996), 'Activist republican trustees change the way public universities see presidents', *The Chronicle of Higher Education*, 9 August, A19–A20.

Holmes Group (1986), *Tomorrow's Teachers*. East Lansing, MI: Author.

— (1990), *Tomorrow's Schools: Principles for the Design of Professional Development Schools*. East Lansing, MI: The Holmes Group, Inc.

— (1995), *Tomorrow's Schools of Education*. East Lansing, MI: The Holmes Group, Inc.

Joyce, B. (1969), *Alternative Models of Elementary Education*. Waltham, MA: Xerox College Publishing.

— (1972), 'The teacher innovator: a program for preparing educators', in Catelli, L and Weil, M, *Perspectives for Reform in Teacher Education*. New Jersey: Prentice Hall, 4–22,

Kennedy, D. (1995), 'Another century's end, another revolution for higher education', *Change*, May/June, 27(3), 8–15.

Knapp, M. (1995), 'How shall we study comprehensive collaborative services for children and families?', *Educational Researcher*, 24, 5–16.

LaMonica, B .(1996), 'Suffolk teachers' tenure: permanent or renewable?', *Suffolk Life*, 21 August, 3, 12.

Trubowitz, S. and Longo, P. (1997), *How it Works: Inside a School–College Collaboration*. New York: Teachers College Press.

McKenna, B. (1995), 'States right: the new political landscape – higher education unions brace for change at the national and state levels', *On Campus*, March, 8–9, 11.

Magner, D. (1996), 'Cultures clash as non-traditional college gets a tough-as-nails president: termination of 16 employees sets off a fierce debate at Goddard', *The Chronicle of Higher Education*, 2 August, A12–A14.

National Commission on Excellence in Education (1983), *A Nation at Risk*. Washington, DC: The National Commission on Excellence in Education.

New York State Department (1995), *New York State Curriculum, Instruction and Assessment Frameworks*. Albany, New York: The University of the State of New York: The State Education Department.

Nicklin, J. (1996), 'Elementary partnership: two San Francisco professors team up to save a troubled grammar school', *The Chronicle of Higher Education*, July, A13–A14.

Professional Staff Congress (1995), 'Senate sue to nullify retrenchment: AAUP asked to investigate violation of faculty rights', *Clarion*, September, 1, 3.

Rosenholtz, S. (1991), *Teachers' Workplace: The Social Organization of Schools*. New York: Teachers College Press.

Scott, J. (1996), 'Defending the tradition of shared governance', *The Chronicle of Higher Education*, August, B1–B2.

Schlechty, P. and Whitford, B. (1988), 'Shared problems and shared vision: organic collaboration', in Sirotnik, K. and Goodlad, J., *School–university Partnership in Action: Concepts, Cases and Concerns*. New York: Teachers College Press, 191–204.

Stallings, J. (1995), 'Ensuring teaching and learning in the 21st century', *Educational Researcher,* 24(6), 4–8.

Stoel, C., Togneri, W. and Brown, P. (1992), *What Works: School/College Partnerships to Improve Poor and Minority Student Achievement*. Washington, DC: American Association for Higher Education, Office of School/College Collaboration.

Vandergrift, K. (1990), 'Exploring the concept of contextual void: a preliminary analysis', in Intner, S. and Vandergrift, K., *Library Education and Leadership: Essays in Honor of Jane Anne Hannigan*. New York: Scarecrow Press.

—   (1994), *Teaching: A Primary Role of the School Library Media Specialist*. Chicago, Ill: American Library Association.

von Glasersfeld, E. (1995), *Radical Constructivism: A Way of Knowing and Learning*. London: Falmer Press.

Wilbur, P. and Lambert, L. (1991), *Linking America's Schools and Colleges*. Washington, DC: AAHE.

Wilbur, P. and Lambert, L. (1995), *Linking America's Schools and Colleges:* (2nd Ed). Washington, DC: AAHE.

Zeichner, K. and Gore, J. (1990), 'Teacher socialization', in Houston, W.R., *Handbook of Research on Teacher Education*. New York: Macmillan, 329–48.

2.11 Restructuring initial primary teacher education in Ireland – critical perspectives on policy and practice

Ciaran Sugrue

Introduction

The chapter begins with a brief identification of various trends in international discourses on restructuring and reconceptualization of initial teacher education (ITE). This is followed by a more comprehensive account of the social history and geography of initial primary teacher education in Ireland which includes a critique of the structure of existing teacher education programmes in the setting. A critical analysis of available research on ITE in the setting is provided. The focus then shifts to recent policy statements in relation to reform and restructuring of initial primary teacher education and the concluding section makes some tentative suggestions for initiating debate and for shaping the restructuring agenda.

Trends in initial teacher education – international perspectives

Even a cursory acquaintance with recent literature on ITE indicates that it abounds with terms such as reform, renewal, rationalization and reconceptualization in response to present uncertainties and the rapidity of change (Hargreaves, forthcoming; Goodson, 1995; Wideen and Grimmett, 1995; Elliott, 1993). Due to present flux in this terrain, the term 'trends' rather than models of ITE is more appropriate to indicate the manner in which various efforts are being made to address reform issues.

The tradition of apprenticeship or 'sitting with Nellie' (Stones and Morris, 1972) is frequently located in the last century and identified by some as the very antithesis of adequate preparation (Holmes, 1911). Others look with nostalgia to the rational model, which gave hegemonic control to institutions and privileged theory or research-based approaches to teaching. More recent emphases seek, in various ways, to address the relationship between theory and practice, to heal the 'institutional rift' (Grimmett and Erickson, 1988), whereas others seek to educate a more 'reflective practitioner' in response to complexities of society and life in classrooms (Schon, 1983, 1987 and 1991; Russell and Mumby, 1992). Veering towards the practice end of the continuum, some researchers seek to celebrate and give prominence to 'personal practical knowledge' of teachers (Elbaz, 1983; Clandinin, 1986; Clandinin and Connelly, 1988), whereas others recognize the dangers in such advocacy and seek to reinscribe the theoretical mission of teacher education but in a more collaborative and critically reflective manner (Goodson, 1995).

More conservative forces display what Ball (1994) describes as 'restorationist' tendencies and advocate a 'back to basics' approach with greater emphasis on developing competences both in pupils and student teachers that are reminiscent of traditional apprenticeships with all the attendant injustices and inequalities which were endemic in the past (Stronach et al., 1994; Cohn and Kottkamp, 1993). This more utilitarian tendency, present throughout much of the developed world, has reached 'extreme' and 'hysterical' proportions in Britain with the result that reforms 'seek to embrace practical matters further than has been attempted in most other countries', although similar trajectories are detectable also in North America and Australia (Goodson, 1995:144; Lawton, 1992; Ball, 1994; Smyth, 1993; Williams, 1994; Hannan, 1995). This anti-theoretical and 'common-sense' approach needs to be subjected to 'systematic criticism' (Carr and Hartnett, 1996).

As an extension of the theory/practice dichotomy, still others operate along a collaboration-colonization continuum, and favour the creation of common ground between the distinct cultures of the university or teacher education institutions and schools and schooling through 'partnerships' and 'integration' (Grimmett and Erickson, 1988; Wideen and Grimmett, 1995; Elliott, 1993; Goodson, 1995). However, various emphases along this continuum are readily identifiable from 'institution-led' through more collegial and collaborative partnerships (Scott and Burke, 1995; Dawson, 1995; Bowman et al., 1994) to 'site-based' preparation (Knight, Bartlett and McWilliam, 1993; Shehan and Fullan, 1995). In these circumstances also, particularly where there is an emphasis on basic skills, there is a growing tendency to reinscribe the term 'training' when 'teacher education' had just about become the accepted orthodoxy. How these identifiable trends in the literature on ITE are actually reconstructed in practice depends on various forces and coalitions in particular settings. For as Hargreaves suggests:

> How the enterprise of teacher education looks depends on where you look at it from. From the university, it looks utilitarian. From the schools, it seems intellectually removed. Among core elites of star researchers, their teacher education faculty can feel supportive and scholarly. Among the mass of school practice supervisors with heavy teaching loads and very little research time, the self-same faculty can be a slough of drudgery and dronery. There is no single socio-spatial reality of teacher education.
>
> (Hargreaves, forthcoming:10)

Consequently, it becomes necessary, against this international backdrop, to situate analysis of initial primary teacher education in the Irish context in its own milieu while being mindful of this larger picture which envelopes the local setting.

Social history and geography of initial primary teacher education in Ireland

A socio-historical perspective helps 'one to understand the enduring epistemological gaps between theory and practice and the institutional gaps between training and research that afflict and affect the education of teachers' (Hargreaves, forthcoming:4). At the same time, a social geography of teacher preparation also occupies particular 'sites and spaces' within or without higher education and its 'marginality' has particular resonances in the Irish context (Hargreaves, forthoming:5). Consequently, '*where* teacher education is situated and distributed is as important an issue as *when* it became and *how* it evolved in any particular setting' (Hargreaves, forthcoming:6).

Table 1 Colleges of education

Name of institution	Management/ Denomination	Relationship with university	Student intake	
			BEd 94/'5	Grad/Dip 95/'6
St Mary's, Marino	Christian Bros (Catholic)	Recognized College, TCD	37	20
Froebel College, Dublin,	Dominican Nuns (Catholic)	Recognized College, TCD	45	20
Church of Ireland, Dublin	Church of Ireland (Protestants)	Recognized College, TCD	31	
St Patrick's, Dublin	Order of St Vincent (Catholic)	Constituent College Dublin City University	177	80
Mary Immaculate Limerick	Mercy Nuns (Catholic)	Constituent College Limerick University	167	60
Total			457	637

The denominational nature of initial primary teacher education in Ireland is immediately apparent even in the detail of its nomenclature (see Table 1). All colleges are privately owned but publicly funded. While the three smaller colleges have been affiliated to Trinity College since the advent of the Bachelor of Education (BEd) in 1974, the two larger colleges which were (after 1974) 'recognized' colleges of the National University of Ireland, have both become 'constituent' colleges of new universities since 1991. Becoming constituent colleges of universities which were technological institutes until very recently, increases the marginality of teacher education rather than enhances its status. The physical spaces occupied by students destined for primary classrooms are physically separate from all other university students. All except the Church of Ireland College were single sex institutions until 1971, thus reflecting a management preoccupation with suppression and control of sexuality. Students from the three smaller colleges attend lectures on campus in Trinity Colleges two days per week and this division of labour tends to enshrine divisions between theory and practice by locating courses in the disciplines of education in the university, whereas curriculum and pedagogy courses remain domains of the colleges, thus reinforcing their traditional mission as 'training' institutions.

One of the major changes in nomenclature in relation to colleges was their redesignation as colleges of education in 1974 to mark a departure from more narrowly focused 'training', which was their official designation until then. A report on teacher education in Ireland published by the Organization for Economic Co-operation and Development (OECD) in 1991 suggests that these new alliances substantially improved 'the subject and educational theory components of the college courses' and that 'the formal divide between the universities and the colleges was also reduced as the former became responsible for validating the new degree' (Organization for Economic Co-operation and Development, 1991:93). However, affiliation with the university system does not alter the spaces occupied by initial primary teacher education. Consequently, it continues to occupy a marginal space – separate from mainstream university activities but also increasingly isolated from the profession. The same report commented that in the absence of greater collaboration between colleges and schools 'the colleges ... of education will become isolated' (Organization for Economic Co-operation and Development, 1991:92).

When colleges did forge closer links with the universities more than 20 years ago, significant staffing increases resulted to deliver a more diverse and in-depth programme. Staff in these colleges have remained remarkably stable during the intervening period. There has been very little recruitment throughout the 1980s, so that teacher educators are already a 'grey' and 'greying' community – with obvious consequences for reform. In my own institution, for example, less than 10 per cent of academic staff is under 40 years of age and 40 per cent will retire within the next 10 years. However, this may provide a significant opportunity for restructuring.

Since the major colleges became constituent colleges of adjacent universities, they have been obliged to diversify and provide a Bachelors degree in Humanities and also have commenced higher degrees, although numbers of staff have declined. In these circumstances, where workloads have increased, it is difficult to encourage academic staff to reconceptualize ITE. Those who work in academic departments in colleges of education and who, until now, supervised teaching practice and taught some education courses, are increasingly withdrawing their services in these areas resulting in further burdens for education staff. Due to a dramatic decline in the birthrate in the past 15 years, student intake to ITE is set to decline dramatically so that, of necessity, greater emphasis will be placed on induction and in-service programmes, all of which serves to discourage reconceptualization of ITE when such an approach may be necessary and vital for its future.

Structure and provision of initial teacher education programmes

More than 80 per cent of student teachers – those who attend the major colleges – receive their ITE in a concurrent three-year BEd awarded at pass and honours levels, and this degree includes an academic subject taken to degree level. The remainder of student teachers who study in the three smaller colleges take an education-only degree. Ironically, they must complete a fourth year part-time for honours. Students studying for honours complete a fourth year during their first year of teaching and it is based in the university rather than the colleges of education. A smaller number can qualify through a postgraduate diploma of 18 months duration and this is essentially the education component of the BEd. The graduate programme became available in 1995 for the first time in 15 years as part of a policy commitment to provide an alternative route into primary teaching. Table 2 indicates the basic structure of the three-year programme in which the vast majority enrol.

This degree, negotiated by the colleges of education with the university sector in the mid-1970s, is effectively a 1960s British model, where the disciplines of education hold sway – courses in curriculum and teaching studies are part of the programme as is block release for school experience. Additionally, all students pursue one academic subject to degree level, while BEd graduates are licensed to teach in primary schools only. Existing programmes reflect a dated linear theory-to-practice conception of ITE, which is increasingly called into question by much of the literature cited at the outset. When the major colleges became constituent colleges of universities in the 1990s, their respective BEds were accepted without scrutiny for accreditation, thus an important opportunity was missed for critical appraisal of current provision.

Table 2 BEd structure

BEd	Academic	Education
Year 1	50% (two subjects)	50%
Year 2	40% (one subject)	60%
Year 3	40% (one subject)	60%
Total	**43%**	**57%**

There is a growing awareness of the dated nature of these programmes and a lack of fit between the changed and changing context and complexity of schooling and the manner in which initial preparation is approached and executed. It is necessary, therefore, to turn to available research in the setting to interrogate current practice of ITE.

Initial primary teacher education in Ireland – research evidence

There is extremely little research evidence in the Irish context which relates specifically to initial primary teacher education. It is both significant and salutary that no available research has been conducted collectively or individually by teacher education institutions or by individuals or groups of teacher educators on teacher education. There is much anecdotal evidence within the system on the strengths and weaknesses of existing teacher education programmes, and my previous life as classroom teacher, schools inspector and my on-going contacts with primary principals as well as being an insider as a teacher educator provide a certain vantage point in this restructuring debate – an 'enlightened eye' rather than 'immaculate perception' (Eisner, 1991).

Recent studies conducted by the Irish National Teachers' Organization (INTO) suggest that many practising teachers are dissatisfied with ITE as a preparation for their subsequent teaching experience (Irish National Teachers' Organization, 1994 and 1995). In particular they identify 'inadequate preparation' for teaching multigrade classes, teaching in disadvantaged contexts and special needs (Irish National Teachers' Organization, 1995). Teachers also cited additional weaknesses:

- inadequate teaching practice
- overemphasis on academic subjects
- irrelevant educational theory.

Others mentioned a lack of attention to realities of teaching such as stress, isolation, burnout, discipline problems, time management, communication and interpersonal relationships both internal and external to the school (Irish National Teachers' Organization, 1994 and 1995). It is generally accepted among teacher educators in the setting that overload, overlap, fragmentation, overteaching and overexamining are endemic to ITE programmes. Perceptions of overload and fragmentation are confirmed by the OECD report when it states that 'by now these curricula are overcrowded and unable to provide the full range of knowledge and skills that students need', while the challenges presented by the changing context of schooling 'cannot simply be met by adding yet further elements to an already overcrowded teacher education curriculum' (Organization for Economic Co-operation and Development, 1991:96–8). Because of the accelerated pace of change, Coolahan (1994) indicates clearly that a more proactive stance from teacher education institutions is vital to meet these changing circumstances. He states, 'new approaches and responses are required from initial and inservice teacher education' (Coolahan, 1994:85).

The report continues that courses such as the BEd have 'adapted flexibly to changing needs', but such an approach is reactive and has a tendency to contribute to additional fragmentation of course provision and overload in the form of further coursework and examinations (Coolahan, 1994:85). Existing inadequacies may be exacerbated by continuing reactively to adapt when more fundamental restructuring and reconceptualizing are necessary.

Despite perceived shortcomings in present provision, the more fundamental inadequacy with present programmes is in the actual structure of degree programmes. These structures privilege theoretical knowledge to the virtual exclusion of the 'experienced' (Hunt, 1987) or 'practical' knowledge of practitioners (Clandinin, 1986; Connelly and Clandinin, 1988). The INTO comments:

> In the mid-sixties in the UK there was similar dissatisfaction among teachers at the way in which the establishment of the BEd course was seen as the proper domain of the universities and the colleges of education to the exclusion of practising teachers.
>
> (INTO, 1995:9)

This fundamental imbalance between theory and practice or the continued privileging of research-based theories of teaching over practical knowledge of practitioners, requires rethinking as well as restructuring of ITE that promotes a more collaborative approach. However, in the Irish context, with the presence of academic disciplines as a significant dimension of BEd programmes for the vast majority of students, the possibility of reconceptualization is more difficult.

At a recent symposium on the structure and content of ITE where the presence of academic disciplines was questioned, those who teach these subjects, not surprisingly, gave a spirited defence of their retention on the grounds that they were much more than a 'specialization' and were intended to contribute significantly to students' personal development (Sugrue, forthcoming). Nevertheless, within a professional degree which is already overcrowded, it is necessary to question their presence and their apparent exclusive claim to foster personal development when this too could be achieved through the disciplines of education. Ironically, within the Humanities degree in my own institution, human development has become a much sought after 'subject' and it is taught by those in the disciplines of education and consists of an amalgam of philosophy, psychology and sociology. It would be unreasonable to suggest that the personal development of that minority of student teachers who pursue an education-only BEd suffers significantly due to the absence of an academic discipline.

This is not to be dismissive of the important contribution that academic subjects can make to students' development. Many students indicate that they derive more satisfaction from their study of them, and devote more time to them than the fragmented offerings in education. However, there is something fundamentally wrong with a professional programme if this is how it is received and perceived by students. There is little doubt that the presence, some would say dominance, of the disciplines of education in addition to academic subjects places too many constraints on time for curriculum and pedagogy in preparation for being a classroom teacher and reduces flexibility for more regular and on-going contact with schools.

Despite the universal presence of teaching practice or the practicum as integral to ITE programmes, few institutions if any would claim to have got the 'fit' right between college-based and school-based work. The past 20 years have been characterized by much tinkering without substantial development (Grimmett and Erickson, 1988; Kagan, 1992; McNamara, 1995; Cornbleth and Ellsworth, 1994; Stark, 1994; Johnson, 1994; Townshend, 1994). Teaching practice arrangements in the Irish context indicate a linear theory-to-practice mindset, where little attention is paid to selection of co-operating teachers and schools, and classroom teachers have no formal role in supporting and assessing students. This remains the domain of teacher educators and perpetuates the privileging of theoretical perspectives (Irish National Teachers' Organization, 1994 and 1995). There is some anecdotal evidence to suggest that after initial school experience, when students are shocked into realizing the discrepancy between the culture of teacher education and the harsh realities of classroom life, they become cynical about theoretical perspectives and very pragmatic about what works in classrooms. This approach frequently reinforces their own prejudiced and narrow lay theories of teaching – practice makes perfect (Sugrue, 1996; Britzman, 1986).

Although some efforts have been made to involve the profession in teaching practice supervision, these arrangements have been criticized by the profession as they have been *ad hoc*, relying on retired school principals and others who happen to be available, when a more structured mentoring programme seems more appropriate (Sugrue, forthcoming). Some teacher educators in the setting espouse a more critically reflective approach to ITE, and are well disposed towards greater collegiality and partnerships. These intentions are unlikely however to have much impact within existing structures.

It is appropriate and timely, therefore, to ask, 'What structures and policies have been put in place to advance reconceptualization and restructuring of ITE in Ireland?'

Initial teacher education – policy perspectives

Despite an unprecedented amount of policy and policy-related debates, consultations, fora and publications in Ireland since 1990, ITE has remained intact and relatively undisturbed (Coolahan, 1994; Organization for Economic Co-operation and Development, 1991; Ireland, 1992 and 1995). This relative tranquility, some suggest stagnation, is partly a consequence of:

- historical and geographical location
- ageing and declining staff
- lack of 'new blood'
- increasing workloads
- uncertainties around new relationships with universities.

Teacher education, therefore, has been left to its own devices and has grown comfortable in its relative isolation.

Successive Irish Governments have demonstrated a significant lack of capacity or inclination to engage in serious planning and this situation was reflected recently in the editorial of a prominent daily paper. It states, 'there is no policy-based approach to ... areas such as health, education or social services – of identifying priorities, of coordinating programmes and resources or of defining objectives' ('Politics of Crime', 1996:13). In these circumstances, it is not surprising to find that recent policy statements lack coherence and direction and reflect a number of trends in ITE identified in the introduction. In general, these statements focus on pragmatic issues without any serious attempt to reconceptualize the enterprise of ITE, although it is reasonable to suggest also that this task is primarily the responsibility of teacher educators, whose voices have been remarkable by their silence in this debate to date. The recent White Paper on education states that:

> there will be an emphasis, in pre-service courses, on combining academic study with the study of educational theory and practice directed towards the requirements of primary schools.
>
> (Ireland, 1995:122)

This statement at once provides succour to those who wish to retain academic subjects within the BEd, to those with a vested interest in the disciplines of education and to those who are more focused on the practical aspects of teaching. It is a recipe for maintaining the status quo rather than promoting restructuring, and no indication is given as to how a programme such as this could be given coherence and focus or what its underlying principles would be.

Following the OECD (1991) and subsequent Irish reports (Ireland, 1992; Coolahan, 1994), the White Paper makes clear the Government's commitment to conceptualizing the teaching career as a 'continuum', where 'initial teacher education cannot be regarded as the final preparation for a life-time in teaching' (Ireland, 1995:121). There is general welcome and approval for recognition of initial, induction and in-service professional support as benchmarks on this career-long continuum. There is commitment to retention of the concurrent model of teacher education in the White Paper and recognition that structured induction has implications also for the initial phase. The White Paper states:

> It is envisaged that newly appointed teachers will be supported by both teacher education institutions and schools. Teacher education institutions will maintain links with the newly qualified teachers by providing additional opportunities for learning to supplement those already provided in initial training courses.
>
> (Ireland, 1995:125)

One benefit of this will be to allow teacher educators, in collaboration with the profession, to set priorities and set aside the 'rucksack' approach which, teacher educators justified in the absence of clear commitment to induction and in-service provision (INTO, 1995). Though teacher educators generally welcome expansion of their role into the induction phase, they are seriously concerned that the resource and staffing implications of this policy position have not been addressed. When the implications of these policy initiatives remain unaddressed, teacher educators remain reticent about committing to additional work, as it appears to be an implicit demand of more for less. It is disappointing that a commitment to lifelong learning for teachers is not accompanied by an appropriate conceptualization of the task of teacher educators, while such a commitment may be interpreted as an endorsement of creating a more critically reflective profession (Wideen and Grimmet, 1995; Elliott, 1993; Day, 1993). Neither does it reflect particularly well on teacher educators if they do not address the challenge of reconceptualizing and restructuring ITE.

Commitment is given also to 'the development of a broader range of competences' and, within this, greater attention will be paid to 'the arts, European awareness, health promotion, music, physical education and science, and on catering for children with special needs' (Ireland, 1995:123). However laudable, these appear more like a recipe for further fragmentation and overload than rationalization. They also include shades of a 'competency based approach' (Cohn and Kottkamp, 1993). As well as being more broadly based, there is commitment to more specialization and, significantly, the presence of the academic subject in the BEd is regarded as 'an academic specialization' when until now its presence has been justified for personal development (Ireland, 1995:123). There is certainly a case for specialist teachers in schools, but to pretend that three years of engagement with an academic subject equips students as curriculum leaders is difficult to sustain. The case for specialization during the initial phase needs careful articulation rather than mere assertion.

Shades of the 'new right' managerialism are present also in recent policy statements where the White Paper states that colleges will identify 'students' teaching potential ... at the earliest possible point' particularly those who 'are unsuited to teaching', although this seems more like an attempt to socialise student teachers into early acceptance of performance indicators and appraisal (Lawton, 1992; Ball, 1994). Further evidence of giving greater prominence to appraisal is manifest in the role envisaged for teacher educators during initial and induction phases. The White Paper states:

> As part of the induction programme, teacher education institutions will prepare profiles of student teachers for the schools. These profiles will include details on training already undertaken, indicate personal strengths and particular expertise, as well as areas requiring

further development. These profiles will be updated at the end of the induction period and will form the basis for the preparation of personal development plans for the newly qualified teachers.

(Ireland, 1995:126)

All of this, it appears, will be achieved within existing BEd structures without any additional resources. This is fantasy!

The convention report advocates greater partnership between teacher educators and the profession 'in the interests of improving the school-based training experience of student teachers' (Coolahan, 1994:86). Adequate recognition of the experienced knowledge of practitioners, however, needs to extend much further than merely expanding their role as mentor teachers. Such partnerships are likely to remain peripheral and tangential to the socialization of student teachers unless there is shared conceptual understanding of where such experiences fit within a reconceptualized teacher education programme. By far the most important issue raised by the OECD report has been ignored in the White Paper. The former states, 'It is a corollary of accepting the necessity of lifelong teacher education that the very model of schooling and its organization needs to be reconstituted' (Organization for Economic Co-operation and Development, 1991:103). Consequently, in the opinion of the examiners, 'We do not see how teacher education is to undergo the necessary transformation that we have outlined unless some kind of centralised machinery is established' (Organization for Economic Co-operation and Development, 1991:107). Four years after the publication of this report, these structures have not been put in place, and this inaction is all the more surprising since the convention report also advocated the creation of such structures 'at an early stage' to address programme issues in relation to initial preparation and induction (Coolahan, 1994:87). In the absence of such structures, piecemeal reform is the best that can be anticipated. The absence of the voices of teacher educators in this debate is also lamentable.

Not for the first time in relation to issues of professional concern to primary teachers, their union is to the fore in making demands to promote reform and to honour policy commitments to a partnership approach that has potential for greater collegiality and collaboration. Following INTO's own report on teacher education (Irish National Teachers' Organization, 1995), at its annual congress earlier this year a motion which demanded 'the establishment of a review body on teacher education' was passed unanimously ('Teacher Education', 1996:11). The motion also sought to address items such as programme content of ITE, the possibility of a fourth year being added to the three-year BEd, reform of teaching practice and the development of a structured mentoring system, as well as representation on the governing bodies of colleges of education ('Teacher Education', 1996:11). Though some teacher educators are alarmed by these demands as the influence and power of the union engenders anxiety which tends to silence teacher educators, they nevertheless represent an important opportunity for creating the necessary structures for significant reforms in ITE. More recently, the standing committee of heads of education and the teachers' unions have put restructuring of teacher education on its agenda, but this forum excludes important stakeholders such as department of education officials and inspectors.

Restructuring and reconceptualization?

I write this concluding section as a teacher educator and as a former classroom teacher, with a passionate belief that schools can be better places for pupils and teachers only if restructuring and reconceptualization of initial primary teacher education is undertaken as a matter of urgency. It is not an exaggeration to suggest that, in Ireland, initial primary teacher education, although not without its strengths, has lost its way. I share Grimmett's concern that:

> if ... this challenge is not met quickly and decisively, teacher education will become increasingly subjected to the kind of harsh political restructuring that precludes any form of reconceptualization around educational purposes. Such restructuring would, I fear, represent the *coup de grace* for university-connected teacher education.
>
> (Grimmett, 1995:222)

Clearly, there is an immediate need in the Irish setting for a structure in which the reconceptualization debate can begin in a spirit of collaboration, but representativeness rather than elitism needs to inform the selection of a group to lead debate. It is not in any sense peremptory to suggest that teacher educators should take a lead, but omens are not hopeful in this regard. There is an urgent need also for a number of research initiatives to be undertaken individually and collaboratively by practitioners and teacher educators as there is a dearth of material on a whole range of issues from teaching practice and mentoring to the role of academic subjects, disciplines of education, induction, etc. The structural location of teacher education and the profile of teacher educators also requires scrutiny. Yet much of this work – however beneficial for those involved – will have little impact at the levels of policy and practice, if reforms are not accompanied by serious reconceptualization of the underlying assumptions of ITE. This is a challenging, worthwhile and, for those committed to the education of pupils and teachers, an unavoidable task.

References

Ball, S. (1994), *Education Reform: A Critical and Post-structural Approach.* Buckingham: Open University Press.

Bowman, J., Ellis, P., Smart, D. and Wiens, W. (1994), 'Review of teacher education in British Columbia', *Journal of Education for Teaching,* 20(1), 9–21.

Britzman, D (1986), 'Cultural myths in the making of teachers: biography and social structure in teacher education', *Harvard Educational Review,* 56(4), 442–56.

Carr, W. and Hartnett, A. (1996), *Education and the Struggle for Democracy: The Politics of Educational Ideas.* Buckingham: Open University Press.

Clandinin, J. (1986), *Classroom Practice: Teacher Images in Action.* London: Falmer Press.

Clandinin, J. and Connelly, M. (1988), *Teachers as Curriculum Planners: Narratives of Experience.* Toronto: OISE Press.

Cohn, M. and Kottkamp, R. (1993), *Teachers: The Missing Voice in Education*. New York: State University of New York Press.

Coolahan, J. (ed) (1994), *Report of the National Education Convention*. Dublin: Government Publications.

Cornbleth, C and Ellsworth, J. (1994), 'Teachers in teacher education: clinical faculty roles and relationships', *American Educational Research Journal*, 31(1), 49–70.

Dawson, A. (1995), 'Reframing the clinical professor role: the faculty associate at Simon Frazer University', in Wideen, M. and Grimmett, P., *Changing Times in Teacher Education: Restructuring or Reconceptualization?* London: Falmer Press.

Day, C. (1993), 'Research and the Continuing Professional Development of Teachers'. An inaugural lecture delivered at The University of Nottingham School of Education.

Eisner, E. (1991), *The Enlightened Eye: Qualitative Inquiry and the Enhancement of Educational Practice*. New York: Macmillan.

Elbaz, F. (1983), *Teacher Thinking: A Study of Practical Knowledge*. London: Croom Helm.

Elliott, J. (ed) (1993), *Reconstructing Teacher Education*. London: Falmer Press.

Goodson, I. (1995), 'Education as a practical matter: some issues and concerns', *Cambridge Journal of Education,* 25(2), 137–48.

Grimmett, P. (1995), 'Reconceptualizing teacher education: preparing teachers for revitalized schools', in Wideen, M. and Grimmett, P., *Changing Times in Teacher Education: Restructuring or Reconceptualization?* London: Falmer Press.

Grimmett, P. and Erickson, G. (eds) (1988), *Reflection in Teacher Education*. London: Teachers College Press.

Hannan, A. (1995), 'The case for school-led primary teacher training', *Journal of Education for Teaching*, 21(1), 25–35.

Hargreaves, A. (forthcoming), 'Towards a social geography of teacher education', in Shimahara, N.Z. and Holowinsky, I.Z., *Teacher Education in Industrialized Nations*. New York: Garland.

Holmes, E. (1911), *What Is and What Might Be*. London: Constable and Company Ltd.

Hunt, D. (1987), *Beginning with Ourselves in Practice, Theory and Human Affairs*. Toronto: OISE, Press.

Irish National Teachers' Organization (INTO) (1994), *A Career in Teaching: Develop – Recognize – Reward*. Dublin: INTO.

— (1995), *Educating Teachers: Reform and Renewal*. Dublin: INTO.

Ireland (1992) *Education for a Changing World: Green Paper on Education*. Dublin: The Stationery Office.

— (1995) *Charting Our Education Future: White Paper on Education*. Dublin: Government Publications.

Johnson, S. (1994), 'Conversations with student teachers – enhancing the dialogue of learning to teach', *Teaching and Teacher Education*, 10(1),71–82.

Kagan (1992), 'Professional growth among preservice and beginning teachers', *Review of Educational Research*, 62(2), 129–69.

Knight, J., Bartlett, L., and McWilliam, E. (eds) (1993), *Unfinished Business: Reshaping the Teacher Education Industry for the 1990s*. Rockhampton: University of Central Queensland.

Lawton, D. (1992), *Education and Politics in the 1990s: Conflict or Consensus?* London: Falmer Press.

McNamara, D. (1995), 'The influence of student teachers' tutors and mentors upon their classroom practice: an exploratory study', *Teaching and Teacher Education*, 11(1), 51–61.

Organization for Economic Co-operation and Development (OECD) (1991), *Reviews of National Policies for Education: Ireland*. Paris: OECD.

'Politics of Crime' (1996), *Irish Times*, 29 June, 13. Dublin: D'olier Street.

Russell, T. and Mumby, H. (eds) (1992), *Teachers and Teaching: From Classroom to Reflection*. London: Falmer Press.

Schon, D. (1983), *The Reflective Practitioner. How Professionals Think in Action*. New York: Basic Books.

Schon, D. (1987), *Educating the Reflective Practitioner: Toward a New Design for Teaching and Learning in the Professions*. London: Jossey-Bass Publishers.

— (ed) (1991), *The Reflective Turn: Case Studies In and On Educational Practice*. London: Teachers College Press.

Scott, J. and Burke, H. (1995), 'Collaborative teacher education: a merging of agendas', in Wideen, M. and Grimmett, P., *Changing Times in Teacher Education: Restructuring or Reconceptualization?* London: Falmer Press.

Shehan, N. and Fullan, M. (1995), 'Teacher education in Canada: a case study of British Columbia and Ontario', in Wideen, M. and Grimmett, P., *Changing Times in Teacher Education: Restructuring or Reconceptualization?* London: Falmer Press.

Smyth, J. (ed) (1993), *A Socially Critical View of the Self-managing School.* London: Falmer Press.

Stark, R. (1994), 'Supervising teachers and student teachers: roles and relationships in primary initial teacher education', *Scottish Educational Review*, 26(1), 60–70.

Stones, E. and Morris, S. (1972),*Teaching Practice: Problems and Perspectives.* London: Methuen.

Stronach, I., Cope, P., Inglis, B. and McNally, J. (1994), 'The SOED "competence" guidelines for initial teacher training: issues of control, performance and relevance', *Scottish Educational Review*, 26(2), 118–33.

Sugrue, C. (1996), 'Student teachers' lay theories: implications for professional development', in Goodson, I. and Hargreaves, A., *Teachers' Professional Lives.* London: Falmer Press.

Sugrue, C. (ed) (forthcoming), *Rethinking Initial Teacher Education and Induction, Symposium Proceedings.* Dublin: Educational Research Centre.

Teacher Education (1996), *Tuarascáil,* May, 11. Dublin: INTO.

Townshend, J. (1994), 'Developments in school-based initial teacher training', *European Journal of Teacher Education*, 17(1/2), 49–51.

Wideen, M. and Grimmett, P. (eds) (1995), *Changing Times in Teacher Education: Restructuring or Reconceptualization?* London: Falmer Press.

Williams, E.A. (1994),. 'Roles and responsibilities in initial teacher training – student views', *Educational Studies*, 20(2), 167–81.

2.12 Development and under-development in teacher education – African perspectives

John Pryor and Janet Stuart

Post colonial societies inherit the gross inequalities of the colonial system along with a view of the world that tends to the acceptance of this arrangement and an education system which works to perpetuate it.

(Manley, 1974: 132)

Introduction

This quotation provides important background for any discussion of educational issues in the context of North–South relations. Conditions and practices in the South[1] grew out of colonial relationships whose purpose was to maintain power differentials as a means of government and where educational systems with features modelled on those of the North were introduced. This had the effect of sustaining uneven distributions of power and influence well beyond the colonial period, in particular through the examination system (Rodney, 1972; Jansen, 1989; Kellaghan and Greaney, 1991). In many places teacher education for the schools where indigenous children formed the majority was either non-existent or formed part of the secondary rather than tertiary phase, a state of affairs which has continued in many countries. As a result, initial teacher education (ITE) syllabuses can be found resembling those of England in the 1950s. In this chapter we contend that these and many of the practices that derive from them constitute a form of underdevelopment in teacher education. Wideen and Grimmet (1995) suggest that much change in teacher education in the North is 'restructuring', rather than 'reconceptualizing' the process by which young people are inducted into the profession. We wish to engage with this issue by looking at some of the recent and on-going changes in teacher education in some anglophone countries of sub-Saharan Africa, to explore how far the changes are appropriate and sustainable and to consider what a reconceptualization of teacher education might involve.

Trade in educational ideas

The currently dominant metaphor in education, as in most fields, is that of the global market place. Although we would contest the application of this analogy to the process of teaching and learning, it has a certain aptness with respect to the trade in educational ideas that form the basis of teacher education. Whereas colonial education systems were imposed ultimately as a result of military superiority, currently the economic and cultural power of the North is more critical – educational ideas are displayed, exchanged, bought and sold, imported and exported. In this situation the dominance of the North tends to create an aspiration in the South to import the artefacts of the dominant culture. However, in education as in other fields, the key question is, 'Who benefits?' Undoubtedly considerable profit accrues to Northern higher education institutions (HEIs) from student fees, many resulting from tied aid, and through less tangible means – see UK Department of Trade and Industry's Exporting Education Initiative, (Universities Council for the Education of Teachers, 1996). HEIs have also been involved in various capacities with development projects, where the current concern (at least at a rhetorical level) is with 'capacity building' in which the flow of ideas is of crucial importance (Leach, 1996).

World-wide confidence in the importance of education for national development and a shift from the inflexible demand system of manpower planning to a less overtly instrumental human resource development approach, have been influential in starting a redeployment of resources towards universal primary schooling and basic education, entailing a requirement for many more teachers. Faced with the underdevelopment of the post-colonial systems of teacher education, many countries are actively searching for new ideas, but as educators and administrators look North there may be danger that the next set of models are as inappropriate as those they are seeking to replace. On the one hand, aid programmes and consultants might be offering the ideas that we ourselves are discarding, such as child-centred learning and resource-based primary school work. On the other hand, they might be promoting newer ideas such as those derived from the school effectiveness movement or competence-based assessment, which are as yet not properly tested, and many would claim, of dubious worth (Angus, 1993; Davies, 1994; Ball, 1995).

In the field of teacher education some of the ideas originating in the North and currently being exported to the South are:

- school-based initial teacher training
- the use of competence-based assessment
- the association of teacher training with higher education
- the introduction of action research with the idea of the teacher as researcher.

Will such imports lead to further underdevelopment or can some of these ideas help reconceptualise teacher education in ways that are appropriate and sustainable? A key criterion is how far they enable teachers to build a professional understanding, based on the integration of theory and practice. In discussing some of these issues, we will draw both on our experience as teacher educators in England and our links with teacher education in sub-Saharan Africa.

The African context

Historically, teacher training has been a very neglected part of the education systems of the South. As recently as 1990, the Declaration resulting from the World Conference on Education for All at Jomtien made only two brief references to it. However, as mentioned above, the shift in emphasis, at least at a rhetorical level, towards Education for All has meant that teacher education is at last becoming an important issue. Ministries of Education are now realising that universal enrolment cannot happen without a rise in quantity of teachers and high-quality schools demand the preparation of high quality teachers. However, policy takes very different forms in different countries.

Malawi

The Malawian Government has introduced a form of school-based teacher training in order to cope with a unique situation. In September 1994 free primary education was introduced. With classes already overcrowded, the Ministry took the unusual step of recruiting 17,000 untrained teachers from the pool of unemployed secondary school leavers, gave them a two-week induction course and sent them into the schools. Headteachers and primary education advisors were asked to support them in learning to teach in a purely practical way, 'on the job'.

Researchers from Malawi and Sussex University have followed a sample for a year to evaluate their progress (Kunje and Stuart, 1997). The new entrants have remained in post, 'delivering the curriculum' more or less as specified, but as they receive little support or training, their practice remains at a basic level, drawing solely on their own experience. The comment of one headteacher, 'I advised them to teach the children just as we taught them', although an extreme case, highlights the notion that school-based training, unless very carefully structured, tends to be a conservative practice, an issue explored in detail by Drake and Dart (1993).

With foreign aid, a huge in-service programme is being set up for these Malawian teachers, comprising a rolling programme of short residential courses followed by distance learning and school-based support – a bold attempt to find a new structure for teacher training in a situation of severe resource constraint. It is, however, a pragmatic response to crisis rather than a careful reconceptualization of how young teachers learn to teach. In principle, the mixture of theory and practice, with opportunities to reflect and to try out new ideas with tutorial support, could be very effective. However, the schools are not conducive environments – the qualified teachers themselves underwent a watered-down colonial type training and the classrooms hold up to 200 children seated on the floor, often with no textbooks and sometimes no blackboard. What elements can be built on to improve the quality? Where will new ideas come from? What are the training models that are appropriate and sustainable in such circumstances? A recent, small-scale experiment with action research suggests that teachers can be encouraged to undertake such studies even in these unpropitious circumstances, but that a massive input of both physical and human resources is necessary to undergird the development (Kunje and Stuart, 1997).

South Africa

The special situation of post-apartheid South Africa poses different problems. The new Government is attempting a reconceptualization of teacher education of unprecedented breadth and depth. Under apartheid, teacher education was almost entirely theoretical. The basic conceptual framework, drawing on a mixture of Calvinism and nineteenth century phenomenology, was known as 'fundamental pedagogics'. It purported to be a value-free 'science' of education with the central tenet that the teacher is to take the unformed – and potentially evil – child and mould or lead him or her into adulthood. This was taught in a formal and abstract way without reference to the reality of the classroom, and assessed mainly by regurgitatory exams, together with a brief and often ritualistic period of teaching practice.

There was a strong political need for a fundamentally different approach. The Committee on Teacher Education Policy (COTEP) decided on a competence-based model of teacher education, drawn apparently from a mixture of Scottish, Australian and New Zealand models (COTEP 1996). They issued guidelines containing a list of over 100 competences, classified under 'knowledge', 'skills' and 'attitudes', but without examples of how to translate these into a new form of professional curriculum.

Furthermore, in deference to university pressures (the teacher training colleges are poised uncertainly between the further and the higher education systems at present, with a directive to affiliate themselves loosely to the university of their choice), the three-year diploma course has to contain courses 'equivalent to first year university standard'. To complicate matters further, teacher training has to fit into a new National Qualifications Framework (NQF), which has a slightly different definition of 'outcome' and 'competence'; and at the same time, there is a loudly proclaimed call for 'learner-centred approaches' to teaching, whereby teachers and college lecturers must become facilitators of learning, and for training partnership with schools.

Moreover, the COTEP term 'competence' does not differentiate between global 'competence' and more specific 'competency'. Performances are roughly equivalent to 'outcomes'. This terminology seems to beg a number of questions concerning the validity of the assessment criteria, that is the relationship between the task, the competency and competence, and to privilege a more behaviouristic approach which is less concerned with the integration and co-ordination of competences. In the present context, this may seem a sensible, pragmatic approach because of the traditional adherence to fundamental pedagogics, which lacks an appreciation of the complexities of teaching and learning. However precisely because what is needed is a widening and an acknowledgement of that complexity, there are considerable dangers.

Our experiences so far through links with South African universities and colleges suggest that these policies are facing considerable problems. The only form of assessment practised so far has been formal examinations. Can competence-based assessment, which is still far from being universally accepted as successful in its original contexts (Wolf, 1995) be transplanted? Even now, trainee teachers are being taught in college about student-centred learning through transmission style lectures. They have never themselves experienced anything different and when they arrive in schools they discover strongholds of the old fundamental pedagogics where teaching is dominated by 'chalk and talk' (Department of Education of the Republic of South Africa, 1996). Success in passing exams is the main criterion for judging education. For the reform to achieve any success, restructuring will need to be accompanied by reconceptualization in the minds of all stakeholders – not only teachers and lecturers, but also the learners and their parents.

The competences will have to be interpreted in such a way that they do not act as a screen behind which the old practices continue to lurk. They will need to provide a support for a new notion of professionalism. Even then, the term 'professional' may not be acceptable as it is culture-laden and context bound. In South Africa, one of us had a debate with a young radical teacher who explained that the image of a professional there was someone who was politically neutral and who, therefore, worked with apartheid – a collaborator (see Walker, 1996).

Ghana

Ghana is another special case, having been remarkably successful in educational achievement during the early years of independence, but then going through a rapid decline (Peil, 1995), primarily the result of economic collapse.[2] Although there have been great improvements made as a result of on-going educational reforms since 1987, the ability of the system to make the most of these changes has been seriously impeded by the degeneration of the previous period – for example, an increase in untrained teachers. Another important effect of this as far as teachers are concerned is that a month's salary will often feed a family for no more than a week. Teachers must, therefore, of necessity have at least one other source of income, in rural areas usually farming, which needs to be attended to often at the expense of teaching, a phenomenon by no means unique to Ghana (Davies, 1994). Apart from the obvious practical problems, it can lead to a vicious circle of diminished self-esteem as teachers face the shame of being ineffective in providing for themselves and their families and guilt in the lack of time they have to give to their teaching duties.[3]

Ghana too has now embarked on a programme to reform its teacher education. A new university college of education has been established and there are plans to upgrade teacher training colleges by bringing them into the higher education sector. As elsewhere, these policies present problems as well as opportunities, but structural changes such as these are not enough. Teachers' paper qualifications are meaningless if they do not have an adequate conceptualization of their role. We will, therefore, use the situation in Ghana to focus on the issue which is at the root of many of the issues of quality that face teachers and teacher education, namely the question of professionalism and teachers' understanding of their own agency within the school and the classroom and to consider how teacher education can facilitate the development of this.

Ghana – a case study

According to one Ghanaian university lecturer, 'the Ghanaian teacher is the person who waits for the top hierarchy to say, "You are to do this, you are to do that" and they implement it' (Ackumey, 1996). In other words, Ghanaian teachers do not see themselves as agents, merely as operatives. This is not unexpected in an authoritarian system with colonial roots in which a transmission model of teaching is prevalent. However, Fuller (1991) has developed an analysis of education in the South, ascribing this problem to current rather than historic circumstances. States in the South are what he calls 'fragile' – lacking the resources and structures of those of the North, yet desperately trying to 'catch up'. His analysis results in a *signalling theory*, whereby the fragile state defends its own legitimacy by using the symbols of Northern society (e.g. mass schooling) to demonstrate that progress towards a more modern society is being made, whilst still being dependent on more traditional bases of power. Fuller's theory is complex and shows how the effects of this situation result in rigid hierarchies and are felt right down the system into the classroom:

> Teachers may rely on lecturing at pupils, assuming that the mass of youngsters will stay engaged, and on signalling that control will be maintained. This has little to do with boosting levels of achievement; but it signals that the teacher is credible and doing what he or she is expected to do.
>
> (Fuller, 1991:133)

Our own experience would not only support this notion, but we would claim that in many cases it is understated. For example here are some extracts from field notes made in a Ghanaian school:

> Some of the children appeared to be working in exercise books, the majority were just sitting there. I asked the teacher why this was and she went to a cupboard at the back of the classroom. Children came to the cupboard then and searched for their exercise book. The teacher explained that the books had been mixed up. In a quarter of an hour some of the children had still not found their book.

> In the P2 class the children were preparing for their home reading. Since they did not on the whole have books, this involved copying a page off the blackboard into their homework books. At least two of the class had lost their books and were just sitting there.

> Once again the children appeared to be working at a very slow pace with little direction or interaction from the teacher who was just waiting in her place for them to complete the work. I asked one or two children whether they could read the words and they said "no".

Even allowing for the effect of the presence of a stranger, these observations suggest that, for at least some Ghanaian teachers, their lack of agency goes right to the roots of their understanding of their role in the classroom. It is unclear what the goals of these teachers might have been, but we would speculate that they saw teaching more in terms of their presence in the classroom, telling the children what the prescribed work was to be and putting ticks on the bottom of pages rather than actually facilitating learning. When there is a need to react, nothing happens, because the teacher is merely going through the motions of 'being a teacher' rather than operating from any notion of professional practice. Thus, schooling consists of signalling and is conceived in ritual rather than principled terms.

Such an approach is not universal, but it may well be widespread in Africa. This impression is confirmed by other research evidence (Mhlongo and Prew, 1995) and would explain, at least in part, why the overwhelming majority of Ghanaian children after five years of schooling were considered by one account (Unites States Agency for International Development, 1996) to be functionally illiterate and innumerate. We would contend that this ritualization of education is reinforced not just by the fragility of the state, but by the rigid hierarchy of the system. Teachers may seem to pupils to be making decisions, and so may headteachers to the staff, but the implications of a hierarchy are that any exercise of power at all but the top level is severely constrained not only by the degree of autonomy that each level allows to that below it, but also by the degree of autonomy that each lower level perceives itself to enjoy and thus feels able to take. [4] Anderson claims that 'teachers have absolute veto power over innovation and change even in the most highly centralized systems of education' (Anderson, 1991:14), but this power of veto is derived from inactivity rather than activity and does not, therefore, contribute to a sense of enhanced agency and professionalism.

Prospects for development

However, there are signs in Ghana that the rigid hierarchy may be softening. The introduction of continuous assessment with a greater decision-making role assigned to teachers is significant. Devolution may also occur as a result of the increased role that communities, as elsewhere in Africa, are being asked to take in providing funding for schools, particularly for capital expenditure, which is leading to some sense of local ownership. However, even if this tendency develops momentum, there is a paradox: if, in order to create more agency and professionalism in teachers, greater autonomy is made available, teachers are unlikely to be able to access this autonomy because their conceptualization of teaching does not embrace a sense of agency or professional practice. Breaking into this circle will not be easy, but it is here that teacher educators can play a crucial role.

The movement of teacher training into higher education presents several opportunities. Improved self-esteem derived from the enhanced status of teacher education and educators is liable to increase their sense of agency, although we would not concur with the idea that extra teacher education necessarily results in extra quality (McLaughlin, 1996).

Alignment with a more powerful interest which is outside the Ministry and potentially at least not in a directly hierarchical position with respect to schools should also enhance autonomy. However, the best possibility for change in the new situation is that a culture of inquiry set up in the university stands a chance of gradually seeping into the rest of system.

The most hopeful signs of this happening in Ghana are through the interest of some education lecturers in action research. Projects are developing on a small scale involving lecturers working with teachers in schools. Whether this is actually action research or not in the purest sense is debatable, but it does introduce to teachers the idea that they can make principled interventions in the learning of their pupils. This different approach, that of an inquiry that 'makes both the ends and means of education problematic' (Noffke, 1994) and seeks, thereby, to improve individual practice is at the opposite extreme from the signalling mode of teaching. Given the lack of agency amongst teachers and tutors, such projects would seem pointless at first sight. However, it is precisely because of the ritualized conception of education that they hold so much promise. One committed researcher can begin to involve a larger number of teachers in collaboration. Because it stresses the function of the practitioner as the agent, all those who participate in the research may gain confidence in their capacity to make decisions and begin to develop a sense of professional autonomy. Such an approach takes account of the subjective meaning of change, that is, how the participants actually experience it (Fullan, 1991).

The projects we have seen have involved university teacher education staff, but interest is now being expressed by tutors in the training colleges (still in the secondary sector). These developments seem to suggest that there is a chance that restructuring may make possible a reconceptualization of teacher professionalism. This will only happen if there is a large enough critical mass of lecturers and tutors involved with the new approach and, more importantly, if it is not only mediated to trainee teachers but also becomes embedded in the practice of pre-service education. The notion of teacher agency must not only enter the curriculum of teacher training, it must also be overtly displayed in its pedagogy and assessment. This would be no small achievement.

As yet, there have been few other examples of action research projects in African contexts. A similar approach has been used in Lesotho (see Stuart et al., 1997, for a detailed account of the project), in what is historically a less hierarchical system. However, the extent of its impact remains modest. In other parts of southern Africa pockets of action research are developing, particularly around Cape Town (Walker, 1993) and some pilot NGO sponsored projects have taken place in East Africa (Archer and Cottingham, 1996). In many respects, an approach deriving from action research has great potential. Although it might be seen as an import from the North, the strongest claims of action research theory are made about its 'situated understanding' and ability to develop ideas from local practice. These features are seen as inherently empowering to the individual within a framework of social action (Elliott, 1991). In this sense, it is well placed to be transformed into a truly African form.

There are also many potential problems. The greatest of these is probably the question of control. A policy of greater teacher agency and responsiveness is a difficult one to implement through directives. Other, more subtle approaches are needed. Ministries of education need to recognize that if they are to encourage higher quality teaching, they need to devolve some of their rigid control of decision making. Although increased quality of teaching may be a present Government priority, if it comes to a choice between effectiveness and docility in the teaching force a future Government may have different priorities. In addition, the upgrading of teacher qualifications may set a time bomb of increased teacher salaries which could put a premature end to the initiative. This perspective makes it all the more important that training should result in better quality and that higher salaries are not given just for useless paper qualifications.

In summary, the problems are great, but there are some encouraging signs. Necessary as it may be, reconstruction in education is unlikely to fulfil its goals if not accompanied by teachers' reconceptualization of their own agency within the classroom and the school – a notion of professional practice. This would involve a conception of schooling based on both pedagogical and curricular understanding and, above all, a sense of self-respect and confidence stemming from a view of themselves as professional agents. Without this, teachers will always be dependent on someone else's judgement. Collaborative inquiry initiated by teacher educators and influenced by action research offers one way forward towards the development of a conception of professionalism grounded in an African context.

Lessons for the North?

Our argument so far has been concerned almost solely with African issues. However, looking elsewhere can also be instructive in demonstrating that there are other ways of working apart from one's own. However, are the issues which are so strongly evident in the African case-study material cited here so very different from those confronting us in other continents? Lack of resources and poor teacher:student ratios, centralized control of education which prescribes syllabi overloaded with content and takes away the autonomy of the professional, beginning teachers learning on the job from teachers without the time or space to reflect on their work, a ritual rather than principled understanding of the process of teaching and learning, where the external trappings of education replace critical thought and action – it is instructive to see African colleagues grappling with these problems and to reflect that maybe their concerns are our concerns too.

As we go about the global marketplace, we may well see that the goods we are preparing for home consumption are not so very popular. It is worthwhile re-evaluating what we are doing and not just for commercial reasons, for there is a chance that we may be underdeveloping ourselves. There may be ideas that the South can advantageously acquire from England, but an understanding of what is happening there may well be very instructive for us.

Notes

1   Throughout this chapter we follow the practice initiated by the Brandt Report (1980) of using the terms 'North' and 'South' to denote respectively the more developed countries and the less developed countries.

2   In the years between 1970 and 1982 real per capita income in Ghana
     declined by 30 per cent whilst inflation was running at an average of 40
     per cent per annum. This put the country third in the list of fastest rates
     of economic decline (Colclough and Lewin, 1993).

3   This is a predicament whose implications are clearly traced in another
     African context by Ahlenhed et al. (1991, pp 58–9).

4   This theme might be developed by reference to Bourdieu's notions of
     habitus, which although arising initially out of his anthropological
     studies in Algeria have to our knowledge yet to be developed in
     relation to the field of sub-Saharan education.

References

Ackumey, M. (1996), Seminar given at the University of Sussex Institute of
    Education, 27 September.

Ahlenhed, B., Callewaert, G., Gissóko, M. and Daun, H. (1991), *School
    Career in Lower Primary Education in Guinea-Bissau,* Stockholm:
    Swedish International Development Authority.

Anderson, L. (1991), *Increasing Teacher Effectiveness*. Paris: UNESCO
    International Institute for Educational Planning.

Angus, L. (1993), 'The sociology of school effectiveness,' *British Journal of
    Sociology of Education,* 14(3), 333–45.

Archer, D. and Cottingham, S. (1996), *Action Research Report on Reflect.*
    London: Overseas Development Administration.

Ball, S. (1995), 'Intellectuals or technicians? The urgent role of theory in
    educational studies', *British Journal of Educational Studies*, 43(3),
    255–71.

Brandt, W. and members of the Independent Commission on International
    Development Issues (1980), *North-South: A Programme For Survival:
    A Report*. London: Pan.

Colclough, C. and Lewin, K. (1993), *Educating All the Children: Strategies
    for Primary Schooling in the South.* Oxford: Oxford University Press.

Committee on Teacher Education Policy (COTEP) (1996), *Norms and Standards for Teacher Education.* Pretoria: Department of Education.

Davies, L. (1994), *Beyond Authoritarian School Management: The Challenge for Transparency.* Ticknall, Derbyshire: Education Now Books.

Department of Education of the Republic of South Africa (1996), *South African National Education Audit Summary Report.* Pretoria: Department of Education.

Drake, P. and Dart, L. (1993), 'School-based teacher training: a conservative practice?', *Journal of Education for Teaching,* 19(2), 175–89.

Elliott, J. (1991), *Action Research for Educational Change.* Buckingham: Open University Press.

Fullan, M. (1991), *The New Meaning of Educational Change.* London: Cassell.

Fuller, B. (1991), *Growing-up Modern: The Western State Builds Third World Schools.* New York: Routledge.

Jansen, J. (1989), 'Curriculum reconstruction in post-colonial Africa: a review of the literature,' *International Journal of Educational Development,* 9(3), 219–31.

Kellaghan, T. and Greaney, S. (1991), *Using Examinations to Improve Education: A Study of Fourteen African Countries.* Washington DC: World Bank.

King, K. (1990), 'The character of schooling in sub-Saharan Africa', in Entwistle, N, *Handbook of Educational Ideas and Practices.* London: Routledge.

Kunje, D. and Stuart, J.S. (1997), *The Emergency Teacher Training Programme in Malawi: Final Report.* Zomba, Malawi: CERT/ODA.

Leach, F. (1996), 'Failed matrimony: educational projects and their host institutions', in Turner, J., *The State and the School: An international Perspective.* London: Falmer Press.

McLaughlin, D. (1996), 'Who is to retrain the teacher trainers?: a Papua New Guinea case study', *Teaching and Teacher Education,* 12(3), 285–301.

Manley, M. (1974), Keynote address, Sixth Commonwealth Education Conference, Kingston, Jamaica, Sixth Commonwealth Education Conference Report, London: Commonwealth Secretariat, 130-137.

Mhlongo, N. and Prew, M. (1995), *Evaluation Report of the Link Africa –
Vulani Project.* Nongoma: BDDSA.

Noffke, S. (1994), 'Action Research: towards the next generation',
Educational Action Research, 2(1), 9–21.

Peil, M. (1995), 'Ghanaian education as seen from an Accra suburb',
International Journal of Educational Development, 15(3), 289–305.

Rodney, W. (1972), *How Europe Underdeveloped Africa.* London: Bogle-
l'Ouverture.

Scadding, H. (1989), 'Junior Secondary Schools – an educational initiative in
Ghana', *Compare,* 19(1), 43–8.

Stuart, J.S., Lefoka, J.P. and Morojele, M. (1997), 'Improving our practice:
collaborative classroom action research in Lesotho', in Crossley, M.
and Vulliamy, G., *Qualitative Educational Research in Developing
Countries.* New York: Garland.

Stuart, J. (1991), 'Classroom action research in Africa: a case study of
curriculum and professional development', in Lewin, K. and Stuart, J.,
Educational Innovation in Developing Countries. London: Macmillan.

UNESCO (1989), *Statistical Yearbook.* Paris: UNESCO.

United States Agency for International Development (1996), *Ghana Strategy
Survey (Draft).* Accra: USAID.

Universities Council for the Education of Teachers (UCET) (1996), *Annual
Report No.3.* London: UCET.

Walker, M. (1993), 'Developing the theory and practice of action research',
Educational Action Research, 1(1), 95–109.

Walker, M. (1996), 'Academic Positions'. Paper at the Annual Meeting of the
American Educational Research Association, New York, April.

Wideen, M. and Grimmet, P. (eds) (1995), *Changing Times in Teacher
Education.* London: Falmer Press.

Wolf, A. (1995), *Competence-based Assessment.* Buckingham: Open
University Press.

Part 3: Changing key for changing times – issues in practice

'Good practice proceeds not from a theory but from reflection on the characteristics of practice itself. This highlights the crucial significance of circumstance and more particularly of ethos in the development of initial teacher education.'

(Conference Notes Sept. 1996)

A key principle, identified by the conference organizers in their call for papers, underpinned the Exploring Futures in Initial Teacher Education Conference. The editors have endeavoured to ensure this theme is carried through in the chapters in this section. The chapters demonstrate that effective vision in teacher education is grounded in educational practice itself.

The work included in this section sets out to encompass:

- the efficacy of 'new' and devolved models of teacher education (Harris and Shelton Mayes, Struthers)
- the primacy of mentoring in new models of teacher education (Williams et al., Drake and Dart, Heilbronn and Jones)
- the position of profiling and its effective development (Harrison, Griffiths et al.)
- an approach to a psychological understanding of teachers in training (Vallance)
- a concern for the development of deep subject understanding (Prentice).

3.1 The role of open and distance learning in enhancing teacher professionalism

Alma Harris and Ann Shelton Mayes

Introduction

The 1990s witnessed an increasingly interventionist stance by successive Conservative Governments towards reform across the educational spectrum. Legislation signalled the Government's determination to redefine the role of teachers. Policies to control and manage the professional training and development of teachers have played a fundamental part in this process. For example the national regulations for initial teacher training (ITT) in England and Wales – Department for Education (DfE), 1992 and 1993 – introduced the notion of teacher competences for entry into the teaching profession. In 1996, the Government announced plans to tighten up on standards in teacher education by imposing a national core curriculum on all universities and colleges (*Times Educational Supplement*, 20 September 1996). As Hoyle and John point out:

> it is ironic that during the present century, when established professions of medicine and law have gradually developed extensive and sophisticated methods of professional preparation, the education of teachers faces a legitimacy crisis: one which calls into question the very basis upon which professionalization has traditionally been founded.
>
> (Hoyle and John, 1995:129)

For those involved in initial teacher education (ITE) the changes that have taken place in the last decade have been largely unprecedented in both scope and impact. ITE has been subject to radical change from a Government intent on removing teacher training from higher education and keen to locate it unambiguously in schools (Talbot, 1991). Indeed, the Government's pursuit of 'theory free', practical, teaching skills has meant the link between higher education and professional training has been seriously weakened.

The long-term effect of this loosening of higher education influence in pre-service training is difficult to gauge. In the short term, it is clear that the traditional independence of higher education institution's (HEI) teacher training and education courses has gradually been eroded. The emergence of alternative routes into teaching, such as the school-centred initial teacher training (SCITT) schemes, which are not required to enter into any partnership with higher education, understandably, met with some resistance. Indeed, some have viewed these initiatives as a further attempt to de-professionalize teaching (Hoyle and John, 1995; Ozga, 1988; Harris, 1997).

In practice, the central outcome has been the fragmentation and diversification of formal teacher preparation. Bridges (1995) describes this diversity of pre-service models with corporate (school-centred) and collaborative/professional (HEI-based) lying at either end of a continuum. He argues that in the short term corporate models extend the teacher's professionalism through involvement in providing pre-service training. However for the trainee, professionalism is diminished if access to alternative ideas is restricted.

The 'social market' and teaching

The chief ideological driving force behind this redefinition of the profession is what Elliott (1993) has termed the 'social market' view of teaching. This social market ideology is framed by certain basic assumptions, which have been transferred from the economic to the social cultural sphere of human activity. In essence, the major characteristic of the social market model of professional learning is that it views appropriately trained teachers as products which may be valued by consumers (in the form of school managers, parents and governors). This valuing is informed by immediate short-term requirements to meet specific needs or through the appointment or provision of appropriately targeted training. As Elliott argues:

> Products have to have markets and consumers. From a social market perspective, schools conceived as individual consumers of the products of teacher education are the market. And since these products are behavioural Outcomes in the form of practical skills schools also become the main sites for training activities at all phases (from this perspective professional learning is an Outcome of training rather than education).
>
> (Elliott, 1993:17)

The underlying principle entailed in this 'needs-driven' or 'social market' view is that of behaviourism. This basically assumes that required outcomes can be pre-specified in performance terms and that knowledge can be defined in output terms. Within such a behaviourist application, theoretical knowledge in training takes on a purely technical or instrumental significance. It is not highly valued and to a certain extent, is viewed as largely irrelevant in comparison with the acquisition of practical skills. At the core of this 'social market' perspective, therefore, is a desire to define with increasing accuracy those practical behaviours which lead to successful outcomes. The logic of the 'social market' model is premised on a narrow definition of performance. Consequently, teachers' professional development simply becomes the acquisition of further practical 'know how'.

The 'social market' model conveniently ignores the value base and the situational knowledge base encompassed in professional practice. Instead, it offers a narrowly instrumental assessment of teachers and teaching, which is wholly inadequate for reflecting the cognitive nature of professional activity. It is a model premised more on technical competence than intellectual development. Not surprisingly, the introduction of national competences for entry into the teaching profession has been viewed as further evidence of the de-profession-alization of teachers (Hyland, 1992). The central argument against a competency-based model largely revolves around the value placed on experience and the ability to demonstrate teaching skills. This is strongly reminiscent of an appenticeship model and tends to underline a craft-based approach to learning to teach.

A more optimistic view, however, has been offered by Whitty and Wilmott (1991) in support of broadly constructed competences in teacher education. They point to the positive aspects of these changes which they argue have led to:

● the clearer definition of role for both school and HEIs

● the improved confidence from employers in the outcomes

● the clarity of goals for students.

The redefinition of teaching

The net result of these changes has been to re-define ITE and, by association, to redefine the role of the teacher. Important transformations have occurred within teaching which have collectively contributed to a redefinition of the processes and practice of teaching. It has been suggested that these interventions have reduced the ability for teachers to control their own work and have largely separated conception from execution (Ozga and Lawn, 1988). This constitutes an attack on the professional nature of the teaching role, but one that can be resisted if teacher educators choose to make use of the flexibility that resides within the regulations in designing pre-service courses. Furlong (1995) has argued that the national competences are so loosely constructed as to offer teacher educators the opportunity to avoid a narrow mechanistic approach and use them to provide a helpful framework for developing the curriculum, pedagogy and assessment areas in pre-service courses.

The remainder of this chapter will focus on the Open University's (OU) Post Graduate Certificate in Education (PGCE) – a pre-service teacher education and training programme. It will argue that the OU

PGCE team has seized the challenges of recent legislation to design a course that reaffirms the professional dimension of teaching and, in working in partnership with teachers to deliver all aspects of the programme, enhances the professionalism of serving teachers. In particular, it argues that three distinct features of this course support the development of teacher professionalism. First, that the educational approach adopted in the OU's open and distance learning PGCE demands the student teacher take responsibility for his or her own professional development. Second, that the assessment model requires the student to demonstrate professional qualities as an essential dimension of teaching competence. Third, that involvement in a partnership that genuinely involves school staff as teacher educators in all aspects of a pre-service programme leads to enhanced professionalism of serving teachers.

The Open University's Post Graduate Certificate in Education

In the current UK climate of *diversity* and *choice*, there exists a wide range of ITE courses being offered from a greater variety of providers than ever before. A major stakeholder in this new provision is the Open University. In 1994, a pre-service programme was launched by the OU. Since then, over 1,000 graduates each year have entered the programme leading to the PGCE and qualified teacher status (QTS).

The OU's move into ITE preceded the highly political debates about teacher education of the early-1990s. Pressure from the student body was one of the main driving forces of this initiative. Research undertaken by the OU in the late-1980s revealed a substantial interest in an OU part-time PGCE among many undergraduates taking OU courses (Bourne and Leach, 1995), who, due to geographical isolation or personal commitments, were unable to access conventional routes for ITT. The remit for a new route with a substantive open and distance learning dimension and partnership with schools therefore fell within the OU's commitment to broadening access and opportunity.

The development of the OU PGCE involved the development of new approaches to ITE and ITT. Although the national criteria for initial teacher training in England and Wales (Department for Education, 1992 and 1993) had to be met, the means of doing so inevitably departed from conventional provision. It was impossible, and largely undesirable, to replicate all aspects of the practice of conventional providers. Consequently, OU PGCE differs in a number of distinctive ways from other types of ITE and ITT provision.

The framework for professional growth

First, the course structure (OU, 1994a). The OU PGCE is an 18-month part-time course divided into three stages. Each stage is characterized by a full-time block placement in the partner school. This together with a placement in a second school and a flexible school experience component to introduce breadth meets the DfE requirement for 18 weeks of school experience (Department for Education, 1992 and 1993). The student is given responsibility within a clear framework to organize these placements – once the school has been accepted on to the OU PGCE partnership. A common course framework allows for subject and phase development, but ensures a logic and coherence to the development of partnerships with over 1,000 schools each year and progression and continuity for students programme-wide.

Second, the resource frame (Open University, 1994a). Students are provided with a subject- and phase-specific self-study programme using a wide range of resources including AV and text; and a personal computer for the development of Information Technology (IT) capability, including electronic communication. The study programme is fully integrated with school experience. It encourages the development of high-level skills in personal time management and supports the student in systematically auditing and reviewing personal progress.

Third, the school experience guide (OU, 1994b). This is an extensive element of the course providing a coherent framework for school-based experience. The notion of a prescribed school-based curriculum ensures integration of school and self-study components of the course, and ensures a consistent set of learning opportunities are provided despite variable school contexts. It explicitly gives the student the major responsibility for organizing school-based activities and provides detailed guidance to support the student in completing them. The staged activities are designed to progressively develop the full range of teaching competences and professional qualities required for a newly qualified teacher.

Fourth, the Assessment Strategy (OU, 1994c).This explicitly requires students to produce evidence at each stage of the course of development of teaching competences and professional qualities. The evidence arises out of critical analysis of school experience using the educational ideas and issues explored in the linked study programme. The student engages in regular, systematic reviews of progress in teaching competences and professional qualities with the school-based mentor and undertakes formal self-assessment activities at each stage of the course.

Fifth, the support framework (Open University, 1994d and 1996). Students are supported by a network of partner school and university staff. Subject- and phase-specific mentors and tutors have a comparable role in training, supporting and assessing. Senior school and university staff have comparable monitoring and quality assurance roles. The inclusive nature of the partnership model which school staff a role in all aspects of ITT and ITE is critical in ensuring the enhanced professionalism of serving teachers working as teacher educators. In addition to a conventional tutorial programme, students are in direct phone and electronic link to tutors, subject co-ordinators and other students nationally.

The central tenet of the OU's open and distance learning PGCE course is that students take responsibility for their own learning but within the context of an explicit and supportive framework that provides the students with the management and analytical tools to achieve it. The features of the course already outlined clearly puts the onus on the student to take responsibility for their professional growth. As mature and independent adults they are expected to:

- organize their study programme
- manage their time
- negotiate working relationships with mentors and other school staff
- reflect critically on their work in a systematic way

- self-evaluate against criteria
- provide evidence to demonstrate professional growth.

The Open University's professional development and assessment model

The model of competency-based assessment adopted by the OU's PGCE takes into account the complexity of teaching which includes a professional values dimension. In making values an explicit dimension of the competence framework, other models of professional assessment were initially drawn on (Moon and Shelton Mayes, 1995). Winter (1992) had previously developed a competency-based assessment model for social workers which sought to integrate a values dimension.

A number of key principles guided the development of the assessment model. These were that:

- explicit learner outcomes must provide a structure for formative, diagnostic as well as summative assessment purposes
- outcomes presented in broadly defined competences terms must incorporate an explicit values dimension
- students had to be responsible for presenting evidence of achievement.

The OU PGCE model of assessment is conceptualized in terms of two dimensions of assessment. The first dimension comprises five areas of teaching competence which are recognized by teachers as defining their professional activities:

- curriculum/subject planning and evaluation
- classroom/subject methods
- classroom management
- assessment, recording and reporting
- the wider role of the teacher.

These are elaborated into a further four or five sub-categories to support systematic training, diagnostic assessment and self-assessment.

In parallel, the student is required to demonstrate professional qualities in the way that teaching competence is displayed. The demonstration of professional qualities is the second dimension of the OU's assessment model. There are some important points to be highlighted here. First, the defined professional qualities (the values dimension to the assessment scheme) are not assessed separately from the normal day-to-day tasks of the teacher. Professional qualities cannot exist in a vacuum, they require some context for realization. The model can, therefore, be conceived as a matrix. In this model, as students demonstrate growth within the defined areas of competence, they will simultaneously develop a foundation of evidence for their capability in relation to professional qualities.

Second, the model is viewed as primarily formative during the students' progression through the course. Finally summative judgements are made at the point when all necessary information is accumulated. Judgement on end-of-course competence is made at the holistic level, where students must demonstrate teaching that integrates all components. This stresses the importance of the interrelation of the various competences and professional qualities. Furthermore, it disavows an attempt by assessors to simply 'tick off' competences in a discrete and isolated way.

The whole assessment model is premised on the interplay between teaching competence and the demonstration of professional qualities. In this respect, evidence must be provided of professional competence and professional qualities simultaneously. Consequently, the OU PGCE assessment model is not based solely on narrow instrumental outcomes. Instead, it is premised upon the widest interpretation of professional development and teaching standards.

The model is primarily formative and diagnostic during the student's progression through the course. The explicit status of professional qualities in this model means that discussion of issues of values becomes part of the student's self-assessment activity and part of the assessment dialogue with tutors and mentors. This raises the profile of critical reflection on practice as integral to competence in teaching. Initial reactions by mentors and students on the PGCE course suggests that they find this explicit competency model supportive in structuring individual training activities during school placements and assuring summative judgements (Shelton Mayes, 1994). Furthermore, there is research evidence which demonstrates that the assessment model provides students and mentors with opportunities for reflection and self-analysis (Harris, 1995).

While the OU PGCE model of assessment is in its early stages of development, it opens up the possibility of teacher assessments which are school-based and student-led and specify clear standards for entry into teaching. These standards contribute to teacher professionalism in two ways. In public and societal terms it demonstrates that the teaching profession, like other professions, has explicit and demanding entry standards, and that teachers are involved in gatekeeping for their profession through their role in summative assessment. At the same time, this explicit formulation of outcomes creates an entitlement to the learner which places obligations and responsibilities on the teacher educator and on the schools. The incorporation of the values dimension, focusing on professional qualities within the model ensures an holistic approach to assessment and one that emphasizes the unique significance of preparing for entry into a profession.

The partnership model

The concept of partnership between schools and HEIs has been of central importance to the Government's plan for initial training. Unlike other PGCE courses, the OU's model does not project different weighting of time to university and school based time. As Blake et al. (1997) point out, students tend to view the one-third university and two-thirds school-based balance as evidence that 'experience and practice had been elevated above taught courses' (1996:22). In contrast, there is no such obvious division between theory and practice implicit in the OU's model of partnership. Clearly, the quality of the training provision is delicately balanced on the quality of the partnership arrangements. Establishing more teacher training in schools has forced, and continues to force, new roles for teachers and college tutors in the training of students. The OU's PGCE demands quite different roles and responsibilities within the partnership arrangement than full-time taught courses dictate.

An important distinguishing feature of the OU partnership with schools is the extent to which the notion of partnership pervades all aspects of the pre-service course. Schools and HEIs have defined roles in the selection of students, in training, in support and for formative and summative assessment. Uniquely, partnership extends to issues of quality assurance and monitoring. Mentors and tutors have parallel roles in relation to student training, support and assessment. This network of roles and responsibilities is clearly defined and articulated (OU, 1994b) for schools at point of entry to the partnership. Clarity in defining the partnership offers teachers a proper role in pre-service teacher education – one that carries genuine responsibility and offers opportunities for enhanced professionalism.

Conclusion

The OU's PGCE is premised on the highest tenets of profession practice. Its open and distance methodology and its mode of assessment demand that students place greater reliance on self-evaluation, critical reflection on practice and their own professional judgements. Within this model, there is greater scope and opportunity for on-going professional training and far greater potential for self-determination. The new *professionalism* characterized by the OU's approach to competency-based assessment offers a partnership approach to professional development in schools. It is aimed at encouraging self-initiative, independence and autonomy and ensuring students engage in debate and critical reflection on professional values issues as well as teaching skills.

As a result of the OU's involvement in ITE, many more schools are now involved in a partnership arrangement. The systematic evaluation and monitoring data collected by the OU, indicates that teachers perceive mentoring to have enhanced their own teaching and many have embarked on further professional development as a result of their involvement in the PGCE. In 1995 the OU's MA module in mentoring had a number of applicants who had mentored on the OU's PGCE. Involving schools in ITE and ITT partnership programmes represents one way forward for professional renewal and regeneration.

The process of collaboration with schools is still in its infancy. Yet, it may prove to be the basis on which the future professional development of teachers can be built. As Hoyle and John point out for this to occur, 'teacher educators have to make it clear to both policy makers and school personnel that the changes are beneficial and preferable to a wholly school centred conception of teacher preparation' (Hoyle and John, 1995:161). Furthermore, that involvement in teacher education has the wider purpose of enhancing professional expertise and professional development.

Thirty years ago, professional expertise tended to be identified with propositional knowledge and theoretical content, regardless of whether such knowledge was ever used in practice. Similarly, until very recently a separation between initial and continuing professional development was encouraged. If we are to move to a re-definition of teacher professionalism, such a separation can no longer be justified. As Eraut has argued:

> more interaction between the two and more explicit discussion of professional development during the post-qualification period would better prepare young professionals for their future problems and obligations; and awaken the interest of mid-career professionals in facilitating the 'on the job' training of their younger colleagues.
>
> (Eraut, 1994:58)

On a similar theme, Fullan has suggested that:

> teacher development and institutional development (of universities and schools) must go hand in hand. You can't have one without the other. If there ever was a symbiotic relationship that makes complete sense it is the collaboration of universities and school systems in the initial and ongoing development of educators.
>
> (Fullan, 1993:121)

It is suggested that open and distance learning has such a role to play in forging such relationships and in ensuring that a continuum of professional development is both achieved and sustained.

References

Blake, D. (1997), 'The place of higher education in teacher preparation', in Watson, K., Modgil, C. and Modgil, S. (eds) *Teachers, Teacher Education and Training*. London: Cassell.

Bourne, J. and Leach, J. (1995), 'Open learning and the PGCE: a primary experience', in Griffiths, V. and Owen:, *Schools in Partnership: Current Initiatives in School Based Teacher Training*. London: Paul Chapman.

Bridges, D. (1993), 'School-based teacher education', in Bridges, D. and Kerry, T., *Developing Teachers Professionally*. London: Routledge.

Department for Education (DfE) (1992), *Initial Teacher Training Circular 9/92*.

— (1993), *The Initial Training of Primary Teachers Circular 14/93*.

Elliott, J. (1993), 'Three perspectives on coherence and continuity in teacher education', in Elliott, J., *Reconstructing Teacher Education*. Lewes: Falmer.

Eraut, M. (1994), *Developing Professional Knowledge and Competence*. London: Falmer Press.

Fullan, M (1993) *Change Forces*. London: Falmer Press.

Furlong, J. (1995), 'The limits of competence: a cautionary note on Circular 9/92', in Kerry, T. and Shelton Mayes, A., *Issues in Mentoring*. London: Routledge.

Harris, A. (1995), 'Mentoring in Open and Distance Teacher Education'. Paper at ECER Conference, University of Bath.

— (1997), 'The de-professionalization and de-skilling of teachers', in Watson, K., Modgil, C. and Modgil, S. (eds) *Teachers, Teacher Education and Training*. London: Cassell.

Hoyle, E. and John:D. (1995), *Professional Knowledge and Professional Practice*. London: Cassell.

Hyland, T. (1992), 'Expertise and competence in further and adult education', *British Journal of In-service Education*, 18(1).

Moon, B. and Shelton Mayes, A. (1995), 'Integrating values into the assessment of teachers in initial education and training', in Kerry, T. and Shelton Mayes, A., *Issues in Mentoring*. London: Routledge.

Ozga, J. (1988), 'Teaching professionalism and work', in J. Dega (ed) *Schoolwork Approaches to the Labour Process of Teaching*. Buckingham: Open University Press.

Ozga, J. and Lawn, M. (1988), 'School work: interpreting the labour process of teaching', *British Journal of Sociology of Education*, 9(3), 289–306.

Open University (OU) (1994a), *The Open University Post Graduate Certificate in Education: Course Guide.*

—   (1994b), *The Open University Post Graduate Certificate in Education: School Experience.*

—   (1994c), *The Open University Post Graduate Certificate in Education: Assessment Guide.*

—   (1994d), *The Open University Post Graduate Certificate in Education: Handbook For Partner Schools.*

—   (1996), *The Open University Postgraduate Certificate in Education: School Co-ordinator's Guide.*

Shelton-Mayes, A. (1995), 'Mentoring and Assessment'. Paper at ATEE Conference, Prague.

Talbot, C. (1991), 'Towards school-based teacher training', *School Organization*, 11(1): 11-23.

Times Educational Supplement (1996), 'Shephard orders training re-design', 20 September, p.1.

Whitty, G. and Wilmott, E. (1991), 'Competence-based teacher education: approaches and issues',*Cambridge Journal of Education*, 21(3): 27-32.

Winter, R. (1992), The Asset Training Programme, Essex County Council Social Services Department and Anglia Polytechnic.

3.2 An alternative route to qualified teacher status – collaborative partnerships with the licensed teacher scheme (a personal view)

d'Reen Struthers

Introduction

The Licensed Teacher (LT) Scheme, introduced in 1989 by the Conservative Government of Britain was a new initiative that was intended to give more power to schools and assist with staffing problems in shortage subjects. If over 24, and with two years of higher education or the equivalent, with GCSE maths and English (or the equivalent), instructors in schools could become 'licensed to teach' if an appropriate training plan were submitted by the recommending body. After a training period of up to two years, the recommending body can apply for qualified teacher status (QTS).

The Government in 1987 used the words 'freedom, choice and responsibility' to characterize its vision for education in all public speeches and papers. With particular reference to initial teacher education (ITE) routes, it is evident that the LT Scheme was to honour this view – seen as one 'alternative route' into teaching which would give new freedoms (and responsibilities) to schools, and offer choice for entrants to the teaching profession.

This chapter begins with an historical overview, followed by the voices of two LTs from secondary schools. What were their experiences of the scheme at Middlesex University in 1996? Arising from their stories, I shall begin to tease out some of the issues which the LT Scheme raises for the teaching profession, before looking in more detail at the scheme which is now run at Middlesex University. Reference will also be made to the LT route available to overseas trained teachers (OTTs) to gain QTS.

From the 'Middlesex Experience', I will then consider some of the implications for the future of this 'alternative route' into teaching, with reference to the now tabled consultation document from the Department for Education (DfE) on the Graduate Teacher Programme and its proposals to 'reform' the LT, OTT and Registered Teacher Programmes.

Historical overview

When the Green Paper on the LT Scheme was published in 1988, the main teaching unions came out strongly against the proposals. The National Union of Teachers (NUT) deplored the development and argued that 'the absence of a professional qualification for all teachers cannot maintain, let alone improve standards in Education' (McAvoy, 1988). The National Association of Schoolmasters and Union of Women Teachers (NASUWT) described it as 'an attempt to get around the problem of shortages by dilution instead of responding to market forces by increasing pay to attract better teachers' (de Gruchy, N. 1988). The Assistant Masters and Mistresses Association (AMMA) suggested that the use of the licensed teachers represented an admission that the National Curriculum could not be delivered without a reduction in the quality of the teaching profession (*Times Educational Supplement*, 1988).

Indeed by July 1989, as the local education authorities (LEAs) made explicit their concerns about the scheme and the additional costs involved, more governmental money was made available through the LEAs training grants schemes. The draft regulations had also addressed LEA concerns about entry requirements, duration and nature of the required training and the QTS recommendation procedure.

With this context, Middlesex University began negotiations with LEAs, who in turn were looking at local agreements with the teaching unions. Sharing similar concerns, Middlesex University formed a consortium with LEA partners who endorsed the notion that only graduates would be considered for the LT route.

By 1992 Middlesex University staff had developed a unique ITE course for graduate LTs, which was validated in 1993 as a *classroom-based* Post Graduate Certificate in Education (PGCE). The design of the course was heavily influenced by the Oxford Internship Scheme (1990). As part of the overall course design, the final module was to function also as a 'stand alone' module to be taken by OTTs. The first group of OTTs came on the two week course in the summer of 1992.

LEAs at this time were still involved in managing the employment of all teaching staff. It was, therefore, easy for the LEAs in the consortium, to monitor those teachers employed without QTS.

Similarly with close school links, the LEAs were involved in working with schools to agree appointments of graduates to shortage subject posts, knowing that they would be eligible for the LT Scheme with Middlesex. This liaison role which LEA staff performed, was very important. Not only were they able to influence the selection of graduates to school positions, but Link Advisers and Inspectors were able to support the LT and the school, with LEA-provided in-service education and training (INSET) programmes. Their role also involved observing and assessing the LTs, as at this time, the LEA was recognized as the recommending body for QTS. Funding for the scheme was done through the Government Education Service and Training (GEST) budget which included funding for the LT scheme.

Peter's story

During my combined sports and science degree I worked with young people in various summer camps here and in the USA. On completion of my course, I continued working as a sports coach and instructor in various contexts in England, USA and Europe. Throughout this time I was told frequently 'you should go into teaching'. So I looked at various options to become qualified – from the Open University route, the one year PGCE route to the LT Scheme. I thought the idea of 'training on the job' was appealing, especially as I heard Middlesex offered a course for graduate LTs that led to a PGCE anyway.

I found a school that was not closed to the idea of the scheme, but who first wanted to give me a trial period. After a term, the school made connections with Middlesex who worked closely with the school to draw up a programme that had both a school and university element. My mentor went on a training course. Mondays were timetabled as free – so in the autumn term I was able to go and watch other teachers, work in other departments and watch colleagues in my own department. When the course started at Middlesex in the spring term, I was surprised how different the other school contexts were to my own. This helped me understand how supported I was, and indeed to appreciate my school context more. Being with other LTs is also good because you get to hear about other situations, far broader that your own situation. I think this broader perspective is important, especially when considering becoming a true professional. As part of the course, I have to write a journal. I sometimes look back on what I have said and it is good to feel as if I have moved – 'Gosh did I used to think that?'. It helps you feel as if your ideas are changing and something is happening. I have talked to other PGCE students and I am still glad I am on this course. At least my experience is consistent and happens daily rather than in blocks of time. It is easier to step back from your experience perhaps once a week with others in the same boat than having to jump in the deep end and sink or swim.

Nicole's story

After my high school in Germany I attended a university course for three years as part of a programme to gain a degree and teaching qualifications in Germany. The opportunity for me to work on an exchange programme in England looked attractive – I could improve my English and work as a German teaching assistant in an English secondary school.

For personal reasons I decided to stay in this country and eventually had a full-time assistant's post in a school in Essex. Keen to stay and having heard about the LT Scheme, I approached the school. A training programme was developed with Middlesex University on the understanding that my German qualifications could be transferred to a British work-based learning degree.

My mentor is head of a shrinking department, which has failed to maintain a consistent level of staffing for the past two years. He has not been trained as a mentor. Although I have been given some free periods (part of the Middlesex requirement for the course) my shift from 'assistant' to 'licensed teacher' has been very traumatic because of almost non-existent support within the school. Suddenly I find myself teaching 10 different classes, including the requirement that I teach French (not studied since my own high-school days) to a year nine class (GCSE) and most recently, being expected to take on even more classes with the sudden resignation of another teacher from the department. So, I have been 'teaching' 7 weeks, have not had one visit from my school mentor and the school now seems more concerned with 'crowd control' than my ability to 'class-control and teach'. My tutor at Middlesex is trying to negotiate with the school that the situation changes. Meanwhile, I enjoy the university sessions – having the chance to talk with other LTs, to get ideas about classroom approaches and to begin to contemplate why and how I am doing things. As part of the course I am required to write a journal – a time-consuming activity, which at first I resented. However, I am beginning to appreciate that while the school gives me no support, my own journal acts as a reminder of how I am improving. I read back over past week's entries and I have to laugh. Did I really think that? This helps reminds me that yes, I am developing and indeed I am able to make sense of both the practice and the theory.

I am still awaiting the start of the school-based sessions. I gather Middlesex will have to step in, to ensure the joint programme as agreed by both partners is carried out. Thank goodness the university is keeping an eye on the school! I wonder what it is like for LTs who just have a school programme – who checks the school is doing the job it said it would do? If nothing gets resolved at the school, I think I will lose my motivation. How can Middlesex give credit for a school-based programme that is missing? What will I gain at the end? The school will, I think, try to exploit the situation, but hopefully quality control measures from Middlesex and the Teacher Training Agency (TTA) will save me. But I want to become a teacher.

Both of these stories highlight some of the very real dilemmas and concerns about the LT Scheme. Peter is a graduate, working in a school department with a trained mentor who not only participated in the preparation of the training programme, but who, as a senior manager in the school, has been able to advocate on Peter's behalf for timetable space, etc. Nicole on the other hand, is a non-graduate, with very little 'teaching experience', who is now facing the reality of full teaching responsibilities, within a department where there is limited support and an inexperienced mentor. Both, it is hoped, will receive QTS. Peter is on the PGCE route for LTs which Middlesex offers, and Nicole is more than likely (with the accreditation of her previous studies in Germany, her experience and the course credit gained on the LT course at Middlesex) to receive a Work-based Learning Degree (Education/ German). The recommendation for QTS is made by their respective schools.

For both of these LTs, their needs were assessed and, together, the respective school and I (as the university tutor) drew up a training plan. Both parties identified what they felt their strengths were in terms of provision. The school offered on the spot 'craft knowledge'[1] about the job. What Middlesex offered was a structured developmental course programme into which this craft knowledge could be easily placed. Both parties realized that their instructors would be able to experience broader aspects of teaching with the involvement of a higher education institution (HEI). The LT would be learning alongside others, while at the same time being able to have a distance from his or her immediate context within the school, to contemplate other alternative approaches teased out during the Middlesex programme which would complement the school. In this way, the collaborative partnership ensures that the LT's school-based experiences and training are integrated with the university course.

In both of the above instances, the school considered the scheme as a way to meet staffing shortages and retention problems in the subjects these particular LTs both offered. The Modes of Teaching in Education (MOTE) Project commissioned to survey the LT Scheme throughout the country, reported that from the 1990–1 figures, 'the most frequently reported reason for introducing the LTS was to reduce teacher shortages ... reflecting the traditional problem of recruiting and retaining teachers in particular subject areas' (Barrett et al., 1993:15).

However, in addition to this with inspections by the Office for Standards in Education (OFSTED) prompting schools to look at the qualifications of all staff, schools are now approaching Middlesex University with stories of 'teachers' who have been working in the schools for many years, but often with no formal teaching qualifications. These schools are keen to show that all their staff, if not trained,are attached to training programmes. Some of these 'instructors' (not fully qualified teachers) may have two years of higher education, others may not.

The Middlesex Scheme can accommodate such demands

Phil's story

Phil has been a PE instructor in a school for six years – having left school at 16 to become a professional footballer for Millwall. He had no formal qualifications whatsoever, apart from GCSE English. However his many years of experience working within the sports area and with young people meant that he was able to submit a profile of his experience, learning and sporting qualifications to Middlesex University for accreditation. The head of the school of education, who assessed his portfolio was 'impressed not only with Phil's breadth of experience, but also with his insightful understanding of what was involved in teaching and learning'. Initially of course, he first had to complete an equivalence test for GCSE maths. (One of the basic entry requirements for teaching in England.) In Phil's case, the school was very concerned to promote this 'wonderfully dedicated teacher', who was clearly an asset to the profession.

Selection criteria for the Scheme

Because the Scheme is now under TTA authority, and totally school-driven, I am (as an ITE provider), very conscious of a whole number of issues around selection. Of course what I perceive about a candidate, might not be wholly visible to the school and vice-versa. The school might want to promote someone into the Scheme because 'he or she fits' into the culture of the school. Yet I have to address a broader issue of 'a new entrant for the teaching profession'. How would this person measure up in another context? Is the recommendation based solely on how the school perceives the potential LT's *relationships with pupils*, with no account of the quality of his or her professional approaches, which may be inconsistent?

As part of our approach, the programme leader will always interview the candidate in question, and for some, an observation of his or her teaching will be made. A professional dialogue between all participants is then entered into, which develops mutual trust between the school and Middlesex. For example, the educational language we are using is clarified. In this way, the personnel from both institutions involved in the partnership, begin to create a relationship that is transparent. Therefore, when dilemmas arise, we have mutual grounds to raise questions. This approach is important because both parties have significantly different roles to play in the ITE of an LT.

When describing the Middlesex LT Scheme to the schools, the potential LT is always asked what he or she hopes to be doing in five years. If he or she is keen to pursue a career in teaching, the school is encouraged to consider the award-bearing course – pointing out the implications of how a potential new employer may view a totally school-based route to QTS. The Middlesex experience is that no graduates have rejected the offer to gain a PGCE with Middlesex, as well as QTS via the LTS. Indeed, some schools and instructors who initially imagined this was an 'easy route', have expressed their gratitude to Middlesex University for the rigour and challenge they experienced which helped to ensure the quality of the school-based component, and provided the successful LT graduate with the status of a PGCE award which is acknowledged as the professional qualification for teaching in England.

This has been a very important factor for ethnic minority teachers, entering the teaching profession through this route.

Changes to the scheme

With the take-over of the GEST[2] budget by the TTA, many changes occurred. From the TTA literature, the scheme allows maintained schools and non-maintained special schools to appoint individuals with suitable qualifications who, after a period of employment and training under license, can be recommended to the DfEE, where appropriate, for the award to QTS.[3]

Effectively therefore, in keeping with other Government legislation, LEA participation has been significantly reduced. LEA involvement is now initiated by the school, who might seek the advice and support of such Link personnel.

Change in legislation has also had an impact on the functioning of the Middlesex Scheme. In the past, the LEA approached Middlesex about potential LTs or OTTs for the scheme. It was the LEA which completed all the necessary qualification and background checks. Checks still need to be done however, and from experience, we have learned not to assume that the individual school has looked into these thoroughly. Thus, to ensure our own standards and quality control at the point of entry, Middlesex staff have often been involved in time extensive checks, especially for OTTs.

Similarly, in the absence of LEA liaison, all paperwork is the domain of the schools, an intimidating reality for some schools, although Middlesex staff do their best to assist.

However perhaps what is most significant, is the additional monitoring role the Link adviser/inspector used to offer. As part of a school visit, the LEA adviser might discuss the progress of the LT, classroom observations would take place and the school-based programme (mentor discussions, induction programmes, etc.) would be reviewed. Indeed, although Middlesex tutors would only visit twice a term, Link Advisers would be frequently in the school and be able to report back to Middlesex when necessary.

Although we at Middlesex hold tightly to our mission to uphold rigorous quality assurance procedures and standards, given the award-bearing nature of our courses, what now happens in schools is often out of our hands. The Memorandum of Co-operation between the school and the HEI may be a point of reference for us both, but timetable constraints, staff shortage and quality of 'in-house' delivery within the school, all impact on the equality of opportunity which the Scheme theoretically tries to promote. After all, we, as the HEI partner, are really employed by the school to provide just one or two aspects of the training programme – course design and input and assessment of teaching.

The context for the shift away from HEI and LEA involvement has been described by McCulloch (1993), according to whom over the past decade there has been the evolution 'of policies designed to limit the influence of higher education institutions on initial teacher education programmes'. In a consultation document (DES, 1992), the then Secretary of State for Education and Science announced that 'schools should play a much larger part in initial teacher training as full partners of higher education institutions' (p.1, para.1). In that same year Circular 9/92 (Department for Education, 1992) gave schools a much stronger voice generally in partnership training, arguing for joint responsibility for course planning and management, selection, training and assessment of students. The LT Scheme however, was still an alternative because, joint responsibility under the Scheme was not considered necessary. Elliot (1991) suggested that the LT Schemes were precursors of this school-based thrust of ITE and argued that the schemes produce 'a craft model of the occupation, and an apprenticeship model of training' (1991:310).

Thus, with policy initiatives that implied a transfer of power from HEIs to schools, there was an underlying implication for what should be taught and how learning should take place. Now situated in schools, the term 'apprenticeship' was being used. Students would learn from experts on the job, practical experience being preferable and certainly more likely in schools, than the more reflective, awareness-raising practices provided by HEIs. The underlying question was about the relationship between theory and practice. The new Government initiatives seemed to be promoting the importance of practice at the expense of theory and demoting the place of theorizing about practice.

The course at Middlesex University however attempts to address this dilemma. In the first term, the focus is on classroom perspectives. The second term takes a step back, looking at whole-school issues. The aim of the third module is to 'enable students to gain theoretical perspectives for their own classroom practice'. Almost everything we call teaching is underpinned by theories of how human beings learn and what constitutes human knowledge. However, because we are part of a tradition of schooled learning which has developed over the past century, much of this remains implicit. In this module, entitled 'Theoretical Underpinnings of Classroom Learning' we make explicit some of the main theories which have informed those traditions. We ask LTs to relate these to their own classroom strategies as well as examining the theories themselves, in order to assess their relative strengths and limitations from practical perspectives. The final module, 'Historical Perspectives and Recent Developments' addresses the English educational context. Possible to be taken as a 'stand alone' module for OTTs, this module also offers an opportunity for beginning teachers to talk with OTTs about their experiences and understandings of the profession and is always very illuminating.

Running concurrently throughout the year is also an Information Technology (IT) strand and a generic curriculum module, along with blocks of assessed teaching. There are three major assignments expected across the 18-month course and students are also required to keep a journal throughout the duration of the course. They will frequently call on these journal reflections in specific workshop/dialogue sessions, where students are encouraged to share their contemplations with colleague, teasing out themes, issues and professional dilemmas that have arisen.

The school-based programme, which is drawn up by the school and Middlesex staff, takes account of the individual's needs and the opportunities for the school to contribute to the professional education of the LT. Sessions are arranged to integrate the student's learning. From mentor sessions within the school, the LT is able to raise issues discussed with other LTs during their one-day-a-week release to attend the Middlesex course. Similarly, ideas and strategies discussed on the course are taken back into the school and deliberated and contextualized.

The true collaborative partnership?

McIntyre (1991) argues that for a collaborative partnership to be effective, there should be a commitment to developing a training programme where students are exposed to different forms of educational knowledge. Certainly, in the Middlesex Licensed Teacher Scheme, the opportunity for schools to work alongside an HEI and indeed involve other agencies is possible. Many of our schools work in consortiums which provide NQT induction programmes – the sessions being conducted by a range of teachers from the consortium. Some will make use of LEA personnel (advisory teachers, inspectors and subject consultants). Others will make use of LEA induction programmes (where they are still available). In this way, the students are expected to make use of a range of different learning opportunities and perspectives, reflecting on their own growing body of professional knowledge.

Planning and monitoring are certainly a collaborative effort. Initial planning is concerned with the preparation of the training programme for the TTA. Once the framework has been agreed, the school is then expected to organize the detail of the school-based sessions and collaborate with other staff where appropriate. The Middlesex course documentation is shared with schools and meetings are held for LT mentors and Middlesex tutors to get together at least once a term to discuss any concerns about the course and the various roles of people involved. These mentor clinics have proved a very valuable way for those involved in the programme to discuss professional questions, for example the frequency of mentor meetings, ways of monitoring progress and issues about giving feedback to students.

The assessment of the LT is covered from three different angles. School mentors regularly observe the LTs and will make two assessed teaching visits a term. Middlesex tutors will visit at least once a term and there are two periods of assessed teaching where two visits are made within a six week period. Finally, triangulation is completed with an external assessor, often from an LEA, coming to visit the LT three times across the six terms. Each term, reports from each are circulated and the dialogue continues. In addition, the school has an assessment portfolio for each LT where reports are made of the LT's competences – both his or her general competence as a teacher and also subject-specific knowledge and subject application as per DES Circular 9/92.

In this way, at the end of the LT course, evidence is available to support the school's recommendation for QTS from Middlesex University, the school and an external assessor. The mentor training course the University offers, complements the collaborative partnerships we hope to be able to develop with schools. During the course, mentors are encouraged to talk about their views of good practice and to make explicit their own understandings about their personal professional knowledge. Ways of observing colleagues and working to promote change are also included in the course along with other issues relating to the role of mentor. The university staff who work on these courses are also tutors on the LT Scheme. In this way too, mentors attending who will be working with LTs have an opportunity to participate in professional dialogue with HEI staff. Mutual trust and personal relationships are established which is vital not only for successful collaboration, but for the individual LT.

A future way forward?

What has been presented in this chapter is a personal view of one scheme which has successfully been running in the south-east of England since 1992. The quality of the course has become well respected by the TTA. All partners benefit from the scheme, not least the graduate LT who has the opportunity to gain a classroom-based PGCE or for non-graduates, a Work-Based Learning Degree. The OTT Package has also gained recognition within and around Greater London. Students come from as far afield as Kettering, Northamptonshire, and Clacton, Essex. Numbers are modest, 8-10 per year on the longer LT course and 10-15 teachers twice a year, for the OTT course. Hardly a challenge to the present forms of ITE in England.

However, the TTA has recently tabled a consultation document which looks set to challenge not only the above model, but also to potentially threaten the existing PGCE routes led by HEIs at present. The proposed Graduate Teacher Programme it is claimed, will provide a new employment-based route to QTS, alongside the LT and OTT Schemes which will be 'merged and reformed'. In actual fact, it would appear that the proposals are to offer two different routes for graduates and non-graduates. With the underlying assumption that there are many potential teachers out there who would prefer to join the teaching profession via these alternative routes, the possibilities look set to again threaten standards and professional training and education of teachers. Rather than making the existing pathway more flexible, the suggestions promise to throw all those involved in ITE into another round of defending strategies to protect the rigours of the professional preparation of teachers. Further, this new Graduate Teacher Programme assumes that many more schools than are now participating are eager to be involved in the professional preparation of teachers. From my experience, this is not true. Indeed, when challenged to consider the impact of having unqualified staff, who often have very limited experience of schools and classrooms, schools have expressed their concerns about the amount of support they would need to give. So although at first it might appear that this option will relieve the pressure on overburdened staffing budgets, the rest of the staff are often called on to add the support of an instructor to their job descriptions. You can imagine the resentment and the consequences!

Personally, I think there are lessons to be learnt from the LT Scheme. As the New Right are pursuing their policies with rigour, ITE providers must themselves reassess the traditions and authority they have enjoyed in the past. Perhaps there are ways in which both schools and HEIs could benefit from considering more truly collaborative partnerships? I believe the profession as a whole needs to respond to the challenges of the new Government initiatives. Rather than defending existing traditions, we should all be exploring ways to increase open dialogue about what we consider is important in the preparation of teachers. In the process, colleagues in schools may begin to have ownership over their own needs for reflection, critical thinking and continued 'professional' development. For those of us in HEI, we may begin to respect the reality of class and school demands – so different from our own working environments. Certainly, I feel very privileged to work closely with schools involved in the LT Scheme. The mutual respect and understanding of our different skills, knowledge and experience can only lead to a greater unity in the teaching profession.

Of course we need unity not only about our professional views and standards, but also about the resourcing of education generally. Under threat, no-one feels open to reframe their ideas and visions. Could responding more openly to new initiatives, while not losing our professional integrity actually provide opportunities to bring more capital, resourcing and creative energy to a tired and demoralized teaching profession? The future is perhaps more in our own hands than we realize?

Notes

1   A term used to describe what teachers actually do in the classroom and referred to in McNamara and Desforges (1978).

2   GEST budgets were delegated to LEAs when it became apparent that there would be little support for the scheme from unions and LEAs unless reasonable funding was available.

3   TTA Licensed Teacher Schemes: Recommendation Pack for Teachers 1995.

References

McAvoy, D. (1988), *Times Educational Supplement*, 25 May.

Barrett, E. et al. (1993), *The Licensed Teacher Scheme*. Modes of Teacher Education Project Survey, 15.

DeGruchy, N. (1988), *Times Educational Supplement*, 25 May. *Times Educational Supplement* (1988), 11 November.

Department for Education (DfE) (1992), *Initial Teacher Training (Secondary Phase) Circular 9/92*. London: DfE.

DES (1992), *Reform of Initial Teacher Training: A Consultation Document*. London: DES.

Elliott, J. (1991), 'A model of professionalism and its implications for teacher education', *British Educational Research Journal*, 17, 309–18.

McCulloch, M. (1993), 'Democratization of teacher education: new forms of partnership for school-based initial teacher education', in Gilroy: and Smith, M., 'International Analysis of Teacher Education', *Journal of Education for Teaching*. Oxford: Carfax Publishing Co.

McIntyre, D. (1991), 'The Oxford internship scheme and the Cambridge analytical framework: models of partnership in initial teacher education', in Booth, M., Furlong, J. and Wilkin, M., *Partnerships in Initial Teacher Training*. London: Cassell.

McNamara, D. and Desforges, C. (1978), 'The Social Sciences, teacher education and the objectification of craft knowledge', *British Journal of Teacher Education*, 4(1), 17–36.

3.3 Aspects of the mentoring process within a secondary initial teacher education partnership

Anne Williams, Graham Butt, Sue Butterfield,
Carol Gray, Sue Leach, Alan Marr, Allan Soares

Introduction

This chapter uses data gathered during the first phase of a study of mentoring to generate an agenda of questions about the process. The work described here represents the first steps in the development of a theory of the mentoring process which seeks to inform effective practice through a better understanding of how mentoring style relates to learning needs. The chapter will outline the context for the research, summarize the findings and discuss a possible model for mentoring styles. More detailed accounts of the findings from this project may be found elsewhere (Williams, Leach and Marr, forthcoming; Williams et al, forthcoming).

The importance of an improved understanding of mentoring as a process lies in the potential significance of a match between mentoring style and the learning needs of individual beginning teachers. This has implications on two levels. First, a serious mismatch may lead to the withdrawal of a Post Graduate Certificate in Education (PGCE) student from initial teacher education (ITE) altogether. Second, it may limit opportunities for beginning teachers to reach an optimum level of competence which is clearly of significance in the context of a perceived need to improve the classroom performance of newly qualified teachers (NQTs).

Literature in this area alludes both to the stages of learning through which student teachers are said to pass and to the existence of different approaches to mentoring. Calderhead (1987) characterizes phases in the process of learning to teach as 'fitting in', 'passing the test' and 'exploring'. Furlong and Maynard (1995) also identify developmental stages which they describe as 'early idealism', 'personal survival', 'dealing with difficulties', 'hitting a plateau' and 'moving on'. They go on to make the point that, while stages of beginning teacher learning can be identified, this does not necessarily lead them to think about different things at different phases of practice. Rather, as Guillaume and Rudney (1993) have noted, student teachers have a number of concerns which they continue to hold simultaneously. Maynard and Furlong do, however, propose a conception of mentoring as a developmental process when they suggest four stages of mentoring: model, coach, critical friend and co-enquirer. This suggests the existence of variations in mentoring style which is also alluded to by other writers.

Rikard and Veal (1996) characterize the styles of co-operating teachers in the USA as 'do it your way', 'do it my way' or 'we'll do it together'. Saunders, Pettinger and Tomlinson (1995), in an analysis of interviews with 29 mentors, suggest that mentors can be placed loosely into one of four 'types' (although they do not suggest that these types are necessarily discrete):

- the hands-off facilitator
- the progressively collaborative mentor
- the professional friend
- the classical mentor.

Copeland (1982) analyses student teacher supervision in terms of the use of directive or non-directive approaches by supervisory teachers. He suggests that, not only may students have a preference for one style over another, but, more importantly, student preferences and needs may change over time. If, as he suggests, and consistent with the notion of phases in the student learning process, many beginning teachers tend to move from a need for a fairly directive approach early in their practical experience to a much less directive one during the latter stages, then the need for flexible approaches from mentors becomes crucial to the continued progress of the trainee teacher. Saunders, Pettinger and Tomlinson (1995) suggest that the extension of the repertoires of individual mentors could be desirable.

It appears from the above that a variety of perspectives have been used in this country and elsewhere in order to discuss approaches to mentoring, but that the development of a typology of mentoring styles parallel to those used to analyse teaching remains at a rudimentary stage. It has been noted by several writers that good teachers do not necessarily make good mentors and that helping adults to learn is not the same as teaching children (Koerner, 1992; DES/HMI, 1991). Brooks, Fitch and Robinson (1994) partially account for this when they draw attention to the culture of dependency often encouraged in institutions such as schools where child–adult relationships predominate. These may inhibit the development of a more equal relationship between co-tutors/mentors and beginning teachers. Teaching styles have been characterized and analyzed through observing interactions between teachers and pupils. In seeking to understand better what a style of mentoring might involve, access to the interactions which take place between students and mentors was, therefore, considered to be essential.

The study

The work outlined in this chapter grew from an interest in the nature of the interactions which take place between beginning teachers and their co-tutors/mentors during the weekly discussion meetings required by the PGCE secondary course which was the focus of the investigation. Dialogue between mentors and trainees is essentially a private process which has hitherto tended to be reported second-hand (e.g. through accounts of meetings from students or mentors), if at all.

The project involved recording and transcribing conversations between mentors and beginning teachers to generate an agenda for subsequent interviews with the participants and a framework from which the beginnings of a theory could be developed. Thus, the outcome of this project would become the basis for future work. Mentors were asked to tape record their conversations with beginning teachers during weekly meetings. Following preliminary analysis of the transcripts, interviews were conducted with the beginning teachers and their mentors. A total of 34 discussions was finally transcribed involving eight mentors and 15 PGCE students. Six of the mentors and 11 students were interviewed later. Not all mentors were able to tape all meetings for a variety of reasons, but in all cases at least three recordings were made and all spanned several weeks during the course of a one-term placement.

Findings

Preliminary reading of the transcripts revealed three issues which seemed worthy of closer scrutiny. First, different mentors talked about different things and with differing degrees of focus. At opposite ends of a continuum, one meeting consisted of dialogue focused almost exclusively on classroom management, while another included a review of the whole range of competences specified in Circular 9/92. Second, mentors appeared to vary considerably in the 'role' which they were playing. One seemed to proffer advice, whether this was solicited or not. Another used questions to encourage the student to think out her own solutions to issues which had arisen. A third spent a significant amount of time providing encouragement and reassurance. Third, the proportion of dialogue provided by the mentor varied considerably, as did the form of the dialogue, that is balance between questions, directive statements and exposition of some kind. Each of these aspects is taken in turn.

The focus of mentoring

One would expect the competences outlined in Circular 9/92 (Department for Education, 1992) to emerge during discussions between mentors and beginning teachers, implicitly if not overtly, since it is against these that were expected to fit in to the school. The mentors were equally anxious to avoid rocking the boat. It seemed that the equilibrium of the school would be disturbed if pupil learning were disrupted (an even greater worry in an era of league tables), if ITT impeded the other role functions of mentors, or if the students made over-reaching demands on an already stretched set of colleagues. Yet the mentors also received vast amounts of advice from higher education on the extent of their new roles as mentors.

We explored, as a subsidiary study, the role or identity construction of 10 primary school mentors in interviews with them and their headteachers. In none of the schools were adjustments being made at school level to accommodate the new and extended demands of the mentor role. At the same time, none saw any advantage for the school in involvement ITT other than the new ideas already mentioned. When we looked at what was happening, it seemed that mentoring was operating as an extension of previous supervisory practices in essentially conservative ways (Edwards and Collison, 1996b). There had been no metanoia within the schools. Hence any transformational potential of initial training in schools had not been recognized.

A possible future for initial teacher education for primary teachers

It is at this point that I have to move from the data to become speculative and simply indicate possible developments centred on ITT and their potential for the educational continuum. Senge (1990) argues that metanoia can be transformational for the organisations concerned. If followed through, it can move them out of spirals of difficulty or stagnation into new ways of operating. At the centre of the idea of transformation in ITT lies a reconception of the relationship between host schools and universities. Currently, the quality of partnerships depends largely on the potentially vulnerable and fragile but pivotal relations of teacher mentors and the university-based link tutors who work closely with specific schools. The linkages are potentially vulnerable because the connections that hold the training programme together are at the level of individuals and not institutions. The fragility

It is not always easy for tutors to move between the communities to which they belong. However, as they move back and forth, they are able to inform each community with data from the others. Of equal importance, when they work with teacher mentors and student teachers they might be doing three things. They can lead mentors into the community of practice of teacher educators, they are able to gain understandings which will inform their research and can illuminate discussions of practice with theoretical reasoning which will inform both teachers and students.

What I have described places enormous demands on teacher mentors and is a considerable extension of the mentors' role. As Maynard (1996) has indicated, mentoring as currently operating in primary schools is by comparison quite limited in function. Nevertheless, to return to the theme of dialogues as a counter to fragmentation, discussions between teachers, university-based colleagues and students about practice are clearly important opportunities for countering fragmentation.

Connecting initial teacher training to wider educational developments

Our data suggest that a useful first stage in the process of connection would be to end the isolation of mentoring for ITT from other aspects of school life. We found that the majority of the mentors in our study saw their mentor function to be just another demand on their time. Some felt an element of conflict. Being 'torn in two' between students and pupils was too prevailing a metaphor for comfort in our interviews with mentors in the first year of the study. However as the schools became more attuned to the requirements of the programme, mentors did look to, for example, curriculum co-ordinators for support in their work with students. Although this might be a useful step which would enrich students' experiences, it did not seem to do much to reduce the potentially stressful and obviously pivotal role of the mentors as the point at which the HEI connected to the school.

The mentors together with their students found themselves in quite paradoxical positions. The students were welcomed for their fresh ideas and were expected to develop as practitioners. Yet simultaneously they personal support role. Tensions are also noted between the supporting and assessing roles demanded of the mentor (Dart and Drake, 1994; Jacques, 1992; Hill, Jennings and Madgwick, 1992), between the needs of the pupils and those of the beginning teachers (Back and Booth, 1992) and between the need to support and to challenge (Daloz, 1986; Martin, 1996).

As with the focus of the meetings, the transcripts were read in order to produce a list of mentors' behaviours which would be analyzed and related to particular roles. In addition notes of interviews with beginning teachers and mentors were scrutinized for further indicators of roles mentioned. The roles have been grouped into the broad areas identified within the literature related to teaching, evaluation and personal support.

Teaching related

These relate to the mentor's role as teacher, trainer or facilitator of learning. At various times, and in varying amounts, mentors provided trainees with advice and guidance about what they could or should do with:

- various kinds of information
- practical strategies for use in specific situations
- general learning opportunities through encouragement to approach their work in one way rather than another
- particular learning opportunities by setting up situations to meet a specific need
- access to their own experience or insights into their personal philosophies
- encouragement to think and reflect
- non-judgemental feedback on lessons
- role models.

The role of *adviser* or *guide* was mentioned by all mentors and beginning teachers interviewed. What emerged from the transcripts was the very considerable variation in the subject-matter of advice offered, although several topics recurred. There was also some diversity in the way advice and guidance was given. The latter point will be explored more fully in the next section.

Provision of information was also mentioned by all mentors and by almost all beginning teachers, although some of the latter's comments took the form of criticism of the mentor who, in their judgement, had not given sufficient information. Transcripts revealed information about a wide range of school procedures or policies, about issues related to subject teaching and, in some cases, about wider aspects of the teacher's role.

Offering practical strategies refers to the mentor role in offering help with how to achieve particular ends in very specific contexts. Again it was mentioned by all mentors and by most beginning teachers, although one referred to a lack of help with practical strategies. Most examples here were about work in the classroom, management of pupils or different teaching strategies.

Other aspects of the mentor's role referred to ways in which the mentor could facilitate trainee learning more indirectly than in the examples given hitherto. Some mentors talked to beginning teachers about their own concurrent experience of teaching a particular topic.

Other remarks concentrated on the mentor's personal approach to a particular teaching strategy. Sometimes personal beliefs were offered, instead of examples of the mentor's own practice.

All the mentors mentioned their role in *offering learning opportunities* during interviews as did many beginning teachers. This often took the form of encouraging trainees to see their placement as offering opportunities to experiment and to try things out. Sometimes this was introduced very early in the placement. At other times it was encouraged at a later stage. Some were also encouraged to try new things by acknowledgement by the mentor that doing something differently was acceptable. At other times the mentor encouraged the beginning teachers to identify issues for future discussion or action.

Reflection is a much over-used term. The term is used here to refer to aspects of mentor–trainee interaction, which provokes thought on the part of the latter, so that he or she is actively involved in his or her own learning rather than receiving information or guidance passively. All the mentors referred to this in some way during interviews. Most beginning teachers also mentioned it, although some did so critically – either because they wanted more of this kind of help or because they would have preferred to be told what to do. Sometimes mentors encouraged the beginning teachers to think through the implications of what they were planning either for them as teachers or for individual pupils. Sometimes there was encouragement simply to consider alternatives. Beginning teachers were also encouraged to evaluate alternatives which they had used. They were encouraged to consider the purpose of a specific strategy as well as focusing on its effectiveness. Some trainees were asked to reflect on their own progress as well as the progress of their pupils.

Feedback on lessons came into two categories. Most feedback was judgemental to some extent and this is described later. There did appear to be occasions when non-judgemental feedback was offered, generally in the form of a commentary.

The mentor as *role model* is not one which would emerge in transcripts, but it is included because, during interviews, two mentors and three students mentioned it as being significant for them. Its wider significance, therefore, merits further investigation.

Evaluative roles

Given the tensions between support and assessment identified in the literature about mentoring, it came as no surprise that this group of roles emerged both from the transcripts and from interviewing mentors and beginning teachers. Four aspects of evaluative activity emerged:

- praise or censure which could be about any element of practice
- feedback about lessons, which might be positive or negative
- target setting, which involved identifying future priorities
- the formal assessment of the beginning teacher's performance.

The balance between giving *praise* and *censure* would obviously depend on performance and progress as well as on the predisposition of the mentor. Most examples that emerged were of praise, although critical comment was evident. Praise could be about the beginning teacher's general approach or it could be quite specific.

Much *feedback on lessons* also involved praise or criticism. It could take the form of an overall comment on what had been observed. Many comments began with an evaluative remark and went on to explain why that particular judgement had been made. Some feedback tempered praise with a suggestion that there was scope for improvement. Critical feedback could also be diluted by reassurance that the issues raised were not major ones.

Target setting was undertaken by the mentors in some cases where targets were very clearly based directly on a judgemental observation by the mentor, whether general or very specific. Other mentors put the onus on the beginning teacher to identify his or her own personal targets.

Assessment is characterized separately because the comments included relate to judgements that were more summative in nature than the preceding ones in this section, although there was not always a clear distinction between summative and formative feedback. Sometimes mentors made specific comments related to the assessment of the beginning teacher, which is according to criteria laid down on a report form which has to be completed and returned to the university. At other times the mentor summarized the overall assessment made.

Personal support

All beginning teachers made it clear during their interviews that the personal support received was of prime importance to them. This aspect of support was also mentioned by all mentors although they did not appear to attach quite the same importance to it.

Much support took the form of assuring the beginning teachers that what they were experiencing was to be expected. Some mentors used comparison with their own practice in order to reassure. Others emphasized that it was all right to ask for help. At times reassurance took the form of contradicting the beginning teachers' self-criticism. It could take the form of acknowledging that advice had been taken.

The importance of *listening* was not revealed by the transcripts, but was mentioned during interviews by two mentors.

For some the issue of *personal knowledge* emerged during interviews. For one mentor, interpersonal issues were the key to good mentoring and crucially the importance of getting to know the beginning teacher.

Some saw discussion of personal issues as a part of the role, while for one trainee, the fact that the mentor did not appear to share such a view had been a problem when he had had personal difficulties.

The form of mentor–student interaction

This dimension can be seen in terms of general mentoring styles (McIntyre and Hagger, 1993; Saunders, Pettinger and Tomlinson, 1995) or in terms of specific exchanges drawing on discourse analysis (Coulthard, 1992; Coulthard and Brazil, 1992). Several writers have drawn on discourse analysis in order to analyse and interpret classroom exchanges and, although these are not without their critics, it may be that similar work on the dialogue between mentors and trainees could help our understanding of the mentoring process. For the purposes of this chapter, analysis of the mentors' use of directive, elicitive and informative exchanges were chosen to identify one aspect of difference in mentoring style. Further categories of exchange were needed in order to differentiate between exchanges which, although of the same basic form, were clearly not the same in purpose or impact. Following careful reading of the transcripts, the framework in Table 1 was drawn up.

'Exchange forms' of mentors rather than trainees are the focus and the exchanges of two of the mentors were analysed to test the usefulness of this approach. Both are female and both are working with pairs of beginning teachers. Names have been changed. Two taped discussions were analysed from each, all of which took place during the early part of a whole term placement which had begun in January.

Informative exchanges are those which do not require a response (either in words or in action) from the beginning teacher. Elicitive

Table 1

Basic exchange form	Extended exchange form
Mentor elicits	information
	judgement
	reflection
Mentor directs	the discussion agenda
	future action with reference to pupils' learning
	future action with reference to students' learning
Mentor provides	information
	justification
	feedback/evaluation
	reassurance
	access to own professional thinking/expertise

exchanges refer to those which imply that a response is expected of the students. They will, therefore, generally, though not necessarily, be expressed in a question form. Directive exchanges refer to any which imply that some action should be taken by the beginning teacher.

Both Jacky and Sarah used informative exchanges more than the other two exchange forms. Many of these simply provided information, about the school, departments, pupils, teaching resources and so on. Some had an evaluative element. Jacky and Sarah included a similar proportion of such exchanges, although Jacky's comments were more likely to be critical than positive, whereas Sarah's were the reverse.

Elicitive exchanges were used by Sarah far more than by Jacky. Not only does Sarah make greater use of questions, she makes much greater use of questions which seem to invite reflection and to demand evaluative responses rather than one specific answer. Jacky's questions, in contrast, seem to demand very concrete answers. When directive exchanges are analysed, the positions are reversed – with Jacky making much greater use of this exchange form than Sarah, whose use of directives is minimal.

Discussion

The three dimensions of mentoring which have been discussed may be represented diagrammatically (Figure 1) in order to model mentoring

Figure 1 Modelling mentoring style

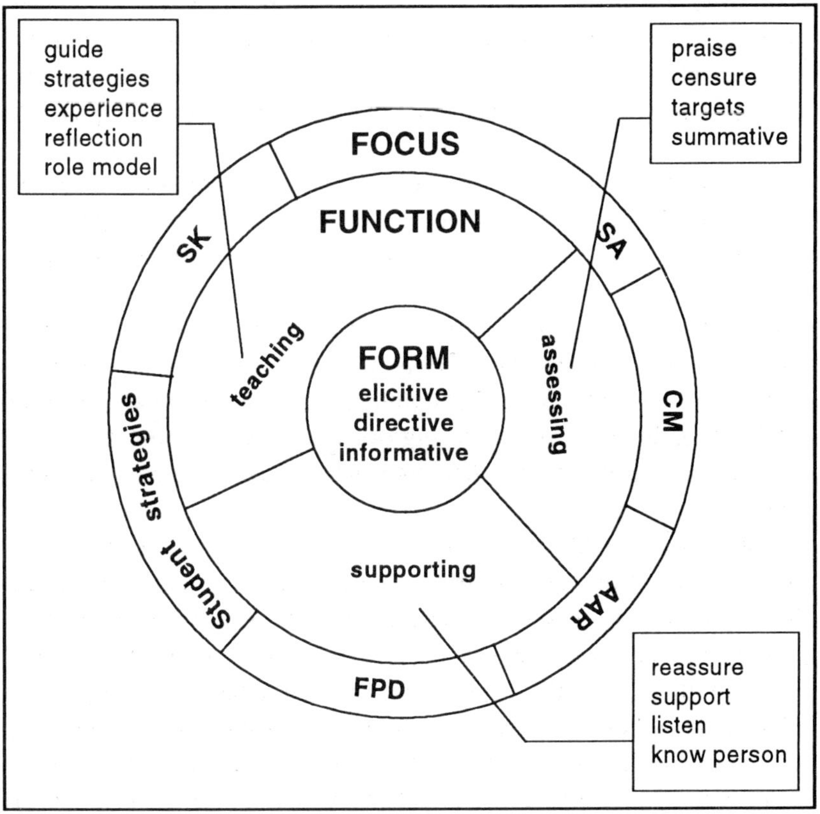

style. Different juxtapositions of the three concentric circles may combine form, function and focus in ways which suggest different kinds of mentor and styles of mentoring. If this model is applied to the data presented here, examples of different styles of mentoring can be proposed with reference to particular interactions. Where one kind of interaction appears to predominate consistently, a particular type of mentor is suggested who may work in a different way from another who favours a contrasting form of interaction.

For example, one mentor might focus predominantly on class management issues, provide a great deal of advice, guidance and practical strategies and make much use of the directive exchange form. In contrast, another could refer to many different competences, encourage reflection and provide learning opportunities, and use mainly elicitive exchange forms. Further work is needed to establish how much flexibility in style is needed if mentors are to be able to meet the differing learning needs of beginning teachers or to adapt to changes in their needs as a placement progresses.

A related issue is the extent to which mentors and beginning teachers attach equal importance to different roles. The interviews conducted here suggest that beginning teachers value the support role more highly than mentors, but this issue needs further investigation. They also suggest that a mentor can fulfil several roles which seem to match the needs of one beginning teacher while failing to meet the needs of the other. The individuals in each pair of beginning teachers had markedly different preferences in terms of mentoring practice. There is no evidence that the mentors involved varied their approaches to accommodate differences in needs.

The detailed analysis was of dialogue taking place fairly early in a placement. Scrutiny of other transcripts reveals little evidence of change in approach as the practice progresses and, thus, little accommodation to changing needs of trainees suggested by Copeland (1982). Mentors who are directive in their approach appear to remain so throughout the placement, although the limited amount of data available to substantiate this suggestion means that it can only be made tentatively. This is another issue worthy of further investigation, which might also include the question of how beginning teachers might cope with changes in mentor tactics during the course of a placement.

Concluding remarks

This analysis has focused on the mentors' contributions to discussions rather than those of the beginning teachers. Questions, therefore, remain about the extent to which the mentors' exchanges are affected by the beginning teachers' input and how much mentors' exchanges would vary depending on the individuals with whom they were working. There is some evidence here from interviews that one of a pair of beginning teachers found their mentor's approach more valuable than the other. This may indicate an inability on the part of the mentor to vary style according to individual need, but this suggestion needs further investigation in the light of the Saunders, Pettinger and Tomlinson (1995) suggestion that extension of the repertoires of individual mentors could be desirable.

References

Back, D. and Booth, M. (1992), 'Commitment to mentoring', in Wilkin, M., *Mentoring in Schools.* London: Kogan Page

Barker, A., Brooks, V., March, K. and Swatton: (1996), *Initial Teacher Education in Secondary Schools: a study of the tangible and intangible costs and benefits of initial teacher education in secondary schools, Final report of research commissioned by the Association of Teachers and Lecturers.* Warwick: Institute of Education, University of Warwick.

Blake, D., Hanley, V., Jennings, M. and Lloyd, M. (eds) (1995), *Researching School-based Teacher Education.* Aldershot: Avebury.

Brooks, V., Fitch, T. and Robinson, M. (1994), 'Positive mentoring and the novice expert', in Reid, I., Constable H. and Griffiths, R., *Teacher Education Reform, Current Research.* London: Paul Chapman Publishing.

Burgoyne, G. and Wiggans, J. (1994), 'Supporting learning in the workplace', in Little, B., *Supporting Learning in the Workplace, Conference Proceedings*. Leeds: Leeds Metropolitan University.

Calderhead, J. (1987), The quality of reflection in student teachers' professional learning', *European Journal of Teacher Education*, 10(3), 269–78

Campbell, R. and Horbury, A. (1994), 'Mentoring articled science teachers', in Reid, I., Constable, H. and Griffiths, R., *Teacher Education Reform, current research*. London: Paul Chapman Publishing.

Copeland, W.D. (1982), 'Student teachers' preference for supervisory approach', *Journal of Teacher Education*, 33(2), 32–6.

Coulthard, M. (ed.) (1992), *Advances in Spoken Discourse Analysis*. London: Routledge

Coulthard, M. and Brazil, D. (1992), 'Exchange structure', in Coulthard, M, *Advances in Spoken Discourse Analysis*. London: Routledge.

Daloz, L. (1986), *Effective Teaching and Mentoring: Realizing the Transformational Power of Adult Learning Experiences*. San Francisco: Jossey-Bass

Dart, L. and Drake, P. (1995), 'Mentors in English and mathematics', in Reid, I., Constable, H. and Griffiths, R., *Teacher Education Reform, Current Research*. London: Paul Chapman Publishing.

DES/HMI (1991), *School Based Initial Teacher Training*. London: HMSO.

Department for Education (DfE) (1992), *Initial Teacher Training, Secondary Phase Circular 9/92*. London: DfE

Elliott, J. (1991), 'A model of professionalism and its implications for teacher education', *British Educational Research Journal*, 17(4), 309–18.

Furlong, J. and Maynard, T. (1995), *Mentoring Student Teachers*. London: Routledge.

Guillaume, A. and Rudney, G. (1993), 'Student teachers' growth towards independence: an analysis of their changing concerns', *Teaching and Teacher Education*, 9(1), 65–80.

Hawkins: and Sholet, R. (1989), *Supervision in the Helping Professions*. Milton Keynes: Open University Press.

Hill, A., Jennings, M. and Madgwick, B. (1992), 'Initiating a mentorship training programme', in Wilkin, M., *Mentoring in Schools*. London: Kogan Page.

Jacques, K. (1992), 'Mentoring in initial teacher education', *Cambridge Journal of Education*

Jowett, V. (1995), *Working for a Degree – Mentoring Project*. Leeds: Leeds Metropolitan University.

Koerner, M.E. (1992), 'The co-operating teacher: an ambivalent participant in student teaching', *Journal of Teacher Education*, 42(1), 46–56.

Martin, S. (1996), 'Support and challenge: conflicting or complementary aspects of mentoring novice teachers', *Teachers and Teaching*, 2(1), 41–56.

McBride, R. (ed.) (1996), *Teacher Education Policy, Some issues arising from research and practice*. London: Falmer Press.

McIntyre, D. and Hagger, H. (1993), 'Teachers' expertise and models of mentoring', in McIntyre, D., Hagger, H. and Wilkin, W., *Mentoring: Perspectives on School-based Teacher Education*. London: Kogan Page.

Nolder, R., Smith, S. and Melrose, J. (1994), 'Working together: roles and responsibilities in the mentoring process', in Jaworski, B. and Watson, A., *Mentoring in Mathematics Teaching*. London: Falmer Press.

Rikard, G.L. and Veal, M.L. (1996), 'Cooperating teachers: insight into their preparation, beliefs and practices', *Journal of Teaching in Physical Education*, 15, 279–96.

Saunders, S., Pettinger, K. and Tomlinson: (1995), 'Prospective mentors' views on partnership in secondary teacher training', *British Educational Research Journal*, 21(2), 199–217.

Shaw, R. (1992). 'Can mentoring raise achievement schools', in Wilkin, M., *Mentoring in Schools*. London: Kogan Page.

Williams, E.A., Butt, G.W., Butterfield, S., Gray, C., Leach S., Soares, A. and Marr, A. (forthcoming) *Form Function and Focus in Mentor Student Dialogue: An Exploratory Study*.

Williams, E.A., Leach, S., Marr, A. (forthcoming), *The Form of Mentor Student Dialogue within a Secondary Initial Teacher Education Partnership*.

3.4 Different perceptions of 'teacher competence' – trainees and their mentors

Pat Drake and Lisa Dart

Introduction

This chapter presents a preliminary discussion of how the relationship between the school co-tutor/mentor and the beginning teacher interacts with notions of teacher competence. We draw on our previously published work on mentoring in secondary English and maths, on work currently in progress and on the specific case of one relationship between a mentor and trainee in English. We work on the Post Graduate Certificate in Education (PGCE) at our own institution, the University of Sussex, where we are both heavily committed to teaching on the programme and to programme development and organization. Inevitably, our discussion is contextualized within current developments in initial teacher education (ITE) in England and Wales since 1992 – the centrally driven shift towards a school-based or 'partnership' model of postgraduate teacher training, and the requirements for newly qualified teachers (NQTs) to be 'competent' as assessed according to criteria laid down initially in Circular 9/92 (Department for Education, 1992), and subsequently adopted by the Teacher Training Agency (TTA).

Our first project was an action research programme which, by pairing experienced mentors in English and maths with inexperienced mentors in the same subjects, sought to develop the mentors' skills in mentoring beginning teachers. At the same time, specific describable aspects of mentoring, including tensions for mentors, were elicited and transferred to a mentor training programme which was being developed at the time (McIntyre and Hagger, 1994), and to the redefined partnership criteria. To our surprise, it seemed that mentoring then was being generally interpreted as generic activity, more or less independent of subject specialisms (Dart and Drake, 1993; Prentice, this volume).

Following on from this was a study in which mentors in English and maths were tracked during the academic year 1994–5 to investigate the extent to which their mentoring activities were subject specific (see Drake and Dart, 1994). In this project, we investigated similarities and differences between school mentors of trainee teachers of English and maths with respect to their attitudes towards the respective school subjects. We then explored how these attitudes impinged on the interactions between the mentors and the beginning teachers for whom they had responsibility.

In the research, several lists emerged: lists of mentoring activities and lists of concerns (Dart and Drake, 1993); differences between maths and English mentors in what they perceived made a 'good' teacher, differences within both maths and English between mentors, for example attitudes to grammar in English and attitudes to mathematical knowledge between maths mentors (Drake and Dart, 1995). In our sample of mentors, it was clear, for instance, that a necessary condition for being a 'good' teacher of maths was perceived to be a liking for children. On the other hand, English teachers prioritized 'a love of literature'.

We were also able to identify differences in interpretation of teaching experience between trainees themselves and their mentors (Dart and Drake, 1995). For example, the attitude of a maths trainee to a lesson in which the pupils used computers was very different to that of his mentor. The trainee, a mature man, was so caught up in his own perception that using computers per se in school was a considerable treat in itself that he simply did not recognize his mentor's subsequent advice on how to make the lesson more of a directed learning experience for the pupils.

Despite the range of views that mentors were happy to articulate, the suspicion grew that, notwithstanding all our lists and revelations, we were not really getting to the heart of something important regarding the way that mentors and trainees interact with each other and with teaching. We felt that some trainees may be being labelled as weak or unsuitable on the grounds of their failure to resonate with the attitudes and perspectives of their mentor. Other trainees, however, whose attitudes were in sympathy with their mentors' views were judged far more favourably in terms of competence.

Competence and capability

Eraut (1994) develops a useful argument describing the potential for a concept he calls 'capability' as a parameter for assessing professional aptitude across a number of professions, including engineering, healthcare, business and management as well as teaching. He writes:

> We found it useful to discuss evidence of professional competence under two main headings: performance and capability. Performance evidence does of course provide evidence of capability; but the term 'capability evidence' is used to refer to evidence not directly derived from normal performance on the job. Sometimes the purpose of capability evidence was to supplement performance evidence, sometimes it was to ascertain the candidate's potential to perform in the future.
>
> (Eraut, 1994:200)

This is entirely consistent with the view of the maths mentor who, when questioned on the importance of specific mathematical knowledge on the part of beginning teachers, said:

It's perfectly possible for people to come in without big rafts of areas. That's not a problem in the sense that people who have got degrees we assume are capable of learning.

What began to bother us was that a picture seemed to be emerging where some beginning teachers were indeed assumed to be capable of learning, when others were not. This would not be surprising if the trainees had not been through a selection process before beginning the

PGCE course. However at Sussex, PGCE entry qualifications are high, with the majority of English trainees having degree classifications of 2.i or above. Maths trainees at Sussex were also well qualified at the time of this work, with approximately one-third of the cohort in any one year between 1992 and 1996 having attained a similar level.[1] All had also been through a selection interview with a mentor and university tutor, with many of the interviews having been conducted in a partnership school.

It seems reasonable to suppose that the qualities which mentors believe to characterize good practitioners in English and maths teaching respectively are likely to be the ones that mentors look for in their trainees. It is less clear when and how trainees learn what these qualities are explicitly, even though it is likely that they are under pressure to exhibit them. One mentor reflected that she had, on a rare occasion when the content was similar to that studied at university at degree level, neglected to clarify with the trainee her view that a different approach would be required.

> She put a Shakespeare sonnet in front of them. I was sitting in the cupboard listening to this and she launched straight into work on the structure of the sonnet, rhyme scheme with syllables, two lines, all different stresses in the line. And it never occurred to me that she would look at the structure rather than the meaning. And of course you've got to look at the meaning of a poem first, especially something like a Shakespearean sonnet which as far as they were concerned had just landed from the moon.
>
> (English mentor, female)

Here, both mentor and trainee were able to recognize and use a language – 'university English' and 'school English' – to identify a context where training would make a difference. It is not always as easy, as is demonstrated in this extract from the writing of a maths mentor in the first project, at a time when partnership was in its very early stages.

> We've had a lot of difficulties this year trying to assess A ... She has actually taught for 12 years I believe in her own country, so she

is an experienced teacher which presents problems because an experienced teacher isn't so receptive to being told that they are not doing their job in the way you want them to.

(Mathematics mentor, female).

Here, despite the trainee teacher being experienced 'in her own country', there is considerable doubt on the part of the mentor that competence in her terms is being achieved and anxiety expressed about providing for what are seen as the trainee's training needs.

Recent work

Our more recent work is not directly with school co-tutors/mentors, but with university tutors. Interested in how beginning teachers come to be deemed competent or, more particularly, 'weak' (or 'At Risk', to use the Sussex nomenclature), we joined forces with two personal tutors who between them covered about 30 beginning teachers. Our aim was to build up an evidence base of instances when trainee teachers were described in judgemental terms without reference to the formal competence criteria written in the course documentation. Our sources of evidence for this work are:

- the written profiles on the cohort of beginning teachers

- diaries which the personal tutors kindly agreed to keep during the year in which details of conversations with and about beginning teachers were recorded

- and some correspondence from school tutors received during the course of the work.

In this recent project, we were concerned to try to unravel more clearly the reasons why some trainees were considered 'weak' or 'good'. We were especially interested in how the informal judgements and comments were made outside the reporting process, but which, in our experience as tutors on the course, had an impact on decisions about competence. It would seem from this project, that the kinds of expectations that trainees and their mentors have about a variety of areas (e.g. teaching styles, subject knowledge and beliefs, and the understanding of professional attitudes) all influence assessment of competence. Inevitably, the influence that informal comment has on formal assessment procedures, as well as the form it takes, is context-bound. Such possible differences in trainee experience call into question the efficacy of a competence model as a method of assessing trainees' suitability for teaching.

One of the interesting results of the project is the way in which it appears that professionals look for personal, but undefined, characteristics when communicating their concerns about trainees. These characteristics include notions of: charisma, sparkle, gender, personal eccentricity and/or being oneself, dress/appearance and intelligence. It appears that these characteristics can each be applied in both a pejorative and positive sense and used indiscriminately to apply to both 'weak' and 'strong' trainees. For example, one person can be 'very intelligent' but do 'little work', with this being viewed as a skilful interpretation of the competence requirements – they simply do enough to get by. Another, in a different subject, school or department, despite being described as 'very bright', is doing 'little work' and is categorized as 'lazy' or 'uncommitted to teaching'. Furlong et al. (1988) identify four levels of training:

- direct practice
- indirect practice
- practical principles
- disciplinary theory.

In a partnership model of training, direct practice (i.e. the development of knowledge, skills and understanding through immediate first-hand experience) is afforded considerable importance, with beginning teachers being implicitly trained to act according to practical principles exemplified in the pragmatics of everyday classroom practice. In the shift nationally since 1992 towards school-based teacher education, a plethora of commentators have identified in more detail aspects of the process which is expedited by school professional tutors, for example Wilkin (1992), Dart and Drake (1993), McIntyre, Hagger and Wilkin (1993) and Heilbron and Jones (this volume). Wiliam (1994) points out that tuition on school-based schemes is costly, and so it is of fundamental importance that the interaction between trainee and mentor is effective.

In the field of subject knowledge, the evidence is less clear. Ruthven (1993) suggests three forms of professional knowledge are drawn on by expert teachers:

- tacit expertise, with which skilful teachers make sense of and act in teaching situations

- pragmatic wisdom, by which is meant the generally accepted perceptions of good practice which permeate the teaching fraternity in a subject

- grounded science, which indicates a basis for action which takes account of research into the teaching and learning of, in the context of Ruthven's work, school maths.

He suggests that expert teachers manage a repertoire of teaching activities implicitly drawing on and relating their knowledge in these domains. Furthermore, he argues that unless a novice teacher has access to these forms of knowledge, he or she will be unable to make sense of the classroom behaviour exhibited by experienced teachers. This point is supported by Cooper (1990), who, in a study of mathematics PGCE students, revealed specific anxieties in the area of investigational maths. These anxieties are consistent with the inexperience that typically novice teachers have of doing investigational work at school themselves, and the inaccessibility of the practice of their experienced colleagues in school. The experienced teacher, on the other hand, in making judgements about the progress of trainees and deeming them to be competent, will bring to bear his or her own beliefs and value system about the teaching of the subject (Crosson and Shiu, 1994). As well as this, Sanders (1994), in her examination of mentors' personal views of maths teaching, draws attention to the wide ranging philosophies held by maths teachers about maths itself. She reminds us of our own experience as pupils on the receiving end of these philosophies, and how our perceptions of the subject are shaped by teachers who, for example, insisted on following the rules, or, in contrast, encouraged us to find our own errors and to thereby develop our own understanding. In an earlier phase of our own study (Drake and Dart, 1994), English mentors expressed beliefs which were for some formulated in terms of a traditional approach to literature, an awareness of the need to teach National Curriculum and to tackle issues arising from basic skills of punctuation, spelling, grammar, etc., a knowledge about the impact of theories such as post-structuralism and their potential for offering alternative explorations of text, and also the skills of being organized, a manager and an effective member of a team.

A case study

We would like to turn to a close examination of the relationship between one beginning teacher in English and her mentor which broke down after the trainee had been in school for one term. Study of the written report (a longer one than was usual was accepted since the mentor felt there was so much that needed to be communicated) and the trainee's written response to it, allow some of the above issues to be explored. In particular, it is possible to see the effects of expectations about professional behaviour in a training situation. The co-tutor/mentor had a clear idea of what she expected from a new trainee. The beginning teacher too showed a clear, but different, set of pre-occupations and expectations. The consequence of the breakdown of the relationship was that the beginning teacher was moved to another school. In the second school the trainee went on smoothly to gain QTS and secured a job before the course had finished.

The first mentor cites a number of examples of ways in which the beginning teacher was cause for concern. After the trainee had seen the report, she felt it was unfair and wrote a lengthy reply. It could be suggested that the conflict between the two of them is merely the result of inexperience on the part of the co-tutor/mentor and misunderstandings on the part of the beginning teacher. However, an analysis of the situation reveals some interesting assumptions about expectation of the nature of being a teacher generally, and an English teacher specifically.

The co-tutor/mentor reports considerable negativity in the beginning teacher's attitude. In the mentor's opinion, the beginning teacher had not understood anything of the nature of the sixth form lessons she had observed.

> She had failed to understand the nature of any of the sixth form lessons I had specifically arranged for her to attend. She dismissed as 'reading' the intense grappling with psychological insights that were going on ... and her own apparent lack of interest and clock-watching were intrusive to the intimacy of the group ... as to my own A level lit. group, their sessions have been dismissed as not 'real lessons' as we were 'just talking', i.e. getting to grips with Walcott's poetry.

The mentor suggests that the beginning teacher might familiarize herself with the new material. In her reply, the trainee suggests that she use the time to prepare lessons, which she sees as more useful.

Both of the interpretations of the trainee's reactions may be seen differently. From a trainee's point of view 'real lessons' may be ones where the planning that goes into them is evident. For example, lessons with lots of different activities ranging through a variety of tasks such as written and oral ones. It may mean lessons which involve group work or role plays – indeed, the kinds of lessons that beginning teachers become anxious about planning. Lessons that seem to be just about 'talking about text' may look straightforward and easy and may not seem to the novice to require the same type of intensive planning. Although to an experienced practitioner this is clearly not the case, it may appear that way to someone who is just learning to 'read' classroom interactions. Similarly, this may be why the trainee wanted to prioritize her time for planning – to organize lessons which appeared to her to be more demanding (lessons where she may well also struggle to maintain control of pupils' behaviour).

In particular, the co-tutor/mentor raises the question about the beginning teacher's attitude to her subject.

> I am still unsure whether J has the genuine love of literature which
> I deem vital to successful English teaching ... She did not seem
> responsive to the more intimate Sixth Form Theatre Studies and did
> not involve herself in our two major drama evenings ... her work
> on school poetry has been slight in content so far ... A more obvious
> delight in the poetry would help.

She goes on to discuss the beginning teacher's approach to teaching
novels, but once again notes, 'She does not exhibit much enjoyment in
the reading.' We have already discussed how a love for literature is
deemed by many as an essential quality in an English teacher (Dart and
Drake, 1996) and how it raises questions about how trainees are supposed
to demonstrate that 'love'. In this case, the mentor expects the beginning
teacher to do so overtly, in her reading in the classroom as well as by her
attendance at the drama productions. It is extremely unlikely that either
of these expectations have been made explicit to the trainee, who, clearly
aware of the pressure she is under in the classroom, chooses to prioritize
her time differently. She is, nevertheless, using the time to improve her
practice and her response seems quite reasonable:

> Of course I have a natural and 'genuine' love of literature. Why on
> earth would I have studied for GCSE literature and language, A
> level English and then gone on to study English at degree level ?

She continues by showing how her awareness of what is expected in this
situation is developing:

> Perhaps I must try to convey more enthusiasm in my lessons.
> However I have not yet been struck by other teachers' conveyance
> of their love of literature ... I love reading and do not like the
> insinuation that I read grudgingly. I have spent some time in the
> English office trying to familiarize myself with various books, both
> literature and language-based ones.

Our evidence supports the work of Protherough and Atkinson (1991),
namely, that 'a love of literature is paramount' as a quality for a successful

teacher of English. But what does a genuine love of literature mean? Whatever, it is clear that this love must manifest itself in overt and recognizable ways in schools when you are training to teach. In this instance, it would seem, the beginning teacher is becoming aware of such a requirement.

This small case study illustrates the nature of different perceptions and expectations held by beginning teachers and their mentors. Our research suggests that expectations about teachers generally or subject specific beliefs particularly (or both), which are not shared between the mentor and trainee, may play a significant part in judgements about competence.

Conclusion

All providers of initial teacher training (ITT) have now been inspected at least partly in accordance with the competence criteria. Further, the Office for Standards in Education (OFSTED) inspections have been announced which will check that individual subject tutors within institutions are training teachers appropriately. The requirements for explicit competence look like becoming increasingly complex with a profile emanating from the TTA being piloted across England. This profile demands not only a recognition of competence, but also a description of the strengths of NQTs in different competency areas. It is, therefore, through the competence of its beginning teacher that the fitness or competence of the higher education institution (HEI) to provide ITT is assessed. The recent announcement of a National Curriculum for teacher training by the then Education Minister Gillian Shepherd was for the stated purpose of the further 'improvement' of teaching methods in specific subjects, viz. reading, writing and maths.

However, the substance of our work to date implies that, despite an increasing emphasis on making the process of ITE explicit at all levels, there remain aspects of the trainee and assessor relationship, which invariably exists between mentor and beginning teacher, which are not explicit yet which affect the judgements and assumptions each makes about the other. This suggests there is a muddle over the whole question of competence in relation to subject knowledge and its application. The specificity of a curriculum per se does not alter this situation, and so the question of teaching 'better' or 'more effectively' clearly depends on who is looking and what is being looked for.

As an endnote, it is interesting to relate here the work of Valerie Walkerdine in her study of girls and maths in secondary schools (1988). Walkerdine claims that teacher assessments of pupils' potential maths performance are gendered. She provides evidence to demonstrate how boys are seen as 'bright' but underachieving. Often misbehaviour in such boys is tolerated because of the teacher's belief in their ability. On the other hand, girls who achieve are seen as having done so through 'hard work' rather than through ability. They are not noted for having qualities such as 'flair' or 'natural ability'. Certain descriptions carry concealed meaning, for example, immaturity and maturity. When 'maturity' is applied to girls, it may well denote a limit on their ability (i.e. they have shown their full capabilities). However, for boys who are described as 'immature' the implicit meaning is that their real potential is hidden, yet to be displayed. Walkerdine suggests that girls' achievements are belittled in such cases, and are so demeaned merely because they don't do things in the same way as the boys. It might be interesting to examine how similar thinking may be applied to male and female beginning teachers. For example, our work suggests co-tutors/mentors often look for qualities such as 'charisma' in beginning teachers. Yet, how often is this term actually applied to female trainees as opposed to males? Walkerdine's study leads her to a fundamental critique of 'child centred pedagogy', which she argues is based on a male perception of childhood as a gendered state – the free, exploratory, essentially inquisitive boy child – 'he' as opposed to his mother, 'she'. Teacher training is a very different context, and it would be extremely simplistic to propose that judgements about competence are made on straightforwardly gendered lines. However, it would be interesting to consider the possibility of an analogy, where new teachers' potential is assessed quite early (sometimes within the first week at school) according to quite fundamental beliefs about self and subject. That piece of mischief, reader, is up to you.

Acknowledgements

This work has been supported by the Paul Hamlyn Foundation, Esmée Fairbairn Charitable Trust and the Research Development Fund at the University of Sussex. In addition, we are immensely grateful to those mentors who have bravely allowed themselves to be used as exemplifying particular attitudes to ITT, even though they themselves may have altered their approach since the evidence was collected. In particular, we would like to thank Ella Dzelzainis, Ken Leonard, Lesley Scales, Marian Metcalfe, Janet Stuart and Gill Weller.

Note

1   We understand that this picture is not typical nationally. It is also likely to change as Sussex, along with other providers of ITT, struggles to meet the challenge of increasing the numbers of secondary teachers by 50 per cent by the turn of the century.

References

Cooper, B. (1990), 'PGCE students and investigational approaches in secondary maths', *Research Papers in* Education, 5(2), 127–51.

Crosson, M. and Shiu, C. (1994), 'Evaluation and judgement', in Jaworski, B. and Watson, A., *Mentoring in Mathematics Teaching for the Mathematical Association.* Sussex: Falmer Press.

Dart, L. and Drake: (1993), 'School-based training: a conservative practice?', *Journal of Education for Teaching*, 19(2), 175–89.

—   (1996), 'Subject perspectives on mentoring', in McIntyre, D. and Hagger, H., *Mentors in Schools: Developing the Profession of Teaching.* London: David Fulton.

Department for Education (1992), *The Accreditation of Initial Teacher Education Circulars 9/92 and 14/93.*

Drake, P. (1994), 'Mentoring and mathematics: some issues from a research project', in Dossey, J., *Proceedings of the International Congress of Mathematics Education*. Quebec, August.

Drake, P. and Dart, L. (1994), 'English, mathematics and mentors', in Reid, I., Constable, H. and Griffiths, R., *Teacher Education Reform: Current Research*. London: Paul Chapman.

(1995a), 'Intellectual challenges for partnership', in Griffiths, V. and Owen, *Schools in Partnership*. London: Paul Chapman.

(1995b), 'Subject knowledge and beliefs and the mentor-trainee interview', *British Congress on Mathematics Education , Conference Proceedings,* Manchester, July.

Eraut, M. (1994), *Developing Professional Knowledge and Competence*. Sussex: Falmer Press.

Furlong, V.J., Hirst, H., Pocklington, K. and Miles, S. (1988), *Initial Teacher Training and the Role of the School*. Milton Keynes: Open University.

McIntyre, D., Hagger, H. and Wilkin, M. (eds) (1993), *Mentoring: Perspectives on School-based Teacher Education*. London: Kogan Page.

McIntyre, D. and Hagger, H. (1994), *Mentoring in Initial Teacher Education: Five Research Studies Supported by the Paul Hamlyn Foundation*. Oxford:

Protherough and Atkinson (1991), *The Making of English Teachers*. Milton Keynes: Open University Press.

Ruthven, K. (1993), 'Pedagogical knowledge and the training of mathematics teachers', *Mathematics Review*, 3.

Sanders, S.E. (1994), '"Mathematics and Mentoring' in Javorski B. and Watson, A. (eds) *Mentoring in Mathematics Education*. London: Falmer Press.

Walkerdine, V. (1988), *Counting Girls Out*. London: Virago.

Wiliam, D. (1994), 'I'm sorry but there's not enough money for a third teaching practice visit', in Reid I., Constable, H. and Griffiths, R., (1994), *Teacher Education Reform: Current Research*. London: Paul Chapman.

Wilkin, M. (ed.) (1992), *Mentoring in School*. London: Kogan Page.

3.5 New teachers in an urban comprehensive

Crispin Jones and Ruth Heilbronn

Introduction

This chapter examines some key aspects of the changes that have occurred in initial teacher education (ITE) and training at Hampstead School, an 11–18 mixed comprehensive school, between the years 1992-6. To help frame this examination, some information about the school is essential. The head, Tamsyn Imison, has recently written about the school in the following terms:

> Hampstead School is a true comprehensive, with 1,279 students and 81 teachers. It draws from the full range of attainment, with 25 per cent in the top, 25 per cent in the bottom reading bands and 50 per cent in the centre band. There is a good social and ethnic mix and there also a balance in most years between girls and boys. The name of the school is very misleading, as most of our intake comes from Cricklewood and Kilburn, which are inner-city areas, and not from leafy Hampstead, which is a few miles away ... Fifty-five per cent of the roll speak over 80 different languages between them. These students include about 150 asylum seekers, whose high motivation rubs off on others and who also help to make Hampstead an

international secondary school. On local education authority (LEA) raw and value-added comparative analysis, our school delivers high SATs, GCSE and A level examination results, has high attendance, low exclusion rates and has many students staying on for after-school activities. Girls do particularly well and boys' performance has moved up to match this. Finally, of the year 11 cohort, nearly 100 per cent have been staying on into post-16 education and training, for the last five years. There are 230 students in our own sixth form, which is currently capped at that level because of serious space constraints.

(Imison, 1997)

The head's account points up several features that make inner-city schools, such as Hampstead, particularly challenging places in which to teach and learn. To the wide range of ability common to most comprehensives is added the special elements of a linguistically and ethnically mixed student body, within which the educational needs of refugee students are a constant pre-occupation. Crucially in relation to ITE, the school is seen as successful on a range of measures, from raw scores of league tables to the successful meeting of the complex range of educational needs of asylum seeking and refugee children.

The period of time covered in this chapter has been one characterized by change both in the content and management of ITE in England, and also by interest in the potential educational and economic value of such change (McBride, 1996; Whitty et al., 1992; Wideen and Grimmett, 1995). This environment has provoked much discussion and new practice and this chapter is to be seen as a contribution to this on-going process.

New developments and the role of the school professional tutor

With the advent of partnership training, it was understood that if arrangements were to work in relation to Hampstead, change was required in four key areas of the school's practice:

1 There was a need for greater co-ordination both within the school and between the school and its partnership higher education institutes (HEIs). This meant the involvement of a senior management in the school that was already over extended, because of the wide-ranging changes brought about by the 1988 Education Act and its successors.

2 The changes had significant financial and budgetary consequences for both school and HEI, which was relatively uncharted territory for all concerned.

3 The school's mentors/co-tutors needed proper training and support within the school if they were to work in the manner intended. If nothing else, this had major financial and other resource implications.

4 Related to the above, all involved in the partnership needed to be clear about the assessment criteria for passing the courses. We needed to be consistent in our expectations, including making evaluatory criteria explicit to both beginning teachers and their tutors alike.

How could this be done? One HEI with which Hampstead worked, the London Institute of Education, had started to develop a new extended role for the school-based tutor in the early-1990s. This role became the key for the new partnership arrangements at the school and its subsequent development is at the heart of this chapter. Amongst the most important of these developments were:

• the production of guidelines for monitoring and evaluating the practice of the beginning teachers and clarifying the roles and responsibilities for trainers

• the evolution of more sophisticated and effective support systems between school and HEIs

• the building up of further professional development for teachers involved in ITE, in which the HEI's expertise is shared and exchanged within a practice-based context

- the viewing of professional development as a continuum by the school, beginning at the ITE and initial teacher training (ITT) stage, consolidated in the newly qualified teacher (NQT) induction period and continuing to demand reflection and progression in subsequent stages of a teaching career

- the explicit sharing of assessment criteria in general between all parties involved in ITE

- the consideration and development of the competency model (set out in Circular 9/92) as a basis on which to develop beginning teachers' evaluative skills, using action planning, self-assessment and target setting.

This also involved reflection on practice, research in the school context and the production of 'profile tasks', such as the professional development portfolio. Although many LEAs and schools have their own guidelines and monitoring procedures for NQTs (Earley, 1992; Earley and Kinder, 1994; Office for Standards in Education, 1993), there is very little available on the role of the school professional tutor/co-ordinator in partnership programmes of ITE and ITT. However, certain guidelines for the role need to be made explicit. It is a developing role and one whose extent and value has not yet been mapped. It is essential in pulling together the various aspects of the course for the beginning teachers and in performing complex liaison processes involved in new partnership relationships. For beginning teachers, partnership can seem like being pulled in more than one direction, as they work with HEI providers and school tutors at different times in their training. The school professional tutor, we have found, needs to know and understand the details of all training arrangements to ensure that the school provides the conditions to make them a reality. He or she also has a direct responsibility for the professional development of the beginning teachers in school.

    School-based training in partnership with higher education is a new and developing form of provision, yet partnership itself is already in danger of becoming a catch word, much used, almost a cliché. In the specific context of Hampstead, its use indicates a developing understanding of the need to create, nurture and maintain a good learning institution with the effective and targeted support of many others, particularly colleagues from HEIs and the LEA. From the school's point of view, there has been a need to develop a network of support from within and without, including local authority and HEI for mentor training. All of this needs a focus or a conduit. The school professional tutor is the person best placed to provide this.

The reorganization of teacher education and training within schools

To understand the development of partnership, we need to look back to our starting points. In Hampstead's case, they were typical of other, similar schools at that time. In 1992–3, prior to mandatory partnership, the school was involved with a spectrum of different teacher training programmes, both postgraduate and BEd. Briefly, they consisted of:

1 an important link with the Institute of Education, London, developing an 'area-based' teacher training scheme, which will be described in more detail later in the chapter, since it was the most formative programme for preparing the school for the new role of the school based tutor

2 close liaison with the University of North London's modern languages Post Graduate Certificate in Education (PGCE) and the school's modern languages department

3 collaboration between the University of North London and the school's maths department

4 placement of student teachers from various HEIs on request, arrangements for which varied from year to year.

Although some effective and long-standing relationships between curriculum departments in the school and in HEIs were built up, such ad hoc relationships militated against the evolution of coherent partnership. The onset of formal partnership arrangements precipitated the reappraisal of the school's involvement in ITE. The Institute of Education's so-called 'area-based scheme' (Lambert and Totterdell, 1995) was influential in this process.

The area-based scheme (worked in conjunction with Camden LEA) followed partnership principles, i.e. tutors from schools and the Institute of Education met regularly to shape the content and delivery of the PGCE course. Hampstead School took an active role and the course ran for two years before Circular 9/92 forced modifications to the school-based arrangements. However the area-based link with the Institute of Education had been made. At Hampstead it was maintained by a deputy head and had involved overall co-ordination of the work of several subject departments to ensure consistent expectations across departments. Moreover, a school professional tutor, working in conjunction with an Institute of Education tutor, taught the professional studies elements of the course in the school. At that time, this arrangement was unique, professional studies being still taught entirely by the HEI tutors in all other courses with which we were involved.

Experience of the area-based scheme which foreshadowed the compulsory implementation of partnership, was productive for the school in a range of areas:

- in providing recognition of areas of expertise

- in developing the skills of the school-based tutor

- in establishing shared perceptions of the conjoint roles of school-based and Institute tutor

- in allowing the input of particular and up-to-date practice-based illustrations of the issues in education under discussion.

The area-based scheme was, therefore, pioneering in its attempt to pull together different elements of ITE and to implement coherence and consistency, a process which was evaluated at the end of each year. Resultant changes were implemented yearly, to the overall benefit of the course. The school's experience in developing this course, particularly the experience of collaboration with the LEA, with other schools and with the Institute of Education, was a significant factor in the subsequent development of the role of the school professional tutor and her responsibility for ITE across the school.

When the school previewed successive changes to the ITE programme, the senior management team and the staff generally were committed to a partnership model as was being developed with the Institute of Education. It was also realized, however, that the school needed to consolidate the Institute's way of working across subject areas if the benefits were to be spread beyond the domain of ITE alone. To facilitate a training ethos across the school became the first main task in the evolving role of the school professional tutor.

In 1994–5, a training group of teachers was set up in the school, including all those who were involved with teacher training, those who would be taking on the newly expanded role of subject co-tutor/mentor and anyone else who expressed an interest in being involved. The group met regularly throughout the spring and summer term of 1994 to clarify its aims and objectives for the new PGCE arrangements, which were to come into play in September of that year. Convening and co-ordinating such a training group, which had an interest in in-service education and training (INSET), staff development and NQT induction as well as initial training, seemed to be an excellent way to develop a policy to ensure coherence and consistency of training across departments. Indeed, co-ordinating the work of co-tutors/mentors has become a central aspect of the role of the school professional tutor.

'If I were you, I wouldn't start from here' goes the old joke. Indeed, the training group's early meetings revealed a confusion of paths, a patchwork of different tracks to qualified teacher status (QTS) across different institutions and departments. The whole school had not collectively debated the fundamentals of teacher training before and it was eye-opening to compare experiences across departments and institutions, noting significant differences in assessment between HEIs and between tutors in different departments within HEIs. Through discussion, a common core of concerns for the implementation of the new courses evolved and the principles which should underlie the school's commitment to training beginning teachers agreed. The most essential aspects of their implementation were also worked out, including basic management issues. This work led to the development of a code of practice for beginning teachers in school.

The code of practice came from the collective input of the group (details in Heilbronn and Jones, 1997). It maintains that the school's pupils are entitled to high-quality teaching and that beginning teachers are entitled to good training and education. Classteachers are responsible for the classes taught by the beginning teachers and subject co-tutors/ mentors have overall responsibility for their beginning teachers. Beginning teachers' responsibilities are not specifically outlined in the code, as the school has an academic code of conduct to which all teachers should conform. Careful monitoring of the code ensures that a climate of support and entitlement is built up, which, as has become the case at Hampstead, ensures that responsibilities remain uppermost in the minds of both trainer and trainee.

On a day-to-day level, the role of the school professional tutor is full of small, but important, issues. For example, the timetables of the classes taught by beginning teachers need co-ordination to ensure that there is an even spread of beginning teacher input. It can happen that a particularly 'good' teaching group is given to a beginning teacher by several departments, with the possible result that children receive predominantly novice teachers. This is unacceptable, as the code of practice lays down.

Co-ordination and monitoring across the school is another part of the role of the school-based tutor. Monitoring requires holding meetings to exchange information on practice. It also includes checking that teaching files and mentor logs are kept. The logs are important in providing a record of the focus of particular mentor sessions, and in establishing a key aid for the beginning teacher to set targets on which to work between formal mentoring sessions. If, towards the end of the teaching practice there is any doubt about the amount of support given to a beginning teacher, for example if the beginning teacher felt she or he had cause for complaint or grievance about support time, the log can serve as an important record of work done together. Since mentor time at Hampstead School has been costed and given to the mentor as non-class contact time, having a log also enables the school to ensure that these sessions do take place. In practice, of course, far more time is given to the beginning teacher informally, in snatched moments or longer conversations. Much generously given time and energy is not logged by the co-tutor/mentor, but having a log of the official sessions does provide an essential formal record.

Partnership has provided the opportunity for the school to provide training and development for beginning teachers in areas previously tackled by HEIs. This is particularly true of the link with the London Institute of Education. Again, this gives a new and expanding role for the school professional tutor, aspects of which may be illustrated by examining how beginning teachers receive induction in their school. In all courses, there is an induction period at the beginning of the teaching practice when the school professional tutor needs to put on a programme of introductory activities. (The school has produced a booklet for beginning teachers, containing the school's key policies, for example on student management, which cross-reference to the staff handbook, which they also have.) The induction period may vary according to the HEI involved, but all involve most of the following elements:

- preliminary orientation activities, including a tour of the school, a look at the school context and the statistics which describe this

- introduction to senior staff and to some of the school policies

- tutorial support in researching an 'area study' assignment and provision of a seminar to feed back the results of this assignment.

In the Institute of Education course, the school functions within an area-based cluster. This is a group of schools, usually three or four, often geographically close together, which collaborate on seminars for school-based professional work, pooling resources and expertise. The area-based feedback is usually delivered in the cluster, which enables staff to visit other schools and also, in turn, host other tutors and beginning teachers at Hampstead.

Another element of the early induction period needing co-ordination across the school is tracking. All beginning teachers in their first practice spend one day shadowing a tutor group, one day shadowing a school student with special educational needs and a third shadowing a student with English as his or her second language. The school views these tracking activities as extremely valuable, as they are the beginning teachers' first glimpse of the range of students for whom they will ultimately have some responsibility. Tracking students with particular needs also focuses beginning teachers on issues with which they will have to grapple in their teaching practice and feedback in seminars allows reflection on the challenges of differentiated teaching and learning, and the need to target individuals appropriately. The school professional tutor organizes these tracking exercises and runs the seminars for oral feedback and discussion of issues raised by the exercise. The school professional tutor also monitors the written reports of such activity, which are a formal requirement of some of the ITE courses.

From the period of induction, the school professional tutor supervises all the pieces of work which will build into a final professional development portfolio. In the Institute of Education PGCE a variety of professional development activities ('profiling tasks') form a focus for reflection often resulting in concise, refined pieces of writing. These tasks involve the beginning teacher in writing personal, analytic pieces on topics such as an audit of prior learning experiences, a reflection on the kind of teacher he or she wants to be, accounts of the student observation from the tracking tasks, his or her reflections on teaching practice and the targets for development. Other profiling tasks contain an element of school-based research, a topic covered in greater detail elsewhere (Heilbronn and Jones, 1997). To assist the research process, the school professional tutor also maintains a staff library, using funds earmarked from the PGCE budget. This library is also available to teaching staff and is gradually building into a valuable resource for all school researchers. Some staff are now donating their own texts and resources from higher degrees they have completed.

Conclusion

Hopefully, it will be clear from this discussion that the school has a strong commitment to training and developing teachers. The school values partnership and welcomes the recognition of the expertise involved in largely practice-based teaching and learning. However, it is clear that the funding does not cover the time needed to do the job properly. Co-tutors/mentors continue to be involved in ITE for their own professional development and because they are committed to training the next generation of teachers. However as more demands are made on their time, the school relies more and more on their dedication. The time formally allocated to them clearly is not adequate for the job.

The functions of the school professional tutor outlined in this chapter are also vital to ensure the overall quality of training and assessment. Here too, the hours involved are not adequately funded. This chapter has described how the school professional tutor needs to monitor across departments to ensure consistency, to liaise and intervene in the case of a failing student teacher, to support both co-tutor/mentor and beginning teacher. There may also be cases of difficulty or conflict between them and occasionally there may be a complete breakdown in the tutoring relationship which may take many hours to sort out. Many schools are finding such pressures on staff resources difficult. A recent report, based on a survey of partnerships between universities and schools, carried out by a team funded by the Economic and Social Research Council and covering three-quarters of the courses on offer in 1995–6 found that nearly one-third of respondents reported difficulties in recruiting schools willing to take part in teacher training. The report also criticized the Teacher Training Agency's (TTA) underestimation of the role of higher education in teacher training. It concluded gloomily: 'the scope for many schools to move further towards the TTA model, let alone the SCITT [school-centred initial teacher training] model in the foreseeable future seems decidedly limited' (quoted in Gardiner, 1996).

Financial and resource issues are never easy to resolve. This chapter argues that Hampstead, like many other schools, puts far more time into the training process than can possibly be covered by the funding available. The school staff enjoy all PGCE activities and endorse their value. However, the finances the school receives to undertake them in no way cover the time given to them. Higher education has responded to these concerns by providing support in developing mentoring and tutoring skills and some institutions and some curriculum departments have proved excellent over this. Others still need to do more for the school. Hampstead has to look critically at the support given by HEIs, since the school is under constant pressure to justify its use of resources, of which teacher time is by far the most expensive.

Yet the partnership does seem to work and the school values it. Certainly the context of training and education of the school previously outlined is fundamental to its success. The learning–school context, embodied in the school's aims and having the commitment of the head, governors, senior managers and staff is crucial. There also needs to be a co-ordinator who is sufficiently senior in the school, who is allowed and encouraged to take an overview of developmental needs, in an ethos which values learning in its widest sense. This is the role that has been developed by the school-based tutor in Hampstead. However, having structures and people in place is not what makes the process work. It works only because of this total commitment, particularly that of the co-tutors/mentors.

In conclusion, if concern for high-quality teaching in inner-city schools is genuine in Government, such concern needs adequate support. The system works at present mainly because of such commitment and goodwill. These are the essential foundations for successful ITE, but further development and improvement needs more than current levels of financial support.

References

Department for Education and The Welsh Office (1992) *Initial Teacher Training (Secondary Phase) Circular 9/92*. London: HMSO.

Earley, P. (1992), *Beyond Initial Teacher Training: Induction and the Role of the LEA*. Slough: National Foundation for Educational Research (NFER).

Earley, P. and Kinder, K. (1994), *Initiation Rights: Effective Induction Practices for New Teachers*. Slough: NFER.

Gardiner, J. (1996), 'Teacher training in school no panacea', *Times Educational Supplement*, 19 July.

Heilbronn, R. and Jones, C. (eds) (1997), *New Teachers in an Urban Comprehensive School: Learning in Partnership*. Stoke-on-Trent: Trentham Books.

Imison, T. (1997), 'Hampstead school as a learning community', in Heilbronn, R. and Jones, C., *New Teachers in an Urban Comprehensive School: Learning in Partnership*. Stoke-on-Trent: Trentham Books.

Lambert, D. and Totterdell, M. (1995), 'Crossing Academic Communities: clarifying the Conceptual Landscape.' In Blake, D., Hanley, V., Jennings, M. and Lloyd, M. (eds) *Researching School-based Teacher Education,* Aldershot: Aveburg Press.

McBride, R. (ed) (1996), *Teacher Education Policy*. Lewes: The Falmer Press.

Office for Standards in Education (OFSTED) (1993), *The New Teacher in School: A Survey by HM Inspectors in England and Wales 1992*. London: HMSO.

Teacher Training Agency (TTA) (1996), *National Standards for Teachers* (TTA News No. 11/96). London: TTA.

Whitty, G. et al. (1992), 'Initial teacher training in England and Wales: a survey of current practices and concerns', *Cambridge Journal of Education*, 22(3), 293–306.

Wideen, M. and Grimmett: (eds) (1995), *Changing Times in Teacher Education, Restructuring or Reconceptualization?* Lewes: The Falmer Press.

3.6 Individual action planning in initial teacher education – product or process?

Jennifer Harrison

Introduction

Individual Action Planning (IAP) has been embedded in the secondary PGCE course structure at the University of Leicester School of Education for four years. For a full exploration of the concept of IAP in initial teacher training (ITT) see Tomley (1993). Currently student teachers are asked to complete a regular personal review and to set personal targets at key stages of the training year to address the main subject and professional competence areas. This cycle of 'review, plan, do, achieve, review again' is supported by detailed documentation and boxed proformae for completion by tutor and student teacher at key transition stages of the course. An example of the proforma provided to support the first subject tutorial with the school subject tutor (co-tutor) in early November, about 10 weeks into the course and after two weeks of a block teaching attachment, is given on p.362. A similar process is conducted at four key stages with the school's ITT co-ordinator with respect to developing competence in 'further professional development'. Such documentation when fully completed after the 36-week course can be described as the 'product' – it provides a summary of the subject development action plans or (for professional course work) professional development action plans, which are 'statements of intent', highlighting specific targets, the strategies by which they might be met and a review of the learning experiences encountered.

The IAP process is believed, therefore, to provide rationale and structure for a number of formal tutorial sessions involving key school

---

University of Leicester ● School of Education

First IAP tutorial – after two weeks of mode A block attachment

General review by student teacher
Review your recent block attachment experience and record your reflections. Identify any particular strengths you feel you have developed.

General review by co-tutor
Record your general observations of the block attachment so far.

First action plan (co-tutor and student teacher)

Targets:
Identify the targets for development during the second half of the block attachment.

Strategies:
Identify the strategies to be adopted to meet your targets. Include timings where appropriate.

Signature _____   student teacher

Signature _____   co-tutor

tutors and the student teachers throughout the initial training year. As responsibilities for ITT have been transferred to schools as a result of Department for Education (DfE) Circular 9/92, since 1994 some of the school tutors (the ITT co-ordinators) have gained two years of experience of conducting professional development IAP tutorials with student teachers. The co-tutors have gained one year's experience of subject development action planning with student teachers. Although school tutor training and support have been offered to all school tutors, for some tutors it has, necessarily, been on a limited timescale – there is a contractual requirement of one day per year for the co-tutors and for the ITT co-ordinators.

On the surface, both the IAP products and IAP process appear simple enough. Nevertheless, our anecdotal evidence and evaluations of IAP work done in other educational settings (see Watts, 1993 and 1994), make it clear that the process is complex, that the necessary tutorial skills are wide-ranging, and that broader educational issues for ITT are emerging. In a first year of operation involving 130 subject co-tutors, we might expect varying perceptions of the possible meanings of IAP, some teething troubles and even possible resistance to these new formalized tutorials when working with student teachers. It was in an attempt to conduct a course review of IAP and to explore some of the perceptions of the process, that this paper came to be written.

Course review

A questionnaire survey of all school tutors and student teachers was conducted in June 1996 in an attempt to probe tutors' and student teachers' understandings of IAP tutorials, and their perceptions of the strengths and weaknesses of the IAP process. Full details of this work are described elsewhere (see Harrison, 1996).

Encouragingly there was a positive outcome in that there was consensus amongst all parties (school tutors and student teachers) of the perceived benefits of the IAP. We can conclude that, overall, the IAP process:

- is clear in its aims
- recognizes the skills and experiences brought by the student teachers to the training process
- highlights the positive aspects of student teachers' work
- as a result of tutorial resolutions, allows issues to be addressed by the student teacher in order to bring about a positive change in practice.

The course survey reinforces in several ways, and on a much broader base, the conclusions made by Wall (1993) of the introduction of IAP into the university professional course at Leicester and its follow-up in mentoring work conducted with some newly qualified teachers (NQTs) which were that student teachers' experiences and subsequently the experiences of the NQTs in their first year of teaching, affirmed the IAP process.

In the June 1996 survey, there were also expressed uncertainties about the actual process and varying levels of tutorial preparation by school tutors and student teachers. Clearly for some these have contributed to a lack of clarity and possibly to a lack of commitment to the process by these tutors and student teachers. Indeed as a group of university tutors with responsibilities for course documentation, school tutor training, induction of student teachers and our own tutorial and course work with student teachers, we have already been able to respond in a number of practical ways to the refinement and improvement of the course structures and the ways of working.

The data obtained from the survey, particularly the data extracted when exploring possible differences between seven subject areas, requires careful interpretation – sample sizes vary in different subject areas and, in addition, academic attainments, levels of motivation and teaching competence may all be significant factors in determining student teachers' expectations of themselves and others during the IAP process. Although, on the one hand, Booth (1993) noted a seven-fold increase in numbers of mentors spending time in regular weekly meetings with student teachers compared with numbers found in a survey conducted

11 years earlier (Patrick 1982), we are still very much 'in transition' in terms of the extent to which the school tutors are able, or willing, to engage in a contracted weekly discussion time with the student teachers, and in terms of the quality of the tutorial support during this time. For the purposes of discussion in this chapter a number of broad themes are explored in order to highlight and comment on the complexities of the IAP tutorial process.

Discussion

Perceived main aims of Individual Action Planning

In response to the question, 'What do you see as the main aims of IAP?' for the purposes of analysis all responses were assigned to one of four categories.

These categories are based on the suggestions made by Watts (1993) and are described in Table 1. *(See page 366)*

The percentage of responses which were assigned to each category for each participant group: ITT co-ordinators, co-tutors, student teachers, are shown in Table 2. *(See page 367)*

Substantial differences appear in the way the different parties appear to place emphasis on the four possible broad aims of IAP. From the data for category 1 it appears that ITT co-ordinators perceive the IAP process as having to do with 'student responsibility' more strongly (51 per cent) than the co-tutors (28 per cent) and student teachers (22 per cent). The data for category 2 indicates that co-tutors, and student teachers in particular, appear to perceive IAP as having to do with 'guidance' (71 per cent and 88 per cent).

From the data for categories 3 and 4, there is little evidence that the three parties either perceive or acknowledge the wider educational (lifeskills) or self-empowerment aims of IAP. A small percentage of the ITT co-ordinators (six per cent) recognize the possibility of internalization by the student teachers of the IAP process; a tiny minority of co-tutors (0.5 per cent) did recognize this also. What is noteworthy is that the student teachers at this stage of their professional careers do not appear to recognize these wider aims of IAP and that the large majority

Table 1: Categorization of responses to the question 'What do you see as the main aims of IAP?'

Category 1	Responses include those which indicate a student's 'responsibility' for his or her own behaviour or learning in order to meet them. The student's responsibility includes the setting of his or her own deadlines and some personal endeavour to meet these. The targets set are always short term.
Category 2	Responses include those which indicate guidance of the student to enable the setting of targets at key transition points in the course. The notion of choice is there – choices which can be offered and selected from. Targets are somewhat longer term than in category 1.
Category 3	Responses include those with an overall 'educational' emphasis, in which important and valuable lifeskills are believed to be developed, e.g. it is seen to help future decision-making activity. The IAP process is, thus, internalized. Targets are long-term ones.
Category 4	Responses indicate 'empowerment of an individual' and an operation within the overall management of one's learning. It draws together the first three categories and provides a flexible structure which is responsive to an individual's needs.

From: Watts, A.G. (1993), *Individual Action Planning: Issues and Strategies.*

Table 2: 'What do you see as the aims of IAP?' – a summary of the percentages of responses assigned to each category for the three responding groups

Responding groups	Category 1 Student responsibility	Category 2 Guidance	Category 3 Educational	Category 4 Empowerment
ITT co-ordinators	51	42	6	0
Co-tutors	28	71.5	0.5	0
Student teachers	22	88	0	0

of school tutors with whom they spend most of their time do not seem to acknowledge the wider possible aims either.

It is worth considering here the analysis of the responses to the question, 'Do you use IAPs in any contexts other than in ITT?' There are, not surprisingly, considerable differences between the responses of the three parties. The extent of alternative positive use was indicated by the following percentages:

• ITT co-ordinators, 75 per cent

• co-tutors, 52 per cent

• student teachers, 4 per cent.

Such differences are likely to be due to differences in roles and responsibilities for ITT co-ordinators and co-tutors with differing emphases on staff professional development or on classroom teaching and departmental management. Indeed, by examining the nature of the alternative contexts cited: 'pupil support' and 'in-service training', this appears to be a likely explanation. Through the citing of such examples there appears also to be an acknowledgement by these tutors of the role of IAP in the management of pupils' learning. I believe there is scope here for further recognition by co-tutors and ITT co-ordinators of the existing use of IAP in classroom and in whole-school contexts. If the wider aims of IAP (such as those referred to in categories 3 and 4) are acceptable to tutors, then student teachers need further induction in school in its use in the classroom and as a professional tool for appraisal and so on.

The tutorial process

It is important to explore more fully the expectations and the processes of the tutorial process as well as the provided framework and structures of IAP before we can hope to fully understand underlying issues. We have at Leicester avoided the use of the term 'mentor' because, primarily, it raises complications in terms of competing definitions and contexts. The word 'tutor' represents the teacher who carries the responsibilities for various combinations of supervision and assessment of, and provision of help and guidance to the student teachers.

The IAP process is designed to link with the PGCE 'assessment' process. In September 1995 we transferred for the first time to co-tutors a share in the responsibility for the assessment of subject competences, as well as the framework for the IAP tutorials. The IAP process can and should be linked to the assessment framework, and clearly there is opportunity for, and some expectation of, the use of IAP alongside so-called 'open learning methodologies'. Lewis (1993) in a discussion of the evolution of open learning indicated that assessment is:

- based on competence however acquired
- based on a collection of a wide range of 'evidence'
- uncoupled from attendance on courses
- highly modular (units, elements, performance criteria)
- varied and flexible
- linked to performance in the workplace.

To explore the tutorial process further, it is necessary to consider what benefits there are perceived to be in the IAP process. In the June questionnaire survey (Harrison, 1996) an analysis of the perceived strengths of IAP process was conducted by assigning responses to the given question to one of seven categories as shown in Table 3.

Overall, the data shows many similarities in the way members of the three responding parties have chosen to answer this question. However, there is some indication that the ITT co-ordinators place particular emphasis on 'Talking' (34 per cent of their responses), whereas co-tutors emphasize 'Focusing' (29 per cent). Student teachers emphasize both

Table 3: 'What are the perceived strengths of IAP?' – a comparison of the percentages of responses assigned to each heading

Categories of responses	ITT co-ordinators (n = 50)	Co-tutors (n = 89)	Student teachers (n = 196)
Focusing (supporting target setting)	22	29	21
Self-responsibility	10	7	14
Time management	4	9	4
Talking	34	17	23.5
Reflection and evaluation	10	20	10
Monitoring and assessment	14	18	25.5
Management of (student teacher's) learning	6	0	2

n = no. of responses

'Talking' (23.5 per cent) and aspects of 'Monitoring and assessment' (25.5 per cent). The different definitions I provide for 'Talking' and 'Reflection and evaluation' are given in a later part of this discussion. At this stage it is useful to notice the relatively low importance given by all three parties with respect to 'Self-responsibility' and to 'Reflection and evaluation'.

From the same survey, an analysis of responses to a question about perceived weaknesses of the IAP process is summarized in Table 4. Here

Table 4 'What are the perceived weaknesses of IAP?' – a comparison of the percentages of responses assigned to each category

Categories of responses	ITT co-ordinators (n = 36)	Co-tutors (n = 81)	Student teachers (n = 242)
More guidance needed	27	20	20
Avoidance	17	15	31
Time constraints	25	15	15
Management of IAP difficult	22	38	26
Problems with monitoring and assessment	3	5	4
Teaching is viewed as an holistic activity	3	7	1
Learning process (about teaching) is different from this model	3	0	3

n = no. of responses

responses were grouped according to seven categories for the purposes of comparison.

As in Table 3, many similarities in the percentage responses shown in Table 4 are found across all three parties. The main differences in perceptions of weaknesses can be summarized:

- ITT co-ordinators give particular emphasis to the need for further guidance (27 per cent of ITT co-ordinators' responses) and to time constraints (25 per cent)

- co-tutors raise concerns mostly frequently to do with the management of the IAP (38 per cent)

- student teachers mention most frequently issues which indicate avoidance of the IAP process (31 per cent), which can be interpreted also as 'a lack of real engagement with' the IAP process – student teachers also raise concerns to do with the management of the IAP (26 per cent).

Therefore, we need to provide more support to co-tutors to maximize the potential of the IAP and to enable students to have 'responsibility' for their own learning, in order to overcome the sort of confusion about the nature and aim of IAP which is apparent when a co-tutor writes, '(IAP) ensures that in each school every mentor is setting targets for student teachers to improve'.

This in turn connects with monitoring and assessment issues. From the range of comments received from co-tutors on the 'perceived strengths of IAP' the connections between the IAP and the newly-introduced 'staged reporting system' are made on rather a limited basis. The notion that IAP provides for constant monitoring is just beginning for some: 'progression can be clearly identified and positive achievements are recorded', and is more advanced for others: '(the IAP) enables a co-tutor to monitor progression and communicate expectations'. A quarter of student teachers seem to have made positive connections between the IAP process and the assessment process in terms of monitoring and assessment of teaching competences and overall development. It emerges as the most important perceived benefit by the student teachers overall.

Nearly three-quarters of the co-tutors (see Table 2) saw the primary aim of IAP as one involving the provision of guidance to the student teachers. The proportion of student teachers who saw the primary aim as one of guidance is even higher (see Table 2). It may be that one of the effects of the procedures we have put in place (the structure of key transition points, where the option choices can be explored and help given to prepare for them) is that the very structures we have put in place have precluded a greater awareness of an important and hoped-for aim which is 'personal responsibility for learning'.

In contrast, just over half of the ITT co-ordinators claimed 'personal responsibility' as the primary aim of IAP (see Table 2), and therefore, as co-ordinators, they might play a larger and much needed role in encouraging greater awareness amongst student teachers and co-tutors of the importance of personal responsibility and self-initiative in the IAP process. To this end, opportunities for working with pupils in school could enhance the awareness and the skills being developed in student teachers. Watts (1993) points out that pupils taking more responsibility is a 'pupil-management process', for example, dealing with behavioural problems by working with such pupils to set targets for their resolution, resulting in pupils internalizing forms of behaviour needed for the effective running of the school.

Control or personal responsibility?

Although the wider and hoped-for *aim* of encouraging personal responsibility for one's own learning is not made explicit in our present course documentation, it is often referred to by university tutors as an area which can maximize the potential of the IAP process. We have made more explicit in the next year's documentation and briefing papers the particular responsibilities of the student teacher. We ask explicitly, for example, for student teachers to assume responsibility for preparation for tutorials, to keep up-to-date the IAP documentation, and to prepare in advance for the IAP tutorials. Too many students report and lay blame on factors outside for the incompleteness of the process, for example:

- 'none of the tutors knew what I was supposed to write'
- 'the tutor set the targets – not interesting'
- 'targets can be meaningless – they just have to be done!'

We have a challenge if we are to counterbalance this perception with the wider 'lifeskill' aim and the 'management of learning' aim (i.e. categories 3 and 4 in Table 1). Institutionally, we have chosen to initiate the process and to control it through the use of proformae, prompt sheets and so on. We have set the criteria for choosing the targets – they should be few in number, specific, challenging but achievable. If co-tutors are sustaining the process by writing down the targets, reading them back to the student teachers but not reviewing the targets set thoroughly, then the whole process may be de-valued in the eyes of the student teacher. The balance of input from co-tutor and student teacher in the early tutorials is crucial if the student teacher is to 'own' the process.

The repertoire of required skills on the part of the school tutor becomes increasingly long. It has been widely acknowledged elsewhere that, associated with the particular reponsibilities of the school tutor, are a range of tutoring skills. Others (see Turner, 1993a) have summarized these variously as the range of skills shown on the left hand side of Table 5. *(See page 374)*

To embed action planning in the tutorial work makes the list of required skills even longer (see right hand side of Table 5). Some co-tutors are now beginning to recognize the range of necessary professional skills in carrying out their supervisory and supporting roles with student teachers.

Reflection and evaluation

Action planning thus far at Leicester has provided a rationale and a structure for tutors to spend more individual time with student teachers in a guidance role. Blocked time provides status and is value-added, both in the eyes of the tutor and the student teacher. It clarifies the responsibility of the tutor for helping with target setting. It can now be used more widely as a tool for encouraging personal review by the student teachers.

Table 5: Required tutor skills in tutorial work with student teachers

Interpersonal communication	Counselling
Focused classroom observation	Negotiating
The provision of constructive feedback	Listening
Encouraging personal development	Target setting
A concern for the beginning teacher	
Giving advice	
Demonstrating teaching	
Enabling and encouraging reflection	
Assessing (including understanding and interpreting the teaching competences)	

The data in Table 2 reveals the value to all three parties of 'talking'. 'Talking' is taken to mean time for discussion, negotiation, prioritizing and planning. The quality of the 'talk' is very dependent on who 'controls' the talking, whether there is an imbalance in the right to speak, whether there is adequate thinking time for the learner, whether the learner is keen to give the 'right' answers, and so on.

'Reflection and evaluation' can to some extent be distinguished from 'talking' – they encompass the IAP activity of 'review', and so pre-planning, collation of evidence and a written statement all help to pave the way for a more balanced discussion. All three parties rated 'reflection and evaluation' as one of the strengths of IAP (see Table 2), but it is mentioned less frequently by ITT co-ordinators and student teachers (for each, 10 per cent of responses) than co-tutors (20 per cent), and can be considered a relatively low priority in the list of strengths of the IAP process. The student teachers who said:

- 'for many it is a new way of thinking – it takes time to get used to it'
- 'targets that are not achieved are equated with failure – that's demoralizing'
- 'it depends on the skill of the person guiding you – it needs a good co-tutor who is able to pull out specific targets if the student cannot do this'

have clearly grasped the value of the 'review process' and its role in evaluation of self-development. In such circumstances, the process may become more important than the IAP document (the written record).

In her discussion of the management of Records of Achievement (RoA) with pupils, Broadfoot (1989) recognized the need to provide teachers with opportunities to develop one-to-one discussion skills. The characteristic of the IAP tutorial is likely to have special features which make it quite unlike the usual conversations between teachers and student teachers. A school which already has whole-school policies for RoAs, flexible learning initiatives and so on, is likely to be preparing teachers for such discussion skills.

Issues to do with power and negotiation have to be addressed further. The tutor has to allow the student teacher to self-examine their claimed competences, and, in the context of a range of 'evidence', say what he or she feels about the student's progress; subsequently the tutor will negotiate with the student teacher an agreed agenda for further action. The management of the allocated tutorial time has to continue to be a school tutor training issue. Importantly, as has been acknowledged with RoAs in schools and colleges, the IAP process does pose a considerable challenge to schools and tutors. It makes substantial demands on the time, energy, resources and skills of the tutors.

Involvement

There is evidence (Harrison, 1996) that for some (student teachers, co-tutors and ITT co-ordinators) action planning can be viewed as an administrative chore rather than as an aid to building more effective relationships or supporting the learning process. For some the system is constraining – it lacks necessary flexibility. For others it is over-rational – they don't want to write down their plans. It is important to give some consideration to the perceptions of the IAP documentation. There were many references in the June survey (Harrison, 1996) to the workload associated with the paperwork. The IAP documents have to be accessible and, therefore, public. More clarity is needed about the status of the IAP documentation. It is less a private statement of intent and more one that is mediated, clarifying individual purposes but through a process of guidance and review.

At the heart of the process is the relationship between tutor and student teacher. Most novice teachers will only learn about reflective teaching from a role model. Turner (1993) noted that the personality of the mentor is crucial to the success of the tutor–student teacher relationship. In turn the success of IAP is dependent on the teachers 'owning the process'. Our experience at Leicester is that individual tutors clearly need time and support to work through these many complex issues for themselves.

References

Booth, M. (1993), 'The Effectiveness and Role of the Mentor in School: the students' view', *Cambridge Journal of Education*, 23(2): 185-197.

Broadfoot, P. (1989), *Records of Achievement. Report of the National Evaluation of Pilot Schemes*. London: HMSO.

Department for Education (DfE) (1992), *Initial Teacher Training* (secondary phase) Circular 9/92. London: DfE.

Harrison, J.K. (1996), *Report on Individual Action Planning. A Survey of Understandings and Perceptions amongst School Tutors and Student Teachers*. Leicester: University of Leicester.

Lewis, R. (1993), 'The progress of open learning', *Education and Training*, 35(4), 3–8.

Patrick, H. (1982), *The Structure and Process of Initial Teacher Education within Universities in England and Wales*. Leicester: University of Leicester.

Tomley, D. (1993), 'Individual action planning in initial teacher training', *British Journal of Inservice Education*, 19(2), 41–9.

Turner, M. (1993), 'The role of mentors and teacher tutors in school based teacher education and induction', *British Journal of Inservice Education*, 19(1), 36–45.

Wall, D. (1993), *Action Planning in Teacher Training. Final Evaluation Report*. Leicester: University of Leicester.

Watts, A.G. (1993), 'Individual action planning: issues and strategies', *British Journal of Education and Work*, 5(1), 47–63.

— (1994), 'Developing individual action-planning skills', *British Journal of Education and Work*, 7(2), 51–61.

3.7 Evaluation of a developmental profile in initial teacher education – towards a common entitlement

Vivienne Griffiths, Carol Robinson and Mike Willson

Introduction

This chapter presents some of the findings of an evaluation of a developmental profile designed for trainee teachers on a Post Graduate Certificate in Education (PGCE) course. The background to the profile and how the research was carried out are explained. Positive aspects of the profile are stressed as well as issues and concerns. Ways in which the profile has been changed and implications for the future, are also raised in conclusion.

One of the main strengths of the profile, which has been highly praised by external examiners and the Office for Standards in Education (OFSTED) inspectors, is the way it has been developed jointly by university tutors and school practitioners. This has given the users a strong sense of ownership and reinforced new partnership arrangements which have been formalized under the recently established Sussex

Consortium, as well as meeting Government requirements for initial teacher education (ITE).

Background to the Sussex ITE profile

The University of Sussex PGCE developmental profile was constructed to help the university and partnership schools within the Sussex Consortium improve systems for supporting and monitoring the work and development of trainee teachers. A previous study (Willson and Adamczyk, 1996) within the science component of the secondary PGCE programme had shown that, without formal structures for delivery and assessment, a common entitlement could not be guaranteed. In addition, this study had indicated that the trainees' perceptions of who was delivering what on the course were in many respects at variance with the school perspective. Such discrepancies clearly had implications, not only for ensuring common entitlement, but also for quality control.

One option available for addressing these problems was through the introduction of a competence profile. Circulars 9/92 and 14/93 (Department for Education, 1992 and 1993) have provided those responsible for ITE with a focus for addressing the competences thought necessary for newly qualified teachers (NQTs). In the past, many of these were implicit characteristics of successful teaching, but the respective Circulars extend the repertoire of desirable competences and also bring into focus the issue of entitlement with respect to opportunities for acquiring competence (Furlong, 1992). As Halsall (1995) has indicated, a competency-based approach can focus more systematically on whether opportunities are being provided for trainee development, as well as clarify what aspects of teacher training are delivered by the school and by the higher education institution (HEI) respectively.

A profiling approach in assessment and self-evaluation of the trainee teachers had been in operation in embryo on the University of Sussex PGCE course for some time before the DfE Circulars, based clearly on the principle of the reflective practitioner. The PGCE faculty also had experience of the construction of a competency-based professional development profile for NQTs (East Sussex CC, 1996), designed to build on what had been achieved during initial teacher training (ITT). As a high proportion of our trainees take up their first teaching post in Sussex, it seemed an appropriate starting point from which to consider the construction of an ITE profile. Indeed, as Davies has indicated, 'the strongest case for profiling has been the argument that a structured link is built between initial and in-service teacher education which will enable a teacher to improve continually' (1993:29).

However, when the PGCE team started to develop a profile which would also incorporate the Circular 9/92 and Circular 14/93 competences, many reservations were expressed, and it seemed an enormous task to translate a list of summative statements into a workable, formative profile. We certainly did not want to end up with a mechanistic checklist, an approach criticized by other teacher educators as behaviourist and reductionist (Norris, 1991; Calderhead and James, 1992; Husbands, 1993). Indeed, there was a concern from the outset that a potential tension existed between the demands imposed by a competency-led profile and the need for critical reflection on the part of the trainee teacher (Simco, 1995). We were mindful that competences, in lending themselves to the identification and objective assessment of teaching skills based on a range of prescribed criteria, can as a consequence pay little attention to an holistic view of professional development (Norris, 1991; Pring, 1991). As Hextall et al. argue, 'teaching is not reducible to a set of technical operations' (1991:15).

On the other hand, there was also a growing body of evidence that competence could be interpreted in a broader way (Whitty and Wilmott, 1991; Eraut, 1994; Tomlinson, 1995) and profiles could be developed sensitively which addressed learning processes and incorporated professional qualities (James and Denley, 1992; Davies, 1993) leading to the empowerment of trainee teachers (Murphy et al., 1993).

The strength of the East Sussex LEA model lay in the collaborative process that maintained and enhanced long-standing university–school links, emphasized joint responsibility and involved a local employer of teachers. It was important from the outset that the ITE profile was likewise seen as 'a committed, practical and user friendly document with the language of guidance rather than instruction' (Burrell, Grigg and Levine, 1995:3) with the emphasis 'shifting from summative assessment to continual professional development' (Simco, 1995:269). It was equally important from the outset that the developmental ITE profile was seen as a shared endeavour involving the trainee and both school and HEI-based tutors. Central to the profile was a commitment to critical reflection in the belief that 'good teaching involves the continuous process of self-evaluation and reflection on knowledge, beliefs and practice' (East Sussex CC, 1996:2).

As a result, both the primary and secondary PGCE courses at Sussex University opted for a developmental profile which would link ITE with on-going professional development. With the help of university funding, working parties were set up, consisting of school representatives as well as university tutors, in order to base the profile firmly in classroom practice and make it manageable for the trainees and mentors to use. The underlying principle of the working parties was the need to gain ownership of the Government competences by reworking them according to the structure and philosophy of the course.

On the primary PGCE course, it was decided to keep the same major areas of competence as in Circular 14/93, but to alter 'further professional development' to 'professional qualities', in order to stress that trainees were expected to demonstrate these qualities from the start of the course, rather than some time in the future. Competences were also added in areas felt to be missing, such as equal opportunities and special needs, and within professional qualities competences such as the 'ability to reflect critically on practice' were added (Hextall et al., 1991). Three developmental stages were decided on, to reflect the three terms of the course and the main assessment points. The profile framework was fleshed out by adding descriptors to each developmental stage. As well as writing a detailed description of each developmental stage, the working party built into the profile examples of activities which the trainees might do to exemplify a particular competence, to help guide the mentors in providing a suitable programme of work for each stage. The group also drew up the format for reporting, including both a summary column (achieved, not yet achieved, etc.), a large space for comments and supporting evidence, and a final column in which to write targets for the next stage (Griffiths, 1995).

On the secondary PGCE course a competency matrix within the profile was introduced which encompassed the five areas of competence defined by Circular 9/92. Underpinning the profile itself was a framework of meetings and classroom observations which focused, at different times, on these five areas and for each a range of statements was provided which showed progression through three levels of development. The latter highlighted particular strengths with respect to competence that are likely to be acquired by teachers in their NQT and/or early years of teaching. A total of 32 statements were used at three stages of trainee development, putting the five areas into both a specific school placement and university-based context.

During the pilot year, in a limited number of curriculum areas on the secondary course to begin with, these statements were backed up with evidence descriptors so that clear criteria were available against which judgements could be made in specific subjects. It was hoped in addition that the descriptors, as well as detailing the types of evidence that trainees and school-based mentors could present of concept acquisition, also indicated opportunities during the PGCE course for trainees to acquire particular competences. In doing so it was hoped to address the issue of entitlement.

The profile evaluation – methodology

With the help of university funding, an external researcher was appointed to carry out an evaluation of the profile in its pilot stage. Twelve case study schools (six primary and six secondary) were identified and data collected through observation of mentors and trainees during profiling meetings, interviews with mentors and trainees and scrutiny of completed profile forms. In each school at least two mentors and the professional tutor were involved. In particular, the researcher collected data on the implementation of the profiles in practice. The mentors' and trainees' views of the competences, their interpretation of competence statements, how they made judgements about whether a particular competence had been achieved, and the evidence used to support those judgements, were all looked at in detail. In addition to the case studies, a questionnaire was sent to all trainees and mentors.

As in Davies and Macaro's study (1995), anonymity of participants was assured and the findings were fed back to the case study schools for review and revision before final writing up. The researcher reported back to the profile working parties at each stage and produced both an interim and final report (Robinson, 1996). The director of PGCE and profile co-ordinator have subsequently carried out further analysis of the questionnaires.

Positive findings

> Competence-based approaches can be justified as giving students clear targets of achievement and explicit evidence of their progress, enabling schools to share an understanding of the function of placements and giving employers a clear idea of what to expect.
>
> (Whitty and Wilmott, 1991:311)

In general, the response to the profile was almost universally positive and the findings of the research were very similar to those of other evaluations (Calderhead and James, 1992; Ward and Ritchie, 1994; Davies and Macaro, 1995). Most mentors found the profile 'user-friendly', 'informative' and 'a useful working document,' and the competency statements themselves helpful. As one mentor commented, the profile was a 'vast improvement on the previous reporting procedure'. Although somewhat daunted at first (Tomlinson and Saunders, 1995), the trainees found the profiling approach most helpful, because they felt that they were clear about what they were working towards. The possible tension which we perceived between assessment and self-evaluation was not apparent in the trainees' responses. They emphasized the value of the formative and developmental elements of the process. This was also evidence of the positive way in which the mentors had used the profile with them.

In particular, the profile was seen as valuable because it provided a clear structure to trainee progress (Tomlinson, 1995), through developmental stages, and a series of structured activities for the trainees to undertake at each stage. One of the main values to the trainees was as a 'confidence boosting' exercize and a record of achievement (Murphy et al., 1993), as well as of the progress they were making. As one trainee wrote, 'It allows you to target the things you need to achieve and lets you relish in those already achieved.' Quality assurance was cited as a benefit, because the profile was based on clear criteria, and provided a common framework for monitoring, reviewing and assessing the trainees' progress (Davies and Macaro, 1995). The principle of a common entitlement was, thus, clearly established.

Both mentors and trainees welcomed the early identification of trainees' strengths and weaknesses, which resulted from the regular review of progress. This enabled extra support to be provided where necessary at an earlier stage than before. As in other profiling projects, the profile also provided a sharp focus for mentor–trainee discussions (Davies, 1993), 'facilitating an internal dialogue' (Davies and Macaro, 1995:32) and enabling action plans with realistic targets to be drawn up (James and Denley, 1992). As one mentor wrote, 'I did feel that having done so much together already in our areas of planning and implementation that there would be no surprises on the profile for the trainee.'

For the trainees, this varied very much in line with how well they had got on with their mentor and how fair an opinion they felt their mentor was giving (Davies, 1993). If the relationship was low on discussion, however, the profile was felt useful as a means of finding out what the mentor actually thought. The target section was found to be particularly useful to both mentors and trainees. In praising this, the mentors were endorsing the formative aspect of the profile and its benefit to the trainees' future development, rather than simply using it as an extended summative assessment. The developmental profile model adopted also provided more structure to student progression during placements and was particularly useful for transition from first to second school placement.

A related benefit was the direct link to the East Sussex Profile for NQTs (East Sussex CC, 1996), thus providing continuity between ITE and NQT stages and leading to further professional development. This has been one of the main benefits cited in other profiling research (Davies,

1993; Murphy et al., 1993; Haydn, 1996), and often referred to as 'building the bridge': 'a professional profile which begins in the training institution can overcome the major problem of the disjunction between initial training and early professional development' (Husbands, 1993:116).

As one mentor wrote: '[Trainee] teachers would be aware of own strengths and areas in which they may continue to need support as NQTs.' Although mentors thought the profile could easily be transferred from placement to placement, they did not want it used for reference purposes. Trainees shared this concern and were anxious that the profiles were not used for a different audience in this way.

Issues and concerns

> Competency-led profiles redefine the nature of teaching. They direct attention to technical and managerial components of teacher performance and away from more important issues of teacher effectiveness.
>
> (Husbands, 1993:121)

Many of the problems and concerns cited in other research on profiling (Whitty and Willmott, 1991, Murphy et al., 1993; Davies and Macaro, 1995) were also found on the introduction of the Sussex ITE profile.

Although the principle of common entitlement underpinned the profile, there was some concern that mentors were not implementing it in the same way in practice. Initial problems on the primary profile, piloted the previous year, had been ironed out, but some inconsistency was apparent on the secondary course in its pilot year. This was mainly due to uncertainty arising from a cascade model of induction, the fact that not all mentors had read the accompanying guidelines and initial reservations about the profile itself (Tomlinson and Saunders, 1995). This year, all trainees and tutors have been briefed directly by the profile co-ordinator.

The schedule of meetings attached to the Sussex ITE profile was also found to be ambitious and demanding; implementing the profile took time to organize and self-organize from people under different pressures.

A few of the respondents to the questionnaire offered the opinion that the list of competences risked the danger of being too prescriptive, as well as at times giving the impression of being impersonal, cumbersome and constraining. This echoes others' concerns (Calderhead and James, 1992; Husbands, 1993; Murphy et al., 1993) that a competency-based approach can encourage an over-bureaucratic model of teaching. It could be of course, as others have found (Burrell, Grigg and Levine, 1995) that complaints about too many competence statements may be the 'natural reaction of conscientious and pressured people'. Some repetition of competence statements was certainly evident, arising from the DfE Circulars themselves (Davies and Macaro, 1995), and these have been reduced this year, as well as the paperwork required.

Another difficulty experienced during the pilot phase of the profile was knowing when a competence had been achieved by a trainee. How many times did a particular competence have to be shown by a trainee and in what context, in order for it to have been deemed achieved? As Husbands points out, in cautioning against context-free competency descriptors, 'it would... be possible for a teacher described as exceptionally competent to perform none-the-less in a merely mediocre way in some settings' (1993:119). A related concern surrounded the weightings of different competency statements. Some mentors felt that competences such as classroom management should have greater weighting than others when deciding on successful completion of a school placement. The question of weighting needs further consideration by the working parties.

In some cases, mentors interpreted statements of competence in different ways, which led to differing expectations of trainees. For example, 'reporting to parents' was deemed to have been achieved in some cases if mentors had shown trainees copies of school reports; in other cases it was only achieved if the trainees had written and presented reports themselves. Knowing when a competence had been achieved was sometimes difficult to assess because the wording of the competence was too imprecise. In general, mentors found skills-related competences with clear definitions and observable outcomes easier to address. Some competences were difficult to assess, particularly where attitudes, understanding or awareness were involved, for example with cultural issues or equal opportunities. Where evidence descriptors existed, mentors were more confident about the criteria they should apply, even with attitudinal competences. All curriculum tutors on the secondary course are now developing subject specific evidence descriptors.

A further concern expressed by both university and school-based tutors was that the competency statements did not lend themselves to describing the development of what they called the 'holistic' teacher (Husbands, 1993; Davies and Macaro, 1995). A trainee might be technically competent in the classroom, but fail to demonstrate important professional qualities (Davies, 1993). Qualities such as commitment, presentation and relationships were already included in the primary profile. Secondary mentors also requested space for overall comments on trainees' progress and this has been introduced in the reports at the end of each school placement.

Ways the profile has been changed

> 'Our purpose as teacher educators is to equip our students with effective capability to achieve their own teaching purposes.'
> (Tomlinson, 1995:184)

As well as the changes noted above, assessment has been distanced from the profile in the formative stages and it has been made clear from the outset to both trainees and mentors this year that the profile is not a defining blueprint for trainee behaviour. It is an aid to trainees in a crucial year for their development as teachers.

Mindful of Tomlinson's call for consistency (1995), cross-moderation in geographically-based school clusters has already been established on the primary course and will now be extended to the secondary PGCE. Comparison of completed profile forms and subsequent discussion on how they were completed, leads to an appreciation of the need for a common basis for judgements. This is further enhanced by joint observations from tutor–mentor and mentor–mentor, within and across schools. In this way, common entitlement should be ensured in practice as well as in principle.

The future

The University of Sussex experience has revealed a high level of commitment on the part of mentors and professional tutors in partnership schools to the training of tomorrow's teachers and their continuing professional development (CPD). There has been an admirable appreciation of the need for on-going support and a recognition that regular meetings, with the focus on competences, coupled with honest and critical reflection and action plan targets, are the ways to consolidate development. The overwhelming response from mentors answering questionnaires was that the competence statements are appropriate ones for raising awareness of the attributes of a good teacher, and pointers for better practice for *all* teachers. The profile is seen by both mentors and trainees as providing continuity for further professional development between the PGCE and NQT phases, by encouraging effective reflection beyond the training year. A few respondents even expressed the view that a developmental profile could be useful for negotiating targets and entitlement during staff review and appraisal, but held out little hope that sufficient funding would be provided to act on recommendations.

The role the profile should play in applications for first teaching posts remains to be resolved, as well as the link between the Sussex profile and the proposed Teacher Training Agency (TTA) career entry profile. During our pilot year, the secondary team took part in trials of the TTA profile and it did not meet with universal approval. The summative nature of the TTA profile meant that Sussex University tutors felt that, although they had met a nebulous bureaucratic requirement in a 'fair' way, unlike the Sussex developmental profile it had not materially helped the trainees. The TTA pilot profile was impressionistic, time consuming and was not an adequate record of trainee achievement (Haydn, 1996). It would need considerable restructuring if it were to be used as the summative record of our developmental profile in the future.

References

Burrell, D., Grigg, R. and Levine, N. (1995), *East Sussex NQT Development Profile: Evaluation* Report. Lewes: East Sussex County Council.

Calderhead, J. and James, C. (1992), 'Recording student teachers' learning experiences', *Journal of Further and Higher Education,* 16(1), 3–12.

Davies, I. (1993), 'Using profiles in initial teacher education: key issues arising from experience', *Journal of Further and Higher Education,* 17(2), 27–39.

Davies, I. and Macaro, E. (1995), 'The reactions of teachers, tutors and students to profiling student competences in initial teacher education', *Journal of Further and Higher Education,* 19(2), 28–41.

Department for Education (DfE) (1992), *Initial Teacher Training (Secondary Phase) Circular 9/92*. London: HMSO.

— (1993), *The Initial Training of Primary School Teachers: New Criteria for Courses Circular 14/93*. London: HMSO.

East Sussex County Council (1996), *East Sussex NQT Developmental Profile, (Revised)*. Lewes: East Sussex County Council.

Eraut, M. (1994), *Developing Professional Knowledge and Competence.* London: Falmer Press.

Furlong, J. (1992), 'The limits of competence: a cautionary note on Circular 9/92'. Unpublished paper, Universities Council for the Education of Teachers Conference, Oxford.

Griffiths, V. (1995), *Profiling on the Primary PGCE* Course.Brighton: University of Sussex: Enterprise in Higher Education.

Halsall, R. (1995), 'Assessing competence in teacher education', in Edwards, A. and Knight:, *Assessing Competence in Higher Education.* London: Routledge.

Haydn, T. (1996), 'Career entry profiles in initial teacher education: the art of the possible', *British Journal of Curriculum and Assessment,* 6(3), 41-2.

Hextall, I., Lawn, M., Menter, I., Sidgwick, S. and Walker, S. (1991), *Imaginative Projects: Arguments for a New Teacher Education.* London: Goldsmith's College.

Husbands, C. (1993), 'Profiling of student teachers: context, ownership and the beginnings of professional learning', in Bridges, D. and Kerry, T., *Developing Teachers Professionally: Reflections for Initial and In-Service Trainers*. London: Routledge.

James, C.R. and Denley: (1992), 'Using records of student experience in an undergraduate Certificate in Education course', *Evaluation and Research in Education*, 6(1), 23–37.

Murphy, R., Mahony:, Jones, J. and Calderhead, J. (1993), 'Profiling in initial teacher training', *Journal of Teacher Development*, 2(3), 141–6.

Norris, N. (1991), 'The trouble with competence', *Cambridge Journal of Education*, 21(3), 331–41.

Pring, R. (1991), 'On being competent'. Unpublished paper, Universities Council for the Education of Teachers Conference, Oxford.

Robinson, C. (1996), *An Evaluation of the Sussex University Post Graduate Certificate in Education Assessment Profile*. Brighton: University of Sussex: Institute of Education.

Simco, N. (1995), 'Professional policy and development in the induction year', *British Journal of In-Service Education*, 21(3).

Tomlinson: (1995), 'Can competence profiling work for effective teacher preparation? Part 1: general issues', *Oxford Review of Education*, 21(2), 179–94.

Tomlinson: and Saunders, S. (1995), 'The current possibilities for competence profiling', in Edwards, A. and Knight:, *Assessing Competence in Higher* Education. London: Routledge.

Ward, D. and Ritchie, R. (1994), *Journal of Teacher Development*, 3(2), 105–19.

Whitty, G. and Willmott, E. (1991), 'Competence-based teacher education: approaches and issues', *Cambridge Journal of Education*, 21(3), 309–18.

Willson, M. and Adamczyk: (1996), 'Training tomorrow's science teachers: towards a common entitlement', *Science Teacher Education*, 16 May.

3.8 A psychological profile of PGCE students – implications for initial teacher education

Roger Vallance

Introduction

This chapter is concerned with some psychological information about postgraduate beginning teacher students in England. A sample of approximately 1,000 beginning teachers was taken in the summer terms of 1995 and 1996 in a number of institutions. All were in training for secondary teaching. The data reported concern personality style variables.

The sample was collected from 10 higher education institutions (HEIs), ranging from old universities (three) to some of the more recent ones (six) and one former teachers' college. Three were within London, three on the outskirts of London and four from medium-sized towns in southeast England. All respondents were volunteers. Sometimes whole cohorts were sampled within their normal class times. Other institutions allowed invitations to a research session outside normal classes. Just less than 27 per cent of the sample belonged in this latter category.

It is not possible to claim that this sample represents the secondary PGCE in all respects. It has been limited by the resources of a single researcher and remains a sample of convenience in the strictest sense. It is, however, a wide-reaching sample and is large enough to make valid statements at the very least indicative of the full secondary trained Post Graduate Certificate in Education (PGCE) cohort.

The tasks which form the data for this report were all pencil and paper tasks. Each respondent was asked to complete two forms. The first was a sheet requesting biographic information about education and employment prior to the PGCE course, and present age and qualifications. The second was the Myers-Briggs Type Indicator (MBTI) which is a psychological instrument designed to indicate the personality variables as proposed by Jung's theory of personality.

Jung's theory of personality and the Myers-Briggs Type Indicator

CG Jung's psychology has been steadily gaining academic regard (Spoto, 1995). Jung's theories of the collective unconscious and archetypes are readily acknowledged as important contributions to human understanding (Jung, 1964). Less well-known is his theory of personality (Jung, 1971). Briefly, Jung explained personality as the interplay of three dimensions. The first dimension, the attitude of extraversion versus introversion, reflects the orientation to the external world. The extravert is energized by interaction with the outside world. The introvert pays closer attention to the inner world of personal thought. Jung then describes two dimensions as mental functions. The function of perceiving is that of apprehending what is going on. This can be done in either a sensing or intuitive fashion. By this, Jung refers to the two ways people gather information. The sensing person pays attention to the input of the senses. The extraverted sensing person is interested in what is happening 'out there' in the immediate environment. The introverted sensing person pays greater attention to ideas, emotions and feelings coming from the internal world. The intuitive relates more readily to perception of patterns or connections which are perceived without conscious mental processing. The second function relates to how a person decides how to act or interact. This dimension is thinking versus feeling. The thinking person uses the language of logic and order. Feeling is poorly named. A better translation might be 'valuing', paying respect to the language of values and the aesthetic. Each is a rational approach in the sense that it is a way of reaching a decision – one uses the logic of thinking, the other the logic of valuing (Jung, 1971; Spoto, 1995).

The MBTI attempts to operationalize Jung's theory. The authors of the MBTI started this work in the USA in the 1940s and their instrument has developed further the categories of Jung. The MBTI uses a forced choice format and 95 questions to arrive at scores for four dimensions, the first three of which are Jung's of extraversion/introversion (E-I), sensing/intuition (S-N) and thinking/feeling (T-F). The final dimension is judgement versus perception (J-P), which refers to the mental function that is dominant in the external world for the person (Myers, 1993; Bayne, 1995).

The MBTI as a psychometric instrument is deserving of the attention of educators. While it is not the only attempt to operationalize Jung's personality schema (Karesh, Pieper and Holland, 1994) it does perform well pyschometrically (Devito, 1985; Murray, 1990; Lorr, 1991; Tischler, 1994). It is well normed, with predominately US data (Myers and McCaulley, 1985). Reliability is judged to be good (Carlson, 1985; Johnson, 1992; Rytting, Ware and Prince, 1994) and the instrument demonstrates validity (Tzeng et al., 1984; Schweiger, 1985; Rosenak and Shontz, 1988) across a wide range of circumstances (Howes and Carskadon, 1979; Ware, Rytting and Jenkins, 1994). A comprehensive review of the MBTI is provided by Bayne (1995).

Results

Age and gender distributions

Figure 1 indicates that the present sample is comparable to the base population of 1995 entry to PGCE courses (GTTR, 1995), although it contains fewer younger individuals than the total PGCE enrolment of that year.

Figure 2 shows females outnumbering males – 60 per cent of the sample being female. The age spread of the male sample is greater than that of the females.

Figure 1: Ages of PGCE students

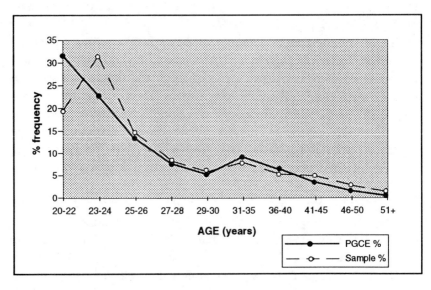

Figure 2: Age distribution of the secondary PGCE sample by gender

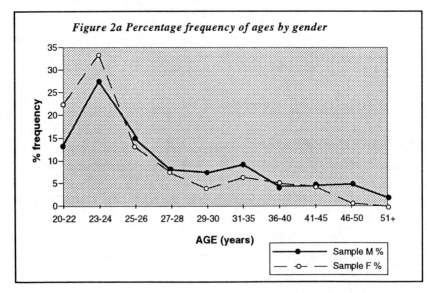

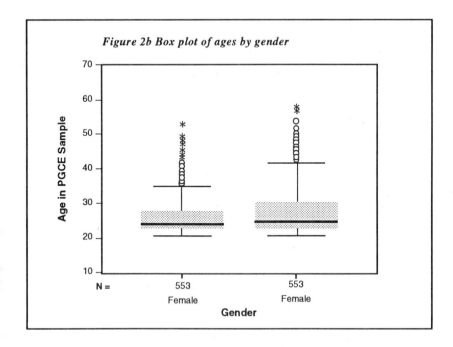

Figure 2a shows that the proportion of females in the sample is greater in the younger groups. After 28 years of age more males enter in the sample. This may indicate a greater uptake of teaching as a second career amongst males. Figure 2b displays the age spread of PGCE students. The box plot shows the median as a thick line, the box being the 25th to 75th percentile. Also shown is the range of ages not considered outliers, the outliers and extreme values. Using a t test for unequal variances, shows that the means are different with a significance at p<0.0001. (Mean difference is 2.177 with a calculated 631.5 degrees of freedom, and the t value of 4.42.) So there is a significant difference between the age distributions of the male and female parts of the sample.

It is clear that the male group is generally older and its spread of age is greater. There is also a longer tail in the male sample of considerably older individuals, many of whom are coming from long-held occupations. The gender ratio in most HEIs was consonant with the overall 60 per cent female, 40 per cent male ratio.

Table 1 Teaching subject by gender

Percentage response by subject and gender			
Subject	*Females*	*Males*	*Total*
Geography	70.4	29.6	2.9
Modern languages	82.8	17.2	12.4
Religious studies	48.9	51.1	5.0
Classics	61.0	39.0	4.4
Chemistry	56.3	43.8	8.6
Physics	43.6	56.4	4.2
Biology	69.8	30.2	9.2
Mathematics	49.2	50.8	13.3
English	70.2	29.8	13.3
History	47.5	52.5	4.3
General science	53.1	46.9	5.3
Physical education	33.3	66.7	5.5
Economics and business	32.1	67.9	3.0
Aggregated subjects	71.6	28.4	8.7%
Total	**562**	**371**	**933**
Percentage Column Total	60.2%	39.8%	100.0%

Table 1 shows dominant female participation in virtually all PGCE subject specialisms. That this also reflects the 1995 GTTR return suggests that the sample is quite representative, at least in this regard, of the whole secondary PGCE cohort.

Myers-Briggs Type Inventory

The typology determined by the MBTI produces a 16-fold classification system; each of the four dimensions has two poles so with four dimensions there are 16 Types. The Type distribution of the sample is presented below as Table 2. The four letter code pertains to the full Type determination scored from the MBTI and the Types are ranked in terms of their frequency within the sample.

Table 2 Type distribution of PGCE students

Type	Frequency	Per cent	Rank
ENFJ	51	5.4	10
ENFP	100	10.7	2
ENTJ	70	7.5	7
ENTP	91	9.7	3
ESFJ	54	5.8	9
ESFP	18	1.9	16
ESTJ	75	8.0	4
ESTP	30	3.2	13
INFJ	43	4.6	12
INFP	71	7.6	6
INTJ	65	6.9	8
INTP	72	7.7	5
ISFJ	45	4.8	11
ISFP	21	2.2	15
ISTJ	107	1.4	1
ISTP	23	2.5	14
Total	936	100	

A Chi-squared test on this data shows that this distribution is not an even one. What is interesting is that the most common Type is ISTJ, which is associated with managerial skills and then the next three most common Types are all extraverts. The least frequent types are –S–P. There are four Types containing SP and these are ranked 13, 14, 15, and 16 in Table 2.

While each Type has a combination of qualities that makes it particularly unique, dealing with a 16-fold classification system is difficult. It is proposed, therefore, to approach the issue of personality principally through the Jungian functions, which yields a four-fold classification – intuitive thinking (NT), intuitive feeling (NF), sensing thinking (ST) and sensing feeling (SF). It is considered reasonable to pay less attention to the attitude to the external world – extraversion/introversion (E-I) – since due to the social and industrial setting of teaching it is by its very nature an activity performed in front of others, pupils, and this setting is presumably anticipated and expected by any prospective teacher trainee. Table 2 also shows that the Jungian Attitude E-I is not associated with the ranking of the frequency of type. (Both E and I hold equal numbers of ranks above and below the median rank.) Finally, the fourth dimension of the external function (judging versus perceiving) is also less helpful in group interactions and more significant within personal development concerns. This last function owes more to Myers and Briggs than Jung (Bayne, 1995). The ranks of Types with P and J are equally spread around the median rank.

The distribution in Table 2 is accounted for by the distribution of the underlying Jungian dimensions. It is expected that gender will influence the distribution of the thinking/feeling function (T-F) as generally 60–70 per cent of males are T and 55–60 per cent females are F (Lawrence, 1993; Myers, 1993). In the published norms for the MBTI there is no correlation between gender with the other dimensions (see Myers and McCaulley, 1985). Table 3 presents the distributions of the Jungian dimensions with respect to gender for the sample of PGCE students. This sample is very different from both Australian and American samples of trainee teachers in that this British sample is more extraverted, intuitive and more thinking (Mallia, 1992).

Clearly, S-N and J-P are not associated in any systematic way to gender. But the sample shows that there is an association with gender for both E-I and T-F. Most of the MBTI literature reports a preponderance of introverts amongst secondary school teachers, a tendency which increases in university and higher education staffs (Myers, 1993). Although this is replicated amongst the males in this sample, the females

Table 3: Distribution of MBTI dimensions with respect to gender

%	Extra/ Introversion		Sensing/ Intuition		Thinking/ Feeling		Judging/ Perceiving	
	E	I	S	N	T	F	J	P
Female	56.7	43.3	41.5	58.5	49.3	50.7	55.8	44.2
Male	45.7	54.3	37.0	63.0	67.3	32.7	52.2	47.8
Total	52.2	47.8	39.9	60.1	56.9	43.1	54.5	45.5
X^2 sig Female versus male	$X^2 = 10.8$ p = .0001		$X^2 = 1.8$ ns		$X^2 = 29.2$ p = .00001		$X^2 = 1.2$ ns	

demonstrate a significant tendency towards extraversion. This may be associated with the younger age of most females in the sample and that 'student life' is characterized by many extraverted type activities, or it may indicate that secondary teaching is starting to attract younger, female extraverts. There is a strong relationship between gender and T-F. Males are predominately T as expected and females more likely to be F but less strongly so than expected. The increase in female participation in the sciences which are generally attractive to Ts might suggest that the availability of these positions is attracting females with strong T mental dispositions.

The distribution of the Jungian functions within the main teaching subjects of the sample is listed in Table 4. From Table 4 it can be seen that there are some distinctive differences within gender for the distribution of the Jungian functions. Religious studies attracts quite different groups as does each of the sciences and economic/business studies.

Table 4 Percentage distribution of Jungian functions by teaching subject and gender

Subject	NF	NT	SF	ST	Female Total	NF	NT	SF	ST	Male Total
Geography	26.3	31.6	15.8	26.3	3.5	12.5	25.0	25.0	37.5	2.2
Modern languages	33.3	22.6	20.4	23.7	16.9	30.0	50.0	5.0	15.0	5.5
Religious studies	52.2	17.4	17.4	13.0	4.2	26.1	47.8	8.7	17.4	6.3
Classics	36.0	28.0	28.0	8.0	4.6	37.5	31.3	18.8	12.5	4.4
Chemistry	35.7	19.0	14.3	31.0	7.7	17.6	47.1	5.9	29.4	9.3
Physics	18.8	18.8	18.8	43.8	2.9	22.7	40.9	9.1	27.3	6.0
Biology	21.7	26.7	20.0	31.7	10.9	28.0	52.0	0.0	20.0	6.8
Mathematics	21.7	21.7	28.3	28.3	10.9	19.0	31.7	12.7	36.5	17.3
English	45.9	30.6	9.4	14.1	15.5	35.1	56.8	5.4	2.7	10.1
History	36.8	36.8	10.5	15.8	3.5	5.3	42.1	21.1	31.6	5.2
General science	20.8	29.2	20.8	29.2	4.4	17.4	21.7	8.7	52.2	6.3
Physical education	35.3	11.8	29.4	23.5	3.1	12.1	36.4	12.1	39.4	9.0
Economics and business	11.1	22.2	11.1	55.6	1.6	26.3	42.1	0.0	31.6	5.2
Aggregated subjects	33.3	38.6	14.0	14.0	10.4	30.4	34.8	13.0	21.7	6.3
Column (n)	178	144	100	127	549	83	148	35	99	365
Total %	32.4	26.2	18.2	23.1	100.0	22.7	40.5	9.6	27.1	100.0

	Female table	Male table
Chi-Squared value	56.8	54.8
Degrees freedom	39	39
Significance	p = 0.032	p = 0.048

Table 4 shows that all Jungian functions occur amongst the trainees for each teaching subject. Further, taking into account the small numbers in some of these cells, the chi-squared values give only tentative grounds to reject the hypothesis that the Jungian functions are evenly distributed across the table (i.e. that the differences we see have occurred merely by chance). This is an important observation. The MBTI literature would suggest that different personalities are drawn to different occupations. Another way of saying this is that different occupations attract different personalities (MacDaid, McCaulley and Kainz, 1986; Myers and McCaulley, 1983; Myers, 1993). However, these data of a wide cross-section of secondary PGCE students show that among teaching trainees each personality occurs within each teaching subject. There is no single personality type that characterizes a teaching subject. This may be interpreted as a good thing – classes in schools have a mixture of types that reflects the total population, for all types are to be found in all 'average' classrooms. Amongst the pupils, each and every personality type will be represented, so it is probably desirable that a full range of types occur within the teaching profession (and probably within all school subject areas). In this way, school pupils experience and gain from the diversity.

Implications for teacher training

What we have done so far is looked at an extensive sample of PGCE students from a variety of HEIs, which seems representative of the PGCE population at large. We have also looked at the results of a psychological instrument of personality. The four personality types described by the MBTI are apparently found in moderate proportions within each teaching subject surveyed. We can now examine some implications of this work in relation to how PGCE students learn, how they relate to different types of learning stimulus and the sorts of needs they have as learners.

There are advantages for those engaged in training teachers to understand psychological type. Some of these advantages relate to their own professional and personal lives. However, it is more the concern of this chapter to focus on the benefits to teachers in training. In this vein, the implications for how different Types approach learning will be addressed in the category of 'Within coursework'. How different Types engage in relationships that could be relevant to partnership matters will be investigated under 'Within partnership schools'. The emphasis of this latter section will be the mentoring relationship.

Within coursework

How can we apply what is known about learning styles and preferred modes of learning to the process of training teachers in PGCE courses? There are two issues here. The first concerns the need to open up the area for explicit examination. Learning styles, how they come about, how to observe them and their impact on the learning process should become part of the content of our courses if they are not already so. This material should be dealt with as an aspect of the richness of the human experience – not in terms of being a problem in learning or relationships, but a matter of individual difference that evokes mystery, interest and experiment. Second, those training teachers should 'practise what they preach' and encourage diversity, cater for differences in learning style and model effective education based on a respect for differences. None of this is meant to sound like 'soft nosed' student centredness. On the contrary, what I suggest makes real demands on tutors which requires a response of integrity and professionalism.

Some authors have written so strongly about individual differences flowing from personality factors that they use the term 'different minds' to emphasize Type differences. There is a sense here of using 'mind' as a verb. There is, however, a danger in such language – for we may be pushed to claim or assume that Type explains everything. This would be to claim too much and it is not the intention here. The emphasis is to acknowledge and honour these differences without negating the best of what we presently do.

The remainder of this paper will focus on aspects of personal learning style which will help in responding to these individual differences. These are general comments and I will try to avoid the presumption of saying what should be done in areas that the reader knows best. The following section incorporates some ideas of Lawrence (1993), Jensen (1987), Myers (1993), and Fairhurst and Fairhurst (1995).

NT learners

People who are NT like working with concepts and ideas. They represent 32 per cent of the beginning teachers sampled. They like to start with the abstract and fit particular pieces of information in later, as examples. The big picture can be like a sketch to locate or position information. The abstract is an opportunity to generalize, make connections and follow intriguing possibilities. They love analysing complex, objective situations and are charged by what is rational and idealistic. They are energized by opportunities to create their own solutions and techniques and prize the innovative and ingenious solution. They like to work individually and also like broad-ranging discussions of a theoretical and general nature. Harmony is not a driving force, as honesty and integrity in argument or discussion are highly regarded.

NT learners accept everything as grist for the mill. All information might be relevant. They like abstract generalizations which are used as maps through the particular cases and examples of learning. They are keenly interested in data, not as facts in themselves, but as evidence to support theories or mental models. Problems are resolved by the application of global theories. For NTs, the language of models and paradigms has immediate resonance. They search for global applications and resist limitations of space and time. They enjoy connecting information and experiences within their mental frameworks. A suitable metaphor would be the conceptual mind.

NF learners

NF learners like situations that allow creative expression. They comprise 28 per cent of the PGCE sample. They are energized by exploring possibilities in relationships and finding situations that value their insights into complex interpersonal relationships. They concentrate on, and are attracted to, issues that involve broad, human values and will see social and group relationships as central to many concerns. They can be motivated by ideals of making the world or institutions more responsive to human needs and are prepared to work to promote harmonious relationships. Harmony is important and, without it, other work demands will be seen to lack value.

NFs enjoy the subtle, personal and 'ambiguous' features of experiences – this is what makes things interesting or valuable. They like mental freedom and 'roam' within a rich experience in which they try to remain open to opportunities. New problems are faced by association with prior experiences and problem solving is associative in this sense. Connections are made between previous and present. Creativity is prized. Learning is perceived as encountering new experiences (Starship Enterprise is a good example – to boldly go where no-one has gone before) and in the sense of swimming in this rich soup which is supportive and nourishing, a suitable metaphor is the oceanic mind.

ST learners

People who are ST like to work within known frameworks. They make up 25 per cent of the PGCE sample. They like to move from the particular and concrete to the general and abstract. They enjoy technical manipulations either in the concrete or with information, for example statistics, and can be very painstaking to ensure details are accurate. They like clearly defined roles and tasks, specific objectives and knowing what is exactly expected of them. When they have a method, they are prepared to put in the effort. Changes in direction or method in midstream can be disconcerting and worrying. They deal well with the concrete here and now and revel in problems that are uncluttered by emotional issues. They can tend not to see emotional overtones in some situations and make decisions on 'objective' considerations of what they see as being right or practical.

STs use their minds as filing systems. They like structuring and storing useful information. They like clear examples, unambiguous situations and theories that deal with objective reality. Knowledge is built up like a building or a scaffold and learning is to erect such a structure. Sequential steps, clear unambiguous instructions, defined goals, a fixed domain of action are all valued in learning and help to increase confidence. A suitable metaphor for this mind set might be the structural mind.

SF learners

Learners who are SF like working in predictable and harmonious relationships. SFs comprise just less than 15 per cent of the PGCE sample. They spend energy on practical contacts that keep personal relationships warm and free of conflict. They are open to the tangible needs of others. They are open to the here and now, spontaneous and often seen as warm. They like a distinctive personal touch to their environment and have a keen sense of what is useful and appreciated, responsive to emotional climates and personal needs.

Their learning is often personal and subjective, at the same time as being grounded in present realities. They esteem experience, especially of an emotional nature or value, take the daily experiences and derive rules of thumb that work with what they know. For SFs the validity of knowledge is grounded in what they know and experience. Life experiences are paramount and it is only from these that abstract principles can be derived (this is the reverse of the NT approach). Learning is about events and information is best experienced. They are in touch with the tangible qualities of events and they know the literal and personal meanings of what happens. The appropriate metaphor is that of relational mind.

Learning styles and the learning cycle

The notion of a cycle of learning is common in discussions about learning skills. It is implicit in the present framework that all learners have most or all learning skills to varying degrees. The issue of learning style is that of preference or what is most easily applied to learning. All learners who are aiming to learn efficiently must bring a range of skills to bear. Learning theory in this regard suggests that by providing stimulus that engages a variety of learning styles, each learner can practice different learning modalities and distinguish which modalities suit different circumstances (Jensen, 1987). Learning incorporates the skills to apprehend, organize, comprehend and assimilate knowledge.

Good teachers have known for a long time that a variety of stimulus material is better than even a very good single style and that different stimuli engage different people for different reasons. Good teachers know that the same tasks can be approached in a variety of ways by a range of learners, often with divergent results. Some students are stimulated by the open-ended question, whereas others are more comfortable with clear guidelines.

Within partnership schools

It is not my intention to suggest that certain schools will be 'better' or 'worse' for certain types of individuals. Of more concern is the nature and character of mentoring that occurs within the school placement. Different Types will have different expectations of the mentoring relationship – this is true for both sides of the relationship. Both mentor and teacher trainee can fall into the same trap of misunderstanding each others' needs. The more that pressures of time and responsibilities impact on the relationship, the more likely it is that difficulties will occur.

NT types will expect a free space, the chance to air different ideas, experience creativity and exchange experiences, approaches and ideas. Professional ethics, individual responsibility and the chance to develop personal approaches will be of high value. Discussion of ideas and concepts may well be the most favoured interaction. Problems can arise if advice is seen to restrict freedoms or compromise 'my way'. It may be difficult to see standard practices, school rules or subject guidelines as valuable and consensus may not be highly valued. The tendency to deal in intellectual generalities might mean that practical issues are not addressed, or even recognized as being of concern or importance.

NF types will be focused on the quality of the relationships within classrooms, staffrooms and the mentoring relationship itself. Acceptance, trust, confidentiality and mutual regard will be of great importance. Differences can be accommodated so long as individuality is valued. The quality of relationships will be the prime focus and how people react, feel, or perceptions of these experiences, will dominate conversations and discussions. Being an accepted part of the school and the teaching profession will be a strong attractant. There may be a tendency to view the content of discussions as secondary to the process itself, general consensus being more important than achievement, being and experiencing more important than thinking and knowing.

For those who are ST, the mechanics of situations are likely to dominate conversations. Recall of incidents and factual recollections will be important. Competence and acceptance, especially in terms of doing the observable behaviours of teaching, will be prized. Often STs are initially seen as organized, well-prepared, and even 'natural teachers'. Many of these skills are surface and have value mainly for the person him/herself rather than for others, such as pupils. Organization can be a way of not engaging with pupils or peers, and busyness an acceptable mode to avoid other issues and responsibilities. Discussions can revolve around incidents and not touch the deeper perceptions and understandings of interactions because it is assumed that these are shared. This is especially so for STs who are introverts.

SFs are the least well-represented in teaching and may struggle with a sense of being little understood, especially if male. While SFs are attuned to sensory information, they make judgements in terms of values and principles of relationship. Discussions can be difficult, as each case is taken as unique. Practices that meet each unique situation can appear arbitrary, inconsistent or chaotic. Planning and organization can be problematic as the perceived needs of others, and sometimes self, make insistent demands for attention. Role perceptions might be restricted to 'meeting needs' and be further reduced to 'keeping people happy'. Emotional freedom may seem to others to be, or indeed take on some aspects of, capriciousness. Some of this concentration on affectivity may be a way of countering a perceived aloneness.

What to do about this?

First, there is the issue of awareness. Trainees who know the signs of ways they do not cope are better equipped to face such problems. If both mentor and trainee teacher are aware that people see the world and its demands in radically different ways, there is increased chance that communication rather than confusion may occur. There may be certain trainees for whom the decision to assign a particular mentor will be informed by knowledge of type and personal development. Course constructors who are sensitive to Type might, with the help of a comprehensible pattern, be able to identify the particular strengths of school personnel and, hence, reinforce the partnership. Knowledge of Type might also allow course personnel to mediate effectively if communication breaks down by understanding the perspectives and needs of the people in the relationship.

For teachers in their daily teaching

And what about effectiveness of teaching? This is really what it is all about: that the beginning teacher develops a professional effectiveness in class and education generally. If trainee teachers are aware of how Type affects their own learning, then there is hope that there will be flow on to the way they prepare and design their own lessons. An understanding of Type is one way, coming from a theoretical framework and grounded in experience, of delivering equal opportunity to all students, of encouraging and prizing individuality, and of developing giftedness across the spectrum of human abilities to be found within a classroom.

References

Bayne, R. (1995), *The Myers-Briggs Type Indicator: A Critical Review and Practical Guide*. London: Chapman & Hall.

Carlson, J.G. (1985), 'Recent assessments of the Myers-Briggs Type Indicator', *Journal of Personality Assessment*, 49(4), 356–65.

Devito, A.J. (1985), 'Review of Myers-Briggs Type Indicator', in Mitchell, J.V., *Ninth Mental Measurements Yearbook*. Lincoln NE: University of Nebraska Press, 2, 1030–2.

Fairhurst, A.M. and Fairhurst, L.F. (1995), *Effective Teaching, Effective Learning*. Palo Alto: Davies-Black Publishing.

HMI (1993), *The New Teacher in School*. London: OFSTED.

Howes, R.J. and Carskadon, T.G. (1979), 'Test-retest reliabilities of the Myers-Briggs Type Indicator as a function of mood changes', *Journal of Psychological Type*, 2, 29–31.

Jensen, G.H. (1987), 'Learning styles', in Provost and Anchors, *Applications of the Myers-Briggs Type Indicator in Higher Education*. Palo Alto: Consulting Psychologists Press.

Johnson, D.A. (1992), 'Test-retest reliabilities of the Myers-Briggs Type Indicator and the Type differentiation indicator over a 30 month period', *Journal of Psychological Type*, 24, 54–8.

Jung, C.G. (ed.) (1964), *Man and His Symbols*. London: Arkana, Penguin.

—   (1971) *Psychological Types*. London: Routledge & Kegan Paul.

Karesh, D.M., Pieper, W.A. and Holland, C.L. (1994), 'Comparing the MBTI, the Jungian type survey, and the Singer-Loomis inventory of personality', *Journal of Psychological Type*, 30, 30–8.

Lawrence, G. (1993), *People Types and Tiger Stripes* (3rd Ed.). Gainesville Center, Florida: Centre for Applications of Psychological Type.

Lorr, M. (1991), 'An empirical evaluation of the MBTI typology', *Personality and Individual Differences*, 12(11), 1141–5.

MacDaid, G.P., McCaulley, M.H. and Kainz, R.I. (1986), *Atlas of Type Tables*. Gainesville Center, Florida: Centre for Applications of Psychological Type.

McGuiness, M., Izard, J. and McCrossin, P. (eds) (1992), *Myers-Briggs Type Indicator: Australian Perspectives*. Hawthorn Vic: ACER.

Mallia, M. (1992), 'The thought... the glimmer... the recognition... that's me!', in McGuiness, M., Izard, J. and McCrossin, P. *Myers-Briggs Type Indicator: Australian Perspectives*. Hawthorn Vic: ACER.

Mitchell, J.V. (ed.) (1985), *Ninth Mental Measurements Yearbook*. Lincoln NE: University of Nebraska Press, 2, 1030–2.

Murray, J.B. (1990), 'Review of research on the Myers-Briggs Type Indicator', *Journal of Perceptual and Motor Skills*, 70, 1187–202.

Myers, I.B. (1993), *Gifts Differing*. Palo Alto: Consulting Psychologists Press.

Myers, I.B. and McCaulley, M.H. (1985), *Manual: A Guide to the Development and Use of the Myers-Briggs Type Indicator* (2nd Ed.). Palo Alto: Consulting Psychologists Press.

Provost, J.A. and Anchors, S. (eds) (1987), *Applications of the Myers-Briggs Type Indicator in Higher Education*. Palo Alto: Consulting Psychologists Press.

Rosenak, C.M. and Shontz, F.C. (1988), 'Jungian Q-sorts: demonstrating construct validity for psychological type and the MBTI', *Journal of Psychological Type*, 15, 33–45.

Rytting, M., Ware, R. and Prince, R.A. (1994), 'Bimodal distributions in a sample of CEOs: validating evidence for the MBTI', *Journal of Psychological Type*, 31, 16–23.

Schweiger, D.M. (1985), 'Measuring managerial cognitive skills: on the logical validity of the Myers-Briggs Type Indicator', *Journal of Business Research*, 13, 315–28.

Spoto, A. (1995), *Jung's Typology in Perspective* (rev. Ed.). Wilmette IL: Chiron Publications.

Thorne, A. and Gough, H. (1991), *Portraits of Type: An MBTI Research Compendium*. Palo Alto: Consulting Psychologists Press.

Tischler, L. (1994), 'The MBTI factor structure', *Journal of Psychological Type*, 31, 24–31.

Tzeng, O.C.S., Outcalt, D., Boyer, S.A., Ware, R., and Landis, D. (1984) 'Item validity of the Myers-Briggs Type Indicator', *Journal of Personality Assessment*, 48(3), 255–6.

Ware, R., Rytting, M. and Jenkins, D. (1994), 'The effect of stress on MBTI scores', *Journal of Psychological Type*, 30, 39–44.

(The Myers-Briggs Type Indicator and MBTI are the copyright of Consulting Psychologists Press, Inc. Palo Alto. California.)

3.9 Creating more contented teachers

Roy Prentice

Introduction

This chapter sets out to explore the nature and role of subject-specific content in courses of initial teacher education (ITE). Issues of concern that are common to primary and secondary courses are identified, whilst the differences determined by each age phase, individual subjects, undergraduate and postgraduate provision are acknowledged. It is prompted by four interrelated factors:

1   a growing concern about the development of school-based courses within which reduced opportunities exist for student teachers to acquire, deepen and extend skills, knowledge and understandings particular to ways of teaching and learning in a given subject

2   the increasing momentum of the national educational and political debates that focus on the relationships between knowledge of subject-matter and pedagogy

3   the introduction of a National Curriculum for ITE

4   an awareness of developing research interests in the area of subject knowledge for teaching.

Increasingly, and from different perspectives, contributors to the debates about teaching and teachers are focusing their attention on subject knowledge. Questions about subject teaching in primary schools raised by Alexander, Rose and Woodhead (1992) have maintained a high profile, reinforced by the findings of the Office for Standards in Education (OFSTED) (1993) and more recent widespread discussions about what teachers need to know in order to raise standards – particularly of numeracy and literacy. It has also been made clear by the Teacher Training Agency (TTA) that a National Curriculum for ITE is expected to provide a powerful means of addressing the issue of subject knowledge.

Ten years ago Shulman (1986) critically analysed what he regarded as 'a sharp distinction between knowledge and pedagogy' that tended to result in the 'identification of teaching competence with pedagogy alone'. Since then, a number of key questions about the complex nature of teachers' knowledge of subject content have been addressed by Shulman and his colleagues at Stanford University (Wilson, Shulman and Richert, 1987; Grossman, Wilson and Shulman, 1989). Action-relevant knowledge, is explored by Calderhead and Miller (1985) and Brophy (1991) draws attention to the influences teachers' personal belief systems about learning have on their approaches to teaching. More recently, and with particular reference to the early years of primary education, Aubrey (1994) makes a useful contribution to the debate about what teachers should know. It is important therefore to ensure that the next phase in the development of ITE – which may include the establishment of a National Curriculum – properly addresses the complex and often contentious issue of subject knowledge; informed by a mounting body of research findings and experience gained by subject-specialist tutors involved in school-based courses.

Under the pressure of a Government-imposed timescale for the implementation of school-based courses, it is hardly surprising that higher education institutions (HEIs), in their collaborations with partner schools, were preoccupied with organizational issues. Most courses, whether primary or secondary age phase, undergraduate or postgraduate, have been dominated by operational concerns linked to financial arrangements, time allocation, assessment procedures and quality assurance mechanisms. Given the prevailing educational climate of managerial rationalism, the concerns such as whole-school policy, local management of schools, OFSTED inspections and the National Curriculum, have greatly influenced the development of school-based schemes.

Underpinned by recent research evidence, it is suggested that a considered shift in viewpoint now needs to be made, in order to place within the wide-angled picture of school effectiveness and school improvement, a more sharply focused image of that which is specific to the content and pedagogy of individual subjects. Critical of the emphasis placed on procedures, management, evaluation and testing by the teacher effectiveness movement, which gathered momentum in the 1980s, Shulman (1986) argues for matters central to an understanding of content to be addressed. Attention is drawn to the fact that the 'cleavage' he identifies between pedagogy and content, both in terms of research activity and policy making, is of relatively recent origin. He makes the point that: 'A century ago the defining characteristic of pedagogical accomplishment was knowledge of content' and reaffirms the view that anyone 'who presumes to teach subject-matter to children must demonstrate knowledge of that subject-matter as a prerequisite to teaching.' Central to Shulman's research are questions about the content of lessons, the issues they raise and the nature of teachers' responses. Writing in a similar vein about the neglect of teachers' subject knowledge in a context of the early years of schooling, Aubrey (1994:5) says, 'Where subject knowledge is richer, deeper and better integrated it is more likely that the teachers will be confident and more open to children's ideas, contributions, questions and comments.'

The position adopted in this chapter is that teachers cannot teach what they do not know, and how they teach what they know is influenced by the way they came to know it. For teacher educators this raises fundamental questions about the nature and sources of teacher knowledge, the acquisition of new knowledge and its relationship with existing knowledge. It cannot be assumed that well-qualified graduates at the commencement of their courses of ITE possess the necessary subject knowledge to teach the requirements of the National Curriculum in their particular subject areas at Key Stages 3 and 4. Within each subject area, intending secondary specialist teachers represent a wide range of highly specialized degree backgrounds. As a result of such diverse provision at undergraduate level, different courses provide students with different experiences of the *same* subject and this has a powerful influence on the stance adopted by secondary specialist teachers towards their subject.

For students following postgraduate courses of primary teacher education, a similar situation exists in relation to their particular degree subjects. However, given the present unrealistic requirement that all primary teachers are prepared to teach the full range of subjects represented in the National Curriculum, their stance towards many subjects will be shaped largely by an assortment of influences (including experiences of their own school days). Undergraduate courses have traditionally provided opportunities for the academic study of a given subject or subjects concurrently with the study of the theory and practice of education. Although they represent perhaps the last vestige of teacher education to be located in a liberal education tradition, in practice such courses too often display a fundamental weakness – a dislocation between subject content and pedagogy. When this occurs, insufficiently explicit connections are made between learning and teaching and it is likely that this shortcoming will be exacerbated as more institutions adopt modular course structures. Whichever route is followed to become a teacher, it must also be remembered that each person's construction of the characteristics of the content of a given subject is an amalgam of beliefs, concepts, facts, attitudes and experiences encountered and revisited in a variety of formal and informal settings and relationships over an extended period of time. The formal curriculum at both school and university level cannot, alone, be held responsible for the ways in which different subjects are perceived, valued, understood – and ultimately taught – by teachers.

It is useful at this point to identify some research findings that help to clarify the relationship between different components of subject knowledge for teaching. According to Shulman (1986), the professional understanding of teachers, on which effective teaching and professional development is founded, relies on a complex combination of knowledge of subject-matter and knowledge of pedagogy. In a similar vein, Leinhardt and Smith (1985) identify two areas of knowledge as a basis for teaching. Using mathematics as an example, lesson structure knowledge is shown to refer to skills that apply in a general way to a given subject and through the application of which lessons, projects and programmes are planned and implemented. Knowledge of subject-matter is seen as being more specific and relates directly to a particular topic being taught.

Differences between so-called knowledgeable and unknowledgeable teachers are identified by Hashweh (1985). Although it is recognized that all teachers use representations to teach particular topics, through which subject content is transformed into teaching material, qualitative differences are observed in the representations chosen by knowledgeable and unknowledgeable teachers. Predictably, unknowledgeable teachers are likely to rely on a thin veneer of knowledge which frequently causes inappropriate or misleading choices to be made that perpetuate inaccuracies, stereotyped and preconceived ideas about a given subject. Knowledgeable teachers demonstrate their deeper understanding rooted in concepts, principles and underlying themes. What is more, the knowledgeable teachers are able to make flexible and meaningful connections between different topics within a given subject. According to Aubrey:

> Knowing about a subject, however, means knowing about the fundamental activities and discourse of a particular discipline, showing an awareness of competing perspectives and central ideas within this field, as well as understanding how seemingly incompatible views can be justified and validated.
>
> (Aubrey, 1994:3)

The concept of transformation is central to distinguishing knowledgeable teachers. The ability to transform subject-matter, through carefully chosen representations, using metaphor, analogy, illustration and demonstration, displays the depth of understanding and capacity to generate alternatives that knowledgeable teachers possess.

From their research into the nature of subject knowledge, Grossman, Wilson and Shulman (1989) provide a theoretical framework within which the interrelationships between three components of subject knowledge in a given discipline are identified.

1   Content knowledge includes:
   - factual information
   - central concepts
   - organizing principles and ideas.

2   Substantive knowledge includes:
   - explanatory models or paradigms
   - conceptual tools used to guide enquiry and make sense of data.

3   Syntactic knowledge includes:
   - relevant forms of methodology
   - ways of introducing new knowledge – justification and evaluation.

This model is incorporated into the following theoretical framework for a professional knowledge base for teaching that embraces both subject-matter and pedagogy.

1   General pedagogical knowledge includes:
   - knowledge of theories and principles of teaching and learning
   - knowledge of learners
   - knowledge of principles and techniques of classroom behaviour and management.

2   Subject-matter knowledge includes:
   - ideas, facts, concepts of the field
   - relationships between ideas, facts and concepts
   - knowledge of ways new knowledge is created and evaluated.

3   Pedagogical content knowledge includes:
   - understanding of what it means to teach a given topic
   - understanding of principles and techniques to teach a given topic.

Pedagogical content knowledge addresses how to teach a particular subject and how learners learn it with reference to subject-specific difficulties, particularities, misconceptions and how curriculum materials are organized. It is informed by both knowledge of subject-matter and general pedagogical knowledge.

Subject knowledge and application in the secondary Post Graduate Certificate in Education

It would seem that such conceptual models of subject knowledge for teaching have had a minimal influence on the design of new school-based courses of ITE. Within the national provision of secondary Post Graduate Certificate in Education (PGCE) courses the relationship between professional studies and subject-specific studies varies. A common criticism of some courses is that too great an emphasis is placed on general pedagogical knowledge – that which is common to all students – at the expense of subject-matter knowledge and pedagogical-content knowledge. Tensions become apparent when the relationship between the general and the particular is ambiguous. On the one hand, generalist tutors are likely to prioritize generic teaching skills. On the other hand, subject specialists frequently argue for an emphasis to be placed on subject-specific knowledge. An oversimplification of two opposing approaches to teacher education might be likened to the same landscape viewed through different ends of a telescope. From one viewpoint, an emphasis is placed on pedagogical issues common to teachers of all subjects and in which subject-specific content is located as detail; while the opposite viewpoint places an emphasis on subject-specific content which is located in a wider context.

In order to demonstrate how subject knowledge and subject application can be addressed simultaneously within courses of ITE, reference is now made to some key features of workshop studies within the secondary PGCE art and design course at the Institute of Education, University of London. Workshops are defined as environments for enquiry into the making of and response to art and design and ways of learning and teaching in art and design. They focus on ways of:

1   recording ideas

2   investigating ideas

3   developing ideas

4   of presenting ideas.

(See Figure 1.)

Figure 1 Workshop studies in art and design education

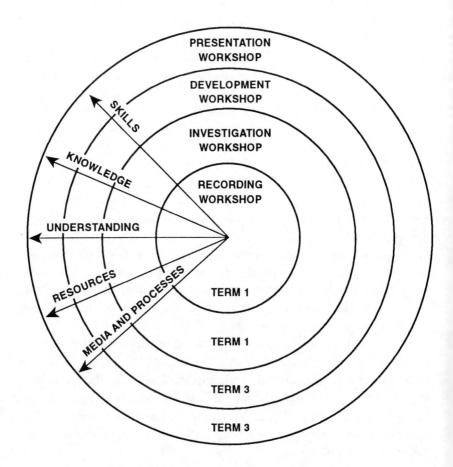

TO RECORD	collect information and data/methodically document/chronicle evidence/preserve in permanent form/find and make equivalents
TO INVESTIGATE	enquire into/systematically examine/ analyse/search/explore
TO DEVELOP	advance/expand/grow/elaborate/work out in detail/unfold/generate/extend/progress
TO PRESENT	communicate/materialize/show/display/ demonstrate/reveal/expose to view/share

From: PGCE Art and Design Course, Institute of Education, University of London.

Through a series of visual displays of the outcomes of practical activity, with accompanying written rationales supported by discussions and guided reading, beginning teachers deepen their understandings of the intricate relationships between concepts and skills and visual and verbal modes of communication and, thus, between the two attainment targets of the National Curriculum for art. Every member of a workshop is a rich resource for learning. Each workshop group consists of students from a wide range of art, craft and design backgrounds. A climate is created in which alternative philosophical positions and working methodologies can co-exist and in which theoretical understandings grow out of engagement in practical activity that is both subject-specific and school-focused. Conceptual clarity emerges through experiential learning and an increasing ability to reflect on it. As Reid reaffirms, 'There is an essential interplay between reflective thinking (which is discursive) and direct intuitive experiences: they need each other (1986:xi)'.

As this PGCE course progresses, workshops provide opportunities for the acquisition and application of a range of reflective skills to apply to content as well as to processes. Records, in the form of personal logs or diaries, visual and written, retain the substance of such reflections through which the implicit becomes explicit. As students evolve strategies to reflect on experience, both individually and in small groups, potential connections between past experience as artist or designer, the present activity and future possibilities as a teacher of art and design become apparent.

In order to avoid students feeling de-skilled, in the first workshop individuals are encouraged to capitalize on their strengths. A structure is provided within which students engage in practical activities that draw on and extend their subject-content knowledge. The brief – to find and invent different ways of recording experience using the processes and procedures of art and design – encourages personal responses that move from familiar towards unfamiliar ways of working. Materials and processes are explored and exploited in new combinations as traditional approaches to craft skills are questioned. Making is informed and enriched by being located in a wider historical, social and cultural context. Everything is subjected to scrutiny. By reflecting on their own creative behaviour and identifying – to the extent that it is possible to identify – the factors which determine their own preferred patterns of working, students gain insight into the nature of the creative process in art and design and the conditions required to support and develop creative responses in pupils.

The ways in which ideas are generated, shaped, developed and refined are explored, along with strategies through which connections can be made between ideas and skills, form and content, process and product. The influence on art and design practice of such constraints as time, scale and materials is addressed, as are ways of dealing with variables of this kind when planning and resourcing lessons and projects for teaching practice. Throughout the workshop, the various means through which ideas about art and design are transformed into curriculum material appropriate to particular groups of learners are brought sharply into focus.

Workshop activities gather momentum and increasingly address pedagogical-content knowledge, alongside a deepening and broadening of understandings about art and design, as work is informed and enriched by school-based experiences. As students gain confidence and competence the agenda is extended to embrace the planning and resourcing of lessons for which they will be responsible. Engagement in such workshops enables students to acquire, develop and apply a range of reflective skills. Written and visual records and displays provide the basis for individual tutorials and group discussions. The intentions and working methodologies of a wide spectrum of artists and designers – pupils included – are critically analysed, clarified and made explicit by being shared. Often long-held assumptions about the functions, nature and content of art and design and art and design education are challenged. Justifications for the adoption of alternative positions are articulated and, in the process of being communicated, ideas and attitudes are open to modification and orientation towards subject-matter and pedagogy change.

In the final term of the PGCE, course projects undertaken with pupils during teaching practice are reflected on further in the light of wider reading and are used as a basis for curriculum development. A key issue is identified to be studied in depth and this becomes the basis for a major assignment in the field of art and design education. The presentation workshop culminates in a series of visual displays which make up a major exhibition supported by written rationales making explicit connections between subject knowledge and subject application through the integration of workshop and teaching practice experiences. Above all, it is the function of workshops to help students gain insight into the factors that influence their own creative behaviour as artists and designers. At the same time, they expose students to alternative ways of thinking and working. As a result, they are better equipped to make informed choices based on an understanding of the range of possibilities available to teachers when representing aspects of art and design to pupils. The value of this kind of approach to subject knowledge in courses of ITE is reinforced by Salmon, who says:

> In teaching we do not merely pass on a free-standing package of knowledge – of the different periods, cultures and traditions in art, say, or the skills involved in working with different materials. What we do is rather to offer, however indirectly, a sense of the personal meaning which our curriculum has for us – its value, its relevance, its implications for us as particular human beings. In teaching we are, in some sense, our own curriculum, because we represent not only our subject, but, more importantly, the stance we take towards it.
>
> Salmon (1995:24)

An acknowledgement of the complex nature of subject knowledge in the context of teacher education is supported by a growing body of relevant research findings and the perceptions of experienced teacher educators. Unfortunately, from the quality of the wider political debates in which this issue is frequently highlighted, a grasp of its complexity is not always apparent. Indeed, it could be argued, to echo Wideen (1996), that the Government's reforms of ITE in the early 1990s in the UK has resulted in a preoccupation with the restructuring of systems rather than a reconceptualizing of content and mode of provision.

The structure of the art and design PGCE course to which reference has been made is supported by two interwoven and interdependent threads – subject-content knowledge and pedagogical-content knowledge. In his quest for more imaginative models for teacher education, Wideen (1996) identifies holistic course structures with client-focused orientations as two vital ingredients. Rooted in personal construct theory, the Institute of Education's art and design education workshops foster an holistic approach to learning that is person-centred. The idiosyncratic baggage of beliefs, ideas, feelings, attitudes and skills that artists and designers carry with them to a PGCE course, and on the basis of which their personal constructs of their discipline operate, provides the growth points for their professional development as teachers. By capitalizing on the strength of subject identity that is evident at the beginning of the PGCE course, workshops help to move beginning teachers from the security of the familiar towards the uncertainty of the unfamiliar. Thus, through a deepening understanding of their particular preoccupations and passions as artists and designers, they become increasingly aware of the range of creative possibilities open to them as teachers of art and design.

The central role of active learning in such workshops is another ingredient to which Wideen (1996) refers. A powerful contribution is made by each member of a group of 20 or more beginning teachers. Through structured discussions about practical processes and visual images, points of view change, as orientations towards art, craft and design are modified as a result of being shared. It is regrettable that such opportunities to benefit from the challenges and in-depth interaction with a peer group in the same specialism are reduced as a result of the shift towards school-based mentoring. Given the range of subjects represented by a group of students attached to a given school, mentoring in group situations in schools inevitably has as its main focus general pedagogical issues. It is widely recognized that most secondary PGCE courses need to raise the profile of, increase the impact made by, and provide more support for, subject-specific mentors. As a matter of urgency, a greater and sustained investment is required in the professional development of subject mentors.

Subject knowledge and the primary Post Graduate Certificate in Education

Within primary PGCE courses it is suggested that beginning teachers' encounters with subject-matter at their own levels are in essence lived through experiences of the same order as those required of secondary specialists. Differences are determined by the knowledge base of beginning teachers, the restricted time available and the appropriateness of chosen representations of the subject for younger children. However, the overriding problem at primary level remains that of curriculum overload. Perhaps at last the unrealistic expectation that all general classroom teachers can meet the sophisticated requirements of the

National Curriculum in all subjects, particularly at Key Stage 2 (seven-to 11-year-old), is being faced full-frontally. Proposed alternatives include differentiating between generalist, semi-specialist and specialist teachers, a drastic reduction in the number of subjects taught and the introduction of a cross-phase Key Stage 2/3 hybrid PGCE course. The breadth and depth of subject-content knowledge demanded of primary teachers to meet the requirements of present core and foundation subjects is clearly an unrealistic expectation. There is an urgent need for the existing one-year PGCE route into primary teaching to be reconsidered. At the present time it seems that the elasticity of a 38 week course is about to snap. One solution would be to restructure the one-year course in such a way that certain components are redistributed over an extended period of time. Another solution is based on the reinstatement of a probationary year as an integral part of an ITE course. Yet another proposal, with far-reaching implications and one which is not devoid of advocates, would see the compulsory National Curriculum at certain stages of primary education reduced to the teaching of literacy, numeracy and science.

Would a narrower curriculum, in the sense that certain subjects would be reduced in the range of content offered at Key Stage 1, necessarily be worse than the present frenetic attempt by classteachers to perform on all fronts beyond a level that can realistically be expected? Might a reduced, more sharply focused and better resourced compulsory curriculum be an improvement? Research into what such developments would entail is essential, particularly the needs of teachers in terms of their subject knowledge and the implications for later Key Stages. Specialist teaching at the upper end of Key Stage 2 would need to be addressed within a new pattern of ITE intent on building more effective bridges between Key Stages 2 and 3.

By their nature, undergraduate courses of ITE should be in a more advantageous position to capitalize on the simultaneity of experience available to students with regard to subject content and subject application. Opportunities should now be grasped to ensure that a new generation of concurrent courses fully integrate these elements within holistically planned course structures; rather than be seduced by modularization and risk greater fragmentation. Compared with decisions based on a consideration of such issues, arguments about the merits of four-year courses over three-year courses seem less important, particularly if entry requirements are more rigorously applied.

Concluding comment

If the centrality of subject knowledge is reaffirmed in courses of ITE the implications for the continuous professional development (CPD) of teachers will also need to be addressed. Provision at MA level will need to include more imaginative opportunities for teachers to reconnect experientially with subject content in a context of contemporary issues and practice. Re-engagements at this level with subject-content knowledge and pedagogical content knowledge enable teachers as a natural part of their professional development to deepen and enrich their understanding of subject knowledge in such a way that, 'knowledge is not divorced from the knower' (Salmon, 1995:24).

References

Alexander, R., Rose, J. and Woodhead, C. (1992), *Curriculum Organization and Classroom Practice in Primary Schools – A Discussion Paper.* London: HMSO.

Aubrey, C. (ed.) (1994), *The Role of Subject Knowledge in the Early Years of Schooling.* London: Falmer Press.

Brophy, J. (ed.) (1991), *Introduction to Vol 2 Advances in Research on Teaching.* Greenwich: CTJAI Press.

Calderhead, J. and Miller, E. (1985), 'The Integration of Subject Matter Knowledge in Student Teachers' Classroom Practice'. Paper at British Educational Research Association (BERA) Conference, Sheffield.

Grossman, P.L., Wilson, S. and Shulman, L. (1989), 'Teachers of substance: subject matter knowledge for teaching', in Reynolds, M, *The Knowledge Base for the Beginning Teacher.* Oxford: Pergamon Press.

Hashweh, M. (1985), 'An exploratory study of teacher knowledge and teaching: the effects of science teachers' knowledge of subject-matter and their conceptions of learning on their teaching'. Unpublished Doctoral Thesis, Stanford University, California.

Leinhardt, G. and Smith, D. (1985), 'Expertise in mathematics instruction: subject matter knowledge', *Journal of Educational Psychology*, 77, 247–71.

Office for Standards in Education (OFSTED) (1993), *Curriculum Organization and Classroom Practice in Primary Schools – A Follow-up Report*. London: DfE.

Reid, L.A. (1986), *Ways of Understanding and Education*. London: Heinemann.

Salmon, P. (1995), 'Experiential learning', in Prentice, R., *Teaching Art and Design: Addressing Issues and Identifying Directions*. London: Cassell.

Shulman, L. (1986), 'Those who understand: knowledge growth in teaching', *Educational Researcher*, February, 4–14.

Wideen, M. (1996), 'Exploring Futures in Initial Teacher Education: The Landscape and the Quest'. Keynote speech at Exploring Futures in Initial Teacher Education Conference, Institute of Education, University of London.

Wilson, S.M., Shulman, L. and Richert, A. (1987), '150 ways of knowing: representation of knowledge in teaching', in Calderhead, J., *Exploring Teaching Thinking*. London: Cassell.

Part 4: Changing key for changing times – prospects

As institutions attempt to adjust to shifting contexts and rapidly changing conditions, we are bound to ask, 'What of the future?'

Marvin Wideen offers a bold and distinctive vision of the future which serves as a powerful and provocative way to conclude *Exploring Futures in Teacher Education*.

He identifies four alternative scenarios for the future, leads us into uncharted territory and new thinking about the future, including Capra's *Web of Life*. A diversity of sources and opinions are gathered up and used to point us forward, dispensing with old models and proposing new ones.

4.1 Exploring futures in initial teacher education: a fin de millennium perspective

Marvin F. Wideen

Let me begin by positing two very simple theories: the purpose of initial teacher education (ITE) is to improve the way beginning teachers learn to teach and the future of teacher education lies in how adequately it accomplishes that task. Faculties of education, where ITE now occurs, clearly have the major formal role to play in this process. How they play that role will be influenced by a complex set of factors, including the actions of policy makers, the thinking of academics, the demands of those who employ teachers and a host of other expectations. But the formal structure of ITE represents only one factor and one set of players in the complex process of learning to teach. The teaching we all experience, beginning in the home and continuing throughout our schooling, entrenches strong images of teaching long before students enter ITE (Weber and Mitchell, 1994). Some of this teaching will be first-rate, but, unless one is extraordinarily lucky, much of it will fall far short of inspiring. When beginning teachers undertake the act of teaching, their own experience of schools and teachers will bear directly on the process of learning to teach. The view of teaching that we hold as a social group also influences how beginning teachers think about teaching. This set of complicated factors, along with others, provides the context in which to explore possible futures in ITE. Those responsible for that education in the next millennium will have to consider the many factors and players involved and will not be able to create that experience on their own terms. An examination of how that experience may be created can take two routes. Technological forecasting offers one route and setting out images of preferred futures another (Livingstone, cited in Lanning, 1994).

Technological forecasting identifies predictions based on trends. Benjamin's (1989) review of the futurists and his series of predictions for trends in society and education provides an example of technological forecasting. He projected specific trends based on the cumulated wisdom (or lack thereof) of futurists. Government bureaucrats and corporate leaders today who produce technical forecasts, directing attention to radical changes stemming from our move to a post-industrial society provide another example. Such forecasts typically emphasize the need to train young people for the changing workforce that will be needed in the emerging global economy (Ministry of Supply and Services, 1991). Clearly, such forecasting plays an important part in alerting us to changes that may well occur in society due to the impact of technological change.

To apply this approach to ITE would involve projecting trends based on the best available information. However, works based entirely on this approach rest on two faulty premises. First, technological forecasters frequently claim a certainty that is totally unwarranted as they make the assumption that today's social trend will be tomorrow's. This assumption represents a flawed attempt to transfer principles from the natural sciences to the social sciences.[1] Critics such as Etzioni and Jargowsky (1990) contend that claims made by such futurists about the impact of a post-industrial society have been greatly exaggerated. Second, such works carry a strong deterministic flavour. For example, Benjamin's work makes virtually no allowance for the choices people make or for unforeseen societal change. We appear as automatons merely following external forces over which we can exercize little control. Livingstone describes technological forecasting this way: 'the enduring image of the future left by such writings is one of irreversible technological trends remote from whatever social and political capacities ordinary people might retain' (cited in Lanning, 1994:181). In short, technological forecasting frequently undervalues the human agency involved in social change.

Setting out alternative futures based on alternative moral images and political expectations provides another approach to thinking about the future. This approach assumes volition and agency on the part of the individual which comes through a critical examination of the present situation and an attempt to link that to the future (Lanning, 1994). This approach also considers alternative futures, recognising that the future social context can take different routes depending on what assumptions one makes about how future events unfold. For example, if one assumes that a crisis in education does exist, then one thinks about the future in terms of reform (McLaughlin and Oberman, 1996). However, if one believes that crisis has been manufactured, as Berliner and Biddle (1995) contend, then a future scenario may look very different. Talking of alternative futures in this way assumes that individuals do exercize some control over their future. Although problems will arise with this approach as single answers will not emerge, as is the case in technological forecasting, it does provide a far more interesting and potentially productive way to think about ITE in the next millennium. Problems arise with this approach as well, because unlike technological forecasting, single answers do not emerge as the participant is thrust into the complexity of considering different futures.

First we must ask ourselves why we should bother about the future of ITE. As I argued in the opening chapter, without substantial changes that will take considerable effort, ITE as we know it could well come to an end. If the problems in faculties of education are so serious, why not shut them down? The reason why ITE is worth fighting for was summed up by Rhys Gwyn[2] when he asked, 'What can be more important than the education of those who teach our young?' I share Gwyn's view in believing that the life chances of our children are best served by the provision of the finest education we can provide. Such an education always has and always will rest on the shoulders of teachers. Thus, their education and preparation for teaching must always be a priority. I further believe that the university provides the best context for exemplary teacher preparation.

The future of initial teacher education

I explore the future of ITE by setting out four scenarios based on alternative moral images and political expectations. The agency of teacher educators remains central to how the different scenarios will be played out in terms of what it means to learn to teach. Figure 1 provides four possible scenarios for the future of ITE. The second, third and fourth scenarios are organised around the context, the institution and what it means to learn to teach.

As a result of the complexity involved in the process of learning to teach and the changes in the institutions where it occurs, exploring ITE demands attention at both the macro and micro levels. Political and social

Figure 1: The possible scenarios for the future of initial teacher education

	The context	The institution	Learning to teach
The status quo			
The corporate culture and the entrepreneurial spirit			
Friendly fascism through bureaucratic control			
Chaos and the power of agency			

developments at the macro level will influence the very existence of faculties of education through resource allocation and institutional priorities. These developments which appear in Table 1 under 'context', ensure that teacher educators do not claim their destiny on only their terms. At the micro level we find the day-to-day struggles of teacher educators who shape the experiences of beginning teachers and the institutions where ITE occurs. Learning to teach remains central to both.

The status quo

Any exploration of the future must recognize the possibility that the current state will continue. Although most people do talk about change as though it were inevitable, typically they assume that someone or something else will be the object of that change. Thus, the status quo option simply means that things, good or bad as they currently are, remain pretty much the same. What we have is what we get. The context within which the status quo will be retained might be something like this. Governments do solve their budgetary problems and a fairly extended period of slow growth occurs. It might also be a period of slow decline, but it will be so slow that no-one will notice. Just as the real wages of those workers without high school education are lower now than they were 30 years ago, we probably will not notice an on-going decline in our standard of living. Even if we do, to whom do we complain? Without sudden economic shifts or Government intervention, the policy makers might leave us alone. Things will go on and we will all live happily ever after (or unhappily, whatever the case may be).

The likelihood of the status quo scenario ushering in the new millennium seems very unlikely indeed. I have three reasons for making this assertion, two at the macro socio-economic level, and one at the micro educational level. First, in both economic and social terms it is hard to imagine the Western countries remaining in a stable state. The economic developments in Western countries point towards very changing times. The Canadian situation provides an example not unlike many Western countries. Richardson (1995) of the Fraser Institute provides data to show that the total debt of all levels of Government along with unfunded social programme liabilities has reached crisis proportions with one-third of all Government revenue going to service the national debt. Although some might argue that the debt crisis has been overstated, the perception has been created that we have a crisis that must be solved. The solution will involve a rethinking of support for social programmes such as education. Another economic factor possibly challenging the status quo rests with the increasing discrepancy between the rich and the poor in most Western nations. That income discrepancy last occurred in the 1920s and was soon followed by a severe economic collapse. I do not wish to join the cadre of 'gloom and doomers' who predict economic collapse, I merely suggest that the growing discrepancy between the rich and the poor signals a period of adjustment and economic shortages. This factor along with the national debt problems will almost certainly change the economic resources available to higher education –unlikely support for the status quo theory. Faculties of education, where ITE now occurs, are likely to see continuing pressure to downsize in the light of the economic shortages. In fact, faculties of education, as newcomers to the university, could well be seen as sacrificial lambs whose cutting loose could save the money needed to preserve the traditional faculties within the ivory tower.

Second, the status quo remains an unlikely scenario because of the pace of change being predicted and the expectations being created for change in educational institutions. Predictions of change abound. Brown (1979) saw the future in terms of compressed change, as he prophesied that the next three decades would bring at least two centuries worth of changes as measured in historic terms. Emberly (1995) recently made this comment when he described some of the pressures being brought to bear on post-secondary institutions: 'Can we today doubt, in the light of the turmoil in Canada's universities, that we are not in the midst of anything less than a revolution that will forever change these institutions?(1995)'[3] With respect to schools, McLaughlin and Oberman (1994) contend that while school reform has been an enduring preoccupation of both educators and the lay public since the Second World War, the current proposed changes, taken together, represent the most comprehensive reform agenda ever undertaken in the USA. Teacher education has not escaped this pressure for reform on either side of the Atlantic. The Holmes Group (1995) begins with the radical premise that institutions preparing educators either adopt reforms or surrender their franchise. Gillian Shepherd, Secretary of State for Education and Employment in Great Britain, outlined sweeping reforms for the ITE. Although critics point out the wrongheadedness in many of these calls for reform, the fact remains that such reports and policy moves create expectations among policy makers and the public that things will change. The status quo can hardly remain within such a context.

Other very different factors suggest the status quo will not continue in ITE. At the micro level, ITE has now become the object of research and development by a group of teacher educators who themselves work with beginning teachers. Their efforts not only bring innovative practices to programmes of teacher education, but also subject those innovations to research, thus creating a culture of inquiry. In fact, as I have argued elsewhere, these efforts by teacher educators in different countries have led to a wedge of improved practice. Clearly, such activity could be snuffed out tomorrow with extensive closures of institutions where they now occur. But, assuming the efforts of these teacher educators continue, I believe that this body of research and development has the potential to energise ITE in such ways that it will never be the same again. The power in this research and development is that it has begun to change the language with which we talk about learning to teach. Oakeshott (1962) described the importance of language some years ago in arguing that, as human beings, we do not necessarily inherit a body of knowledge, but a conversation. It might be that on-going conversation that will enable us to recreate ITE differently in the next millennium. Indeed, in many countries such as Great Britain, that conversation has already begun.

The corporate culture and the entrepreneurial spirit

Context
Any exploration of the future must take seriously the corporate influence which increasingly pervades society. Many practices which have become commonplace in the 1990s would not even have been contemplated 30

years ago. In the 1960s, for example, employers did not fire employees unless as a last resort or in the event of bankruptcy. Society frowned on it. That practice has now become a mark of good management. Corporations that both downsize and make a profit in the same year take on the persona of excellence and frequently reward their chief executive officers. Rifkin (1995) in explaining how technology replaces the workforce, finds the acceleration of corporate downsizing and re-engineering continuing with no end in sight.

The corporate influence has not only made it appear palatable to accept higher and higher levels of unemployment, it also identifies solutions in terms of privatisation and less government. For example, the Fraser Institute, a conservative think tank supported by corporate donors (Richardson, 1995), proposes the sale of all Government business enterprises, the privatisation of all Government services, and the requirement that all students at universities be required to pay full tuition. However unlikely that the Canadian Government will heed the advice of the Fraser Institute, its voice, supported by the corporate sector is heard by policy makers on virtually every social and political issue.

The second scenario, therefore, not only posits the emergence of an even stronger corporate sector, it argues that the corporate spirit will drive the political and social agenda. Competition and individual survival will dominate our social fabric. Educationally, we will see the emergence of a type of pedagogical Lamarkianism, in which schools and higher education institutions (HEIs) will increasingly attend to the need for skills and competences seen to be needed in the marketplace (Barnett, 1994). The successful entrepreneurs will emerge as the icons of success, so we may find ourselves acting accordingly.

The institution
Under this scenario, the corporate sector supported by the State will exert its claims on higher education both in the way education is delivered and what is delivered. HEIs will need to become increasingly competitive and entrepreneurial to survive. Emberly (1995) argues that the corporate right would move higher education to 'virtual universities', where 'outsourcing' and 'modularized curriculum' would replace what we now

understand as a university education. He contends that the corporate right see the university as a business enterprise and will exert continuing pressure to make 'delivery systems' more efficient through technology.[4] Barnett (1994), with reference to the more general trends in higher education, makes a compelling argument that what counts as education and knowledge may well change with the new relationship between society and higher education. In his words, 'those changes may lead to a narrowing of human consciousness. Understanding is replaced by competence; insight is replaced by effectiveness; and rigor of interactive argument is replaced by communication skills' (Barnett, 1994:37).

The survival of faculties of education may depend entirely on how adequately what they offer parallels the corporate ethos, for example, full fee recovery for services. Three possibilities seem reasonable. First, delivery systems of 'virtual teacher education' will become more and more popular. Arguments for such institutional changes will rest on a definition of university teaching as the transmission of knowledge, skills and competences about teaching. As the institutional technology develops to accomplish this transfer, pressure will be exerted to make the delivery of teacher education more efficient through that technology. Second, this resulting modularising of programmes will provide opportunities for export to new markets worldwide. Exporting our expertise to developing countries will occur provided someone pays for it. Governments wishing to make economic advancements into these countries will provide educational resources for ground-breaking that inevitably sets the stage for the sale of our economic products.

The third institutional implication which has already begun involves the shift to new types of institutions for ITE. The recalcitrant professors in higher education who do not wish to play the entrepreneurial game will be used as examples of dinosaurism to argue that universities have become irrelevant in teacher education. Hence, the institution providing teacher education will shift to alternate routes for certification in some parts of the USA, or to the schools as in Great Britain. If skills and competences become the hallmark of teacher preparation, as the corporate ethos suggests, then why not develop them in the schools? Within this scenario, we do find other players in the educational arena. Disney

Corporation has entered the educational scene in the USA aiming both at teacher education and the public schools. Kohl (personal communication, August, 1994) argues that the corporate sector sees public education as a huge market. However, to make inroads there they must first discredit public education – exactly what they have been doing for the last decade or so. That may sound like a paranoid interpretation of events, but it certainly provides one interpretation to what Berliner and Biddle (1995) have termed the 'manufactured crisis' in education.

What will it mean to learn to teach

This corporately-driven scenario points at the vulnerability of our current models of ITE. Teacher education programmes have characteristically been additive in nature to the extent that knowledge is built up layer on layer in preparation for teaching in the classroom. That approach is derived from the notion that learning to teach involves the acquisition of the knowledge about teaching by beginning teachers (Carter, 1990). This definition has invariably led to a transmission model of teaching in many institutions where ITE occurs. With one small technological step, much of what is currently being done through this transmission model may now be possible through technology. If learning to teach continues to be defined in terms of the provision of knowledge about teaching, pressure will be on to shift from the classroom lecture to the computer screen. This clearly sets out a challenge to teacher educators to demonstrate how their provision of ITE provides the added value that warrants having one professor work in a classroom with 30 students when distance education might reach 300 or 3,000. Unless that can be demonstrated, learning to teach under this scenario will increasingly fall into the realm of distance education and tele-learning.

The further challenge to teacher educators will be to demonstrate the role of university-based teacher education as the providers of criticism. As Barnett (1994) argues, the press towards competence implies a shift away from the critical aspect of scholarship. The clear danger in this connection was summarised by Barnett when he argued that, 'the modern university is in danger of reflecting society's own understanding and actions back on itself, or of falling in with society's agenda, that the critical space between the universities' reading of concepts and society's is on the point of disappearing' (1994:51). To accept the corporate ethos might compromise the role that teacher educators can play in offering critique and proposing alternatives to existing practice. The corporate ethos also drives the perception that competences and skills can best be learned in the workplace. That perception, instrumental in the policy to link teacher education more closely to the schools in Great Britain, might soon see teacher education reflect the practice that now exists in the schools. This stance could become a two-edged sword, because the distance that teacher educators once had between themselves and school practice, which had the potential for encouraging reform, might now be on the wane.

Unless teacher educators exercize some form of vigilance within this scenario, it becomes difficult to imagine teacher education as anything other than a concept of learning to teach which focuses on the provision of propositional knowledge about teaching and includes the acquisition of teaching skills in the schools. The roles of the teacher educator as provocateur and critic, innovator of new improved practice in teacher education and reformer of school practice appear at risk in this scenario.

Friendly fascism through bureaucratic control

The previous scenario assumed government support for corporate influence in economic and social policy as has been seen in Great Britain under the recent conservative Government and under the *Republican Social Contract* in the USA. Such support is not a foregone conclusion. The scenario of friendly fascism, which posits the emergence of stronger regulatory agencies who appear friendly on the one hand, but who are fascist in their drive for control, does not run counter to corporate influence. However, it assumes a more aggressive Government response toward corporate influence. The increasing unemployment that Rifkin (1994) refers to may well force governments to take remedial action. Hargrove (1996) may well reflect a growing societal concern over social and economic developments. He points out that over the past decade in Canada, policies have shifted consistently to favour private sector investors and employers. A North American Free Trade Agreement, tax cuts for high-income employers, deregulation, cutbacks in unemployment insurance and other social security benefits to balance the budget, and a scaling back of union influence have all been effected to free up enterprise and enhance business stability in order to create jobs and accelerate growth. Despite all this support for the corporate sector, Canadian investment is down and so is job creation in Canada. Sooner or later, it would seem that Western Governments will intervene to redistribute income and ease the impact of low wages and unemployment.

However, cash strapped Governments heavily laden with debt will have few degrees of freedom within which to operate. Unable to spend their way out of the problem, governments will reach for the levers of control not only to redistribute income, but also to impose accountability on the institutions they support financially. When shortages appear, regulatory processes increase. Such a move by Governments may well usher in a period of what Henchy (1984) called 'friendly fascism'. Bureaucrats and regulatory agencies will be present in our lives even more that they are now. They will be friendly when we agree, but fascistic when we do not.

The institution

One of the means by which to save money is to control the activity that spends it. Under this scenario, we will see our HEIs subjected to increased control, amalgamated, downsized or closed down. Reports from three countries serve to illustrate how institutions could be affected.

The Australian experience provides an image of increased control brought about by groups outside teacher education. Tisher (1995) describes the national pressures for change to teaching and teacher education that have come from the Federal Government, professional associations, as well as business and industrial groups. The policies enacted as a result of these pressures have left that country in a state of disarray. National standards and basic competences have been brought in without much consultation. He describes a reduced school experience for beginning teachers, decreased supervision by university personnel and a phasing-out of concurrent programmes. These procedures occur

Carr, D. (1995), 'Is understanding the professional knowledge of teachers a theory–practice problem?', *Journal of Philosophy of Education*, 29(3), 311–31.

Carr, W. and Hartnett, A. (1996), *Education and the Struggle for Democracy: the Politics of Educational Ideas*. Milton Keynes: Open University Press.

Dewey, J. (1927), *The Public and its Problems*. New York: Basic Books.

Eraut, M. (1995), 'Schon shock: a case for reframing reflection-in-action?', *Teachers and Teaching: Theory and Practice*, 1(1), 9–22.

Fullan, M. (1993), *Change Forces*. London: Falmer Press.

Furlong, J. and Smith, R. (eds) (1996), *The Role of Higher Education in Initial Teacher Training*. London: Kogan Page.

Geertz, C. (1973), 'Ideology as a cultural system', in *The Interpretation of Cultures*. New York: Basic Books.

Gouldner, A. (1979), *The Future of Intellectuals and the Rise of the New Class*. New York: Harper & Row.

Griffiths, M. and Tann, S. (1992), 'Using reflective practice to link personal and public theories', *Journal of Education for Teaching*, 18(1).

Griffiths, V. and Owen, P. (1995), *Schools in Partnership: Current Initiatives in School-Based Teacher Education*. London: Paul Chapman.

Hargreaves, D.H. (1994), 'Initial Teacher Training – Making It Work: Priorities for Action'. Paper at the Longman Conference on Initial Teacher Training, London, 28 November, 1–7.

Harland, J. and Lambert, D. (1997), 'Exploring the role of educational studies: perspectives from the Institute'. *Academic Board Occasional Papers* No.1, London: Institute of Education, University of London.

Hirst, P.H. and Peters, R.S. (eds), (1970), *The Logic of Education*. London: Routledge & Kegan Paul.

Hogan, P. (1995), *The Custody and Courtship of Experience Western Education in Philosophical Perspective*. Dublin: The Columba Press.

in a democratic society requires fairness and tolerance – traditional academic virtues. Fairness reduces our position to a minimum and leaves us vulnerable to our adversary, but this is what it necessarily requires of us. Tolerance, is 'the capacity to listen to an unfair and hostile statement by an opponent in order to discover his sound points as well as the reason for his errors' (Polanyi, 1973:73). Such convicted civility in our 'dealings', combined with a hermeneutics of charity in our 'readings', might better commend our attempts to influence power holders and also allow us to exploit new alliances with others who have a vested interest in teacher education.

References

Alexander, R. (1990), 'Partnership in Initial Teacher Training: Confronting the Issues.' In: M. Booth, J. Furlong and M. Wilkin, *Partnershp in Initial Teacher Training*. London: Cassell.

Barnett, R. (1994), *The Limits of Competence: Knowledge, Higher Education and Society*. Buckingham: Open University Press.

Blake, D. (1995), 'The policy context for school-based teacher education', in D. Blake, V. Hanley, M. Jennings, and M. Lloyd, *Researching School-Based Teacher Education*. Aldershot: Avebury Press.

Blake, D., Hanley, V., Jennings, M. and Lloyd, M. (eds) (1995), *Researching School-Based Teacher Education*. Aldershot: Avebury Press.

Bolton, E. (1994), 'Transition in initial teacher training: an overview', in Wilkin, M and Sankey, D, *Collaboration and Transition in Initial Teacher Training*. London: Kogan Page.

Bottery, M. (1996), 'Some Thoughts on Conceptualizations of Professionalism, and the Implications of this for a Code of Ethics'. In: Universities Council For The Education Of Teachers Occasional Paper No.7, *Code of Ethical Principles for the Teaching Profession*, London: UCET.

A new paradigm

In exploring the future of ITE through the previous scenarios, I have made projections based on trends that have in part at least already begun. I have also drawn on authors whose work bears some elements of technological forecasting. I have assumed that an economic collapse may be about to occur because it always has after a long period of growth. I have assumed that Governments might step in to alleviate shortages and protect the poor in time of need, because they usually have. I assume that the corporations will continue to influence the economic and social agenda in ways that serve their interests because they have done so in the past. My thinking has implied a certain amount of cause and effect which is predicated on my own upbringing as a partially reformed logical-positivist. Such thinking tends to assume a structural-functional theory of behaviour and assumes that organizational cultures explain what people do. Such thinking carries a deterministic flavour, assumes that players work independently and assumes logical action. Therefore, I might have subscribed to an outdated worldview at both the macro and the micro levels.

The previous scenarios do not take into account the emergence of chaos within our society, the individual agency which at times gives the appearance of anarchy, and the benign indifference to social strife on the part of governments and the corporate sector. Nor, perhaps, has a sufficient amount of allowance been given to Giroux's (1983) notion of the 'language of possibility' to conceptualise how individuals and groups are able to challenge systemic barriers and bring about social transformation so that, even if barriers exist, people may simply work around them. As Capra (1996) pointed out, 'most of us, and especially our large institutions, subscribe to an outdated worldview, a perception of reality inadequate for dealing with our overpopulated, globally connected world' (1996:4). So, in this final scenario I attempt to explore the future of ITE within a radically different paradigm which requires a radically different type of thinking.

I will employ the overworked term 'paradigm' (Khun, 1962). Capra draws on Khun's work to describe a paradigm as 'a constellation of achievements – concepts, values, techniques, etc. – shared by a scientific community to define legitimate problems and solutions' (Capra, 1996:5). Science progressed as 'paradigm shifts' occurred within a scientific community. Such shifts frequently took the form of revolutionary, discontinuous breaks with old paradigms, as new data could not be accommodated within previous ways of thinking. Khun's analysis drew on events occurring in the physics community at the turn of the century. Using the concept of a paradigm shift in this chapter assumes that the concept can be applied to explore cultural or educational transformation in general, and the transformation of ITE in particular.

Chaos, networks and personal agency

The work of Capra (1996) provides the background to the context in which I explore this scenario. Capra focuses on science and, in particular, the environmental concerns arising from a whole series of global problems. He contends that the traditional ways of knowing have not been adequate to deal with the problems currently facing society. He traces developments in science from the turn of the century to argue that the paradigm shift in physics identified through Khun's analysis is, in his words, being 'mirrored today by a similar but much broader cultural crisis. Accordingly, we see a shift of paradigms occurring not only in science, but also in the larger social arena' (1996:5). If one entertains Capra's view of the new millennium, then there emerges a vastly different picture, in which ITE will occur. Three areas in particular appear particularly germane to this future context – changes in how we think about power, what constitutes knowledge and how solutions develop and inform other people. I will comment on Capra's notion of power within the discussion of context, knowledge, and solutions under sections dealing with the institution and learning to teach.

The context

Power in social organizations will shift from the hierarchy to the network. We will see a virtual breakdown of most regulatory aspects of society that are based on the power associated with hierarchies. The middle layer of bureaucracy will virtually disappear because it is both expendable and unaffordable. The age of rapid communication through advanced technology will also work to render this middle layer of bureaucracy redundant. Ministries of education will no longer direct or dictate to the masses because those masses simply will not listen. The shrinking global village brought about by improved communication will reduce the need for many of the national and local authorities on whom we have relied in the past. Complex and situated social problems will best be solved through networks and those close to the local situation.

The actions of a local superintendent (whom I will call Paul) illustrates how local control and agency will subvert hierarchies. Paul finds policies from the central provincial authorities completely at odds with his district's policies. The school principals receive directives and forms to be completed from the central Ministerial authorities on which they are hesitant to act because of the differences that occur between the expectations of the Ministry and the local district. So, Paul has the forms sent to his office and he completes them. His actions matter little to the Ministry officials whose benign indifference appears to rest on the view that the Ministry policies will change soon in any case. So, in his district, Paul continues to doctor the forms to side-step central policy for what he believes to be the good of the students in the schools he supervises. Under this scenario, the Pauls of the world will increase, producing a mild form of anarchy.

Within this scenario, the policy makers focus on those things they can, and do need to, control simply to maintain society – money supply, healthcare, law and order, and a very limited safety net. Education will remain an important priority because it will still be deemed necessary to drive economic success in the post-industrial society. However, the structure that now exists may change dramatically or simply cease to exist. We will see considerable diversity within a very modest framework of accountability for most areas in society.

The institution

The institution where ITE occurs will be vastly different from what we know today. The location of ITE within the university will cease to exist, unless radical changes occur both in the mission of faculties of education and in the way teacher educators view knowledge and its relationship to practice. As Capra (1996) argues, knowledge as foundation will be replaced by knowledge as network – a concept very unsettling to traditional academics who have positioned themselves as the 'keepers of content'. Institutions will continue to usurp this traditional role of the professoriate by extending the notion of the virtual university, where tele-learning replaces face-to-face teaching in the traditional sense. Faculties of education that cling to their traditional roles of knowledge makers, keepers and transmitters will likely be closed down or severely downsized.

As a result of the virtual breakdown of traditional hierarchies, alliances created through networking will become increasingly important. Therefore, a concept of a newly created 'boundary spanning' institution, suggested by Zimpher (personal communication, 10 January 1997), offers a possible standard for the next millennium. Resting at the interface between the various players who have a stake in ITE, this boundary-spanning institution will focus on providing access to experiences and learning opportunities to those wanting to learn how to teach. This institution will be conceptualized around the notion of a learning web, a concept mentioned some years ago by Illich (1971), and the premise that candidates for teaching will drive their own learning. Illich's concepts of reference services (libraries, school experiences), skill exchanges, peer-matching and contacts to educators-at-large provide four elements that could become the basis for such a learning web. Such institutions would probably be based on temporary systems whose on-going existence would depend on how well they served those wishing to become teachers and the other groups who claim some stake in the process. Faculties of education could make no *a priori* claim to control such an institution, but would be a player like any other, depending on what they could offer.

The on-going pressure for change implied by this context will dictate that the survival in any form of the current university-based model, whether in existing institutions or newly created ones, will depend on their becoming leaders in promoting improved practice. Institutions will also have to become stronger advocates for what they do. Within a network, power resides with those who participate in it. The docile and silent teacher educators whom Tisher described will be burdens to their institution. As Kiernan (1995) states only the innovative will survive.

Learning to teach

'Chicago', John Dewey wrote to his wife in July of 1894, 'is the place to make you appreciate at every turn the absolute opportunity which chaos affords' (Heffron, McDonald and Cherry, 1996:4). As we enter a period of what appears to be chaos, we may be afforded opportunities we never dreamed existed. Chaos can be a great opportunity. So can anarchy, if you can trust your neighbour. The 1880s in the USA, for example, has been described as a period of great upheaval, originating in and around Chicago where labour, capital, teachers and politicians struggled over the meaning of industrial democracy. Dewey was thrust into turmoil and chaos as highlighted by the World's Fair of 1893, which celebrated the triumph of mechanisation and by the Pullman strike of 1894, one of the worst industrial strikes in that nation's history. It was in Chicago that Dewey did his work. It is there that American Educational Research Association (AERA) was held in 1997, celebrating 100 years of activity. The theme 'Talking together in educational research and practice' reflects Dewey's notion of narrowing the gap between thought and experience, knowledge and action as well as Capra's notion of networking. That chaos of those times produced some wonderful ideas in education. We may be there again.

Programmes designed to assist beginning teachers to learn to teach within this scenario will take many forms. Three challenges will face teacher educators.

The first challenge will be to move beyond the old solutions that have not worked and to take advantage of the freedom to create new ways of thinking within this new paradigm. The advantages are tremendous. An extensive knowledge base of propositional knowledge exists that can be useful, provided it does not merely form the basis for transmission or be used as some type of foundation on which everything else must rest. An extensive literature and experience exists on action research, reflective practice and a theory of constructivism that has changed the conceptualization of learning and knowing.

We have also adopted the view that ITE should improve school–university partnerships. These areas cannot represent a new paradigm in teacher education, particularly if they merely replace dogma with dogma or just tinker with the surface. However, if they become tools to probe the depths of what it means to learn to teach, the process may never be the same. As I am writing this chapter, I have just completed reading a thesis in which the author reflects on her most recent experience in teacher education. I summarize the experience she describes to illustrate the challenges to teacher educators.

Sue and a team of three were assigned to work with a cohort of 30 beginning teachers over two semesters. The first year the team followed the planned curriculum, which had a strong oral culture, in which the practices that seem to work are passed on from year to year during a two-week orientation period. That curriculum drew on reflective practice and constructivist theory and encouraged action research. The team planned and offered the programme to the cohort group of students during that first year. At the end of that first two-semester period, despite some very favourable student evaluations, the teaching team did not believe from their observations of teaching practice that much of a difference had been made to their teaching of those beginning teachers. The students had been socialised into the schools, but the teaching observed by the team was boring, much like watching paint dry.

Planning for the second year at a faculty retreat led to a commitment to doing something different. What seemed central to the difference would be a shift in the power relations and a more deliberate attempt to encourage these beginning teachers in active learning. The team's version of constructivist theory and reflection which were only talked about the previous year had to be modelled. The team broke the administrative rules and gave the students the responsibility for their own evaluation for the first semester. Dropping the gate-keeping function was not popular. The team spent considerable time encouraging students to talk about their own beliefs about teaching, to create metaphors to reflect their teaching, to write about their experiences, and to structure action plans for their own development. They drew heavily on teachers whom they saw as innovative and effective in working with pupils. Many workshops were given and the students read a lot. The team testified that this teaching experience had been the most powerful of their career as it had probed the deep structure of what it meant to learn to teach. Based on student feedback, the team reported having moved beyond the technical aspects of teaching to engage the students such that the worlds of both teacher educators and students had changed.

This team believed they had made a difference in the way they worked with beginning teachers. By taking control of the curriculum and extending the evaluation to the students, they went against the grain. This type of action can become both an opportunity and challenge within the new paradigm.

The further challenge to teacher educators will be to engage within a larger network and move beyond the power they have traditionally enjoyed. Such power has resided traditionally within the coursework structure. However, as Barnett (1994) points out, the systematization of knowledge can no longer be confined to a monopoly possessed by educational institutions and teacher educators. It will no longer be assumed (if it ever was) that teacher educators at universities had the inside track on what it means to learn to teach. The challenge will become to identify the role of the university in ITE. As Sue's team illustrated, the knowledge of the university was only one aspect of the beginning teachers' experience. The team drew heavily on beginning teachers and the knowledge they possessed.

The third challenge – how solutions develop and inform the rest of the community – will be something faced both by teacher educators and by the entire teacher education community. Traditionally, educators thought improvement occurred through implementation, a view that improved practice developed in one setting could somehow be described, packaged and applied in other settings. This view of knowledge utilization is founded on an outdated worldview, to use Capra's terms, of how improvement occurs. Much of the problem lies in that practice in any setting is inextricably bound to the people who work in that setting and to a host of situational factors. However, to suggest that by replacing hierarchies with networks begs a host of further questions regarding how people in different settings actually learn from each other and, indeed, determine what constitutes best practice across settings (if in fact a 'best practice' exists).

ITE within this new paradigm might see the best of times if teacher educators can take advantage of the opportunities that a very different society might afford. On the other hand, for a docile and conservative community of teacher educators, it may be the worst of times.

Reflections and conclusions

In this chapter I have explored futures in ITE by setting out images of preferred futures given different social and economic projections. As such, I intended this chapter to be a type of heuristic journey in which I have explored four possibilities:

- the status quo
- the corporate culture and the entrepreneurial spirit
- friendly fascism and bureaucratic control
- chaos, networks, and the power of agency.

With the pressures for reform being brought to bear on educational institutions from social, economic and educational events, I argued that the status quo option in ITE becomes very unlikely. Change becomes the only certainty. The question is, what kind of change do we want?

The growing corporate culture becomes a preferred future for those whose economic muscle will be felt in the years to come as they seek to influence many aspects of our lives, including Government. Within that context, institutions where teacher education occurs will become increasingly competitive and the tendency in learning to teach will be to streamline the process around competences that can be delivered through tele-learning. Friendly fascism and bureaucratic control become the context in which Governments and their bureaucrats exert increasing control over the lives of people to alleviate hardship arising from financial shortages. Within this context, institutions will become increasingly monitored and controlled by well-meaning bureaucrats. Learning to teach, I argued, may well become the provision of skills to meet predetermined outcomes. Both these scenarios represent trends now underway in many jurisdictions – an observation to which many examples testify. Both scenarios offer major challenges to those in teacher education, not the least of which will be to maintain some agency over what is done in ITE.

In contrast, the fourth scenario sets out a radically different future, based on the replacement of power hierarchies with networks, and knowledge foundations with knowledge based on connections and experiential reflections. Capra's (1996) notion of the holistic web of life provides the context for this metaphor. Many of the traditional notions such as curriculum implementation and improvement will become outdated as traditional structures simply break down and are replaced with individual efforts based on agency. The challenges facing teacher educators within this metaphor will be enormous because much of the ground will be uncharted. The question as to whether this becomes a preferred future depends largely on how teacher educators meet those challenges.

Three points deserve a concluding comment following this exploration of futures in ITE. First, with the tremendous variety occurring in different countries and even amongst provinces and states within some countries, clearly no single future awaits all. Tofler (1975) described what he saw as 'eco-spasms' occurring within the economy of most nations. These were localised conditions in which he projected the occurrence of economic depressions in one area bordered by prosperity in an area near by. Some years later his notion has been proven to be quite accurate. Similarly, the contexts within which ITE occurs may well find bureaucratic control imposed in one jurisdiction, while something akin to chaos may be prevalent nearby. Diversity will probably be much more common in the next millennium than orthodoxy. Such diversity is likely to result from two sources – the global education economy and the breakdown of national barriers and Governmental regulatory agencies. The global educational economy will increasingly see networking capabilities occurring where they never have before, while financial scarcity may well lead to the breakdown of regulatory agencies. The second inescapable point emerging from this analysis casts serious doubt on whether ITE as a university-based activity will survive. The many rounds of criticism have exposed ITE for what it is – a modest, ineffective intervention in the lives of young people hoping to teach. McIntyre's comment with respect to professional education summed up the problem very well:

> more worrying is the readiness of those engaged in professional education to rely on slogans such as 'reflective practice'. Gross as the politician's interventions have been, they have revealed a superficiality in the theoretical rationales on many of those engaged in professional education.
>
> (McIntyre, 1994:ix)

Unless more extensive efforts are made by faculties of education in general and teacher educators in particular, the next millennium may well see teacher education moved back into the schools from where it emerged 100 years ago.

Third, whichever scenario one might prefer, the need for deep thinking about teacher education has never been more apparent. Postman (1995) made a useful distinction between the mechanical side of education and that side which is intended to make one a better person. At one time, we might have required an institution to provide the mechanics of an education, which typically took the form of the provision of knowledge and skills for teaching. Today that function can be done either through tele-learning or apprenticeship within a school. The area that can not be provided by the technology or the workplace involves Postman's notion of 'becoming a different person'. Clearly, the need for reform in our schools requires beginning teachers who think differently about teaching and learning, or who have become different people – providing that experience for beginning teachers becomes the role that teacher educators could fill. Providing that experience goes well beyond the mechanical surface features so typical of the past efforts in professional training.

Clearly, reaching beyond the surface requires much more than the embrace of glib notions of 'reflective practice', 'action research' or 'collaboration'. Changes in one's beliefs is quite a different matter. Here, beginning teachers and those teacher educators who work with them must seek out concepts and experiences that alter the worlds of beginning teachers. That journey is one that needs to be travelled by beginning teachers and teacher educators.

Acknowledgements

I wish to acknowledge Peter Grimmett, Barbara Moon, Jolie-Mayer Smith, Ivy Pye, David Boote and Kathleen Barnard for their thoughtful assistance in producing this chapter. I also wish to acknowledge the suggestions made by the editors. This chapter is based on research conducted under support from the Social Sciences and Humanities Research Council.

Notes

1   I am reminded of the geographical principle uniformitarianism, which states that processes such as erosion that we see occurring today will continue to occur in the future. I have serious doubts that such a principle can apply in the social sciences where the very act of describing a trend may affect subsequent events related to it.

2   Gwyn made this comment at an International Movements Toward Educational Change (IMTEC) seminar on teacher education in Gaustablikk, Norway, 1975.

3   This quotation was taken from an essay published in the Globe and Mail, Saturday, 27 June 1966:D1. This essay was excerpted from Emberly (1995).

4   It should be noted that in his essay, Emberly referred to both the corporate right and the cultural left. He believed that both groups held the universities up to ridicule and scorn and were having their effect on them. For this chapter, I have focused on his description of the corporate right.

References

Barnett, R. (1994), *The Limits of Competence*. Buckingham: Open University Press.

Benjamin, S. (1989), 'An ideascape for education: what futurists recommend', *Educational Leadership*, 47(2), 8–14.

Berliner, D. and Biddle, B.J. (1995), *Manufactured Crisis*. New York: Addison-Wesley.

Brown, L. (1979), *Futuristics and Education: An ASCD Task Force Report. Report No: 1979-1*. Alexandria: Association for Supervision and Curriculum Development (ASCD).

Capra, F. (1996), *The Web of Life*. New York: Doubleday.

Carter, C. (1990), 'Teachers' knowledge and learning to teach', in Houston, W.R., *Handbook of Research on Teacher Education*. New York: MacMillan.

Emberly, P. (1995), *Hot Buttons in Canadian Universities*. Toronto, Ont: Penguin.

Etzioni, A. and Jargowsky, P.A. (1990), 'The false choice between high technology and basic industry', in Erickson, K. and Vallis, S.P., *The Nature of Work*. New Haven, CT: Yale University Press, 304–18.

Giroux, H.A. (1983), 'Theories of reproduction and resistance in the new sociology of education: a critical analysis', *Harvard Educational Review*, 53, 257–93.

Grimmett, P. (1995), 'Reconceptualizing teacher education', in Wideen, M.F. and Grimmett, P., *Changing Times in Teacher Education: Restructuring or Reconceptualization*. London: Falmer, 202–25.

Hargrove, B. (1996), 'No pain from the gain', *Report on Business Magazine*, September 13(3), 37–43.

Heffron, J., McDonald, V. and Cherry, L. (1996), 'Voices: from the 1997 annual meeting program committee', *Educational Researcher*, 25(6), 4–17.

Henchy, N. (1984), 'Futures in Education'. Paper at the Howe Sound Institute, Vancouver, BC, Canada.

Holmes Group (1995), *Tomorrow's Schools of Education*. East Lansing, MI: Holmes Group.

Illich, I. (1971), *Deschooling Society*. New York: Harper-Row.

Imig, D. (1995), 'A Washington Bird's Eye View: Trends in American Education'. Presentation given to members of teacher education (UNITE), Washington, DC, February.

Khun, T. (1962), *The Structure of Scientific Revolution*. Chicago, IL: University of Chicago Press.

Kiernan, M.J. (1995), *Get Innovative or Get Dead*. Vancouver, BC: Douglas & McIntyre.

Lanning, R. (1994), 'Education and everyday life: an argument against "educational futures"', *Canadian Journal of Education*, 19(4), 464–78.

McIntyre, D. (1994), 'Preface', in Eraut, M., *Developing Professional Knowledge and Competence*. London: Falmer Press, viii–ix.

McLaughlin, M.W. and Oberman, I. (eds) (1996), *Teacher Learning: New Policies, New Practices*. New York: Teachers College Press.

Ministry of Supply and Services (1991), *Prosperity Through Competitiveness*. Ottawa, ON: The Queen's Printer.

Oakeshott, M. (1962), *Rationalism in Politics and Other Essays*. London: Methuen.

Postman, N. (1995), *The End of Education*. New York: Alfred A. Knopf.

Richardson, R. (1995), *Inside Canada's Debt Problem and the Way Out*. Vancouver, BC: Fraser Institute.

Rifkin, J. (1995), *The End of Work.* New York: GP Putman's Sons.

Tisher, R. (1995), 'Readjustments, reorganization or revolution? The changing face of teacher education in Australia', in Wideen, M.F. and Grimmett, P., *Changing Times in Teacher Education: Restructuring or Reconceptualization.* London: Falmer, 34–46.

Tofler, A. (1975), *The eco-spasm report.* New York: Boston Books.

Weber, S. and Mitchel, C. (1994), *That is Funny, You Don't Look Like a Teacher.* London: Falmer.

Wideen, M.F. and Grimmett, P. (1995), *Changing Times in Teacher Education. Restructuring or Reconceptualizing?* London: Falmer.

4.2 Endnote

Barbara MacGilchrist

A key theme emerged from the Exploring Futures in Initial Teacher Education International Conference, held at the Institute of Education in September 1996, which has been echoed in many of the subsequent contributions to this book.

There is an urgent need to reconceptualize what we mean by teacher education. Such a reconceptualization, however, will not be easy for at least two reasons. The first is that over-regulation centrally imposed is likely to stultify the debate rather than enable it to fructify. The second is that the restructuring that has and is taking place in teacher education is for the most part a reflection of the past and the present but *not* the future.

It is not looking far enough ahead. It is not taking sufficient account of what the likely futures and the likely future needs will be in the twenty-first century of our ultimate client group, namely the pupils themselves in our schools. It is their future and their needs that in turn should determine the kinds of teachers we require and the kinds of teaching needed for learning in the future.

As Wideen suggests, the world is changing rapidly and we need to ensure that teacher education not only changes with it, but also does its best to anticipate the needs of learners in the future. We will always require high quality teacher education and those involved in teacher education will always need to be held accountable for the quality of what they do. However, those same people also need the ability to be able to innovate, so as to be able to reshape what counts as a professional teacher.

Pedagogy is the heart of the matter and learning is the key. With this in mind, Wideen has thrown the gauntlet down. He has asked us, 'What can be more important than the education of those who teach our children?' He provides insights into ways of engaging beginner teachers, schools and higher education institutions (HEIs) in the quest to redefine – to use Hopkins' words – 'the moral purpose of teaching' and to become much more articulate about pedagogy and what it means to learn to teach.

This book confirms the very real need to keep the 'e' in initial teacher education (ITE). In other words, it is essential that we educate rather than simply train our teachers so that they, in turn, can provide appropriate models for the pupils they teach.

In two years time when we hold our second international symposium at the Institute, I am hopeful that those who have contributed to this book will, in no small measure, have encouraged those involved in teacher education to *change key for changing times*.

List of abbreviations used

AACTE	American Association of Colleges of Teacher Education
AAHE	American Association for Higher Education
AERA	American Educational Research Association
AMMA	Assistant Masters and Mistresses Association
ASCD	Association for Supervision and Curriculum Development
BERA	British Educational Research Association
CATE	Council for Accreditation of Teacher Education
CAUT	Canadian Association of University Teachers
CC	County Council
CNAA	Council for National Academic Awards
COTEP	Committee on Teacher Education Policy
CPD	Continuing Professional Development
DES	Department of Education
DfE	Department for Education
DoH	Department of Health
ERA	Education Reform Act
ESRC	Economic and Social Research Council
EU	European Union
GEST	Government Education Service and Training
GNVQ	General National Vocational Qualifications
GTC	General Teaching Council
GTTR	Graduate Teacher Training Registry
HEI	Higher Education Institution
HEQC	Higher Education Quality Council
HMCI	Her Majesty's Chief Inspector
HMI	Her Majesty's Inspector
IAP	Individual Action Planning
IMTEC	International Movements Toward Educational Change
INSET	In-service Education and Training
INTO	Irish National Teachers' Organisation
IQEA network	Improving the Quality of Education for All network
ISERP	International School Effectiveness Research Project
ITE	Initial Teacher Education
ITT	Initial Teacher Training

LEA	Local Education Authority
LT	Licensed Teacher
MMU	Manchester Metropolitan University
MBTI	Myers-Briggs type indicator
MOTE Project	Modes of Teacher Education Project
NAEYC	National Association for the Education of Young Children
NASUWT	National Association of Schoolmasters and Union of Women Teachers
NATE	National Association for Teachers of English
NCEE	National Commission on Excellence in Education
NCVQ	National Council for Vocational Qualifications
NFER	National Foundation for Educational Research
NNEB	National Nursery Education Board
NVQ	National Vocational Qualifications
NQF	National Qualifications Framework
NQT	Newly Qualified Teacher
NUT	National Union of Teachers
OECD	Organisation for Economic Co-operation and Development
OFSTED	Office for Standards in Education
OISE	Ontario Institute for Studies in Education
OPTET	Occasional Papers in Teacher Education and Training
OTT	Overseas Trained Teacher
OU	Open University
PER Group	Philosophical and Educational Renewal Group
PGCE	Post Graduate Certificate in Education
QSC	Quality Support Centre
QTS	Qualified Teaching Status
RE	Religious Education
RoA	Records of Achievement
SCAA	Schools Curriculum Assessment Authority
SCITT	School-centred Initial Teacher Training
TET Team	Teacher Education and Training Team
THES	Times Higher Education Supplement
TTA	Teacher Training Agency
UCET	Universities Council for the Education of Teachers
UNITE	Urban Network to Improve Teacher Education
USAID	United States Agency for International Development

Index